The Annual of Annuals. Best of European Design & Advertising 07.

The Art Directors Club of Europe

Less

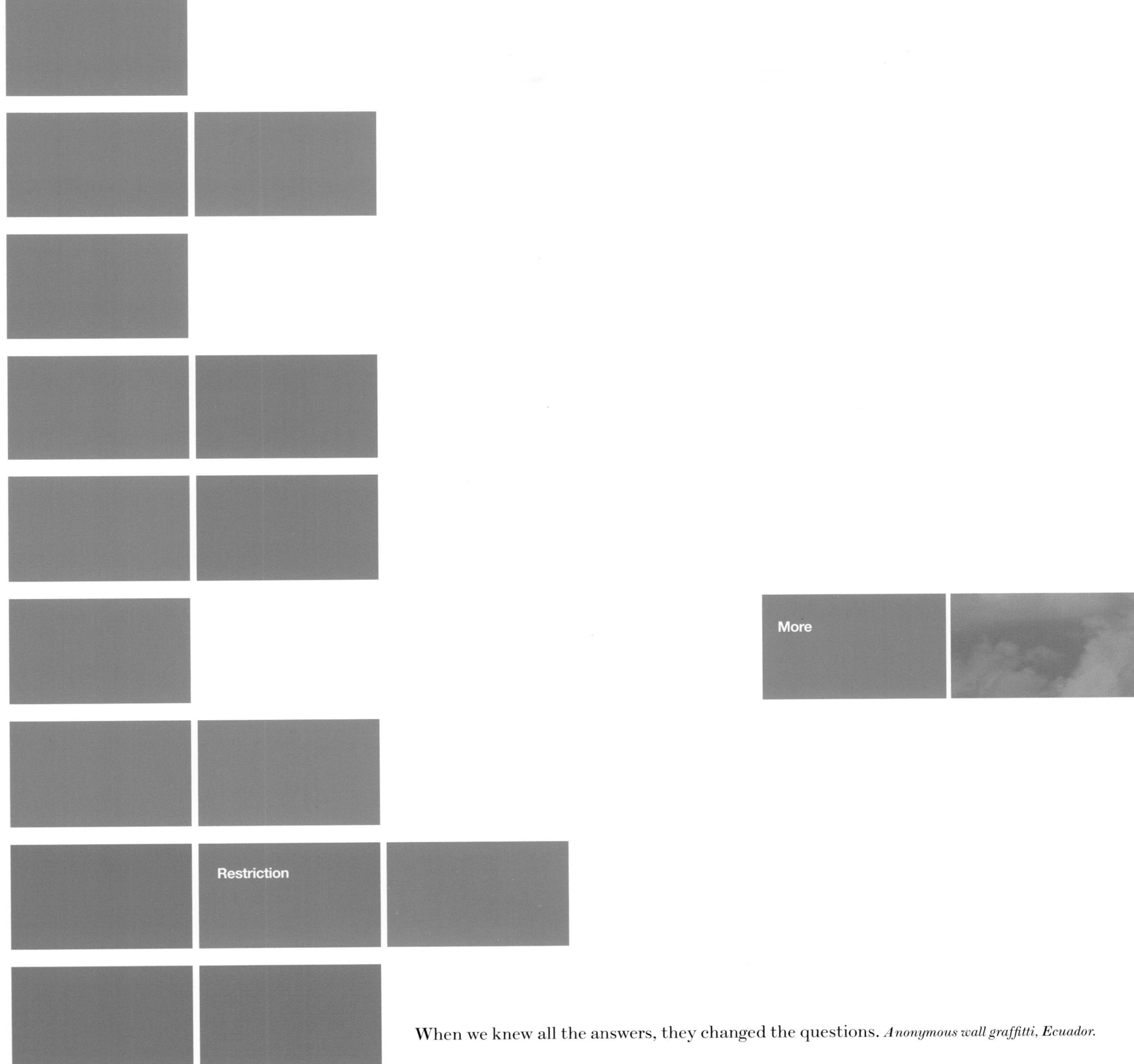

When we knew all the answers, they changed the questions. *Anonymous wall graffitti, Ecuador.*

Q: How much does the system know about me?

Project developed and co-ordinated by ADC*E

Project Manager
Mercè Segú

ADC*E Annual Colaborators
Clara Mas,
Anna Terricabras

Art Direction & Design
Compañía

Layout
Carla Bahna

Text
Compañía
(Thank you: Lewis Blackwell, Louis Rossetto and Marshall McLuhan. And, of course, Tibor "Are you sure?" Kalman)

Other Text
Alexander Alexeev
Mario Mandacaru
Haukur Már Hauksson
Johannes Newrkla

Jury Photographs
Enric Duch Fotografía

DVD Production
Infinia

Pre-press & Printing
Ingoprint

Printed in Spain

Art Directors Club of Europe
ISBN-13: 978-84-612-0001-6
D.L. B-50937-2007

Front Flyleaf
Flash Mob «Yllus 3 2 1»
Le Louvre, 28 août 2004.
Organized by ParisMobs
Photograph
© Jeff Allanson for www.martingraham.com

Back Flyleaf
© VRlab EPFL - http://vrlab.epfl.ch/
Virtual Reality Lab, Real-time Inhabited Virtual Worlds.
Crowd engine: Barbara Yersin, Jonathan Maïm
Design: Helena Grillon, Mireille Clavien
Research Director: Prof. Daniel Thalmann

Very special thanks to Mireille and Martin. And to Max Miedinger and The Buggles, too.

Collaborating Associations & Companies
ADG-FAD
Sappi
Infinia
Hewlett Packard
AD Forum
Pioneer

Collaborating Schools
Miami Ad School Europe

Collaborating Media
Control
d(x)i
Estrategias
Impactos!
Interactive
El Publicista
Visual
Le cool
Point.Ben
La más bella
MediaForum
HMagazine
TIVU
My Marketing Net
El Periódico
Brand Life
The Balde
Briefing

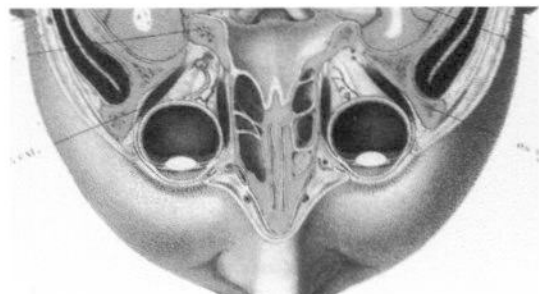

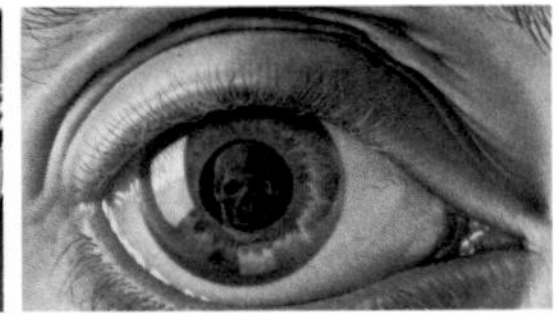
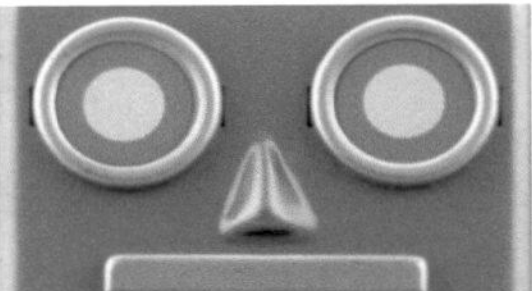

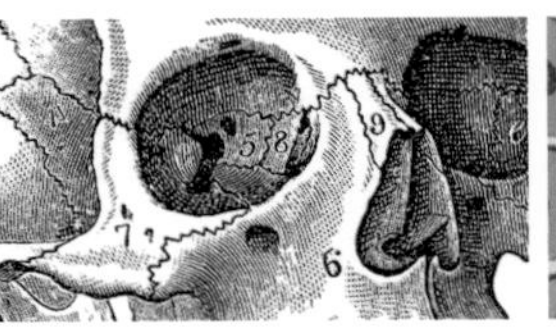
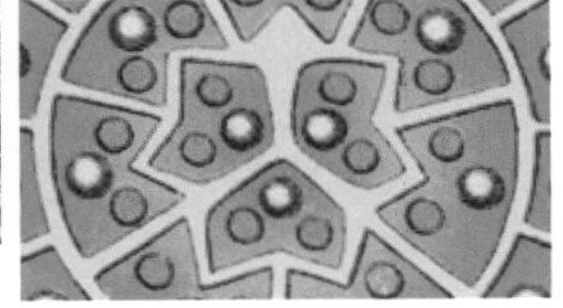

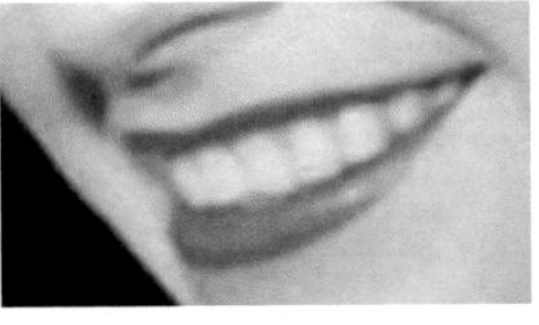
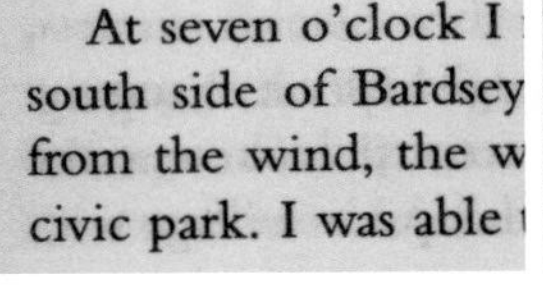
At seven o'clock I
south side of Bardsey
from the wind, the w
civic park. I was able

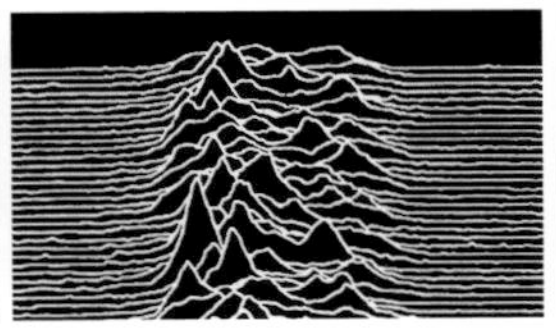

Media

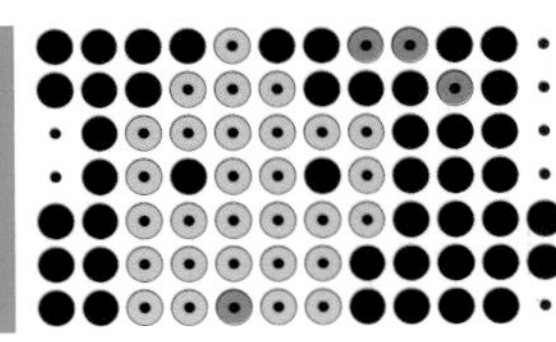

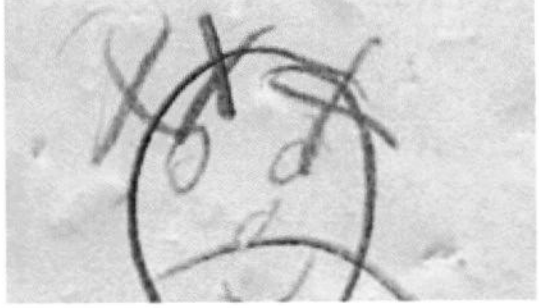
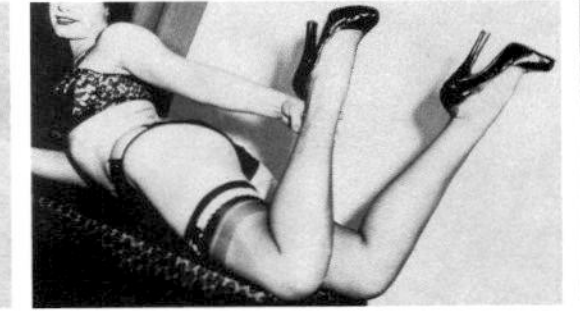

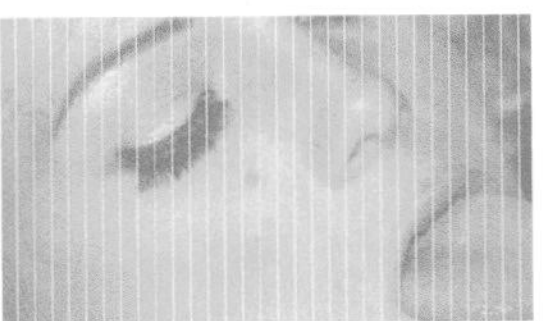

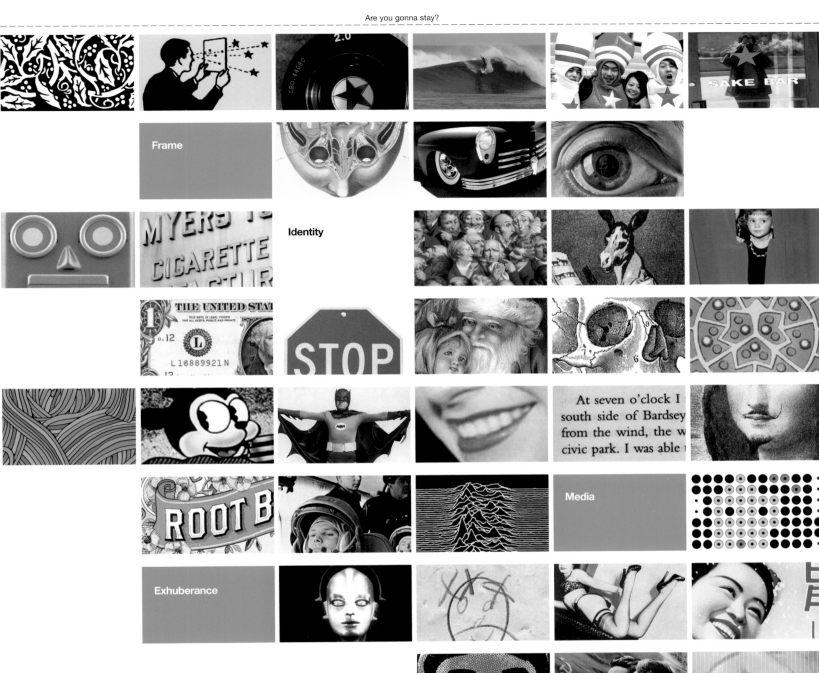

FROM

Q: Is content a luxury?

Manifesto

To those who chase a dream in life - the obstinate, the tenacious, the committed, the sincere, the open-minded. To those who strive for excellence, work to a higher standard and never give up.
To those with passion for crafting detail. To those who place integrity before profit and believe in the triumph of enthusiasm over scepticism. To those committed to honour excellence beyond prejudice, cultural borders and national differences. To those with the vision and ability to challenge what is accepted.

To those who never stop dreaming.

Contents

208 New & Mixed Media

312 Design

458 Epilogue

Q: Are you sure?

Welcome

ADC★E unites the leading advertising and design Clubs / Associations and creatives across Europe.

On Saturday 9th June, 2007, a jury of over 50 top European creatives chaired by the ADC★E President Johannes Newrkla met at the FAD building, the centre of creativity in Barcelona, and judged over 960 Gold, Silver and other awarded pieces of work in 24 categories from 21 countries across Europe. After a long and rewarding day the jury nominated 145 pieces of work. From these 24 Golds were awarded across the different categories and the overall Grand Prix Award, Europe's top creative honour, went to Germany.

The ADC★E aims to unite, excite and inspire European creativity and act as a gateway to its respective community. ADC★E 2007 brings you "the best of the best" in advertising and design.

The following pages are a testimony of the great diversity in creativity that is being done across Europe. We enjoyed bringing the work together and we hope you enjoy reading this book on European creativity as much as we did compiling it.

ADC*E Godfather
Jon Hegarty

President
Johannes Newrkla

Vice-President
Martin Spillmann

Honourable Member of the Board
Michael Conrad

Board
Johannes Newrkla *Austria*
Bojan Hadzihalilovic *Bosnia & Herzegovina*
Eda Kauba *Czech Republic*
J. Margus Klaar *Estonia*
Rémi Babinet *France*
Michael Preiswerk *Germany*
Haukur Már Hauksson *Iceland*
Carol Lambert *Ireland*
Franco Moretti *Italy*
Eriks Stendzenieks *Latvia*
Kot Przybora *Poland*
Mário Mandacaru *Portugal*
Alexander Alexeev *Russia*
Jernej Repvos *Slovenia*
Helena Rosa-Trias *Spain*
Martin Spillmann *Switzerland*

Project Manager
Mercè Segú

Club Co-ordinators
Hans Georg Feik *Austria*
Ekrem Dupanovic *Bosnia & Herzegovina*
Edgar Horcic *Czech Republic*
Tiia Nômm *Estonia*
Nathalie Roland *France*
David Riebner *Germany*
Haukur Már Hauksson *Iceland*
Elaine McDevitt *Ireland*
Gabriele Biffi *Italy*
Zane Berzina *Latvia*
Pawel Tyszkiewicz *Poland*
Maria de Lourdes Matta *Portugal*
Elena Artamonova *Russia*
Eulàlia París *Spain*
Helen Müller *Switzerland*

Members

Q: Will the future be global?

Austria
Creativ Club Austria
Kochgasse 34/16,
A-1080 Wien
T +43 1 408 53 51
F +43 1 408 53 52
office@creativclub.at
www.creativclub.at

Bosnia & Herzegovina
Art Directors Club B-H
Velika Avlija 14
BH - 71000 Sarajevo
T +387 33 272 630
F +387 33 272 660
dupanovic@futuramedia.ba
www.media-marketing.ba

Czech Republic
Art Directors Club C R
V Jircharich 8
110 00 - Praha 1
Czech Republic
T +420 296 334 850-2
F +420 296 334 853
info@adc-czech.cz
www.adc-czech.cz

Estonia
Art Directors Club Eesti
Pärnu mnt. 20A
10141 Tallinn
T +372 6691 950
F +372 6691 951
tiia@korpus.ee

France
Le Club des Directeurs Artistiques
40 Boulevard Malesherbes
F-75008 Paris
T +33 1 47 42 29 12
F +33 1 47 42 59 90
nathalie.roland@leclubdesad.org
www.leclubdesad.org

Germany
Art Directors Club für Deutschland
Leibnizstraße 65
D-10629 Berlin
T +49 (0) 30 59 00 310-0
F +49 (0) 30 59 00 310-11
adc@adc.de
www.adc.de

Iceland
FIT Association of Icelandic Graphic Designers
Félag Íslenskra Teiknara
P.O. Box 8766
128 Reykjavik
T +354 552 9900
fit@loremipsum.is
www.loremipsum.is

Ireland
Institute of Creative Advertising & Design
26 Upper Baggot Street
Dublin 4
T +353 1 6609768
F +353 1 6630026
elaine@icad.ie
www.icad.ie

Italy
Art Directors Club Italiano
Via Moscova 46/3
20121 Milan
T +39 02 655 5943
F +39 02 659 0736
info@adci.it
www.adci.it

Latvia
Latvian Art Directors Club
13 Janvära iela 33,
Riga, LV-1050,
T +371 72 28 21 8
F +371 75 03 61 6
info@adclub.lv
www.adclub.lv

Poland
The Polish Association of Advertising Agencies (SAR)
ul. Lowicka 25 lok. P4
02 - 502 Warszawa
T +48 22 898 84 25
F +48 22 898 26 23
office@sar.org.pl
www.sar.org.pl

Portugal
Clube de Criativos de Portugal
Rua Carlos Testa 1, 1ºA
1050-046 Lisbon
T +351 21 312 15 65/6
F +351 21 312 15 69
M +351 91 756 36 12
clubedecriativos@apap.co.pt
www.clubecriativos.com

Russia
Art Directors Club of Russia
11, Bolshoi Karetnyi Pereulok
Moscow, 127051
T +7 495 9330500
F +7 495 9330501
mail@adcrussia.ru
www.adcrussia.ru

Slovenia
Art Directors Club of Slovenia
StudioMarketing JWT
Vojkova 50
1000 Ljubljana
T +386 1 58 968 10
Jernej.Repovs@smjwt.com

Spain
Art Directors & Graphic Designers Association / ADG-FAD
Convent dels Àngels
Plaça dels Àngels, 5-6
08001 Barcelona
T +34 93 443 75 20
F +34 93 329 60 79
info@adg-fad.org
www.adg-fad.org

Switzerland
Art Directors Club Schweiz
Oberdorfstr. 15
CH-8001 Zürich
T +41 44 262 00 33
F +41 44 262 02 74
info@adc.ch
www.adc.ch

ADCE Board Meeting
Barcelona, June 07

Left to right, top row
Franco Moretti, Michael Preiswerk, Alexander Alexeev, Andris Eglajs, Haukur Már Hauksson, Johannes Newrkla, Martin Spillmann

Left to right, bottom row
Mário Mandacaru, Helena Rosa-Trias, Mercè Segú, Eda Kauba, Maria Bourke Tiia Nömm, Renos Demetriou, Przemek Bogdanowicz

President's Statement

"Predictions are difficult, especially about the future" Karl Valentin, *German comedian*

Everything in life seems to get its own event character, from births to funerals. Entertainment and commerce are merging. Brands are functioning as cultural enabler. The futurologist Peter Wippermann said "the fragmentation of target groups and the atomization of media channels must be reoccupied by themes of overriding importance that can be delivered through entertainment." So media is becoming the glue for our society and the Internet is the experimental field for communication. An idea doesn't give a damn about who had it. It doesn't care if it's a copywriter, graphic designer, or an Internet nerd. In a way we can already see, that low resolution and viral advertising has gone mainstream. Look at the winner of the 2007 Grand Prix and you'll easily understand.

In this years "Book of the books" - the annual of the best of European advertising and design - you will find many other exceptional works that will give you valuable hints of how future communication might change because it is already shaping itself today.

The never-ending cleverness of future advertising and design convinced the Jury, 53 top creatives from across Europe, attending this years Award of Awards Show from the Art Directors Club of Europe (ADC*E), and after a long day and much debate they voted the German "The Make-Believe Story of Ron Hammer" mixed media campaign by Heimat Berlin, the best of the best and awarded it the 2007 Grand Prix. Two weeks ahead of Cannes, the ADC*E Jury sets the pace.

With a new record high of entries and four great European juries, we are proud to honour European diversity in communication with 24 Gold Awards.

ADC*E also aims to encourage young European creatives and we were delighted to award a scholarship to the Miami Ad School, worth 10,000 euros to our European Student of the Year, Eva Klose of Germany. The Young Creative Team awarded Gold was Rafal Gorski, Adam Smerecynski and Konrad Grzegorzewicz of Poland.

I would like to take this opportunity to thank everyone in the jury for his or her enthusiasm, great input and understanding, without this a not-for profit organisation like ours cannot exist. Also thank you to the Board, consisting of all our member countries delegates, for their help in making ADC*E grow every year. We will never stop dreaming of our ability to challenge the future and so improving European communication.

Back in 1991, some enthusiastic creatives founded the Art Directors Club of Europe to encourage and improve European advertising and design. The world has changed since then, but it is still ideas that drive us in our never-ending quest for inspiration. The Art Directors Club of Europe is owned and managed by its, currently, 16 members of leading creative Clubs/Associations across Europe. It is the only Awards scheme in the world to bring all of the European Awards winning work together into one competition.
Two years ago ADC*E opened its doors for more award-winning advertising and design work from around Europe to take part in these exciting and exclusive Awards.

Q: Can we believe in what we see?

Q: What do you want?

The ADC*E winners don't stop in this annual that we call "The book of the books" - all Golds and Nominees will be judged once more by The Cup jury in November. This is the first intercontinental Award Show, where you cannot enter your work, unless the work is already a winner, either at ADC*E, Golden Drum, AdFest or FIAP. The Cup's idea matches our goals 100%, focussing on great regional creativity and committed to honouring excellence beyond prejudice, cultural borders and national differences.

Stay inspired!

ADCE President

Johannes Newrkla

Q: MySpa
the TV Sta

ce Killed ar?

Grand Prix

Q: Is the audience the Demiurg?

Grand Prix

The Make-Believe Story of Ron Hammer

(In DVD)
Germany

National Award
Gold
Agency
Heimat, Berlin
Client
Hornbach AG
Creative Director
Guido Heffels,
Juergen Vossen
Art Director
Tim Schneider
Copywriter
Till Eckel
Designer
Jan Wentz,
Michael Mackens,
Proximity Germany GmbH
Film Director
Jan Wentz
Director of photography
Jo Molitoris
Agency Producer
Kerstin Breuer
Production Company
Markenfilm Berlin/
Treibstoff Pictures
Post production
nhb Berlin /
Niko Papoutsis
Sound Design:
Nima Gholiagha,
nhb Berlin
Web Producer
Proximity Germany GmbH
Other
Executive Producer:
Lutz Müller
Editor:
Piet Schmelz

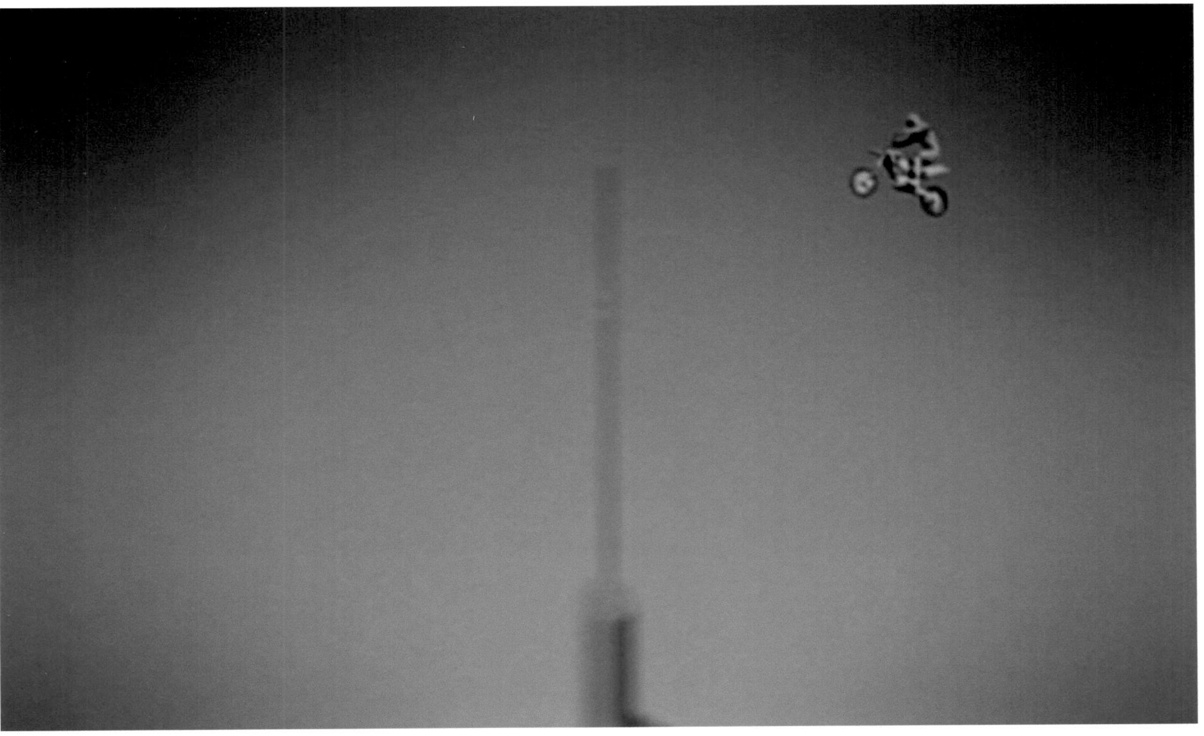

In the run up to a V.A.T. increase, the job was to communicate to D.I.Y. enthusiasts the size of Hornbach Superstores. So we used a yet unknown motorbike stuntman to communicate the size of Hornbach by letting him try to jump over one. An amateur video captured the crash. Usually a campaign like that ends here but this was where the Ron Hammer campaign started to take off. Step by step the media, both on and offline were brought on board to increase the credibility and, gradually, even the non-believers became believers.

Grand Prix

"Is the New and
Mixed Media the
future? Not really,
it is the present.
Let the Grand
Prix in this book
be the answer."

Franco Moretti.
New & Mixed
Media Chairman

Q: Can the media be innocent?

Q: Why does Capitalism want us to be always young?

Film

Q: How far is your client from your beliefs?

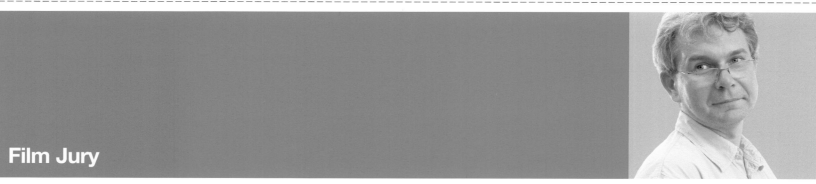

Film Jury

I guess our jury was the least conflicting and the most comfortably settled. Great work. Sometimes very Estonian and always absolutely non-German. Tereza from Prague was giggling at Russian films, thank you Tereza. I still believe the superb Audi 'Designed to thrill' deserves Gold for TV not for print. I was mystified that 'Bocelli' for Zurich Home for the Blind got nothing, stunning work. Johannes just recalled that their film with Stevie Wonder's song took an award last year.
So consistency really matters, watch out for the Golds of 2007.
Still it was quite hard to judge TV graphics, which weren't really graphics for TV, and Film-Any Other because, unlike traditional TV and Cinema commercials, the wide range of digital formats made them more challenging to watch.

But lastly 'Basketball' by VW got Gold for TV because (in my opinion) of its perfect casting and action, 'Incredibly Mini' for brilliant dialogs and natural interaction with TV format, 'Back Seat' got Gold in Cinema, because it delivers with greater on the big screen. And 'The Art of Football' is just hilarious.

One great day full of great work, great impressions, great talks. Thank you, creative officers of Europe.

Alexander Alexeev
Chairman
President ADCR, MD and ExecCD McCann Erickson
Russia

He graduated from the Academy of Print in 1987. In 1994, he worked as an Art Director for the Centre of Contemporary Arts. From 1994 to 1995, he worked at BBDO Moscow. In 1995, he worked for Akademie Der Kunst in Berlin, and from 1996 to 2001 he worked as an Art Director/Creative Director for Adventa Lowe. From 2001 until 2005, he worked as a Creative Director for McCann Erickson Russia. Since 2005, he has served as President of the Art Directors Club of Russia and has been a member of the Union of Artist since 1993. Since 2006, he has been the Managing Director and Executive Creative Director for McCann Erickson Russia.

Christoph Gaunersdorfer
Creative Director
Jung von Matt/Donau
Austria

Born in Vienna in 1976 and graduated from the ViennArt High School in 1995, he studied Journalism and Theory of Drama at the University of Vienna. In 1999, he began work for Demner, Merlicek, & Bergmann as a Copywriter. Since 2002, he has worked as a Copywriter for Jung von Matt in Vienna, and presently, is the Creative Director there.

Tereza Sverakova
Creative Director
Leagas Delaney Prague
Czech Republic

She started her career 13 years ago as a Copywriter. Since then, she has worked for several network agencies. For four years, she was a Creative Director for DDB Prague before she joined Leagas Delaney Prague to work on the Skoda account.

Alvar Jaakson
Creative Director
Division
Estonia

Alvar Jaakson has been creative director in Division McCann-Erickson since 2004. He has also worked as an animated film director and been lecturer of creative advertising in Tallinn University. He has been member of Estonian and Lithuanian national advertising award juries.

Stephan Moritz
Sound Engineer and Composer, Studio Funk GmbH & Co. KG
Germany

He was born in Berlin in 1977. In 1998, he worked as a Sound Engineer, Composer, Sound Designer, Director, and Producer at Studio Funk Berlin. In 2004, he began work at ADC Germany. He has won numerous national and international awards for sound design for television, cinema, and radio commercials, including awards for music, composing, and for directing radio commercials. Such awards include those from ADC, Eurobest, Clio, D&AD, NYF, LIAS, Ramses, ARD, and many more.

Bjarni Helgason
Art Director
EKKERT
Iceland

Graduated with BA in Graphic Design from the Icelandic Academy of the Arts in 2001. In 2004, he graduated from Kent Institute of Art and Design with MA in Media Arts, where he explored the relationship between sound and image. In 2007, he started his own company called EKKERT (eng. NOTHING) working in design, advertising, motion graphics, as well as teaching courses at the Icelandic Academy of the Arts.

Nicholas Pereira
Art Director
Publicis QMP
Ireland

Nicholas Pereira is an Art Director at Publicis QMP in Dublin. A South African living in Ireland, he has worked for agencies such as The Jupiter Drawing Room and TBWA\Hunt\Lascaris in Johannesburg and Ogilvy in Cape Town. He has won enough awards to give him a big(ish) head, but not enough to retire young(ish).

Andris Eglajs
Zoom
Latvia

Andris Eglajs is an inspiring visionary. After marketing and business organisation studies and work experience in Germany Andris returned to Latvia to join one of the best northern European advertising agencies - ZOOM! As the head of his business development department he is responsible for expanding the business into The Business. Born 1980 in Latvia, Andris' life has been touched by different political systems, moral principles and values. "Unique time with outstanding valuable experience," he says.

Przemek Bogdanowicz
President and Chief Creative Officer
BBDO Warsaw
Poland

Born in 1965,he graduated from the Design Department at the Academy of Fine Arts in Warsaw. He joined DMB&B Warsaw as an Art Director in 1993.

In 1997 became an Associate Creative Director, and, in 1999, the Creative Director of the agency. In 2002 the agency changed its name locally into G7 and until 2005 he was the Managing Partner & Creative Director. In August 2005 he joined BBDO Warsaw as the Chief Creative Officer, and since 2006 he has also been the President of the BBDO Group in Poland.

Winner of the national and international advertising festivals. Also, he is a founder and a board member of KTR (Polish Creative Club).

Vasco Thomáz
Art Director
MSTF Partners
Portugal

Vasco Thomáz (25) started working as an Art Director at Young & Rubicam in 2001, and then moved on to MSTF Partners (currently the number 1 National Ad Agency in the Portuguese ranking, according to Media Monitor) where he has been working ever since its foundation until the present day.
Vasco has been awarded in several different national and international festivals, such as: Young Guns of Portugal, Festival de Publicida de Lusófona, Épica, Creative Club of Portugal, Portuguese Language Festival, Cresta Awards, Cannes Lions and several others.

Siscu Molina
Managing Creative Director
Tiempo BBDO
Spain

Member and Creative Director in charge of the Audiovisual Production department at SCPF between 1998 and 2005. He was a Judge of the Laus awards in 2002 and 2007, and Jury Chairman of the Club de Creativos (CDC) in 2006.

Q: Is truth still a value?

Matthias Freuler
Creative Director
Wirz Werbung
Switzerland

Renos Demetriou
Creative Director - Founder
Daedalus CS
Cyprus

Matthias Freuler has been working in advertising since 1982. He has won more than 300 national and international awards, including a Gold Lion, four Bronze Lions, and numerous shortlist entries in Cannes, a Grand Prix Eurobest, a Grand Prize London International Advertising Award, Gold at a New York festival, Gold at the Art Directors Club New York, and ADC Europe.

Born in Cyprus in 1971, he graduated in 1994 in Design and Advertising at the University of North Florida (US). After that he spent two years in Miami as a freelance designer and in 1996 he worked in Atlanta on a project for the Olympic Games at the studio Formation Creative Media. At the same time he studied interactive and broadcast media at the Art Institute of Atlanta. He carried on working with Formation and for 2 years he was the team leader for projects between Atlanta and New York. In 2001 he returned to Cyprus where he founded his own company called Daedalus CS (Creative Services) and also was the founder of the Cyprus Creative Club.

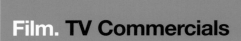

Film. TV Commercials

Austria

Czech Republic

Estonia

Germany: 2 Gold 5 Nominations

Ireland

Italy

Latvia

Poland: 1 Nomination

Portugal

Russia

Spain: 2 Nominations

Switzerland

United Kingdom: 1 Nomination

Gold
Basketball
(In DVD)
Germany

National Award
Silver
Agency
DDB Germany, Berlin
Client
Volkswagen AG
Creative Director
Amir Kassaei,
Wolfgang Schneider,
Mathias Stiller,
Bart Penlacke,
Stephan Shulte
Art Director
Kristoffer Heilemann
Copywriter
Ludwig Berndl
Film Director
Sebastian Strasser
Director of Photography
Rodrigo Prieto
Agency Producer
Marion Lange
Production Company
Radical Media
Producer
Christiane Lochte
Other
CD: Bert Peulecke,
Stefan Schulte
Editor: Nils Landmark

Makes anyone look strong.
The new Polo GTI®.

A couple of huge streetball players are choosing teams. They get into a fierce fight over a small guy, although his athletic abilities are obviously very limited. But he is the owner of a Polo GTI.

Gold
Incredibly Mini
(In DVD)
Germany

National Award
Bronze
Agency
Jung von Matt AG
Client
BMW AG MINI
Creative Director
Oliver Voss,
Goetz Ulmer
Art Director
Julia Ziegler,
Nils Eberhardt,
Till Monshausen
Copywriter
Dennis May,
Fabian Frese
Production Company
@radical.media Berlin

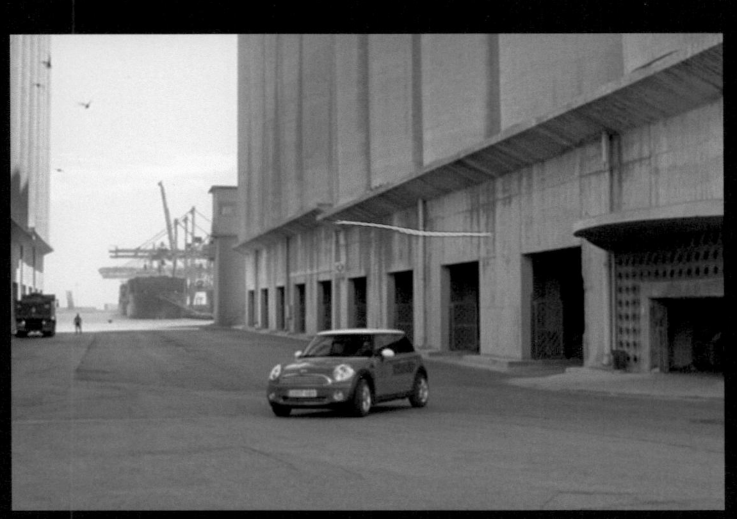

UNGLAUBLICH MINI. DER NEUE MINI.

WWW.MINI.DE

The new MINI is out! A worldwide campaign spreads this great news all over the globe. And tells the people that the new edition of the legend is more driving fun than ever.

Nomination
Back Seat
(In DVD)
Germany

National Award
Shortlist
Agency
BBDO Germany GmbH Team smart
Client
DaimlerChrysler Vertriebsorganisation Deutschland
Creative Director
T. Bazarkaya, S. Hardieck, M. Eickmeyer, S.Meske
Art Director
Szymon Rose, Florian Barthelmess, Jonathan Schupp
Film Director
Markus Walter, Malte Hagemeister
Agency Producer
A. Berkenbusch, M. Ceranna, S. Gentis
Production Company
Cobblestone Filmproduktion Hamburg GmbH
Post Production
Schoenheitsfarm, Hamburg

>> No backseats. The smart fortwo.

www.smart.com

Back Seat
Sometimes it's more secure to drive a car with no backseats. Note: All scenes in the commercial were filmed referring to the cinematic look of the originals.

Nomination
Better Living Starts At Home: Faktum, Besta, Beddinge
(In DVD)
Poland

National Award
Silver
Agency
Leo Burnett Warsaw
Client
IKEA
Creative Director
Martin Winther
Art Director
Jakub Zielecki
Copywriter
Michel Lars
Film Director
Sebastian Panczyk
Agency Producer
Leo Burnett Warsaw
Production Company
Platige Image
Other
Producers:
Agnieszka Trzeciak,
Janusz Wlodarski

Nomination
Motorway
(In DVD)
Germany

National Award
Shortlist
Agency
DDB Germany, Berlin
Client
Volkswagen AG
Creative Director
Amir Kassaei, Mathias Stiller,
Wolfgang Schneider
Art Director
Kristoffer Heilemann
Copywriter
Ludwig Berndl
Film Director
Edward Berger
Director of Photography
Michael Heiter
Agency Producer
Marion Lange
Production Company
soup.film GmbH
Other
Planning: Jason Lusty, Wiebke Dreyer
Sound: Stephan Moritz, André Kón
Editor: Ruxanra Wôltche

Relax. It's the new Polo.

Motorway
A police car next to the highway: an officer incredulously reads out the record of an incredibly spectacular car accident. The driver confirms all that very matter-of-factly. The reason is his car: Relax. It's the new Polo.

Smith and Schmidt
The new Mercedes-Benz S-Class has Pre-safe - an accident prevention system that also helps you to anticipate and react earlier as a driver. It is the automotive equivalent of the modern business leader who thinks two and often three steps ahead of the rest of us. The film shows what happens when two men, both brilliant businessmen and S-class owners, go head to head.

Nomination
Smith and Schmidt
(In DVD)
Germany

National Award
Shortlist
Agency
S&J International B.V.,
S&J Werbegeantur GmbH
& Co. KG
Client
Mercedes-Benz
Creative Director
Murray White,
Tobias Ahrens
Copywriter
Murray White
Film Director
Sven Bollinger,
Murray White
Agency Producer
Hermann Krug,
Mirco Seyfert
Production Company
Tony Petersen Fim GmbH

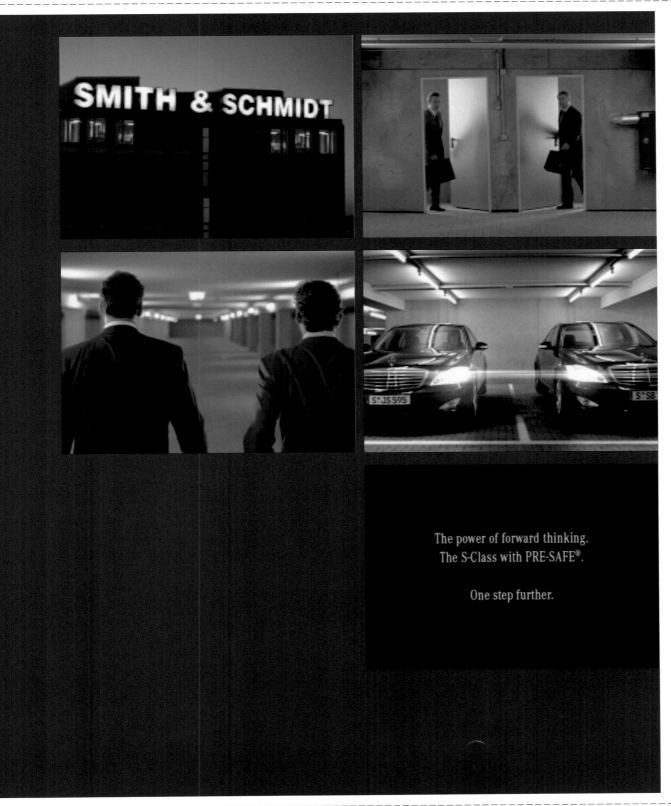

The power of forward thinking.
The S-Class with PRE-SAFE®.

One step further.

Nomination
Turk
(In DVD)
Germany

National Award
Shortlist
Agency
Kempertrautmann GmbH
Client
MTV Networks GmbH
& Co. OHG
Creative Director
Frank Bannoehr,
Daniel Ernsting
Art Director
Frank Bannoehr
Copywriter
Daniel Ernsting
Film Director
Alex Feil
Production Company
e + p commercial
Filmproduktion GmbH

Turk
Police officers are filming a checkpoint with a hidden camera. Their colleagues, ask a foreign resident to perform a completely silly choreographed routine. Meanwhile, the officers in the car turn up the volume on the radio. It appears as if the foreign resident is dancing to "Macarena". When the driver of the car notices that he is being made a fool of, he goes ballistic. Chart: "Not a minute without comedy. COMEDY CENTRAL".

Aus Liebe zum Automobil

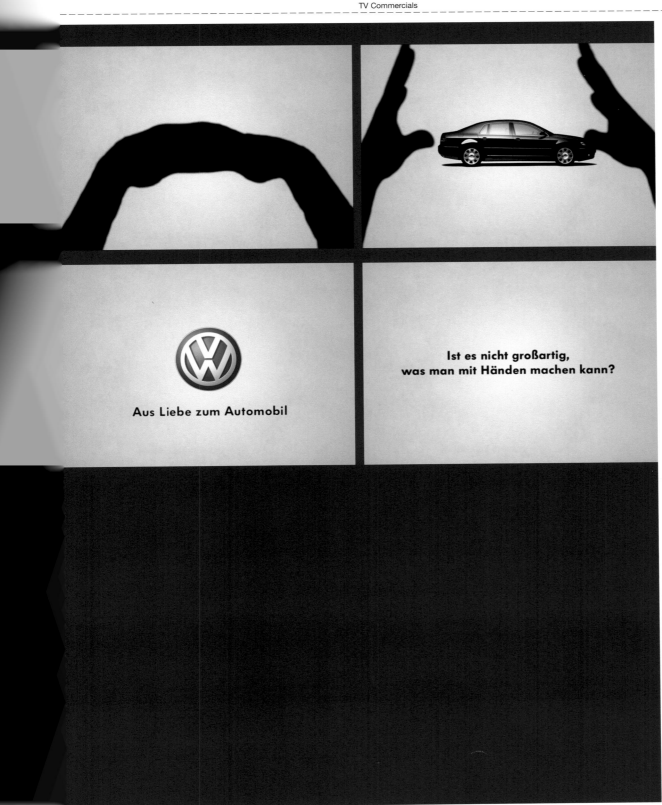

Ist es nicht großartig,
was man mit Händen machen kann?

Nomination
Galanty show
(In DVD)
Germany

National Award
Gold
Agency
Grabarz & Partner
Client
Volkswagen AG
Creative Director
Ralf Heuel,
Ralf Nolting
Art Director
Christoph Stricker
Copywriter
Paul von Muehlendahl
Film Director
Michael Reissinger
Production Company
deli pictures
postproduktion GmbH

Nomination
Hairdresser
(In DVD)
Spain

National Award
Shortlist
Agency
Vitruvio Leo Burnett
Client
Sitges Sci-Fi & Fantasy Film Festival
Creative Director
Rafa Antón
Art Director
Alberto Antón, Javier Álvarez
Copywriter
Alberto Jaén
Film Director
Yuri Alemani
Director of Photography
Pedro del Rey
Agency Producer
Dionisio Naranjo & Guzmán Molín Pradel
Production Company
Lee Films

Hairdresser
Anniversary of Lynch's "Blue Velvet" premier. Time enough to get it.

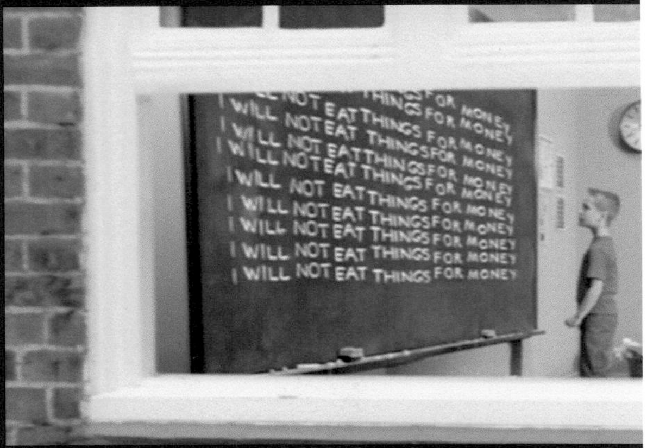

Nomination

Come Home to The Simpson

(In DVD)
UK

National Award
Shortlist
Agency
Devilfish
Client
Sky One
Creative Director
Richard Holman
Art Director
Nik Stewart
Copywriter
Jonny Parker
Film Director
Chris Palmer
Director of Photography
Ian Foster
Agency Producer
Audrey Hawkins
Production Company
Gorgeous
Other
Prod. Co Producer:
Rupert Smythe

Nomination
Commas and full stops
(In DVD)
Spain

National Award
Silver
Agency
DDB Barcelona
Client
V.A.E.S.A.
Creative Director
José Mª Roca de Viñals
Art Director
Quito Leal
Copywriter
Oscar Vidal Larsson
Film Director
Joan Constansó
Director of Photography
Sergi Ventallo
Agency Producer
Vicky Moñino
Production Company
La Iguana

Commas and Full Stops
From the viewpoint of a driver we see, a series of moving images, a series of views. Some grammatical symbols interrupt, stopping and starting the action with no compassion; both the images and the music.

One loves Music - Rock it
ONE LOVES MUSIC is a big multi-media campaign focused on music. In the TV-spots professional breakdancers show their fingerdance skills to the music of Rock it, the breakdance classic.

One loves Music - Princess Superstar
ONE LOVES MUSIC is a big multi-media campaign focused on music. In the TV spot professional breakdancers show their fingerdance skills to the music of Princess Superstar.

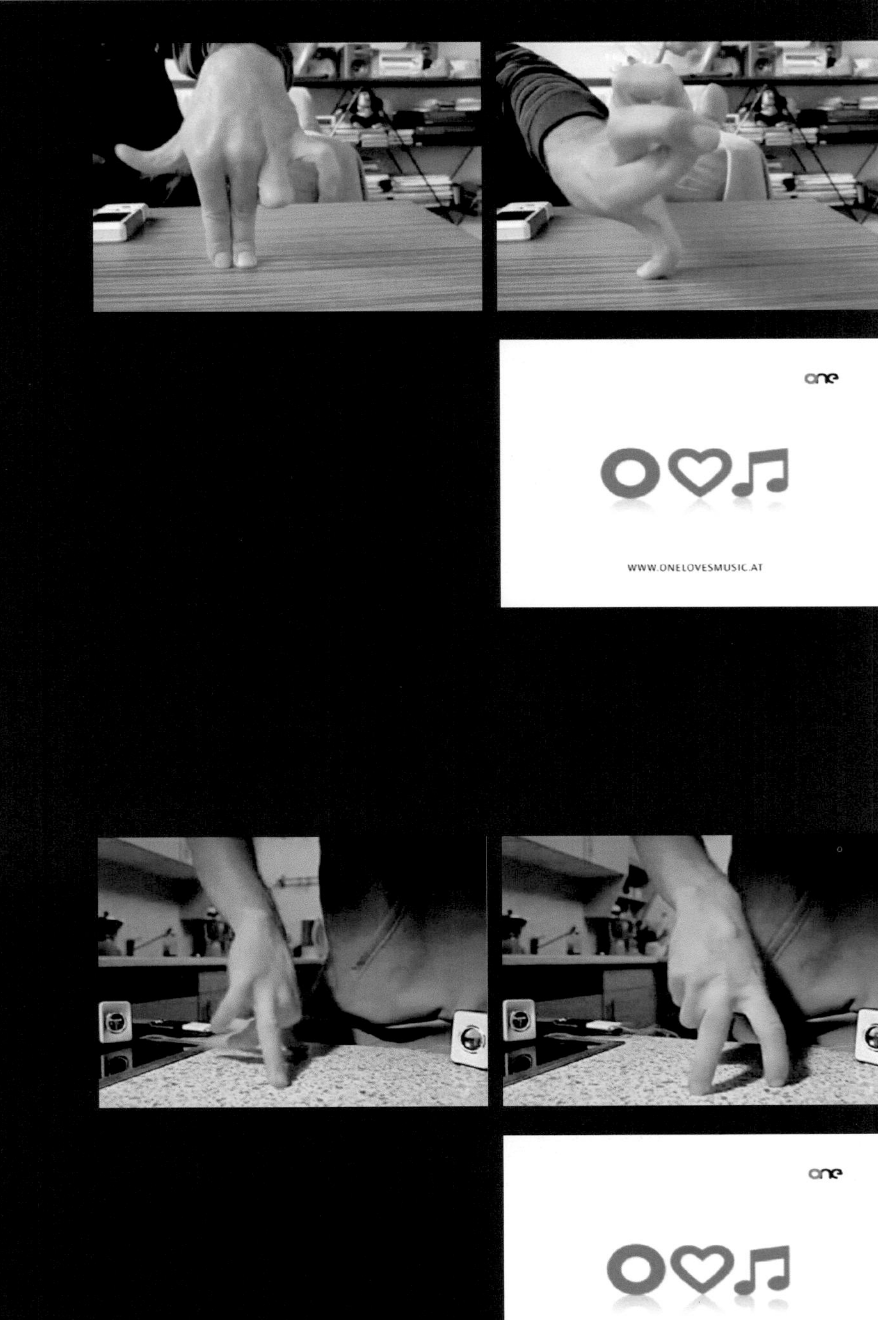

One Loves Music Rock it
(In DVD)
Austria

National Award
Gold
Agency
Jung von Matt/Donau Werbeagentur GmbH
Client
One GmbH
Creative Director
Andreas Putz, Christoph Gaunersdorfer
Art Director
Georg Feichtinger
Copywriter
Christoph Gaunersdorfer, Bernd Wilfinger
Film Director
Niklas Weise
Production Company
Neue Sentimental Film Wien
Other
Producer: Thomas Bogner, Ernst Koth

One Loves Music Princess Superstar
(In DVD)
Austria

National Award
Gold
Agency
Jung von Matt/Donau Werbeagentur GmbH
Client
One GmbH
Creative Director
Andreas Putz, Christoph Gaunersdorfer
Art Director
Georg Feichtinger
Copywriter
Christoph Gaunersdorfer, Bernd Wilfinger
Film Director
Niklas Weise
Production Company
Neue Sentimental Film Wien
Other
Producer: Thomas Bogner, Ernst Koth

Betandwin Magic Moments of Sports
(In DVD)
Austria

National Award
Silver
Agency
Springer & Jacoby Österreich GmbH
Client
BWIN Interactive Entertainment AG
Creative Director
Paul Holcmann, Murray White
Art Director
Katharina Haines
Copywriter
Hans Juckel
Film Director
David Frankham
Director of Photography
Carl Nilsson
Agency Producer
Hermann Krug, Stephan Bandermann
Production Company
STINK London, Springer & Jacoby Hamburg
Other
M. Kloss Zechner, M. Bodner, R. Kober, H.P. Feichtner

Bulgaria
(In DVD)
Czech Republic

National Award
Silver
Agency
Young and Rubicam Prague
Client
Cesky Telecom
Creative Director
Daniel Ruzicka
Art Director
Ondrej Hubl
Copywriter
Jaroslav Schovanec
Film Director
Tomas Masin
Director of Photography
Sebastian Milaszewski
Agency Producer
Jana Kudrnackova
Production Company
GPS Production and Dawson

There are moments when anything's possible.

In the spirit of the game.

Betandwin Magic Moments of Sports
In November 2005 betandwin brought 12 of the greatest athletes of all time together. Legends from all fields of sports discussed the subject of sports in general and their own very personal magic moments as sportsmen and sport fans. Online betting and gaming.

Bulgaria
Cesky Telecom - Internet Express.

Goose
Goose is thanking people for cleaner air.

The Bear
(In DVD)
Estonia

National Award
Silver
Agency
Zavod BBDO
Client
Postimees
Creative Director
Marek Reinaas
Art Director
Marko Kekishev
Copywriter
Toomas Verrev

Goose
(In DVD)
Estonia

National Award
Silver
Agency
Kontuur Leo Burnett
Client
Honda
Creative Director
Henri Jääger
Art Director
Jaanus Meri
Copywriter
Andrus Niit
Film Director
Jaanus Meri
Agency Producer
Karin Sepp
Production Company
Kontuur LB
Project Manager:
Karin Sepp

Hansabank Small Loans
(In DVD)
Estonia

National Award
Gold
Agency
DDB Estonia
Client
Hansabank
Creative Director
Meelis Mikker
Art Director
Erik Teemägi
Copywriter
Rait Milistver
Film Director
Marko Raat
Agency Producer
Reilika Mäekivi
Production Company
Allfilm

Jail Break
(In DVD)
Estonia

National Award
Gold
Agency
Indigo Bates
Client
Puls Brewery
Creative Director
Indrek Viiderfeld
Art Director
Veiko Tammjärv
Copywriter
Indrek Viiderfeld, Alar Pikkorainen
Film Director
Kaido Veermäe
Director of Photography
Mait Mäekivi
Production Company
Rudolf Konimois Film

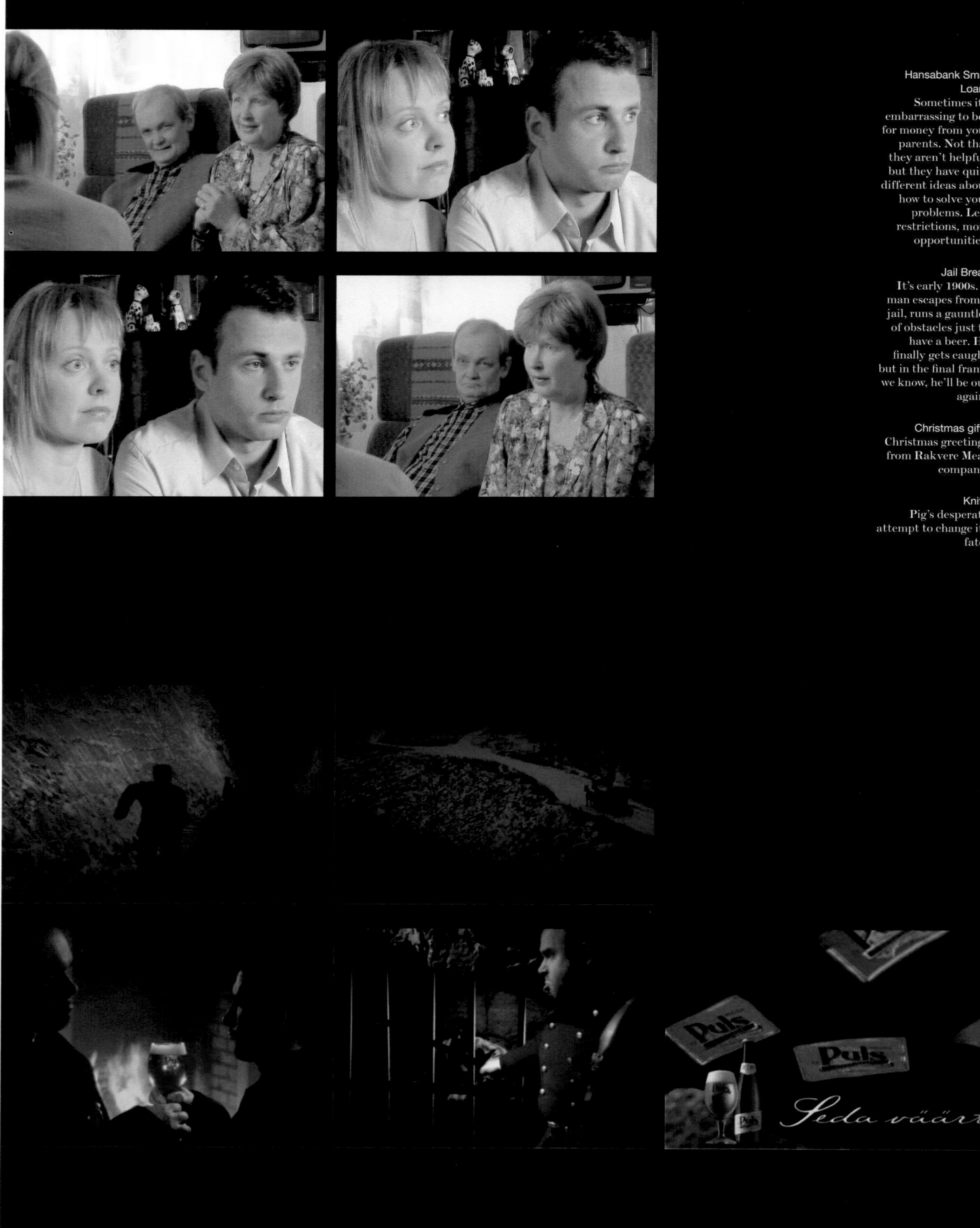

Hansabank Small Loans
Sometimes it's embarrassing to beg for money from your parents. Not that they aren't helpful, but they have quite different ideas about how to solve your problems. Less restrictions, more opportunities!

Jail Break
It's early 1900s. A man escapes from a jail, runs a gauntlet of obstacles just to have a beer. He finally gets caught but in the final frame we know, he'll be out again.

Christmas gifts
Christmas greetings from Rakvere Meat company.

Knife
Pig's desperate attempt to change its fate.

christmas to everybody!
RAKVERE
RAKVERE

Christmas gifts
(In DVD)
Estonia

National Award
Gold
Agency
Kontuur Leo Burnett
Client
Rakvere Meatfactory
Creative Director
Urmas Villmann
Art Director
Jaanus Meri
Copywriter
Andrus Niit
Film Director
Jaanus Meri
Agency Producer
Janika Tobi
Production Company
Kontuur LB
Project Manager:
Peep Pajumäe

Knife
(In DVD)
Estonia

National Award
Gold
Agency
Kontuur Leo Burnett
Client
Rakvere Meatfactory
Creative Director
Urmas Villmann
Art Director
Urmas Villmann
Copywriter
Andrus Niit
Agency Producer
Janika Tobi
Production Company
Kuukulgur; Kontuur LB

Sparkasse
(In DVD)
Germany

National Award
Silver
Agency
Sehsucht GmbH /
Jung von Matt AG
Client
Sparkasse Savings Bank
Creative Director
Oliver Voss, Goetz Ulmer,
Daniel Frericks (JvM)
Art Director
Till Monshausen,
Martin Terhart (JvM)
Copywriter
Dennis May,
Fabian Frese (JvM)
Designer
Ole Peters,
Niko Tziopanos (Sehsucht)
Film Director
Ole Peters,
Tom Abel (Sehsucht)
Agency Producer
Jasmin Bedir (JvM),
Andreas Coutsoumbelis
(Sehsucht)
Production Company
Sehsucht GmbH

Interview
(In DVD)
Ireland

National Award
Silver
Agency
Chemistry Strategic
Communications Ltd
Client
Trócaire
Creative Director
Mike Garner
Art Director
Mike Garner,
Peter Heron
Copywriter
John McMahon
Film Director
Brian O'Malley
Director of Photography
James Mather
Agency Producer
Fiona McGarry
Production Company
Red Rage
Other
***Account Director*:**
Niamh O'Dea

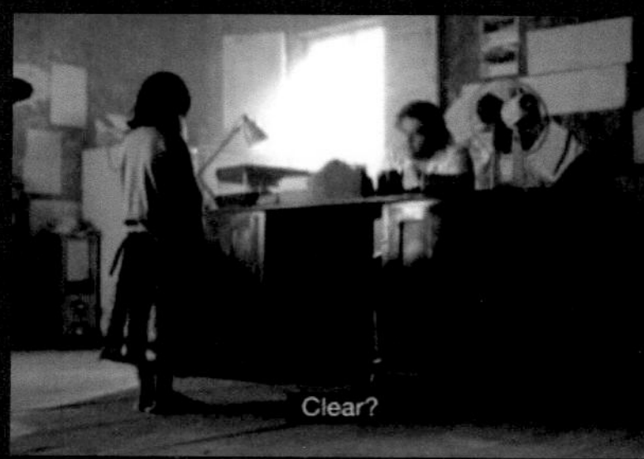

Help end the misery of child labour

www.trocaire.org

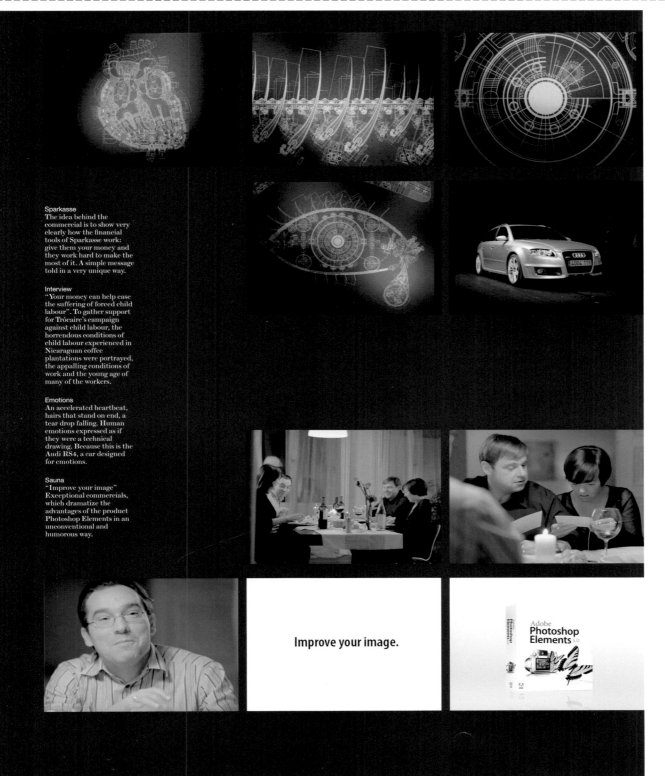

Sparkasse
The idea behind the commercial is to show very clearly how the financial tools of Sparkasse work: give them your money and they work hard to make the most of it. A simple message told in a very unique way.

Interview
"Your money can help ease the suffering of forced child labour". To gather support for Trócaire's campaign against child labour, the horrendous conditions of child labour experienced in Nicaraguan coffee plantations were portrayed, the appalling conditions of work and the young age of many of the workers.

Emotions
An accelerated heartbeat, hairs that stand on end, a tear drop falling. Human emotions expressed as if they were a technical drawing. Because this is the Audi RS4, a car designed for emotions.

Sauna
"Improve your image" Exceptional commercials, which dramatize the advantages of the product Photoshop Elements in an unconventional and humorous way.

Improve your image.

Adobe
Photoshop
Elements 5.0

Emotions
(In DVD)
Spain

National Award
Gold
Agency
DDB Barcelona
Client
V.A.E.S.A.
Creative Director
Alberto Astorga
Art Director
Jaume Badia
Copywriter
Alfredo Binefa
Film Director
David Ruiz
Agency Producer
Vicky Moñino
Production Company
Ruiz + Company

Sauna
(In DVD)
Germany

National Award
Silver
Agency
Jung von Matt AG
Client
Adobe Systems GmbH
Creative Director
Bernhard Lukas,
Arno Lindemann
Art Director
Joanna Swistowski
Copywriter
Caroline Ellert
Film Director
Sven Bollinger
Agency Producer
Nic Heimann
Production Company
Erste Liebe
Filmproduktion GmbH
Other
Editor: Felix Drawe

Low heating costs
(In DVD)
Estonia

National Award
Gold
Agency
Division
Client
Isover
Creative Director
Leslie Laasner
Art Director
Leslie Laasner
Copywriter
Leslie Laasner
Film Director
Jaak Kilmi
Director of Photography
Mart Taniel
Agency Producer
Kaarel Mikkin
Production Company
Kuukulgur Film

Low heating costs
A truck brings the whole winterwood supply that is much smaller than expected. Start saving on heating expenses.

Balta Tears Episode 1
This TV commercial was made for an insurance company with the main idea of reducing potential risks as a sign for a better and safer future, which is emphasized by the campaign's slogan - a calm answer to a nervous world.

Balta Tear episode 1
(In DVD)
Latvia

National Award
Silver
Agency
Food
Client
Balta
Creative Director
Eriks Stendzenieks
Art Director
Maris Upenieks
Peteris Lidaka

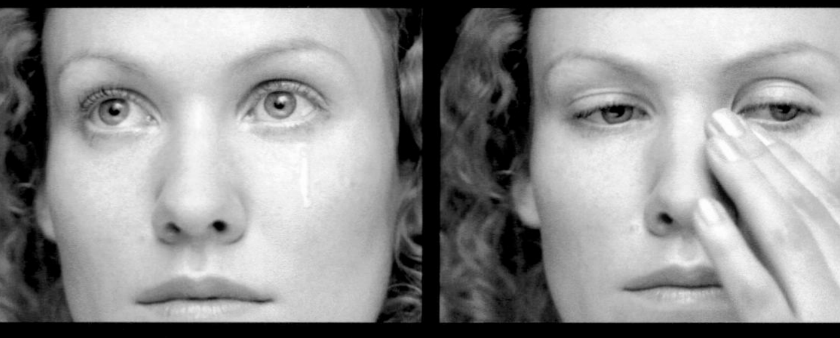

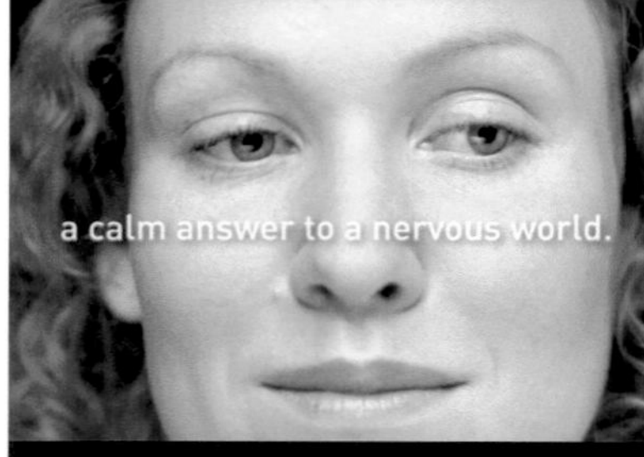

Energy goes beyond what we can see

(In DVD)
Italy

National Award
Silver
Agency
Saatchi & Saatchi
Client
Enel
Creative Director
Luca Albanese,
Francesco Taddeucci
Art Director
Luca Albanese
Copywriter
Francesco Taddeucci
Film Director
Laurence Dunmore
Agency Producer
Manuela Fidenzi
Production Company
H Film
Other
Music: T. Newmand
Producer Production:
D. Cattaneo

Video Testaments
(In DVD)
Estonia

National Award
Silver
Agency
Vatson&Vatson/Y&R
Client
Monetti
Creative Director
Madis Ots
Art Director
Ken Oja
Copywriter
Madis Ots
Film Director
Jan Erik Nõgisto
Agency Producer
Rain Tolk
Production Company
Kuukulgur

Video Testament
During World War II Estonian refugees formed a strong and successful community in Canada. And to their relatives who were left back, the term "rich uncle in Canada" has symbolized financial support ever since. However, a loan via text message is a much faster and simpler way of getting money - just take your mobile phone, send a text message and in a few minutes the money is on your bank account. You won't have to rely on your rich uncle in Canada any more.

Hunt
European bison is a symbol of Polishness and of a beer coming from the heart of Poland's wildlife sanctuary. Another one of a series of commercials featuring the beloved bison.

Hunting
To create an emotional link with the whaling problem this illustrates a simple thought: that extinction of one species must influence other species in the world. Which means it will also influence us.

Thanks
(In DVD)
Portugal

National Award
Silver
Agency
BBDO Portugal
Client
Portuguese Federation of Disability Sports
Creative Director
Nuno Cardoso
Art Director
Fabiano Bonfim
Copywriter
Nuno Cardoso, Nuno Riça
Film Director
José Pedro Sousa
Production Company
Ministério dos Filmes

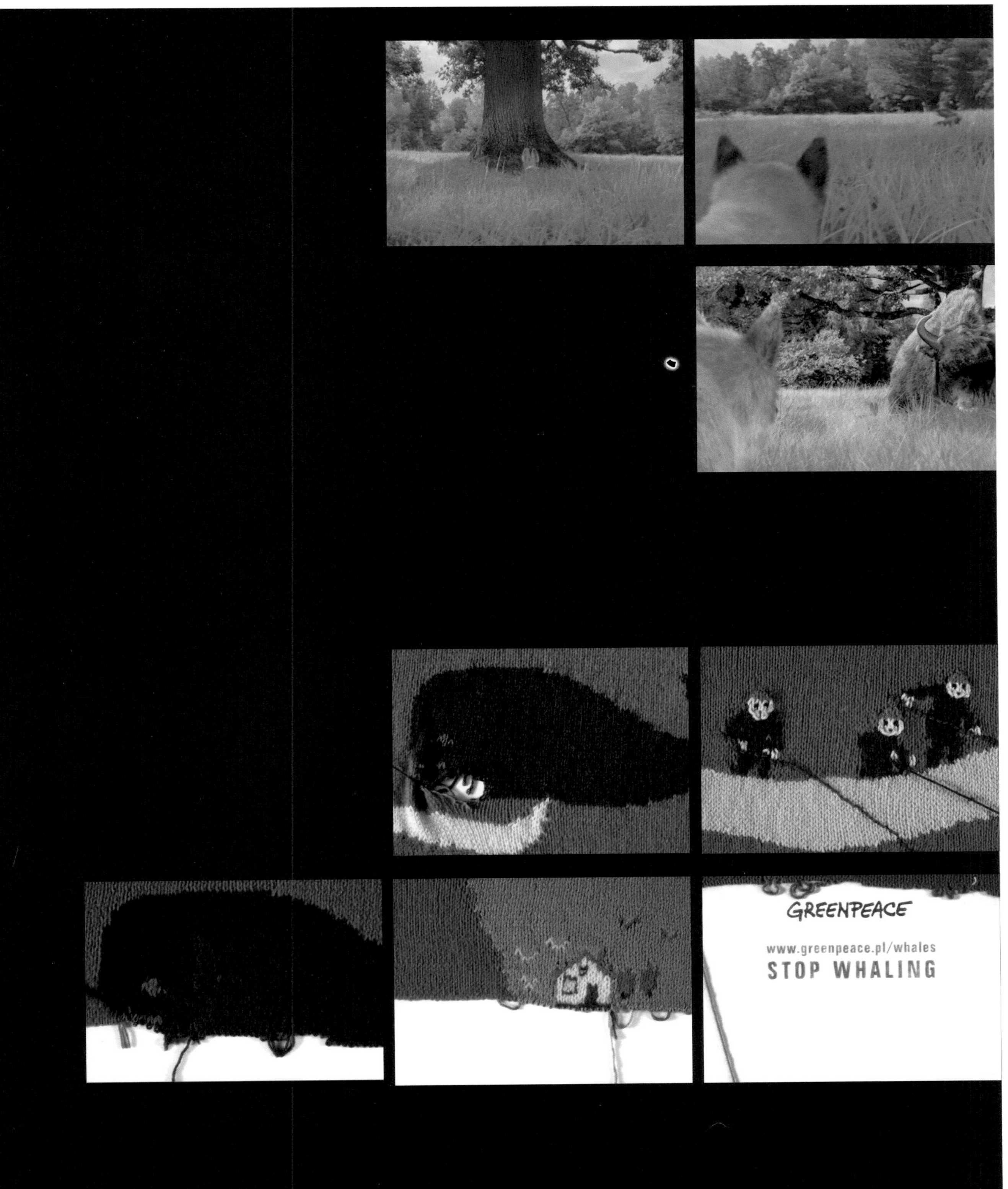

Hunt
(In DVD)
Poland

National Award
Silver
Agency
Pzl Warszawa
(Leo Burnett Group)
Client
Kompania Piwowarska S.A
Creative Director
Iwo Zaniewski
Art Director
Iwo Zaniewski
Copywriter
Cezary Filew
Film Director
Iwo Zaniewski
Director of Photography
Dominik Struss
Agency Producer
Pzl
Production Company
Blast Factor Group

Hunting
(In DVD)
Poland

National Award
Gold
Agency
Saatchi & Saatchi Poland
Client
Greenpeace
Creative Director
Max Olech
Art Director
Bozena Slaga
Copywriter
Radek Kotapka
Film Director
Marek Skrobecki
Director of Photography
Mikolaj Jaroszewicz
Agency Producer
Saatchi & Saatchi Poland
Production Company
Tank Productions/se-ma-for Z Lodzi
Other
Animator:
Krzysztof Brzozowski

Lights
(In DVD)
Spain

National Award
Silver
Agency
DDB Barcelona
Client
V.A.E.S.A.
Creative Director
Alberto Astorga
Art Director
Jaume Badia
Copywriter
Alfredo Binefa
Film Director
Fergus Stothart
Agency Producer
Vicky Moñino
Production Company
ATC

Flash moves
(In DVD)
Portugal

National Award
Silver
Agency
BrandiaCentral
Client
Vodafone
Creative Director
Marco Dias
Art Director
Tiago Prandi
Copywriter
Miguel Martinho
Film Director
Tangerina Azul
Director of Photography
Tangerina Azul
Agency Producer
Rui Pregal da Cunha
Production Company
Tangerina Azul

.ights
Ve see night lights naking beautiful olours and shapes. It s the suggestive world hat one discovers a the vheel of an Audi S4 333 V. A world full of new anoramas...

lash moves
"The world needs Yorn's" Spontaneous lash mobs featuring YORN users. It shows hem changing clothes, loing a workout, lowing bubbles, ointing at the sky and illow fighting.

Play
t is raining inside a ouple's flat. They run or cover. They get to he car, and luckily it sn't raining. As they eave the car park, the un comes out. They ut the roof down and o.

he Make-Believe Story f Ron Hammer
"The Legend of Ron Iammer". The viral hat started the mazing buzz about Ron Hammer, the tunt biker that failed o jump over a Iornbach Home mprovement Superstore. These tores are simply too ig.

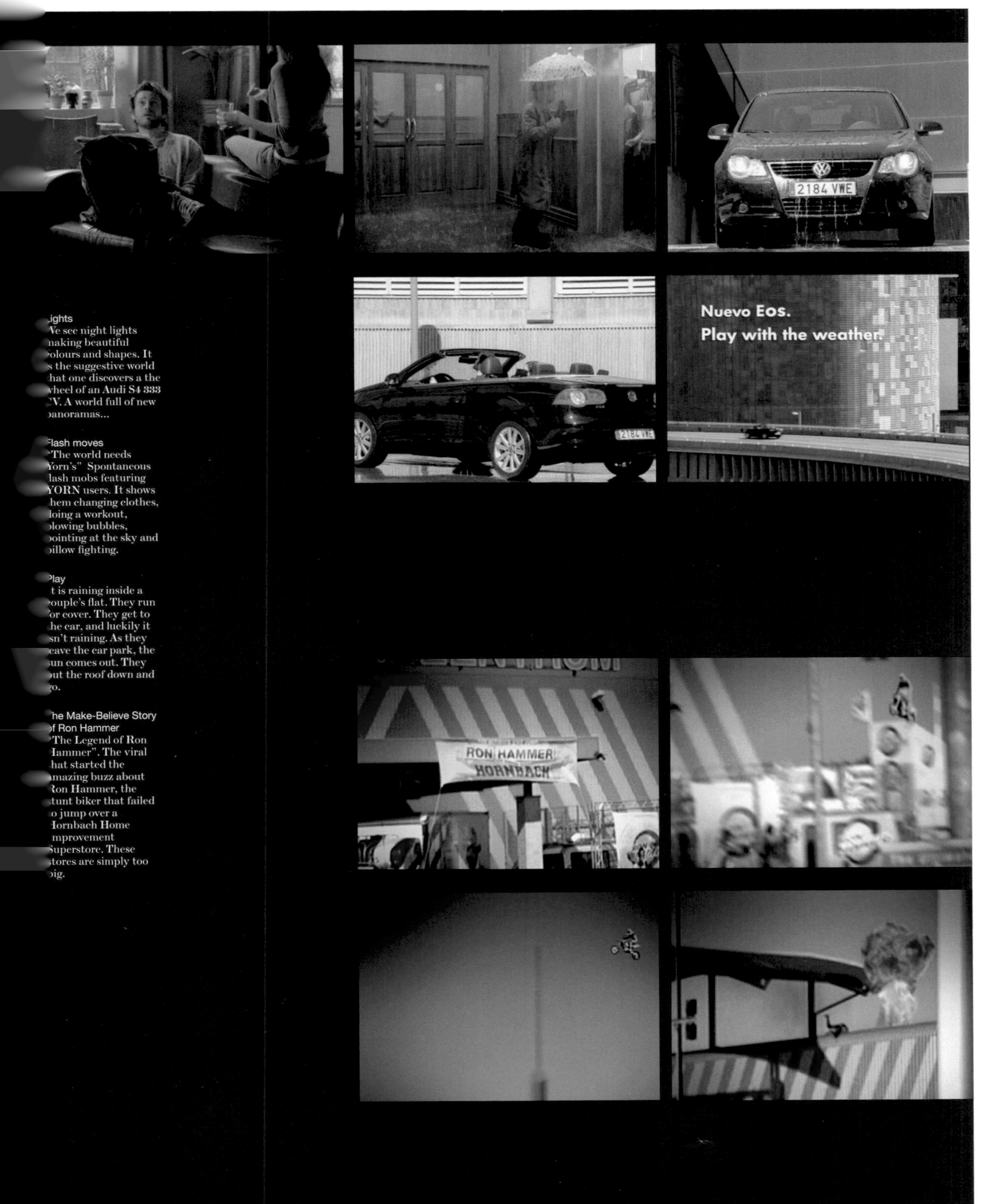

Play
(In DVD)
Spain

National Award
Silver
Agency
DDB Barcelona
Client
V.A.E.S.A.
Creative Director
José Mª Roca de Viñals
Art Director
Quito Leal,
Josep Mª Basora
Copywriter
Oscar Vidal Larsson,
Pepe Colomer
Film Director
Nacho Gayan
Director of Photography
Jan Velicky
Agency Producer
Vicky Moñino
Production Company
Agosto

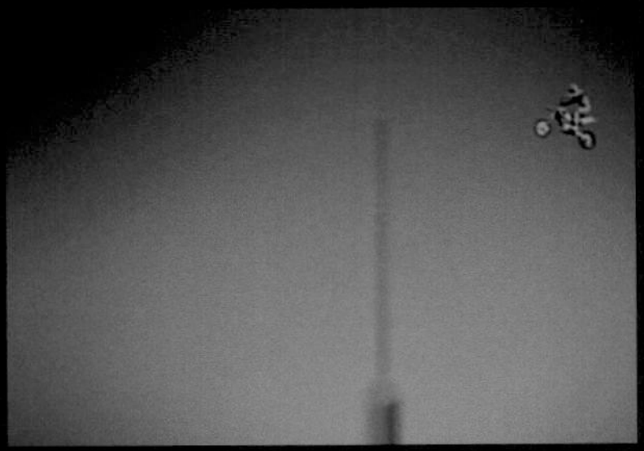

The Make-Believe Story of Ron Hammer
(In DVD)
Germany

National Award
Gold
Agency
HEIMAT, Berlin
Client
Bau- und Gartenmarkt AG
Creative Director
Guido Heffels, Juergen Vossen
Art Director
Tim Schneider
Copywriter
Till Eckel
Film Director
Jan Wentz
Agency Producer
Kerstin Breuer
Production Company
Markenfilm, Berlin

River
(In DVD)
Portugal

National Award
Silver
Agency
BBDO Portugal
Client
Optimus
Creative Director
Pedro Bidarra
Art Director
Raoul Van Harten
Copywriter
Francisco Alves
Film Director
Joâo Nuno Pinto
Director of Photography
Cácá
Agency Producer
Maria Joâo Monteiro
Production Company
Garage Films

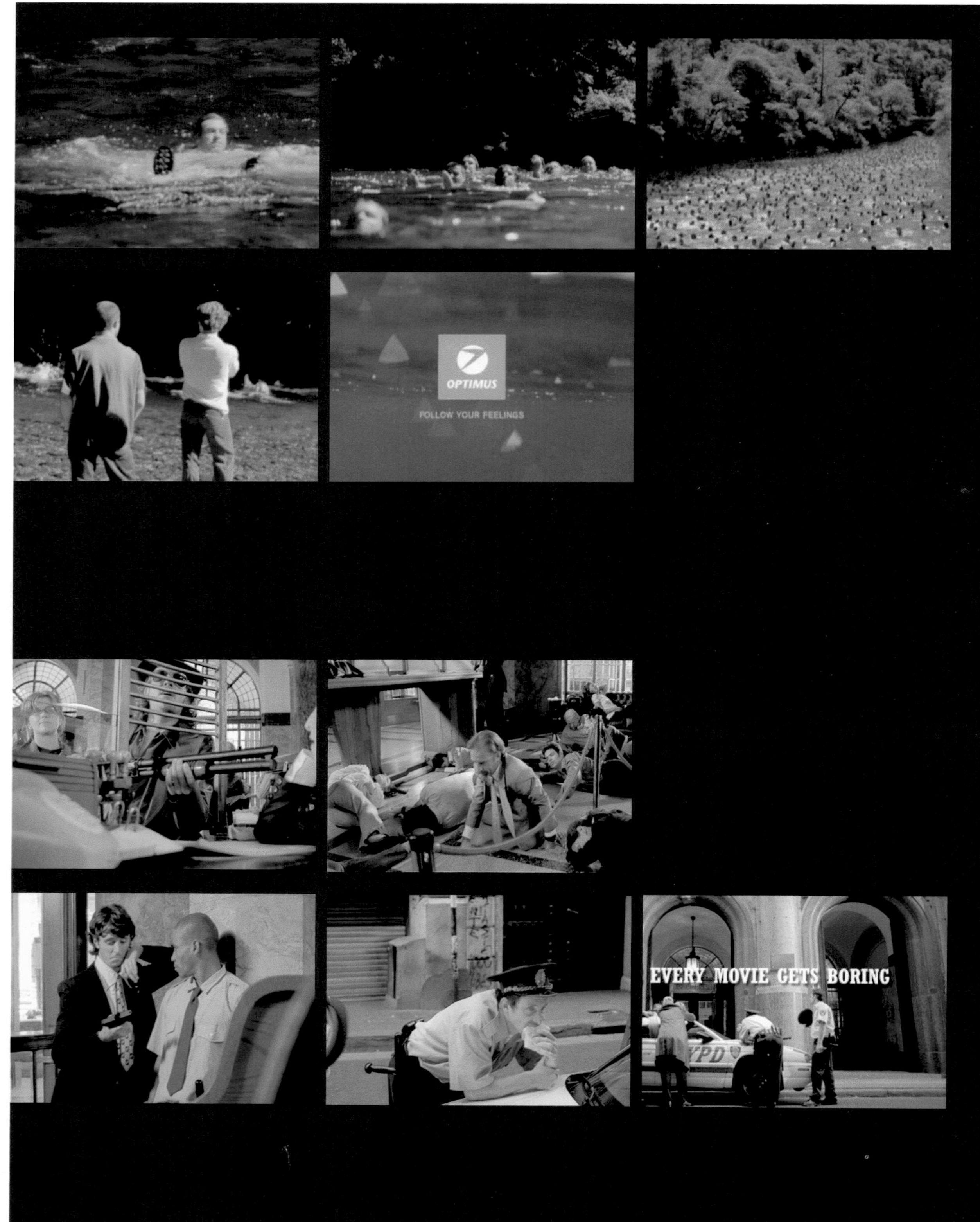

Bank Robbery
(In DVD)
Poland

National Award
Gold
Agency
Grupa66 Ogilvy
Client
Cyfra Plus
Creative Director
Michael Nowosielski
Art Director
Agata Fidler Wieruszewska
Copywriter
Grzegorz Warszawski
Film Director
Czuk Czuk
Director of Photography
Victor Kino Gonzales
Agency Producer
Grupa66 Ogilvy
Production Company
Tango

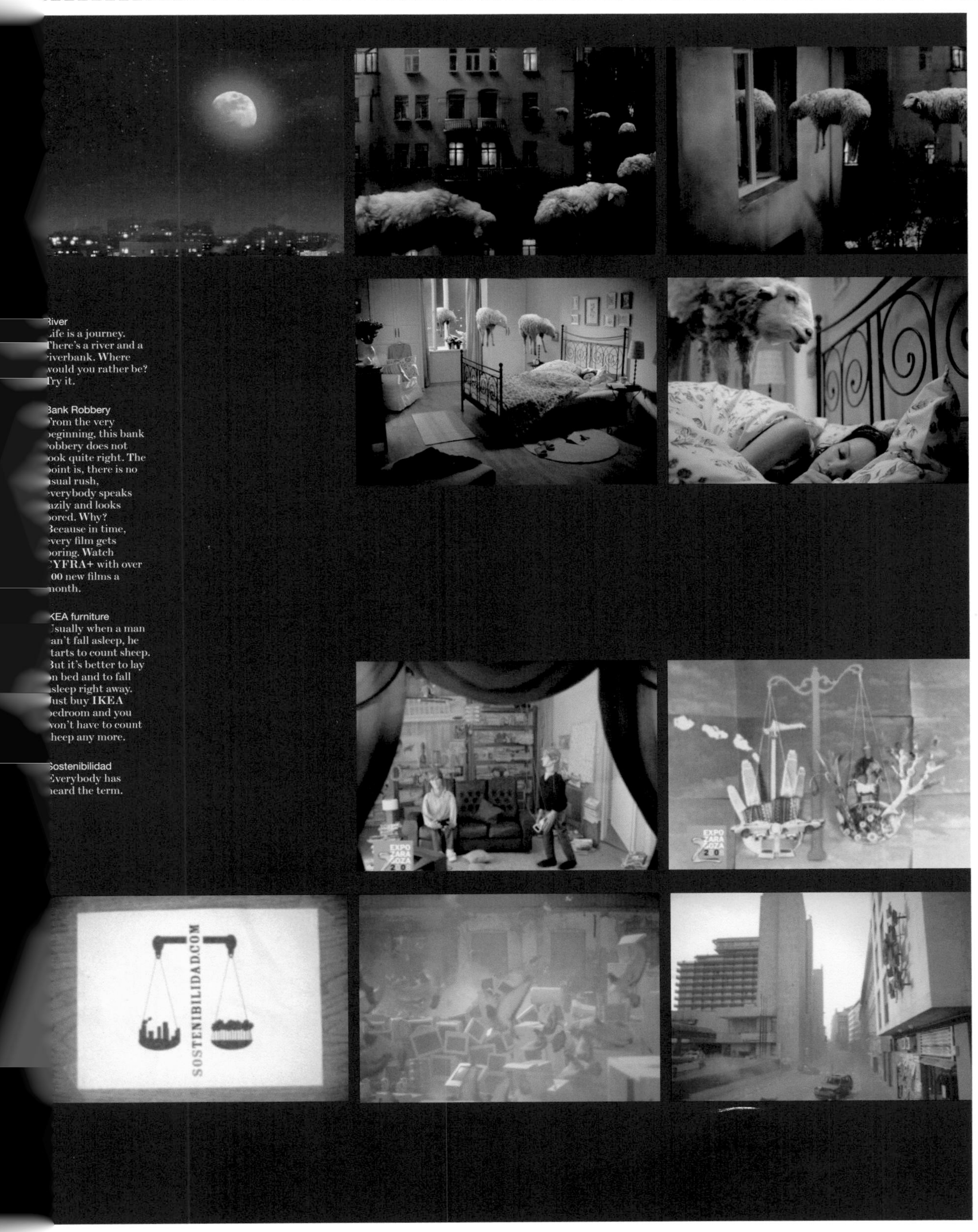
River
.ife is a journey.
There's a river and a
iverbank. Where
vould you rather be?
Try it.

Bank Robbery
From the very
beginning, this bank
obbery does not
ook quite right. The
oint is, there is no
isual rush,
everybody speaks
azily and looks
bored. Why?
Because in time,
every film gets
boring. Watch
CYFRA+ with over
00 new films a
nonth.

KEA furniture
Jsually when a man
an't fall asleep, he
tarts to count sheep.
But it's better to lay
n bed and to fall
asleep right away.
Just buy IKEA
bedroom and you
von't have to count
heep any more.

Sostenibilidad
Everybody has
heard the term.

EXPO ZARA GOZA
SOSTENIBILIDAD.COM

IKEA furniture
(In DVD)
Russia

National Award
Silver
Agency
Instinct
Client
IKEA
Creative Director
Yaroslav Orlov,
Roman Firainer
Art Director
Daniil Ostrovskiy
Copywriter
Igor Ivanov
Designer
Ivandikov Andrey
Film Director
Steve Dell
Production Company
Metrafilms

Sostenibilidad
(In DVD)
Spain

National Award
Silver
Agency
McCann Erickson
Client
Acciona
Creative Director
Juan Carlos Salas
Art Director
Abel de la Fuente
Designer
Sara Fernandez
Film Director
Federico Brugia
Director of Photography
Joan Garrigosa
Agency Producer
The Family

Sustainibility “What Can We Do?”

(In DVD)
Spain

National Award
Silver
Agency
McCann Erickson
Client
Acciona
Creative Director
Juan Carlos Salas
Art Director
Abel de la Fuente
Designer
Sara Fernández
Film Director
Federico Brugia
Director of Photography
Joan Garrigosa
Agency Producer
The Family

Joy of Peeing

(In DVD)
Poland

National Award
Gold
Agency
Saatchi & Saatchi Poland
Client
Procter & Gamble
Creative Director
Max Olech
Art Director
Aneta Szeweluk
Copywriter
Piotr Skarbek
Film Director
Piotr Skarbek,
Aneta Szeweluk
Agency Producer
Saatchi & Saatchi Poland
Production Company
Tps Warsaw

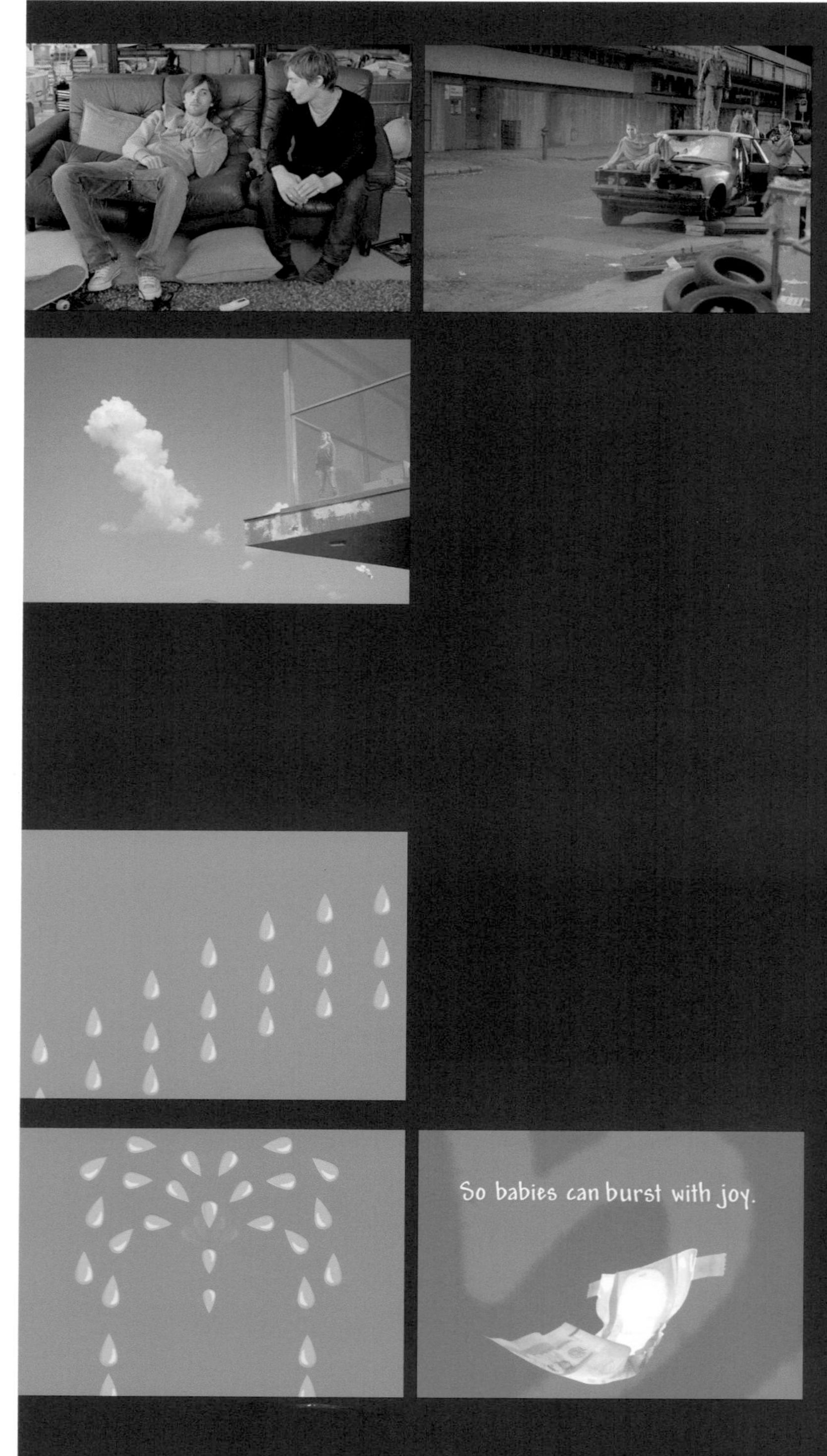

Sustainability “What Can We Do?”
Everybody has heard the term.

Joy of Peeing
Because of pampers, the peeing is now nothing but a joy.

Skittles “Village”
One day a bear appears in the village. People run away from it. And then we find out that the bear is not aggressive, that it has brought skittles and candies to the village.

Him
To launch the “Try it” concept on TV, two directors were asked to improvise from the same script. A communication experience in its own right, that resulted in two visions, two styles, two distinct communication languages and two films that were broadcast at the same time, reinforcing the new concept adopted by Optimus, and acting as a pioneer in trying out new things.

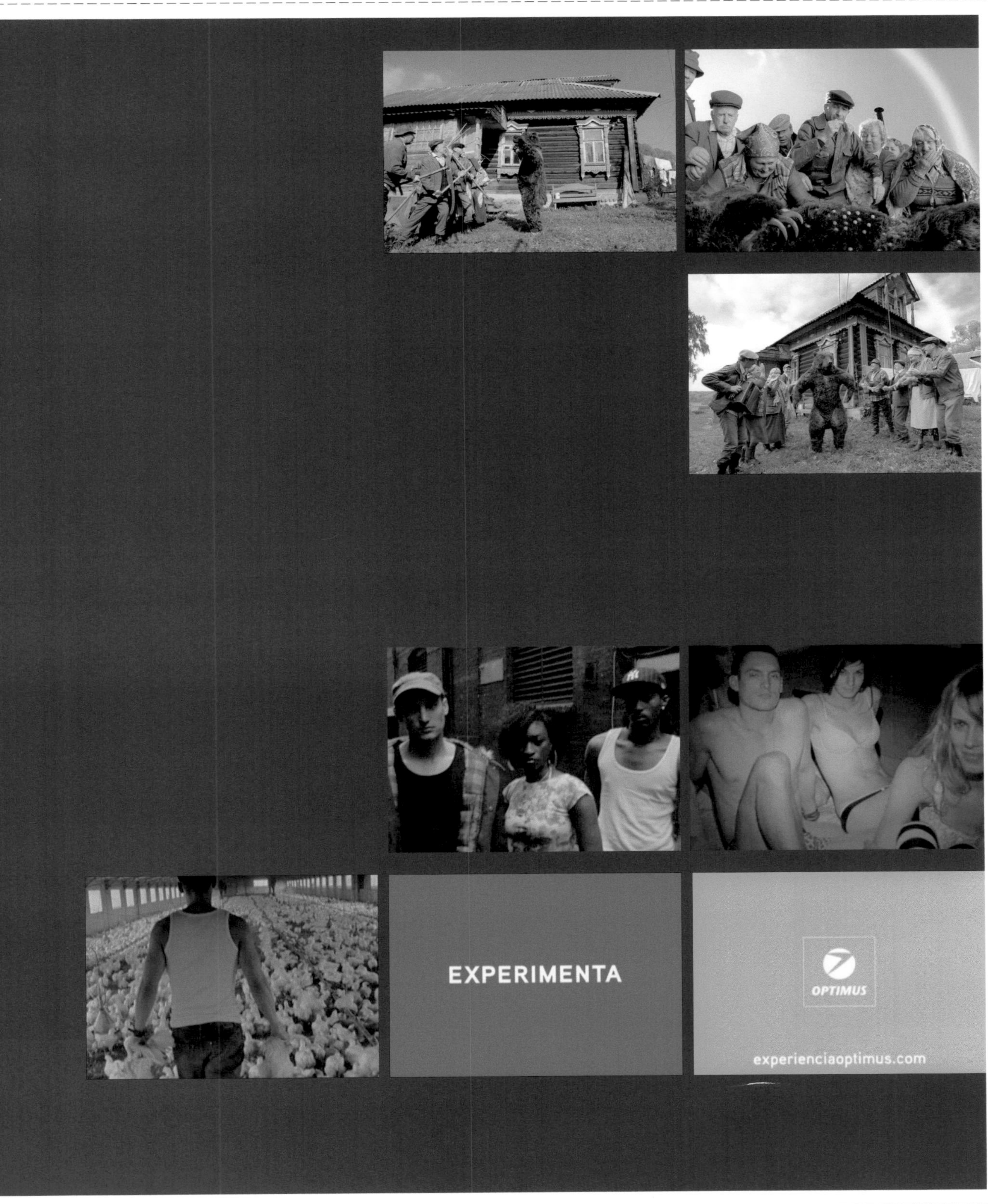

Skittles "Village"

(In DVD)
Russia

National Award
Silver
Agency
TBWA
Client
Mars
Creative Director
Donald Tursman
Art Director
Dmitriy Ovchinnikov
Copywriter
Yuriy Tikhonravov
Film Director
ACNE
Production Company
Workshop

Him

(In DVD)
Portugal

National Award
Gold
Agency
BBDO Portugal
Client
Optimus
Creative Director
Pedro Bidarra
Art Director
Juliano Bertoldi
Copywriter
Hellington Vieira
Film Director
Marco Martins
Director of Photography
Carlos Lopes
Agency Producer
Rodrigo Abreu
Production Company
Ministério dos Filmes

Starlings
(In DVD)
Spain

National Award
Silver
Agency
Villarrosàs
Client
Honda
Creative Director
Oriol Villar,
Fernando Codina
Copywriter
Miguel Angel Elizalde
Film Director
Nacho Gayan
Agency Producer
Melanie Andrada
Production Company
Agosto

Mother's day campaign
(In DVD)
Switzerland

National Award
Gold
Agency
Walker
Client
Fleurop Interflora
Creative Director
Pius Walker
Copywriter
Roger Beckett
Film Director
Axel Laubscher
Director of Photography
Gösta Reiland
Production Company
Cobblestone Hamburg,
Socialclub Stockholm

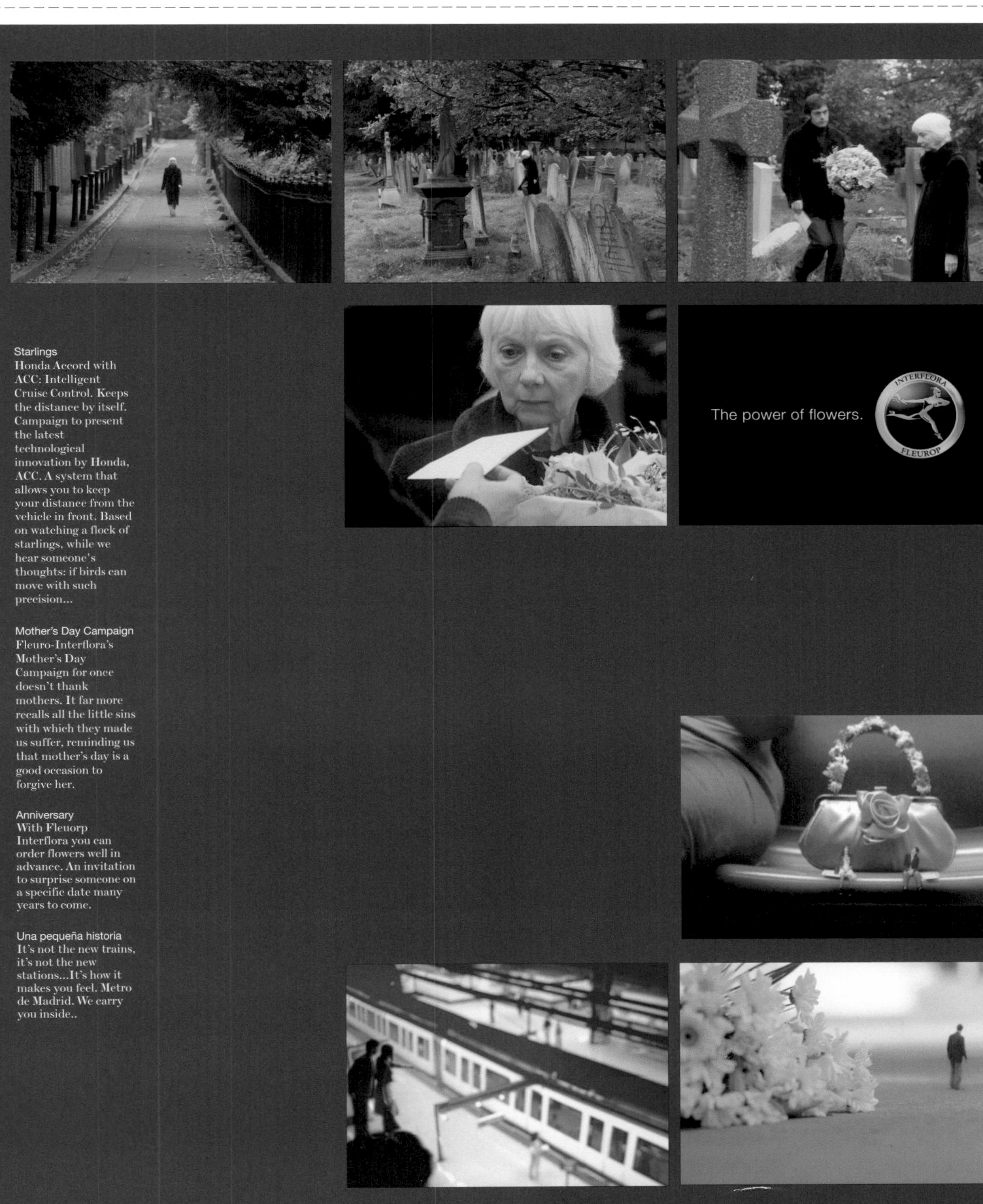

Starlings
Honda Accord with ACC: Intelligent Cruise Control. Keeps the distance by itself. Campaign to present the latest technological innovation by Honda, ACC. A system that allows you to keep your distance from the vehicle in front. Based on watching a flock of starlings, while we hear someone's thoughts: if birds can move with such precision...

Mother's Day Campaign
Fleuro-Interflora's Mother's Day Campaign for once doesn't thank mothers. It far more recalls all the little sins with which they made us suffer, reminding us that mother's day is a good occasion to forgive her.

Anniversary
With Fleuorp Interflora you can order flowers well in advance. An invitation to surprise someone on a specific date many years to come.

Una pequeña historia
It's not the new trains, it's not the new stations...It's how it makes you feel. Metro de Madrid. We carry you inside..

Anniversary
(In DVD)
Switzerland

National Award
Gold
Agency
Walker
Client
Fleurop Interflora
Creative Director
Pius Walker
Copywriter
Pius Walker
Film Director
Anthony Minghella
Director of Photography
Benoit Delhomme
Production Company
Paul Weiland Film Company
Other
Actress: Anna Massey

Una pequeña historia
(In DVD)
Spain

National Award
Silver
Agency
McCann Erickson
Client
Metro
Creative Director
Mónica Moro
Art Director
Ricardo Rovira
Copywriter
Isabel López
Film Director
Sega
Agency Producer
Lee Films

its a giiirrrl
(In DVD)
Portugal

National Award
Silver
Agency
Brandia Central
Client
Compal
Creative Director
Marco Dias
Art Director
Jorge Ferrâo
Copywriter
Joào Freitas
Film Director
Tiago Guedes,
Frederico Cerejeiro
Director of Photography
Janeco
Agency Producer
Ana Romana
Production Company
Take it easy

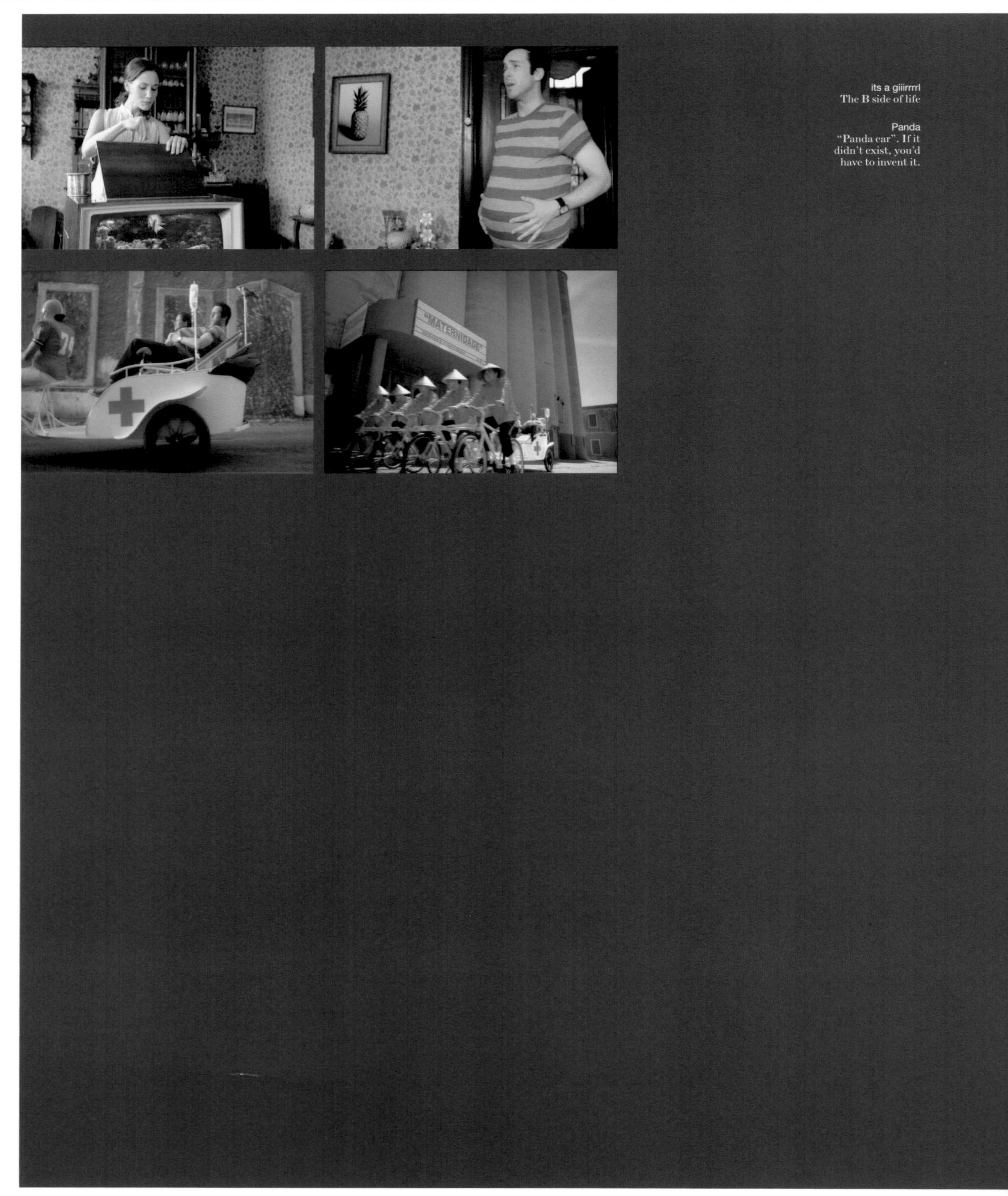

its a giiirrrl
The B side of life
Panda
"Panda car". If it didn't exist, you'd have to invent it.

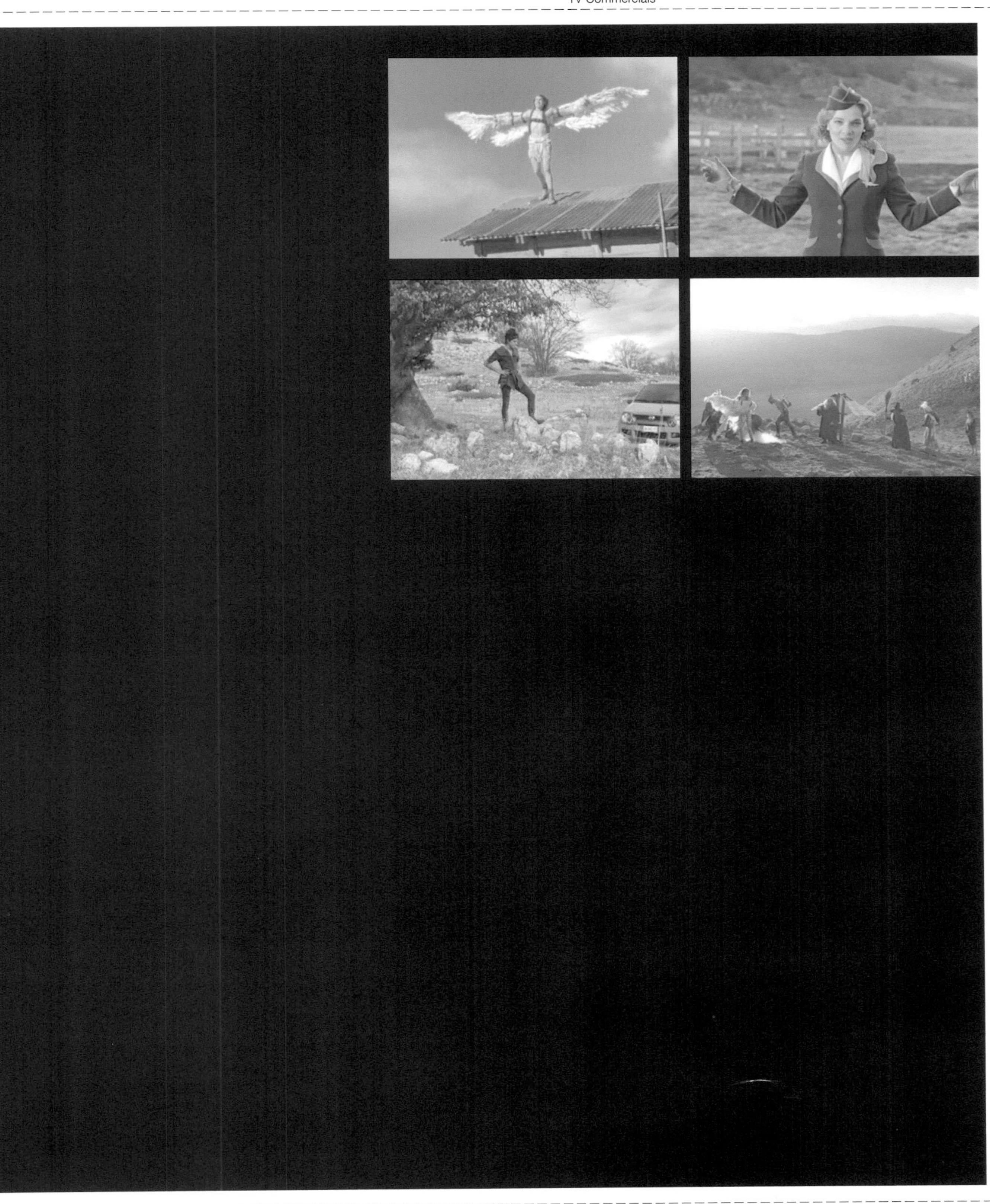

Panda
(In DVD)
Italy

National Award
Silver
Agency
Leo Burnett Company
Client
Fiat Auto
Creative Director
Paolo Dematteis,
Riccardo Robiglio
Art Director
Barbara Ghiotti
Copywriter
R. Robiglio, M. Pieri,
V. Pastore
Film Director
Sebastian Strasser
Director of Photography
Julian Hohnodorf
Agency Producer
Antonello Filosa
Production Company
Indiana
Other
Post Production: Edi

Film. Cinema Commercials

Austria

Germany: 2 Gold 6 Nominations

Switzerland

Gold
Back Seat
(In DVD)
Germany

National Award
Shortlist
Agency
BBDO Germany GmbH / Team smart
Client
DaimlerChrysler Vertriebsorganisation Deutschland
Creative Director
T. Bazarkaya, S. Hardieck, M. Eickmeyer, S.Meske
Art Director
Szymon Rose, Florian Barthelmess, Jonathan Schupp
Film Director
Markus Walter, Malte Hagemeister
Agency Producer
A. Berkenbusch, M. Ceranna, S. Gentis
Production Company
Cobblestone Filmproduktion Hamburg GmbH
Other
Post Production: Schoenheitsfarm, Hamburg

smart
open your mind.
www.smart.com

Sometimes it's more secure to drive a car with no backseats. Note: All scenes in the commercial were filmed referring to the cinematic look of the originals.

Gold
The Vision
(In DVD)
Germany

National Award
Shortlist
Agency
Jung von Matt AG
Client
JesusCenter Hamburg
Creative Director
Arno Lindemann,
Bernhard Lukas
Art Director
Soeren Porst
Copywriter
Tom Hauser
Agency Producer
Anne Ehrig
Production Company
VCC Perfect Pictures
Hamburg
Other
Filmanimation:
Thomas Kordt,
Oliver Maassen

Jesus

www.JesusCenter.de

In this commercial for the JesusCenter for social welfare, following message appears: "Even when you don't believe I'm present, I'm always there for you". Afterwards the message's sender materializes: Jesus, as a vision on the viewer's own retina.

Nomination
Basketball
(In DVD)
Germany

National Award
Bronze
Agency
DDB Germany, Berlin
Client
Volkswagen AG
Creative Director
Amir Kassaei,
Wolfgang Schneider,
Mathias Stiller
Art Director
Kristoffer Heilemann
Copywriter
Ludwig Berndl
Film Director
Sebastian Strasser
Director of Photography
Rodrigo Prieto
Agency Producer
Marion Lange
Production Company
@radical.media
Other
CD: Bert Peulecke,
Stefan Schulte

Makes anyone look strong.
The new Polo GTI®.

Nomination
Curtain
(In DVD)
Germany

National Award
Shortlist
Agency
Jung von Matt AG
Client
IKEA
Creative Director
Arno Lindemann,
Bernhard Lukas
Art Director
Jonas Keller
Copywriter
David Leinweber
Film Director
Gregor Schnitzler
Production Company
Markenfilm GmbH
Other
Konzept:
Jonas Keller,
David Leinweber

Basketball
A couple of huge streetball players are choosing teams. They get into a fierce fight over a small guy, although his athletic abilities are obviously very limited. But he is the owner of a Polo GTI.

Curtain
The cinema-goers were presented with a depressing scene. They were looking through a window onto a dreary, grey courtyard. Suddenly, the screen curtain closed and following text was projected onto the curtain: "Curtains beautify your life. IKEA".

Nomination
Future
(In DVD)
Germany

National Award
Bronze
Agency
Jung von Matt AG
Client
Jamba! GmbH
Creative Director
Mathias Stiller,
Wolfgang Schneider
Art Director
Tim Stuebane
Copywriter
Mirko Stolz
Designer
Friederike Coninx
Film Director
acne
Producer
A. Schildt,
S. von Hacht, G.von Reden
Agency Producer
Nadja Catana
Production Company
Tempomedia Hamburg
Other
Animation: nhb Hamburg

Future
A cinema commercial that treats its own bad image with self-irony to take the wind out of the sails of the numerous Jamba critics and provide support to its own fans. "Have it or hate it. Jamba ringtones".

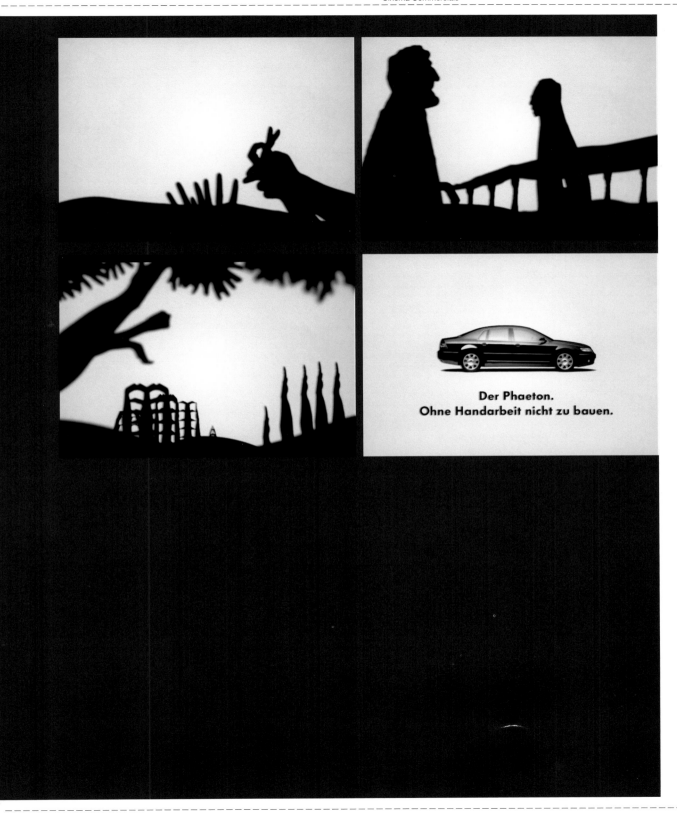

Der Phaeton.
Ohne Handarbeit nicht zu bauen.

Nomination
Galanty show
(In DVD)
Germany

National Award
Silver
Agency
Grabarz & Partner
Client
Volkswagen AG
Creative Director
Ralf Heuel, Ralf Nolting
Art Director
Christoph Stricker
Copywriter
Paul von Muehlendahl
Film Director
Michael Reissinger
Agency Producer
Anne Hoffmann, Patrick Cahill
Production Company
deli pictures postproduktion GmbH
Other
Music: BEATSUCHT (Florian Lakenmacher, David Pauli)

Nomination

Hail. The return of the sun.

(In DVD)
Germany

National Award
Silver
Agency
Jung von Matt AG
Client
Solon AG
Creative Director
Wolf Heumann,
Sascha Hanke,
Timm Hanebeck
Copywriter
Michael Okun,
Moritz Grub
Film Director
Joseph Kahn
Director of Photography
Chris Probst
Agency Producer
Mark Rot
Production Company
Film Deluxe GmbH
(Berlin), HSI Productions

970 Billionen kWh Energie
fallen täglich auf die Erde.

Hail. The return of the sun.
To illustrate the power of the sun and thereby the potential benefits of solar energy, this spot shows what would happen if the world were bombarded with batteries instead of sunbeams.

Nightvision
Objective: BMW invented Nightvision technology. This commercial shows how that system helps the driver to avoid accidents in the dark. Concept: When it's dark at night a lot of strange things happen unseen. We make them visible.

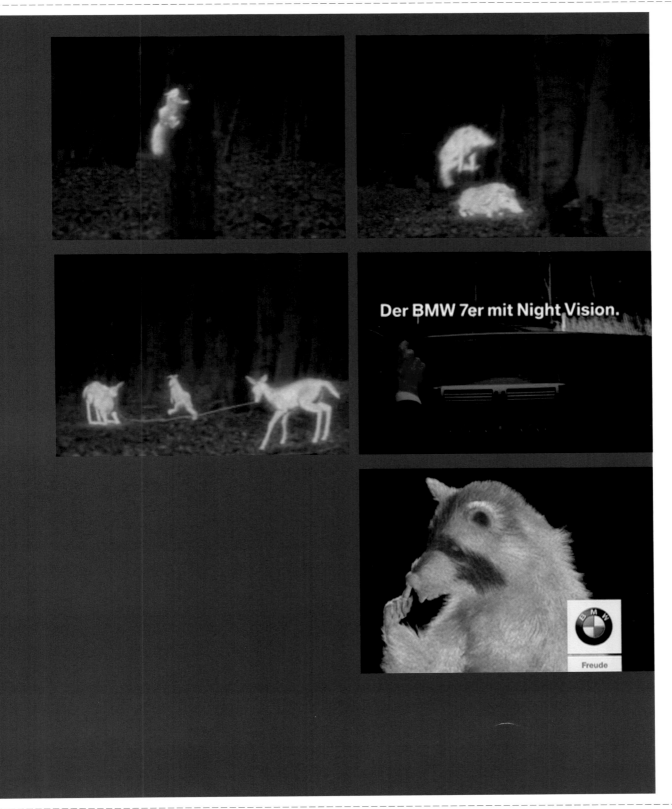

Der BMW 7er mit Night Vision.

Freude

Nomination
Nightvision
(In DVD)
Germany

National Award
Silver
Agency
Jung von Matt AG
Client
BMW AG
Creative Director
Fabian Frese,
Thimoteus Wagner,
Deneke von Weltzie
Art Director
Till Monshausen
Copywriter
Susanne Ostertag
Film Director
Thorsten Herken
Director of Photography
Sebastian Pfaffenbichler
Agency Producer
Mark Rueta
Production Company
Big Fish Filmproduktion
GmbH
Other
Producer:
Henry Rehorek,
Robert Gold

Bet and Win Magic Moments of Sports
(In DVD)
Austria

National Award
Silver
Agency
Springer & Jacoby Österreich GmbH
Client
bwin Interactive Entertainment AG
Creative Director
Paul Holcmann,
Murray White
Art Director
Katharina Haines
Copywriter
Hans Juckel
Film Director
David Frankham
Director of Photography
Carl Nilsson
Agency Producer
Hermann Krug,
Stephan Bandermann
Production Company
STINK London, Springer & Jacoby Hamburg
Other
M. Kloss Zechner,
M. Bodner, R. Kober,
H.P. Feichtner

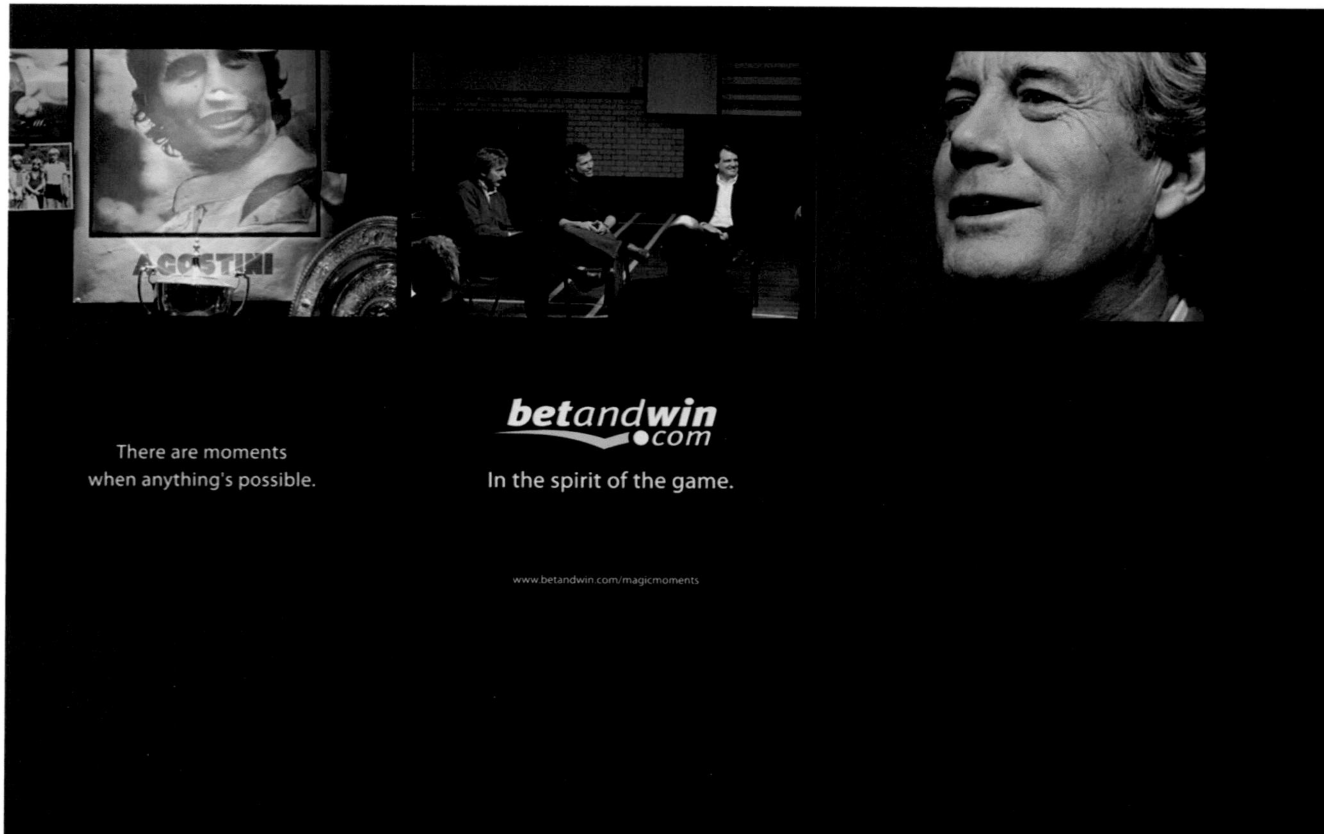

There are moments
when anything's possible.

betandwin.com
In the spirit of the game.

www.betandwin.com/magicmoments

Mother's day campaign
(In DVD)
Switzerland

National Award
Gold
Agency
Walker
Client
Fleurop Interflora
Creative Director
Pius Walker
Copywriter
Roger Beckett
Film Director
Axel Laubscher
Director of Photography
Gösta Reiland
Production Company
Cobblestone Hamburg,
Socialclub Stockholm

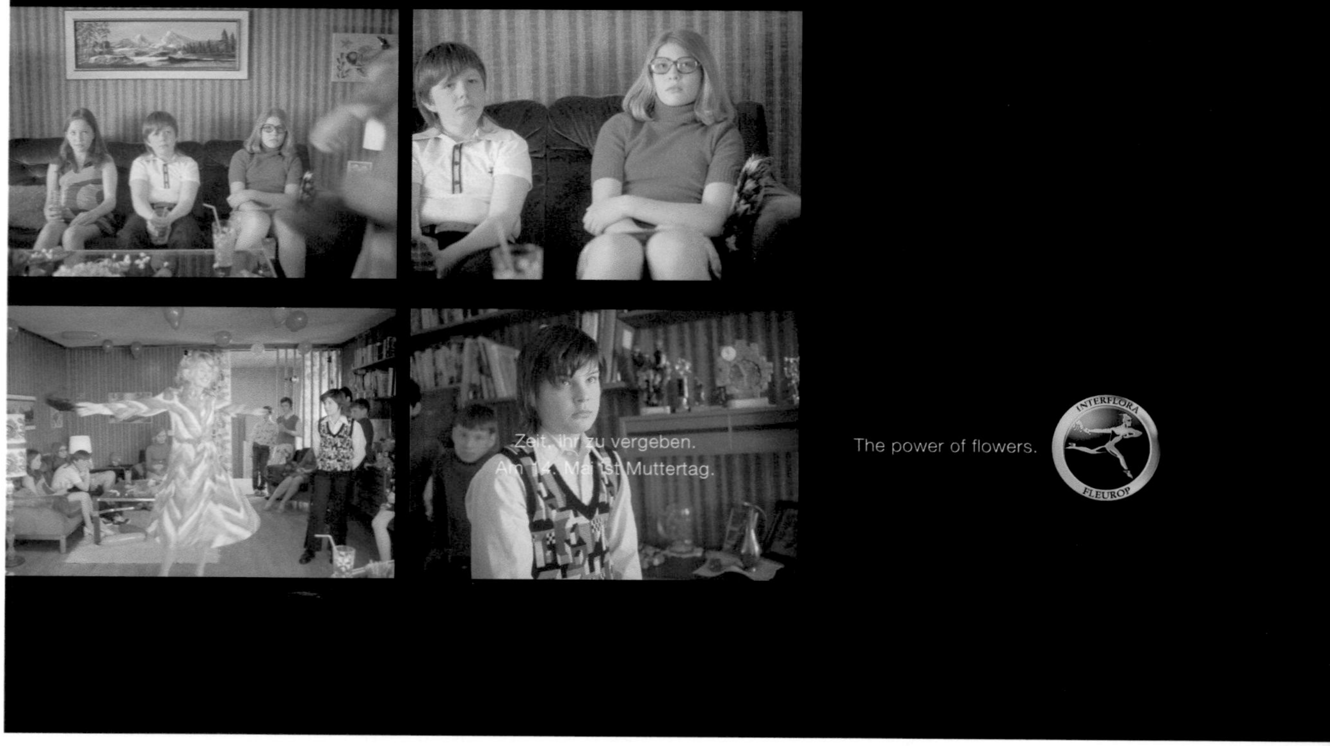

The power of flowers.

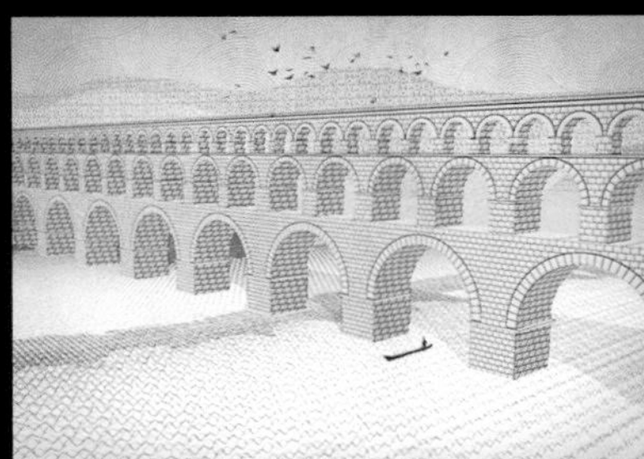

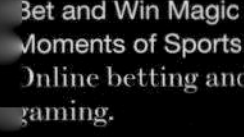

et and Win Magic
oments of Sports
nline betting and
aming.

other's Day Campaign
leurop-Interflora's
other's Day Campaign
or once doesn't thank
nothers. It far more
ecalls all the little sins
vith which they made us
uffer, reminding us that
nother's day is a good
ccasion to forgive her.

parkasse
he idea behind the
ommercial is to show
ery clear and
nderstandable how the
nancial tools of
parkasse work: give
hem your money and
hey work hard to make
he most of it. A simple
nessage told in a very
nique way.

nniversary
Vith Fleuorp Interflora
ou can order flowers
vell in advance. An
nvitation to surprise
omeone on a specific
late many years to
ome.

Sparkasse
(In DVD)
Germany

National Award
Silver
Agency
Sehsucht GmbH /
Jung von Matt AG
Client
Sparkasse Savings Bank
Creative Director
Oliver Voss, Goetz Ulmer,
Daniel Frericks (JvM)
Art Director
Till Monshausen,
Martin Terhart (JvM)
Copywriter
Dennis May,
Fabian Frese (JvM)
Designer
Ole Peters, Niko Tziopanos
(Sehsucht)
Film Director
Ole Peters, Tom Abel
(Sehsucht)
Agency Producer
Jasmin Bedir (JvM),
Andreas Coutsoumbelis
(Sehsucht)
Production Company
Sehsucht GmbH

Anniversary
(In DVD)
Switzerland

National Award
Gold
Agency
Walker
Client
Fleurop Interflora
Creative Director
Pius Walker
Copywriter
Pius Walker
Film Director
Anthony Minghella
Director of Photography
Benoit Delhomme
Production Company
Paul Weiland Film Company
Other
Actress: Anna Massey

Agnus Dei
(In DVD)
Switzerland

National Award
Silver
Agency
Publicis Werbeagentur AG
Client
Schauspielhaus Zurich
Creative Director
Markus Gut
Copywriter
Markus Gut
Agency Producer
Ines Bossart
Production Company
Condor Films Zurich
Other
Account Executive:
Marion Marxer

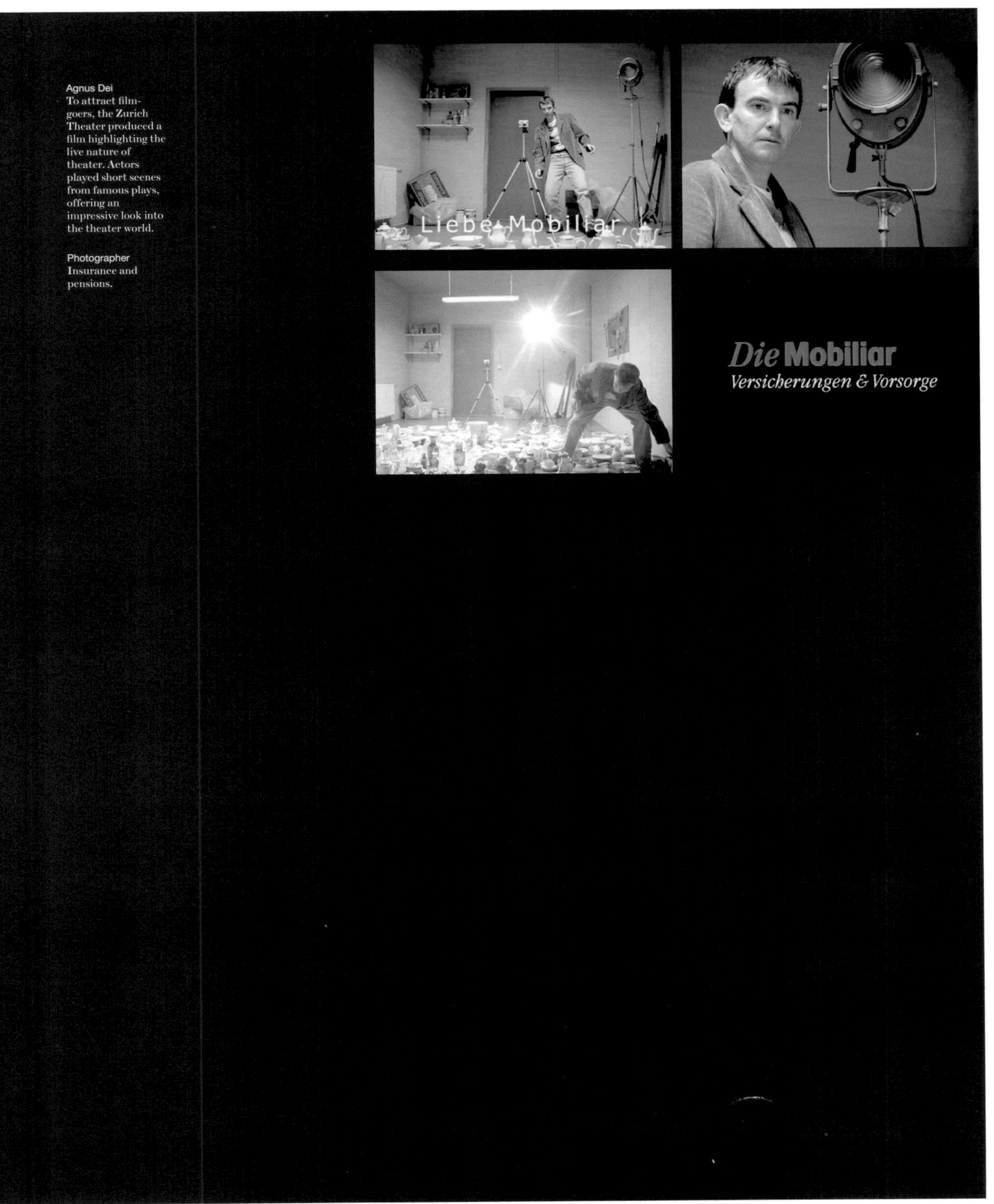

Agnus Dei
To attract film-goers, the Zurich Theater produced a film highlighting the live nature of theater. Actors played short scenes from famous plays, offering an impressive look into the theater world.
Photographer
Insurance and pensions.
Liebe Mobiliar,
Die Mobiliar
Versicherungen & Vorsorge

Photographer
(In DVD)
Switzerland

National Award
Gold
Agency
Wirz Werbung / BBDO
Client
Die Schweizerische Mobiliar
Creative Director
Matthias Freuler
Art Director
Andrea Reinhart
Copywriter
Thomas Kurzmeyer
Film Director
Ernst Wirz
Production Company
Wirz Fraefel Productions
Other
Producer: Stefan Fraefel

Film. TV Graphics

Spain: Gold

Gold
Dark Teuve

(In DVD)
Spain

National Award
Gold
Agency
Comodo Screen
Client
Teuve
Creative Director
Comodo Screen
Art Director
Comodo Screen
Copywriter
Comodo Screen
Designer
Comodo Screen
Film Director
Comodo Screen
Director of Photography
Comodo Screen
Agency Producer
Comodo Screen
Production Company
Comodo Screen

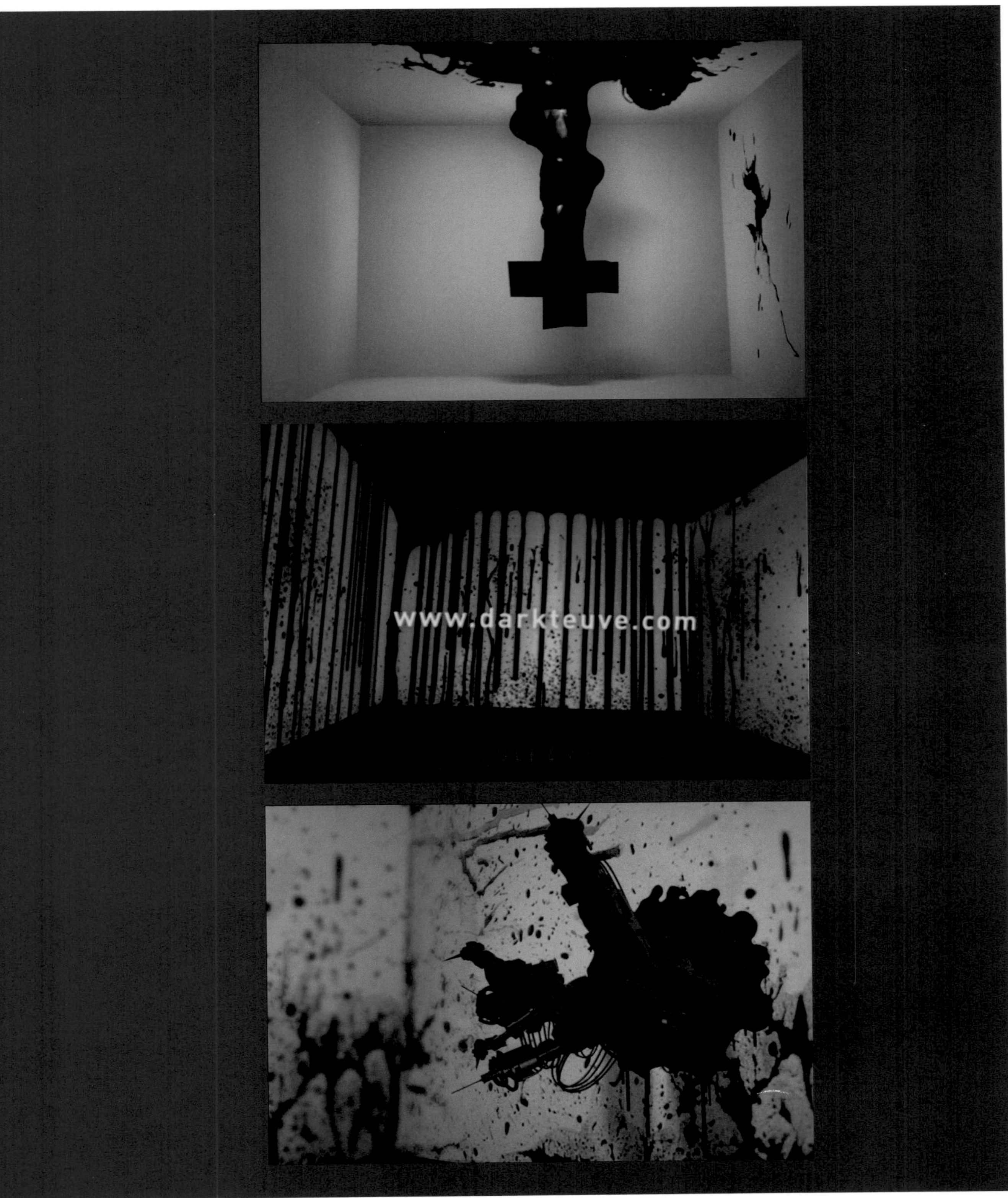

A strong and powerful image based on one of the most primal fears of mankind: The fear of the dark. A clean and almost abstract space was created where everything happens. Then narratives on horror movie themes were applied creating short pieces that work as short stories in themselves, and links were included about the background of horror cinema.

Colors en sèrie
(In DVD)
Spain

National Award
Gold
Agency
TV3
Televisió de Catalunya
Client
TV3
Televisió de Catalunya
Designer
Sira Viñolas
Film Director
Mai Balaguer
Other
Musical composition:
Pascal Comelade

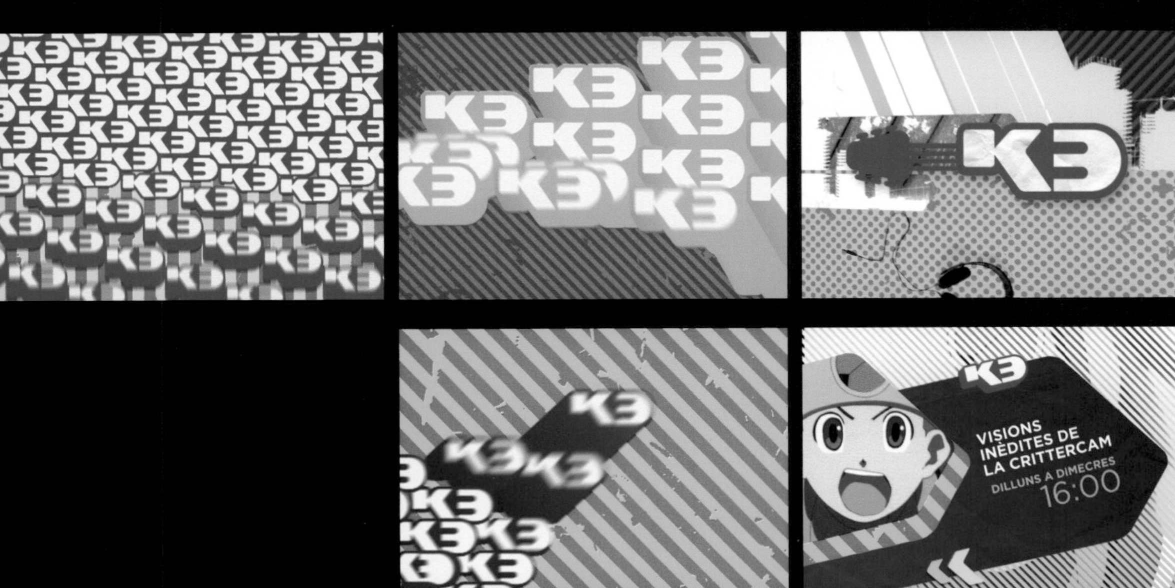

K3 / Branding
(In DVD)
Spain

National Award
Silver
Agency
zeligstudio
Client
TV3 / Televisió de Catalunya
Creative Director
Ana Zelich
Designer
Coaner Codina, Eduardo Testo, Claudio Fresneda
Production Company
zeligstudio
Other
Production: Fabiana Andreatta. *Music*: Trafalgar 13. *Collaboration*: Ignasi Gozalo, David Aynés, Paola Dragonetti

Colors en Sèrie
By focusing on details one can see how colorful every aspect of our daily lives is. When color becomes the star, form loses importance and many surprising symbolic connotations appear.

K3 / Branding
Rebranding K3, the Television of Catalonia kids' channel.

Film. Public Service & Charity

Czech Republic: 1 Nomination

Austria

Estonia

Latvia

Nomination

Sperms
(In DVD)
Czech Republic

☆

National Award
Bronze
Agency
Thamesdown CZ
Client
Greenpeace
Creative Director
Viktor Lelek
Art Director
Jan Pohl
Copywriter
Ivan Peterka
Film Director
Krystof Michal
Production Company
Simply Sirena

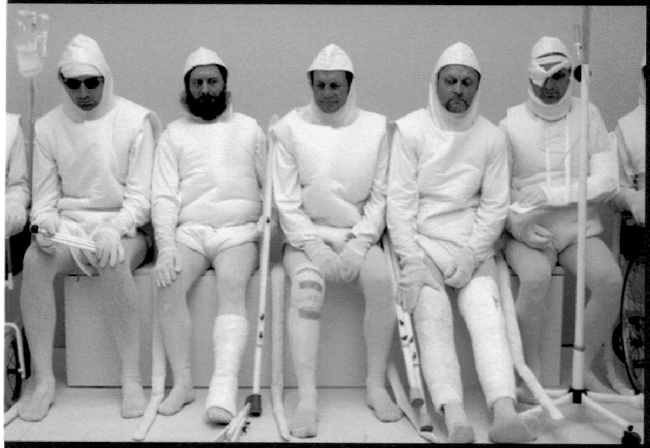

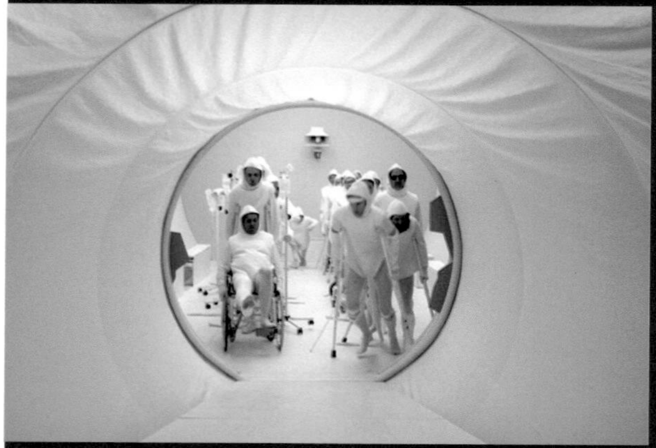

Sperm
Greenpeace warn
the public an
stresses the danger o
chemical liquids fo
huma
reproduction
Chemicals caus
damage to men'
sperm

Stay clean
Shows the dirty
route and places tha
drugs pass throug
on their way to th
final user

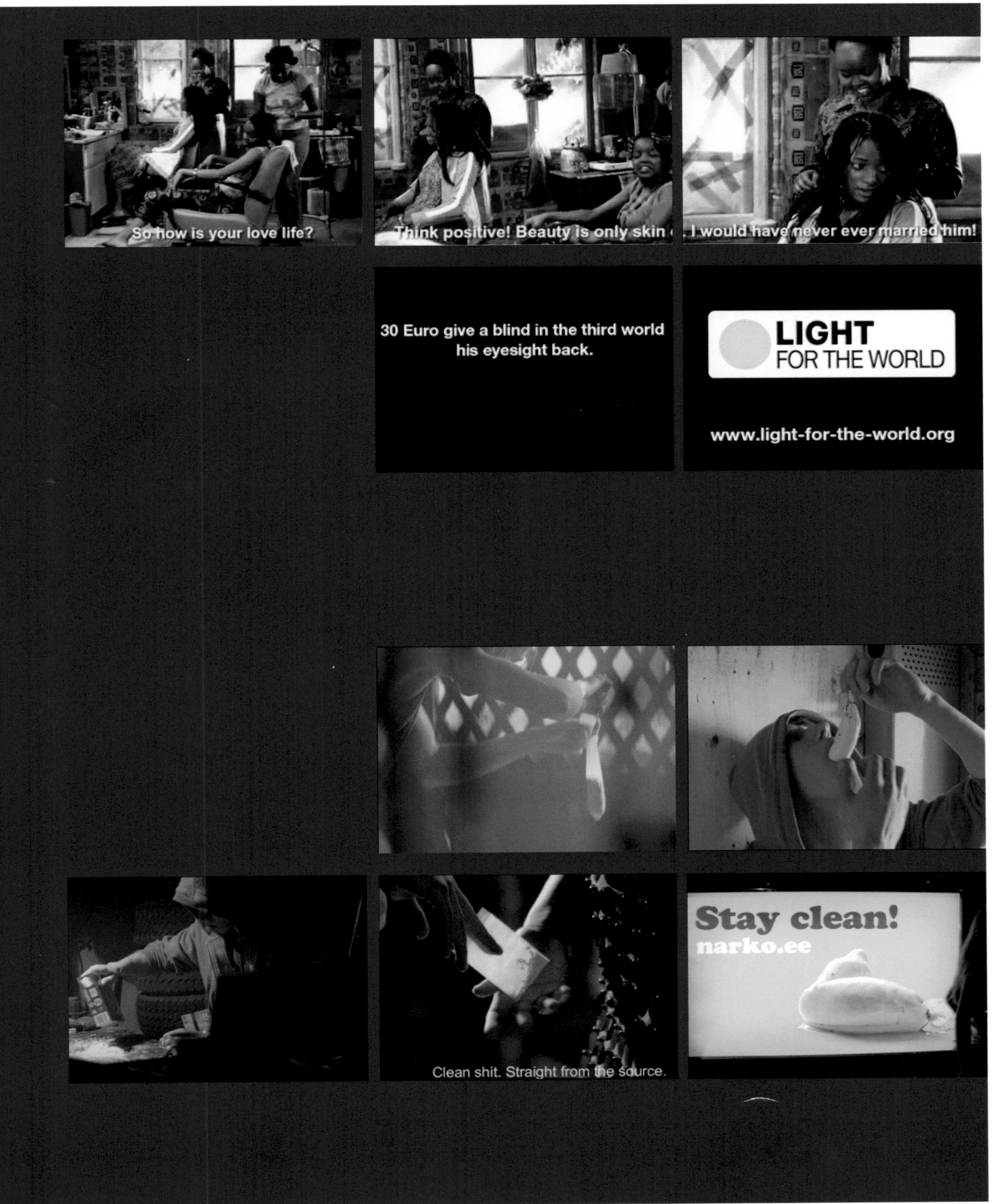

Married girl
(In DVD)
Austria

National Award
Gold
Agency
BBDO Austria Werbeagentur GmbH & CO KG
Client
Light for the world
Creative Director
Christoph Klingler
Art Director
Richard Kaim
Copywriter
Michael Grill
Designer
Christian Brezina, Dieter Oitzinger
Film Director
Antony Guedes
Production Company
Film Factory
Other
Soundstudio:
Tonstudio Holly

Stay clean!
(In DVD)
Estonia

National Award
Gold
Agency
Division
Client
National Institute for Health Development
Creative Director
Alvar Jaakson, Lesile Laasner
Art Director
Lesile Laasner
Copywriter
Alvar Jaakson
Film Director
Andres Maimik
Director of Photography
Mart Taniel
Production Company
Kuukulgur Film

Parliament

(In DVD)
Czech Republic

National Award
Gold
Agency
Mowshe
Client
Mowshe
Film Director
I. Zacharias, M. Dostal, D. Ruzicka, F. Malasek

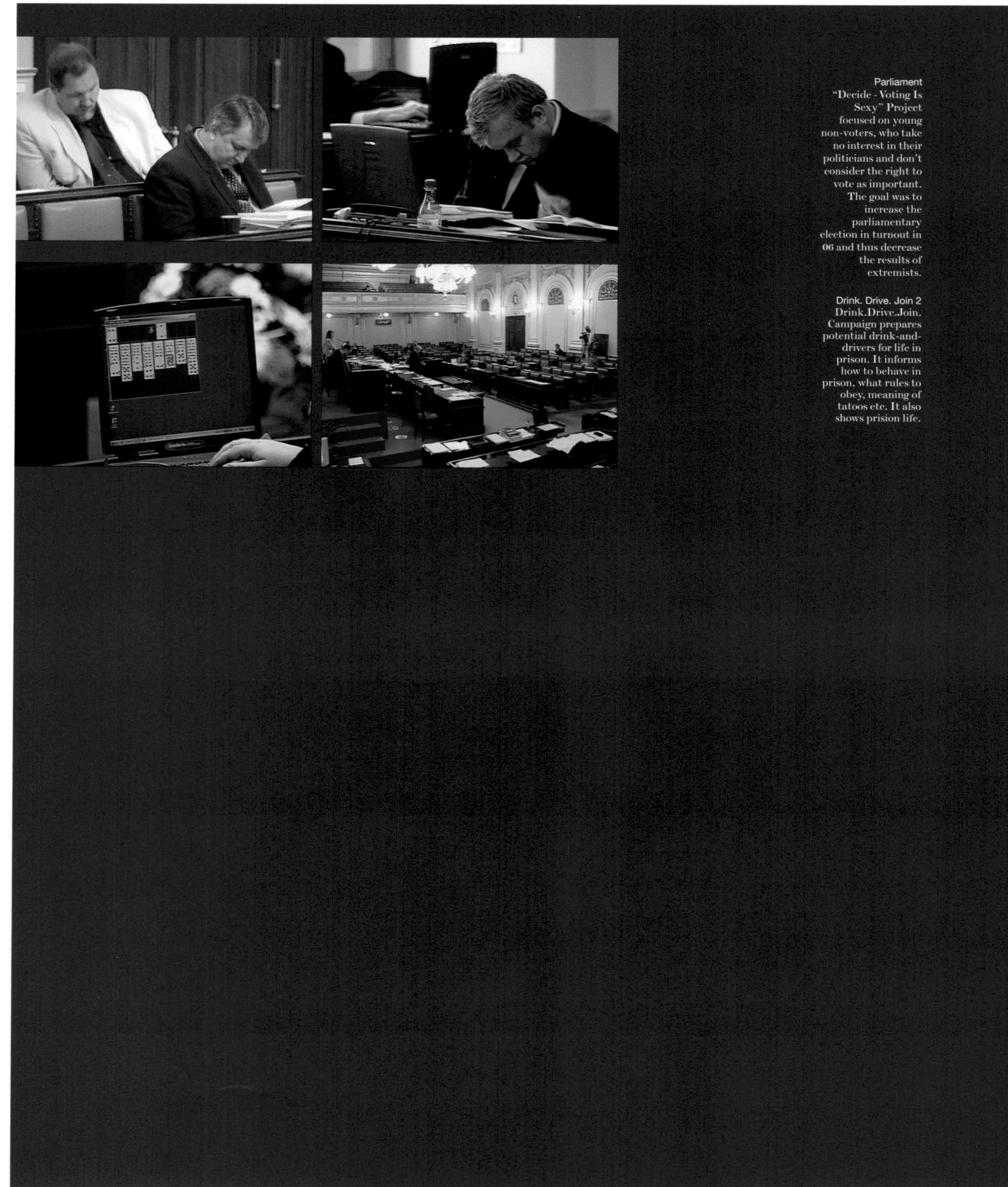

Parliament
"Decide - Voting Is Sexy" Project focused on young non-voters, who take no interest in their politicians and don't consider the right to vote as important. The goal was to increase the parliamentary election in turnout in 06 and thus decrease the results of extremists.

Drink. Drive. Join 2
Drink.Drive.Join. Campaign prepares potential drink-and-drivers for life in prison. It informs how to behave in prison, what rules to obey, meaning of tatoos etc. It also shows prision life.

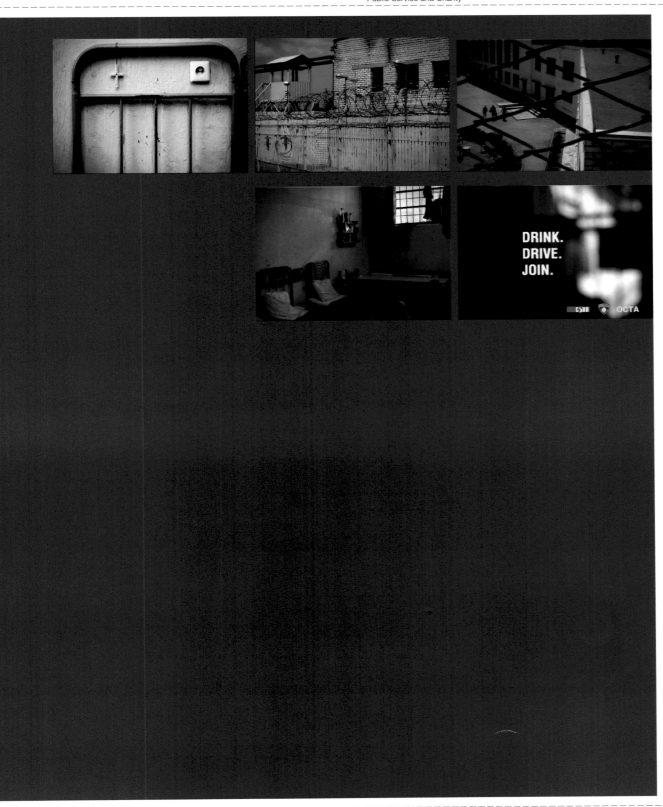

Drink. Drive. Join 2
(In DVD)
Latvia

National Award
Silver
Agency
ZOOM!
Client
Road Traffic,
Safety Directorate
Creative Director
Eriks Stendzenieks
Art Director
Maris Upenieks

Film. Any other

Austria

Germany: Gold 6 Nominations

Portugal

Spain

Switzerland

Gold

The art of Football - C = Creativity, H = Hollywood, O = Offside

(In DVD)
Germany

National Award
Shortlist
Agency
Hermann Vaske's Emotional Network
Client
Studio Hamburg Distribution and Marketing
Creative Director
Hermann Vaske
Art Director
Hermann Vaske
Copywriter
Chris Langham, Hermann Vaske
Designer
Johan Le Tenoux
Film Director
Hermann Vaske
Director of Photography
Mate Toth, Goran Pavicevic
Agency Producer
Hermann Vaske
Production Company
Hermann Vaske's

tisse
Also steht „H" für Hollywood.

STUDIO HAMBURG
DISTRIBUTION & MARKETING

Nomination

Ask Yourself campaign

(In DVD)
Germany

National Award
Silver
Agency
Trigger happy productions GmbH
Client
www.dropping knowledge e.V.
Creative Director
Ralf Schmerberg
Art Director
Andreas Laeufer, Johannes Koblenz
Film Director
Ralf Schmerberg, Sandra Schaede
Director of Photography
Schmidt-Reitwein, Schaede, Kummer, Schmerberg
Agency Producer
Stephan Vens
Production Company
trigger happy productions GmbH
Other
Film Editor:
Robert Kummer

Ask Yoursel
campaig
Since Septembe
2005, droppin
knowledge'
international
multimedia outreac
campaign: "As
yourself" - has bee
empowering peopl
all over the world t
raise the question
about the topics tha
matter to most t
them. "Ask Yoursel
- Donate You
Question

Back Sea
Sometimes it's mor
secure to drive a ca
with no backseats
Note: All scenes i
the commercial wer
filmed referring t
the cinematic look o
the originals

Nomination
Back Seat
(In DVD)
Germany

National Award
Silver
Agency
BBDO Germany GmbH/Team smart
Client
DaimlerChrysler Vertriebsorganisation Deutschland
Creative Director
T. Bazarkaya, S. Hardieck, M. Eickmeyer, S. Meske
Art Director
Szymon Rose, Florian Barthelmess, Jonathan Schupp
Film Director
Markus Walter, Malte Hagemeister
Agency Producer
A. Berkenbusch, M. Ceranna, S. Gentis
Production Company
Cobblestone Filmproduktion Hamburg GmbH
Other
Post Production: Schoenheitsfarm, Hamburg

>> No backseats. The smart fortwo.

smart
open your mind.
www.smart.com

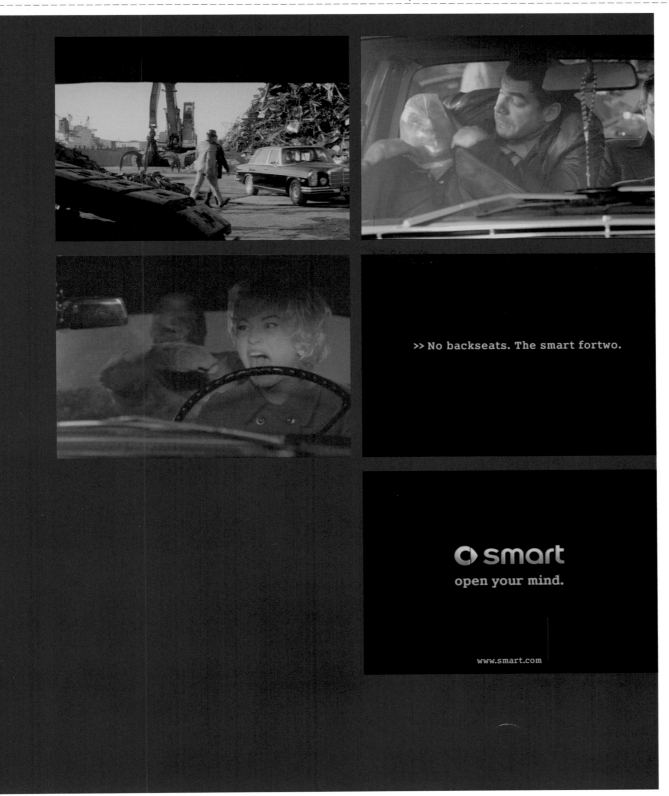

Nomination
Bye Bye Berlusconi
(In DVD)
Germany

National Award
Bronze
Agency
Jung von Matt AG
Client
Jetfilm GmbH
Creative Director
Oliver Voss, Goetz Ulmer, Tobias Bauckhage
Art Director
Jens-Paul Pfau, Martin Terhart, Danny Baarz
Copywriter
Tobias Bauckhage, Judy Stahlberg, Fabian Frese
Film Director
Jan Stahlberg, jetfilm GmbH
Director of Photography
Daniel Reiss, Christian Grund, Nicolais Joray
Production Company
Jetfilm GmbH, Schiwago Film
Others
CD: Jan Stahlberg, Jon Handschin;
CW: Dennis May

Nomination
The Make-Believe Story of Ron Hammer
(In DVD)
Germany

National Award
Gold
Agency
Heimat, Berlin
Client
Hornbach Bau- und Gartenmarkt AG
Creative Director
Guido Heffels, Juergen Vossen
Art Director
Tim Schneider
Copywriter
Till Eckel
Designer
Jan Wentz, Michael Mackens, Proximity Germany GmbH
Agency Producer
Kerstin Breuer
Production Company
Markenfilm, Berlin
Other
Producer: Lutz Müller

Nomination
Kitchen
(In DVD)
Germany

National Award
Shorlist
Agency
Saatchi & Saatchi
Client
A.R.T. Studios
Creative Director
Burkhart von Scheven
Art Director
Nicole Groezinger
Copywriter
Alexander Priebs-Macpherson
Film Director
Alex Feil
Director of Photography
Marc Achenbach
Agency Producer
Michael M. Maschke
Production Company
Element E
Other
Sound: A.R.T. Studios

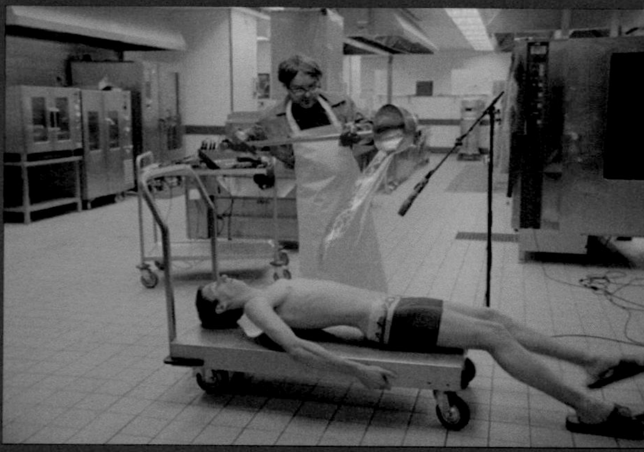

FÜR DEN BESTEN TON
GEBEN WIR ALLES.

Kitchen
A.R.T. Studios wanted to attract attention to film companies and advertisers. The motto at A.R.T.: "We give our best for sound quality".

Urban Stealth Technology
Briefing: Create a spot, that dramatises smart's core characteristic: its ability to park anywhere within the city. Solution: A tarp, which covered the car up and transformed it into a candy machine. Therefore making it invisible to traffic wardens.

Nominatio

Urban Stealthn Technology

(In DVD)
Germany

National Award
Silver
Agency
BBDO Duesseldorf GmbH
Client
DaimlerChrysler Vertriebsorganisation Deutschland
Creative Director
Sebastian Hardieck, Matthias Eickmeyer
Art Director
Patrick Hahne, Michael Dunlap
Copywriter
Elias Kouloures, Dietmar Neumann
Agency Producer
Soehnke Christiansen, Sabine Boenigk
Production Company
Vogelsaenger Film GmbH, Duesseldorf
Other
Director: Benjamin Brettschneider

Karma Hunters
(In DVD)
Spain

National Award
Gold
Agency
el miku
Client
Outstanding records uk ltd
Creative Director
el miku [albert martinez arpa]
Art Director
el miku [albert martinez arpa]
Copywriter
el miku [albert martinez arpa]
Designer
el miku [albert martinez arpa]
Film Director
el miku [albert martinez arpa]
Director of Photography
el miku [albert martinez arpa]
Agency Producer
outstanding records uk ltd
Production Company
el miku [albert martinez arpa]

Swan lake
(In DVD)
Austria

National Award
Gold
Agency
Demner, Merlicek
& Bergmann
Client
XXXLutz Group
Creative Director
Rosa Haider
Art Director
Friederike Ivens
Copywriter
Viktoria Farda
Agency Producer
Sahinaz Agamola-Schauer
Production Company
Franz Kremslehner
Other
Concept: Viktoria Farda

é bom sujar-se
skip
Think yellow.
Put the empty packaging in the plastics and metal containers.
Amarelo
VASENOL FILM
Vasenol
Think yellow.
Put the empty packaging in the plastics and metal containers.
Amarelo
valorsul
Separate. We'll take care of the rest.
1:05
1:43
1:47
0:15

Think Yellow
(In DVD)
Portugal

National Award
Gold
Agency
Lowe & Partners Portugal
Client
Valorsul
Creative Director
Susana Albuquerque,
Joâo Coutinho
Art Director
Tocas
Copywriter
Marcelo Dolabella
Agency Producer
Ana Rondao
Production Company
Pix Mix

Campanades TV3
(In DVD)
Spain

National Award
Silver
Agency
TV3 Televisió de Catalunya
Client
TV3 Televisió de Catalunya
Creative Director
Francesc Fabregas,
JM Andres-Aranya
Film Director
JM Andres-Aranya
Illumination
Mirelec
Production Company
Montse Rovira: TV3
Televisió de Catalunya
Other
Music: Carles Santos

Bob Sound-Logo
(In DVD)
Austria

National Award
Silver
Agency
Demner, Merlicek & Bergmann
Client
Mobilkom Austria AG
Creative Director
Francesco Bestagno
Copywriter
Florian Nussbaumer, Florian Gigler
Film Director
Florian Nussbaumer, Florian Gigler
Agency Producer
Sahinaz Agamola-Schauer
Production Company
Soundfeiler
Other
Composer: M. Wondrak, H. Donaubauer, M. C. Riegler

Voutch: Japonesa / Remeros / Telenoticias
(In DVD)
Spain

National Award
Silver
Agency
Canal Satélite Digital S.L.
Client
Canal+
Creative Director
Cristina Alovisetti
Art Director
Pau Bosch
Illustrator
Voutch
Other
Animation: ISKRA S.L. - Prod: Sioni Aranda

Good grief!

We will row against the current before it is too late.

DISASTER
I'll be the plane with 268 Moldovan passengers completely unaware of the danger and Cristina will be the mountain.

Bob Sound-Logo
In order to give the mobile service provider "bob" a distinctive acoustic feature, an acoustic logo - as simple and recognisable as the visual logo - was developed. The result was a kind of "sound bite" consisting simply of the brand-name "bob".

Voutch: Japonesa / Remeros / Telenoticias
Continuity wipes to separate scheduling blocks. Audiovisual adaptation of cartoons by the cartoonist and humorist Voutch. Laughing is always healthy

Zapatos de España
Spanish footwear. The project consists of catalogue showing the trends for the autumn-winter seasons.

Agnus Dei
To attract film-goers, the Zurich Theater produced a film highlighting the live nature of theater. Actors played short scenes from famous plays, offering an impressive look into the theater world.

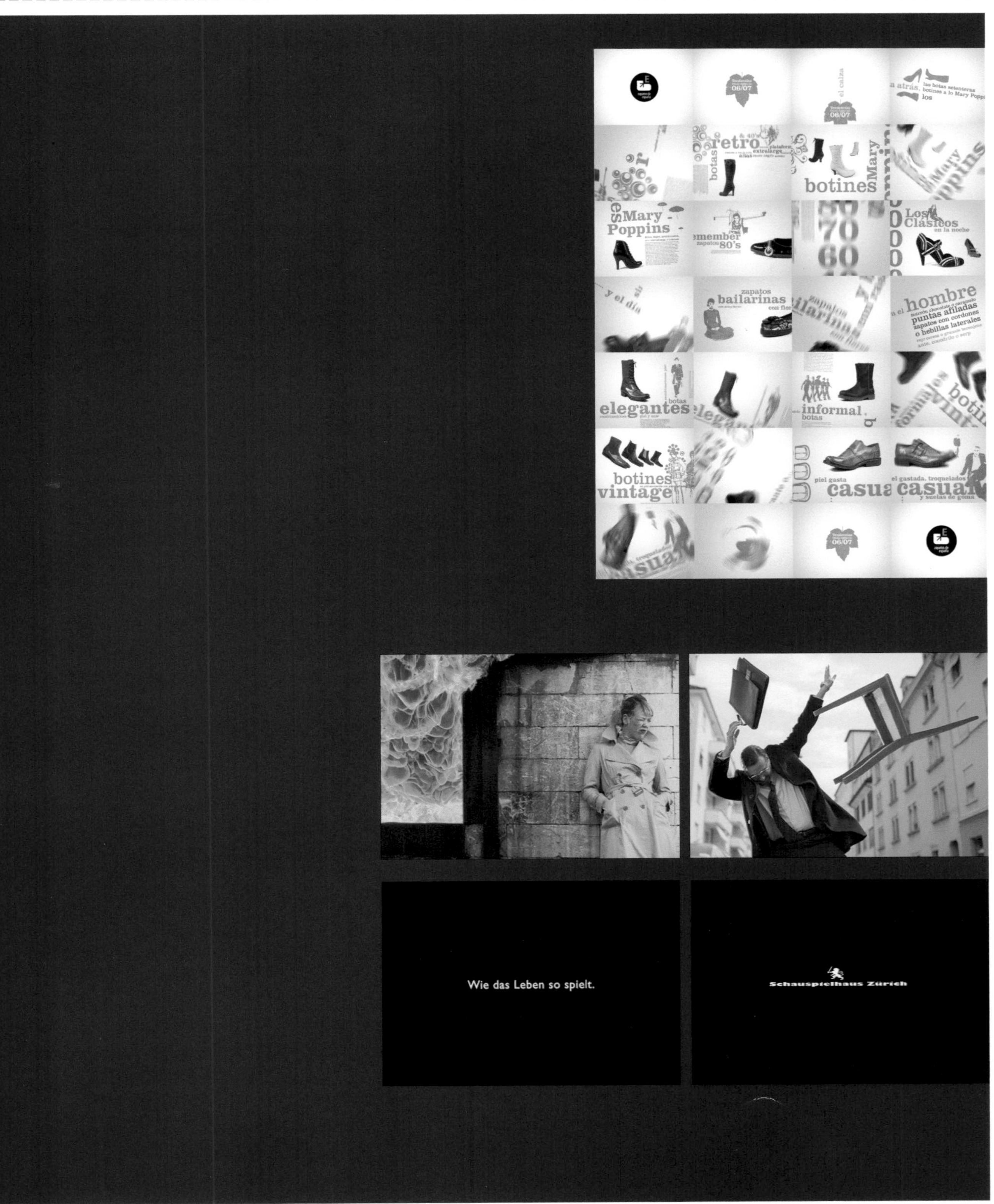

Zapatos de España
(In DVD)
Spain

National Award
Silver
Agency
Kikuru
Client
FICE/Daniel Nebot
Creative Director
Kikuru team
Art Director
Kikuru team
Designer
Kikuru team
Director of Photography
Kikuru team
Agency Producer
Kikuru team
Production Company
Terratremol Produccions
Other
Music: Javi Belda

Agnus Dei
(In DVD)
Switzerland

National Award
Silver
Agency
Publicis Werbeagentur AG
Client
Schauspielhaus Zurich
Creative Director
Markus Gut
Copywriter
Markus Gut
Agency Producer
Ines Bossart
Production Company
Condor Films Zurich
Other
Account Executive:
Marion Marxer

Q: Are you contributing to shape your time?

Q: Do you make things easier or harder?

Q: Could the client possibly be right?

2

Advertising Print

Q: Is consumption equal to welfare?

Advertising Print Jury

There is no magic formula how to do great creativity. We all intuitively recognize good or bad creative work. We are hooked by great work or we just pass over it. Both as juries and as consumers. To be hooked by creativity is like a fish being caught by an angler. Either a fish takes the bait because it believes it is a tasty morsel, or it recognises the fraud and just ignores it. We ignore most work because we recognise that it is fraudulent, but we love to be hooked by great work, because we love tasty creative fare.

Enjoy the best European print and poster menu!

Eda Kauba
Chairman
Creative Director
Euro RSCG
Czech Republic

Eda has been Creative Director for Euro RSCG Prague since 2000. Previously he worked for eight years as Creative Director for Saatchi & Saatchi. He is on the Board of the Czech Art Directors Club and was a jury member at The Golden Drum, Slovak ADC, Rumanian ADC Festivals and President of the Jury for the Moscow International Advertising Festival.

Eda has won more than 35 national and international awards, including a Golden Drum, New York Ad Festival, Golden Hammer, Moscow International Advertising Festival and ADC Czech.

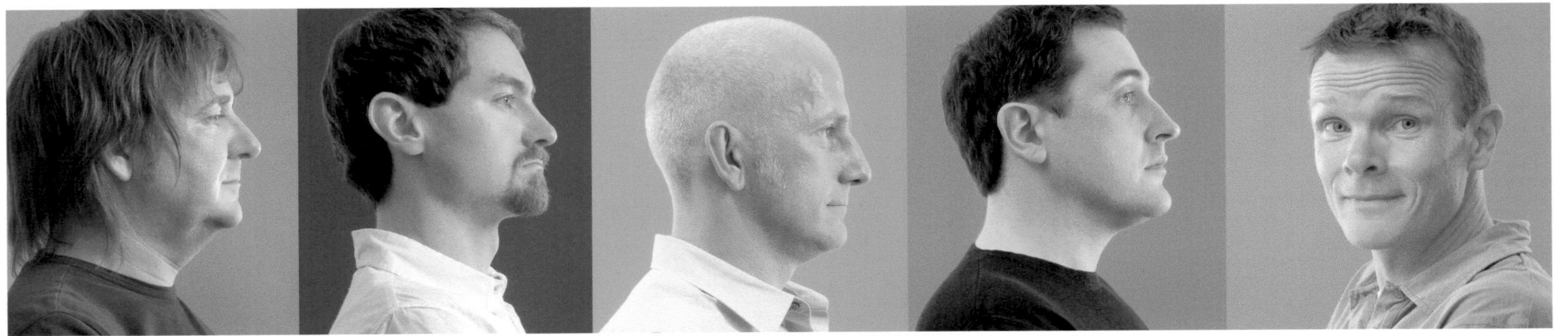

Dieter Pivrnec
Vice Chief Creative Officer
Lowe GGK
Austria

He studied design and obtained his Master of Arts at the University of Arts Linz, and also studied design at the University of Ausburg. Initially, he worked as a Freelance Art Director for various agencies in Germany and Austria. Then he worked for GGK Salzburg as an Art Director, and then, from 1990 until 2005, for Ogilvy Vienna as a Creative Director. Since 2006, he has worked for Lowe GGK Vienna as a Creative Director and Vice CCO.

His talents have been recognized internationally at the Cannes Lions, Golden Drum Festival, New York Festival, Crea Award, Midas Awards, Houston Film Festival and Die Klappe.

Madis Ots
Creative Director
Vatson & Vatson
Estonia

He was born in 1977 in Tallinn and studied advertising and media at Tallinn University. He has been with Vatson&Vatson/Y&R throughout his career - as Copywriter since 1998 and Creative Director since 2005. Has won a couple of dozen Golden Egg advertising awards in Estonia over the years, six this spring. Most recent achievement - Grand Prix, gold in TV, and special prize for 'use of national peculiarity' at Kyiv International Advertising Festival, or KIAF. Besides advertising, he is the author of about 3,000 comic strips of "questionable moral value."

Constantin Kaloff
Creative Director
Scholz & Friends Berlin GmbH
Germany

Constantin Kaloff is Creative Director at Scholz & Friends Berlin. From 1993 to 1995 he worked at Scholz & Friends Hamburg becoming Creative Director later on. Subsequently he went to Springer & Jacoby being responsible for Mercedes-Benz Passenger Cars. In 1999 he came to Jung von Matt becoming Managing Director two years later. Besides his work for BMW he was significantly involved in the highly awarded "steering-wheel" campaign for the Deutsche Bahn and the "Geiz ist geil"campaign for Saturn.

Constantin Kaloff is a member of the Art Directors Club for Germany (ADC). His work has received numerous awards at national and international creative festivals.

Haukur Már Hauksson
Art Director
Pipar Advertising
Iceland

He studied film and photography in the United States before studying graphic design at the Icelandic Academy of the Arts, where he graduated in 1997. Haukur has worked for various advertising agencies in Iceland, both small and large, and is currently Partner and an Art Director at Pipar Advertising. Also, he is the President of the Association of Icelandic Graphic Designers, a board member of FORM ISLAND (the Icelandic Design Association), and board member of ADCE.

Donal O'Dea
Creative Director
Owens DDB
Ireland

Donal O'Dea is joint Creative Director of Owens DDB in Dublin. He has produced a wide range of award winning above and below the line work, including Bulmers, Volkswagen, Carlsberg, Allied Irish Banks, and McDonalds. He is also the co-author of a highly successful series of humorous books on Irish culture called the Feckin' Series, one of which deals with Irish slang. "And they're feckin' deadly".

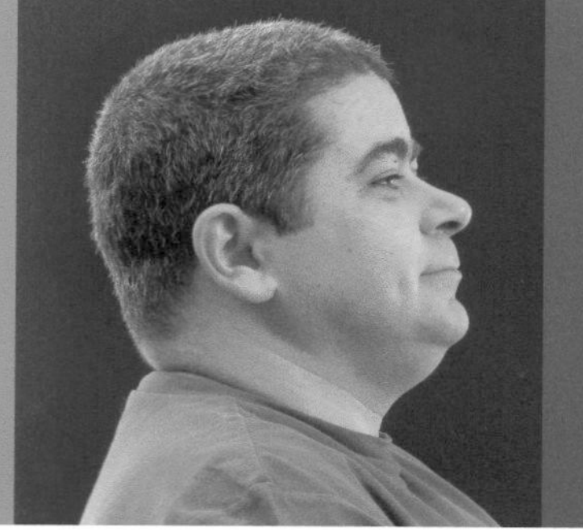
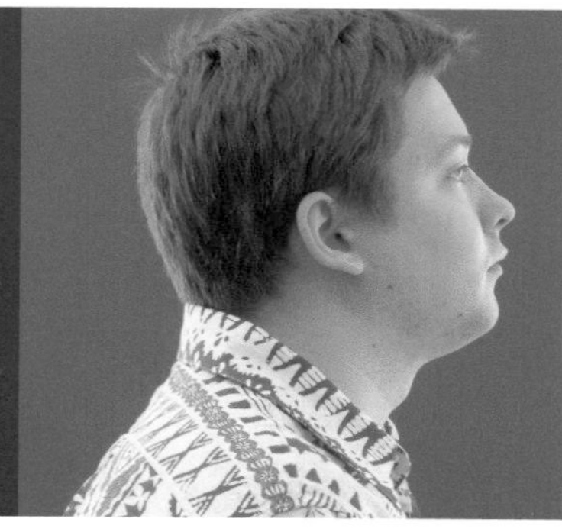

Daniele Ravenna
Freelance
Daniele Ravenna
Italy

He is an experienced freelance copywriter of Italy's major advertising community in Milan. He studied Philosophy and graduated at Università degli Studi in Milan. He has worked for several agencies since 1974; among them, TBWA, Italia/BBDO, Pubblimarket, Leo Burnett, DDB, STZ, Young&Rubicam, BGS, Ogilvy, JWT, and EuroRSCG.
He has been a member of the Art Director Club of Italy since 1988, and was voted 'Copywriter of the Year' in 1990. He was on the ADCE Jury in Vienna in 1994. At the ADCI awards, he has won two Gold, nine Silver, and five Bronze awards.

Martins Kibilds
Creative Director
TBWA/Latvia
Latvia

Since 2000, he has worked as the Creative Director of TBWA/Latvia. Since 2002, he has been in charge of the Latvian version of the television show, "Who Wants to be a Millionaire?" Before that, he was a Marketing Director for the daily "Diena", and a PR advisor for several politicians, and a television and press journalist. He has also studied law and is the father of two sons.

Jakub Kaminski
Partner & Creative Director
Brain
Poland

He was born in 1970 in Warsaw. He studied philosophy on the UW, and, from the second year, he has been involved with advertising. From 1992 to 2001, he worked at the Warsaw branch of Publicis, finishing as Creative Director and board member. During his work in Publicis, he met Asiya Malinowska, his partner in Brain advertising agency.

José Carlos de Campos
Creative Director
Strat
Portugal

He has worked for many prestigious agencies such as Cineponto/Leo Burnett, Young&Rubicam, Z.cdp europe, JWT, TBWA/EPG, Strat and Ogilvy. He has been awarded five Cannes Lions (1 gold, 1 silver, 3 bronze), the Grand Prix Eurobest, 4 Eurobest, 4 Fiap, 3 with New York Festivals, and several awards in the Portuguese Creative Club. He is founder and the first President of the Clube de Criativos de Portugal.

Yaroslav Orlov
Creative Director
Instinct Ad Agency
Russia

Started in small Russian agency as a Junior Copywriter in 97. Shortly after he jumped into medium-weight local full service agency, spent 3 years sharpening texts and radio. Then he went one step further to TV and train his nervous system through experience with P&G in Saatchi&Saatchi Moscow. Finally, he came to BBDO, where he worked-worked-worked to become the youngest Creative Director of Instinct BBDO - a newly started agency. With numerous awards and shortlists at various festivals and mountains of work done, Instinct was recently rated the most awarded creative agency in Russia.

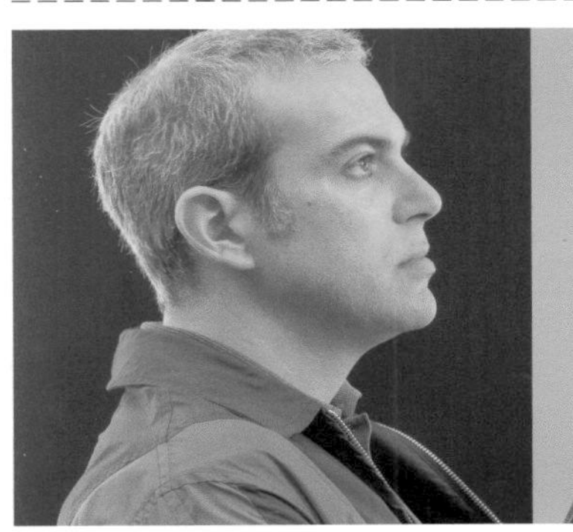

Q: Endless love or sex for fun?

Fernando Planelles
Creative Director
SMÄLL
Spain

Philipp Skrabal
Creative Director
Publicis Werbeagentur
Switzerland

He was born in Madrid and fell in love with Barcelona. He feels he has been very lucky to have the opportunity to work always with people who are enthusiastic about their works (Bassat Ogilvy, Vizeversa, Casadevall Pedreño). He met his partner, Xavi Hidalgo, and is currently embarked on a very exciting project: SMÄLL.

Philipp Skrabal has worked as a Creative Director at Publicis in Zurich since July 2004. Previously he was a Creative Director and a member of the executive management at Matter & Partner, the former local agency of Leo Burnett, as well as an Art Director at EURO RSCG in Zurich and Sydney and at Seiler DDB Zurich, where he began his advertising career 14 years ago.

Advertising Print. Poster Advertising

Austria

Czech Republic: 1 Nomination

Estonia

Germany: 5 Nominations

Ireland

Italy

Latvia

Poland

Portugal

Russia

Slovak Republic

Slovenia

Spain

Switzerland: Gold

Gold
Not here but now
Switzerland

National Award
Gold
Agency
Walker
Client
Amnesty International
Creative Director
Pius Walker
Copywriter
Pius Walker
Designer
Marianne Friedli
Photographer
Federico Naef
Graphics
Florian Fröhlich,
Carolina Gurtner

This campaign shows how human rights are abused each and every day - within only a few hours' flying distance of us. Two worlds collide on 200 posters, each one adapted to match its surroundings. So brutal scenes take place in the middle of Zürich.

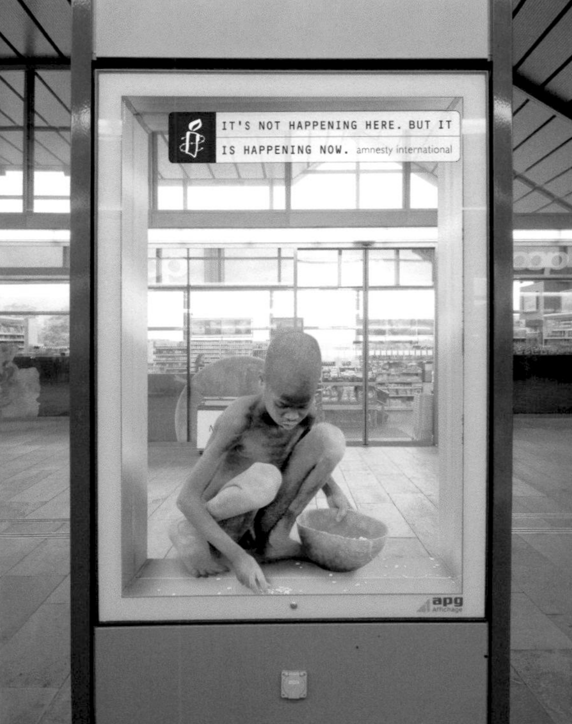

Nomination
Shining
Czech Republic

National Award
Silver
Agency
Mark BBDO
Client
Wrigley
Creative Director
Leon Sverdlin, Martin Charvat
Art Director
Jan Tamchyna
Copywriter
Pavel Brazda
Agency Producer
Pavel Jankovsky
Graphics
Retouching: Drawetc

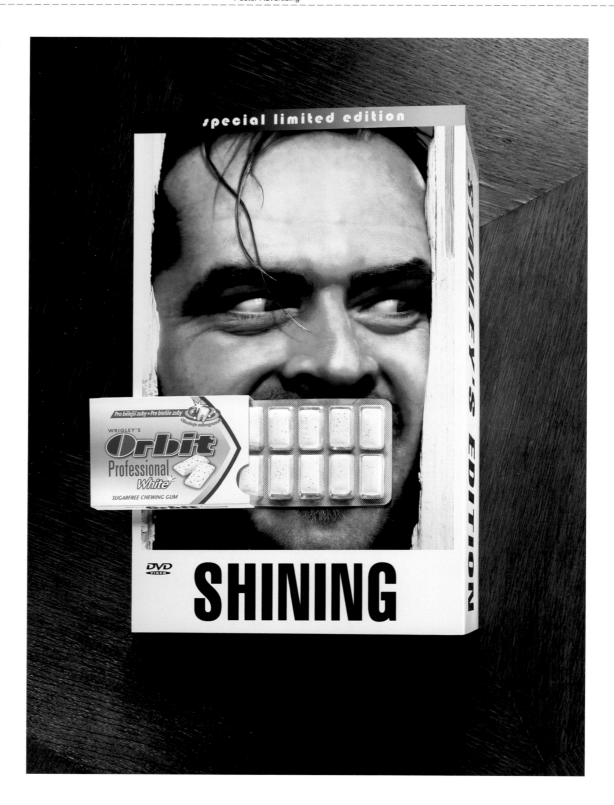

Shining
Orbit White gives you shining white teeth.

Nomination
Audi Open Sky System
Germany

National Award
Shortlist
Agency
Philipp und Keuntje GmbH
Client
Audi AG
Creative Director
Diether Kerner
Art Director
Soenke Schmidt
Copywriter
René Ewert
Photographer
Sebastian Denz
Graphics
Kaloyan Yanev,
Rouven Steiman

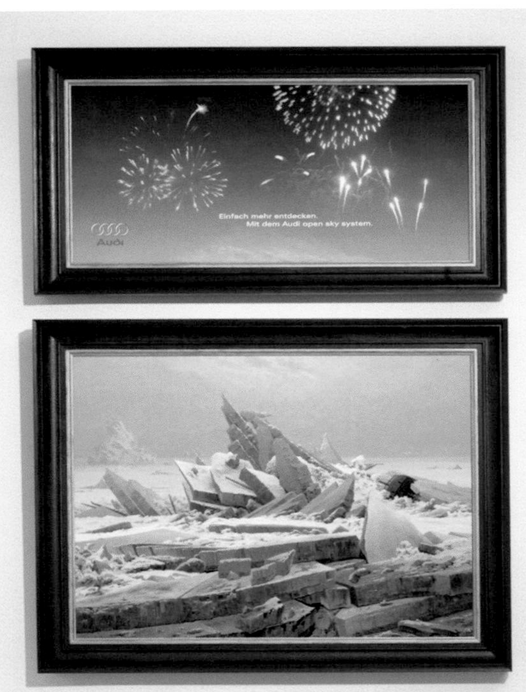

Nomination

Comedy Central Launch Campaign

Germany

National Award
Shortlist
Agency
kempertrautmann gmbh
Client
MTV Networks GmbH & Co. OHG
Creative Director
Frank Bannoehr, Daniel Ernsting
Art Director
Frank Bannoehr, Axel Schilling
Copywriter
Daniel Ernsting, Christian Soldatke
Photographer
Arthur Mebius
Graphics
Tim Belser, Marita Loecmele

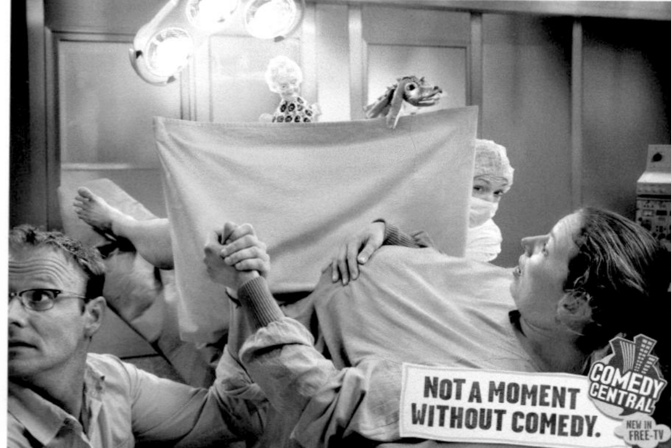

Comedy Central Launch Campaign
MTV Comedy Central Launch Campaign. "Not a moment without comedy".

Living Video
At Google video you can find any film. And that's what Google wanted to promote through non-traditional advertising in German cities like Berlin and Hamburg.
Solution:
It was needed to 'teach' billboards to show moving images. But how to do that? Custom build billboards without content (except the Google Video toolbar with typed in search term) were placed around city centres and airports. So the environment of the billboards supplied the moving images in real time and passers-by were able to interact with the Google Video screen.

Nomination
Living Video
Germany

National Award
Shortlist
Agency
Kolle Rebbe Werbeagentur GmbH
Client
Google Germany GmbH
Creative Director
Lorenz Ritter, Sven Klohk, Ulrich Zuenkeler
Art Director
Nina Zimmermann
Copywriter
Sebastian Oehme
Other
Account manager: Katharina Lechelt, Sike Schilling

Nomination
The Annual Ticket Campaign
Germany

National Award
Bronze
Agency
Scholz & Friends
Client
Zoologischer Garten Berlin AG
Creative Director
Matthias Spaetgens, Jan Leube, Martin Pross
Art Director
Mathias Rebmann
Copywriter
Florian Schwalme
Photographer
Matthias Koslik
Graphics
Heidrun Kleingries, Felix Pfannmueller
Other
Futura Berlin GmbH

Nomination
The Post-it Campaign
Germany

National Award
Shortlist
Agency
Scholz & Friends
Client
Queisser Pharma GmbH & Co.KG
Creative Director
Suze Barrett, Matthias Schmidt, Stefan Setzkorn
Art Director
Marcin Baba
Copywriter
Dennis Lueck, Roman Jonsson
Photographer
Susanne Ludwig
Other
***Postproduction*:**
Metagate GmbH, Hamburg

The Annual Ticket Campaign
The ads show what can happen if one visits the Zoo: the animals are hiding or sleeping in their burrows and just won't feel like posing in front of the visitors.
So sometimes one has to be a little patient to experience all the animals in the zoo. With the annual ticket it is not a problem. One can come back and try again any time.

The Post-it Campaign
"If your memory needs help".
The task was to develop a striking and convincing campaign demonstrating that Doppelherz Lecithin pills strengthen the memory.
The campaign shows people in normal everyday situations - except that absolutely everything is covered with post-its.

Danke, Schwester
Austria

National Award
Gold
Agency
CCP, Heye Werbeagentur GmbH
Client
McDonald's WerbegmbH
Creative Director
Werner Celand,
Peter Czerny
Art Director
Dietmar Kreil
Copywriter
Viola Gangl
Photographer
Thomas Hannich
Graphics
Dietmar Kreil
Other
Account Director:
Philipp Krumpel

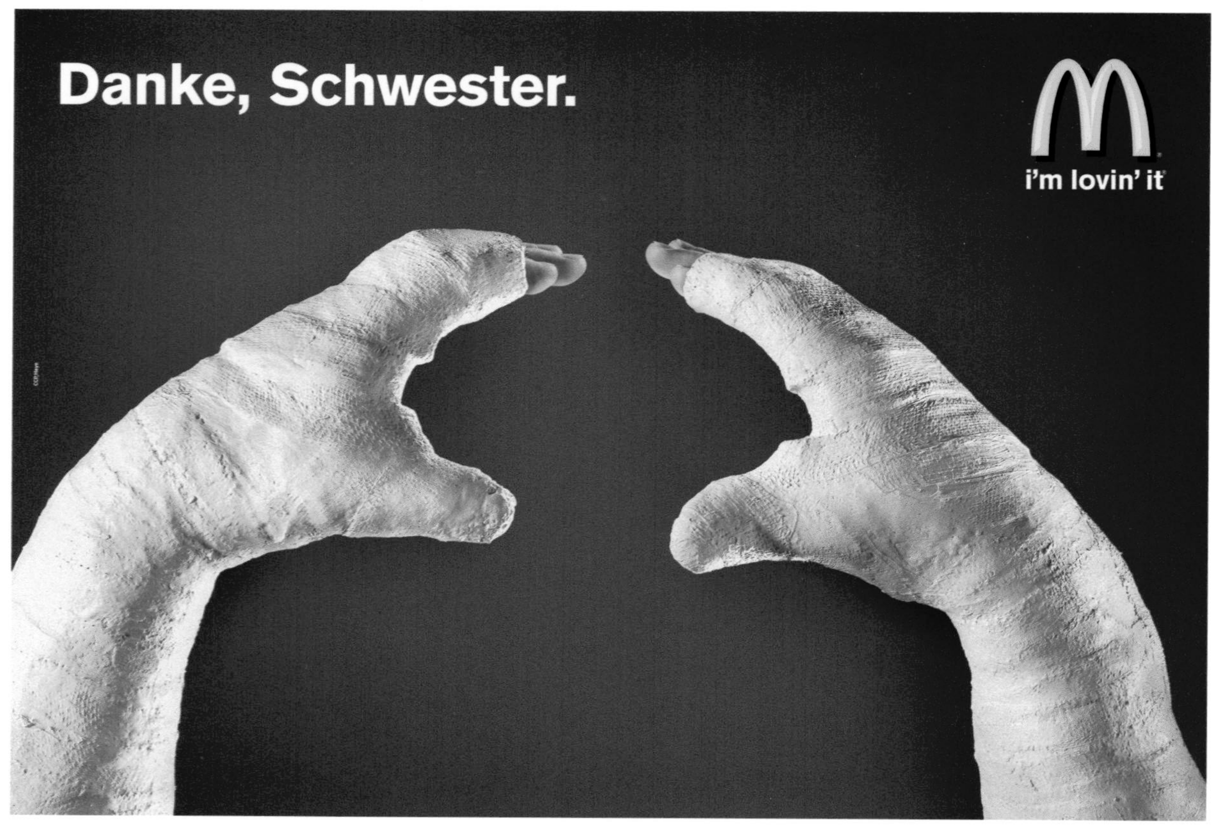

Danke, Schwester
Thanks, Nurse.

Light into the Dark
Donation Box
Light Into The Dark is the name of Austria's most important charity organisation. These special backlit posters were completely dark, until one donated money by inserting a coin to light the poster and thereby literally bring light into dark.

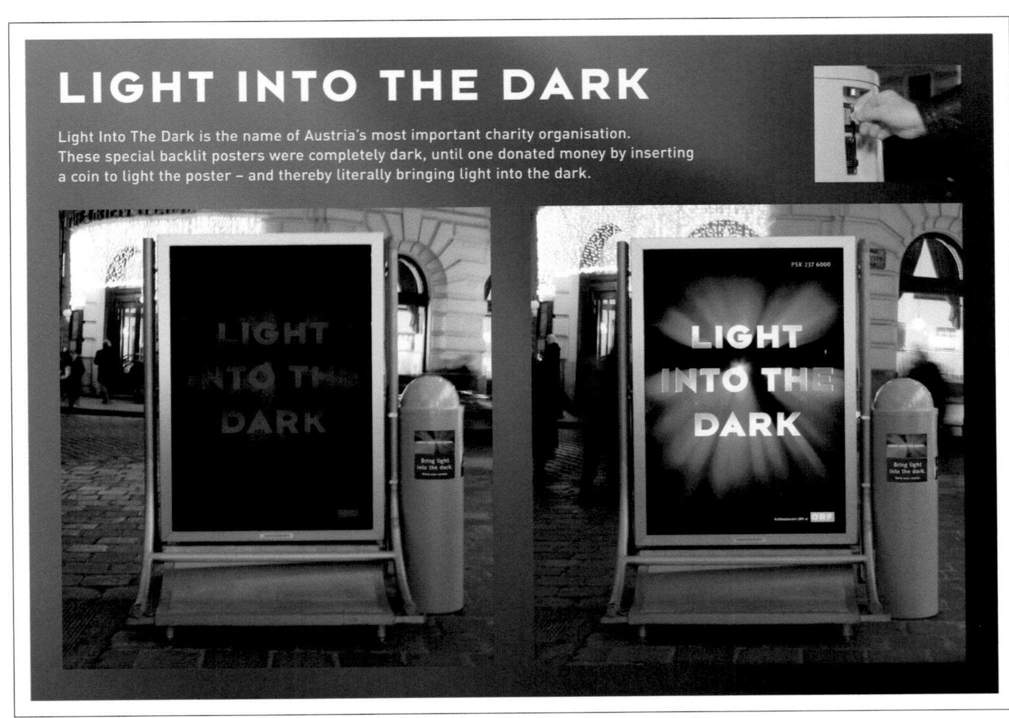

Light into the Dark Donation Box
Austria

National Award
Gold
Agency
Demner, Merlicek & Bergmann
Client
ORF / Licht ins Dunkel
Creative Director
Francesco Bestagno
Art Director
Francesco Bestagno
Photographer
Staudinger + Franke
Graphics
Daniela Schabernak
Other
Digital Imaging:
Natalie Leroy

Coffee to go
Austria

National Award
Silver
Agency
Draftfcb Kobza
Client
Naber Kaffee
Creative Director
Joachim Glawion
Art Director
Tolga Büyükdoganay
Copywriter
Tolga Büyükdoganay,
Jürgen Heel
Designer
Tolga Büyükdoganay

MQ-Man Image Campaign
Austria

National Award
Silver
Agency
Büro X Design GmbH
Client
MuseumsQuartier Wien
Creative Director
Andreas Miedaner
Art Director
Andreas Miedaner
Copywriter
Christian Pott
Designer
Andreas Miedaner,
Sascha Schaberl
Agency Producer
Gertraud Haas
Photographer
Oliver Jiszda
Graphics
Sascha Schaberl

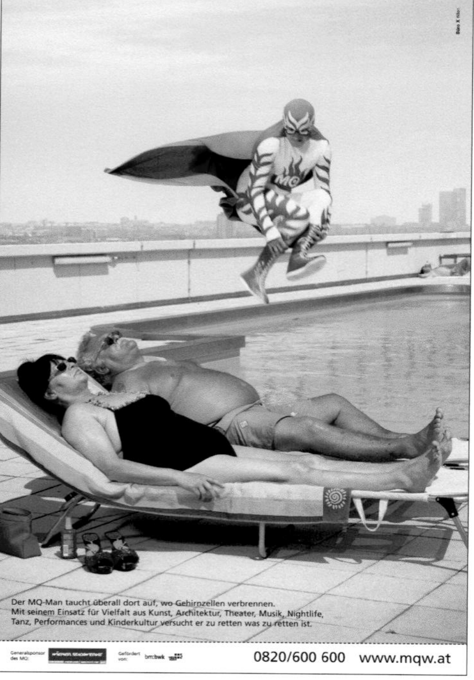

MQ-Man Image
Campaign
Culture for Everyone

Meinl Coffee Decaf
An ad for the decaffeinated variation of Austria's famous Julius Meinl coffee where the Meinl logo, the North-African boy, was slightly altered to fit the new product.

Meinl Coffee Decaf
Austria

National Award
Silver
Agency
Demner, Merlicek & Bergmann
Client
Julius Meinl Austria GmbH
Creative Director
Francesco Bestagno
Art Director
Francesco Bestagno
Copywriter
Claus Gigler
Agency Producer
Norbert Rabenseifner, Daniela Kalmar
Graphics
Daniela Schabernak
Other
Digital Imaging:
Siegfried Duft

The Homeless Aid
Austria

National Award
Silver
Agency
Draftfcb Kobza
Client
Obdachlosenhilfe Wien
Creative Director
Joachim Glawion
Art Director
Michael Köditz
Copywriter
Florian Ludwig
Photographer
Michael Köditz

Horror
Estonia

National Award
Silver
Agency
Kontuur LB
Client
Rakvere Meatfactory
Creative Director
Urmas Villmann
Art Director
Jaanus Meri
Copywriter
Andrus Niit
Designer
Tarmo Talvik
Other
Project manager:
Peep Pajumäe

Hunting
Austria

National Award
Silver
Agency
Draftfcb Kobza
Client
Radatz Fleischwaren
Vertriebs GmbH
Creative Director
Erich Falkner,
Ronni Ronniger
Art Director
Hannes Glantschnig
Copywriter
Dominik Niebauer,
Christoph Reicher
Designer
Tanja Promitzer
Photographer
Robert Marksteiner

THE HUNT IS OVER.
RADATZ
Venison Specialties

Hunting
Autumn is hunting season. Radatz offers a big variety of venison specialties. Therefore modified binoculars serve as key-visual.

+10 Fresco
Football stars like Beckham, Zidane, Raul, Messi, Kaka or Ballack are considered to be real football gods by their fans. They are simply elevated to where they belong anyway - into football heaven.. The world's largest football fresco was created in the main lobby of the Cologne central train station, which happens to be right next to the stunning Cologne Cathedral.

WWF Donations Campaign
Save the world with a few coins. Become a partner of the WWF. Donate at www.wwf.at

+10 Fresco
Germany

National Award
Silver
Agency
TBWA Germany (180/TBWA), Berlin
Client
Adidas AG
Creative Director
Kurt Georg Dieckert, Stefan Schmidt
Art Director
Boris Schwiedrzik
Copywriter
Helge Bloeck
Designer
Felix Reidenbach (Illustrator)
Agency Producer
Katrin Dettmann
Production Company
Methodik Management & Partner

Donate at www.wwf.at
for a living planet WWF

WWF Donations Campaign
Austria

National Award
Gold
Agency
Jung von Matt/Donau Werbeagentur GmbH
Client
WWF Austria
Creative Director
Andreas Putz, Gerd Schulte-Doeinghaus
Art Director
Eva Ortner
Copywriter
Helena Giokas
Agency Producer
Joerg Guenther
Photographer
Graham Westmoreland/ www.enste-jaspers.de
Graphics
Eva Ortner
Other
Illustrator: Hannes Kosina, Friendly Fire Comm.

Mini Loop
Ireland

National Award
Silver
Agency
McConnells
Client
BMW Ireland
Creative Director
Laurence Keogh
Art Director
Michael Creagh
Copywriter
Des Creedon
Photographer
Donal Moloney
Other
Retouching:
Jeff Bennett

Nature calls
Estonia

National Award
Silver
Agency
Kontuur LB
Client
Rakvere Meatfactory
Creative Director
Urmas Villmann
Art Director
Andres Abe
Copywriter
Andrus Niit

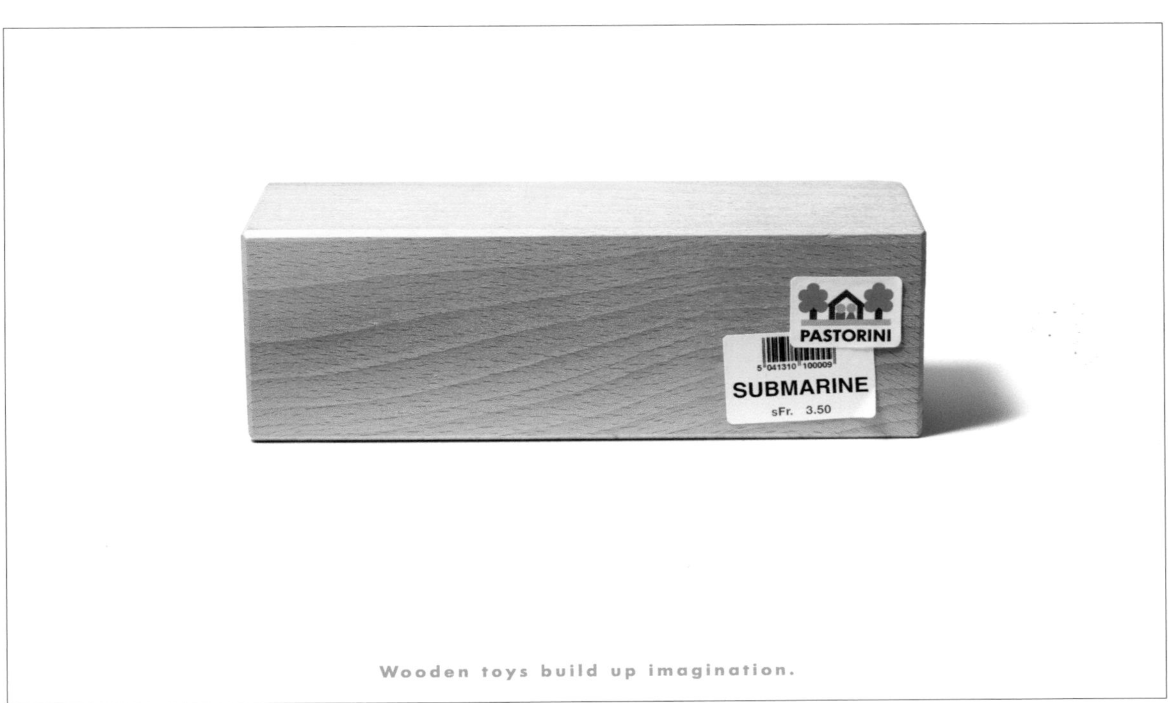

Blocks
Switzerland

National Award
Silver
Agency
Publicis Werbeagentur AG
Client
Pastorini
Creative Director
Philipp Skrabal
Art Director
Simon Staub
Copywriter
Livio Dainese
Photographer
Felix Streuli
Graphics
Moritz Stillhard
Other
Account Executive:
Claudia Camenisch

Mini Loop
The Mini is all about fun and exhilaration. So by rights it should have its own special lane on the motorway.

Blocks
Wooden toys fully come to life in the imagination of children and do not dictate how they should be used. To dramatize this quality, simple wooden blocks that Pastorini sells are labelled with a price tag and a possible use.

Kahn
Task: Adidas asked to create an outdoor spectacle that firstly becomes not only Talk of the town but the Talk of the world and secondly welcomes all guests in the city to the FIFA World Cup 2006 kick-off match: Munich. Idea: A 65-meter wide Oliver Kahn statue was built across a four-lane highway near the Munich international airport.

Kahn
Germany

National Award
Silver
Agency
TBWA Germany (180/TBWA), Berlin
Client
Adidas AG
Creative Director
Stefan Schmidt, Kurt Georg Dieckert
Art Director
Boris Schwiedrzik
Agency Producer
Katrin Dettmann
Production Company
Kinetic World Wide
Photographer
Joerg Reichardt

Touareg Turban
Italy

National Award
Silver
Agency
DDB
Client
Volkswagen Group
Creative Director
Vicky Gitto
Art Director
Giovanni Policastro
Copywriter
Vicky Gitto
Other
Post Production:
Pixelway

Krone Poster
Austria

National Award
Gold
Agency
Lowe GGK
Client
Krone Verlag GmbH & Co
Vermögensberatung KG
Creative Director
Alexander Zelmanovics,
Dieter Pivrnec
Art Director
Hannes Böker
Copywriter
Werner Bühringer
Designer
Justin Nickerl
Agency Producer
Vienna Paint
Photographer
Stockmaterial

Krone Poster
This refers to the daily coverage of the Kronen Zeitung. Don't believe it until you read about it in the Kronen Zeitung.

Cada cosa al seu lloc
"Make no mistake: everything in its place" Roda de Ter Council's intention was to carry on encouraging the townspeople to leave their rubbish in the right kind of bin for selective collection and recycling, a system that had been started up a year before. So we cast around for an everyday image taken to absurd extremes, in order to show how easy it was to do what they were being asked to do: to put each kind of rubbish in the right place. The photo helped to achieve a sense of reality and of proximity to the people, thereby enhancing the message.

The Bovisa Triennial is Born
Italy

National Award
Silver
Agency
Art Directors Club Italiano
Client
La Triennale di Milano
Creative Director
Giuseppe Mastromatteo - Luca Scotto di Carlo
Art Director
G. Mastromatteo, L. Toniutti, G. Valerio
Copywriter
Luca Scotto di Carlo
Photographer
Pier Paolo Ferrari

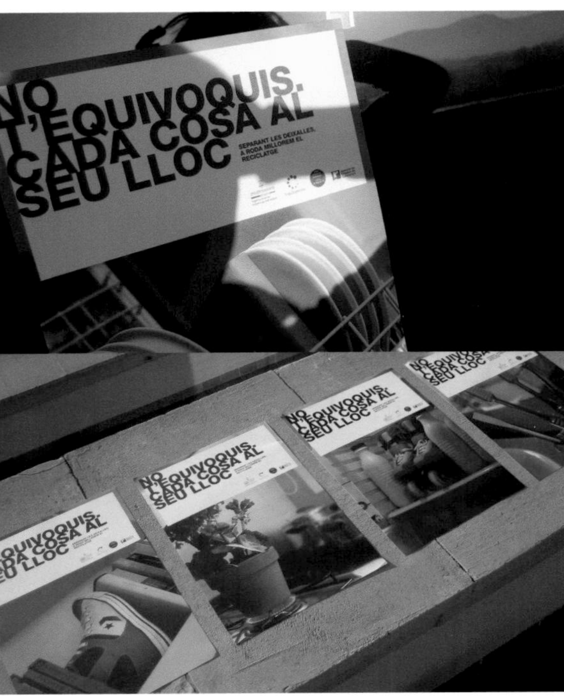

Cada cosa al seu lloc
Spain

National Award
Silver
Agency
Bisgràfic
Client
Roda de Ter Town Council
Creative Director
Bisgràfic
Art Director
Bisgràfic
Copywriter
Bisgràfic
Designer
Bisgràfic
Agency Producer
Bisgràfic
Photographer
Fotodisseny J.E
Graphics
Bisgràfic

Love Yourself catalogue
Latvia

National Award
Silver
Agency
RCL Ltd. TBWA Latvia
Client
Domina
Creative Director
Martins Kibilds
Art Director
Mareks Hofmanis

Couple
Poland

National Award
Silver
Agency
JWT Poland
Client
Amersport
Creative Director
Darek Zatorski
Art Director
Katarzyna Macharz
Copywriter
Kamil Nazarewicz
Agency Producer
Jwt Poland
Photographer
Andrzej Dragan

Love Yourself catalogue
Instead of demonstrating and showing particular prices, products and clothes, it was very important to create the feeling – in this shopping centre there are so many things that I would like. Because when I (and even my alter ego) open the closet on the first day of spring, only one thing is certain – there is nothing to wear. Instead of sending the usual product catalog, Fashion shopping centre Domina sends a fashion poster (with additional descriptions of vintage-style interiors) in order to create the impression of style abundance.

Vienna Art Festival 2006
Vienna Art Festival Campaign 2006. The 250th anniversary of the birth of Wolfgang Amadeus Mozart had released a veritable flood of hype in Austria. Everybody wanted to get in on the act. There was a Mozart Year, numerous events, and the commercialisation even went as far as a Mozart Sausage. It was also a jubilee year for Sigmund Freud. He would have been celebrating his 150th birthday. It is also widely known that in his lifetime he avoided dealing with his birthday. Not only at the Vienna Art Festival are sage people asking themselves: what would they have said about it all? One can only assume that they would have rolled their eyes in disbelief.

boba
Spain

National Award
Silver
Agency
grafica
Client
boba
Creative Director
Pablo Martín
Art Director
Pablo Martín
Designer
Ellen Diedrich
Graphics
Ellen Diedrich

Vienna Art Festival 2006
Austria

National Award
Gold
Agency
Demner, Merlicek & Bergmann
Client
Vienna Art Festival
Creative Director
Mariusz Jan Demner
Art Director
Felix Broscheit
Agency Producer
Norbert Rabenseifner, Sandra Fauster
Photographer
Stockfoto: IMAGNO Christian Brandstätter Verlag
Graphics
Felix Broscheit
Other
Digital Imaging: Vienna
Paint: C. Ruff, R. Macku

Doll, Bear, Bee
Russia

National Award
Silver
Agency
Avrora
Client
Avrora LTD
Creative Director
Pavel Khizhnykov
Art Director
Victoria Lountsi
Copywriter
Anton Zimin
Designer
Victoria Lountsi

STRAYS
Poland

National Award
Gold
Agency
McCann Erickson
Client
MPT Warsaw taxi service
Creative Director
Iwona Kluszczynska, Wojciech Dagiel
Art Director
Lukasz Kotlinski, Iza Przepiorska-kotlinska
Copywriter
Iza Przepiorska-kotlinska, lukasz Kotlinski
Agency Producer
McCann Erickson: Monika Dagiel, Karolina Czplarska
Photographer
Lukasz Murgrabia
Other
Iza Zambrzuska (Tomograf), Marek Lesniak

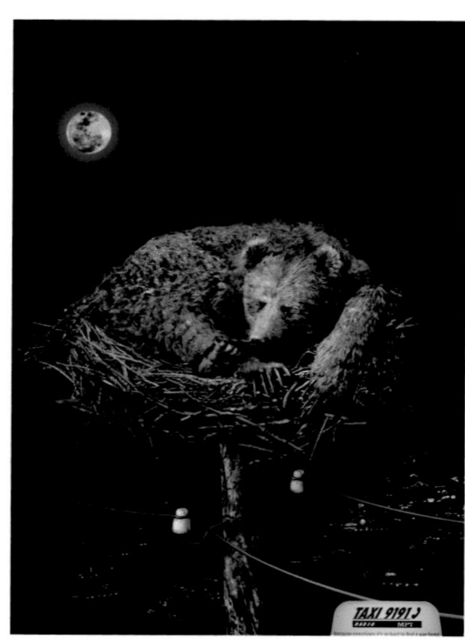

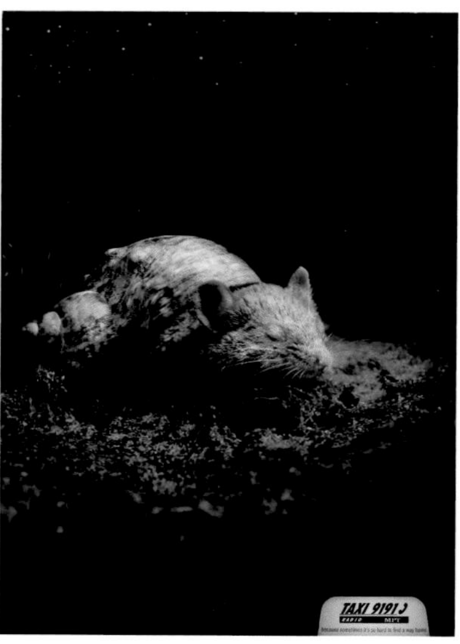

Doll, Bear, Bee
Is it possible to show, how disgusting, when adults use children as sex toys? No. But we did our best.

Strays
When it's so hard to find the right way home just dial 9191.

Find your way
"Enjoy your journey through constructive art". The main aim was to attract the tourists (both Slovak and foreign) to a unique exhibition of constructivist art in the Slovak Republic. How to help them to find the way? Show them the map!

Interferències
Interferences

Find your way
Slovak Republic

National Award
Silver
Agency
Vaculik Advertising
Client
Milan Dobes Museum
Creative Director
Milan Hladky,
Juraj Vaculik
Art Director
Dejan Galovic
Copywriter
Zuzana Hasanova

Interferències
Spain

National Award
Silver
Agency
RUN Design
Client
Ajuntament de Terrassa (IMCET)
Creative Director
Xavier Roca Connétable
Art Director
Xavier Roca Connétable
Copywriter
Xavier Roca Connétable,
Manuel Segade,
Belén Simón
Designer
Xavier Roca Connétable
Agency Producer
RUN Design
Graphics
Xavier Roca Connétable

Earphones
Ireland

National Award
Silver
Agency
Publicis QMP
Client
Hugh Lane Gallery
Creative Director
Ger Roe
Art Director
Ger Roe
Copywriter
Ted Barry
Photographer
Neil MacDougald

MS
Switzerland

National Award
Silver
Agency
Advico Young & Rubicam
Client
Multiple Sklerose Gesellschaft
Creative Director
Daniel Comte, Urs Schrepfer
Art Director
Marietta Albinus
Copywriter
Martin Stulz
Photographer
Peter Hebeisen

Earphones
Earphones promotes the re-opening of the newly refurbished Hugh Lane Gallery and celebrates the return of 8 Impressionist paintings which haven't been displayed together in Ireland for nearly 100 years.

MS
"Multiple Sclerosis affects the nerve tracts". The symptoms of MS are extremely varied, although they have a common cause, the interruption of the nerve tracts through inflammation. These were dramatized in places where actual interruptions occur: in between posters, at doors and so on.

Mercè Artero
This Year No way.

Do you suffer
Do you suffer more when you run or when you don't?

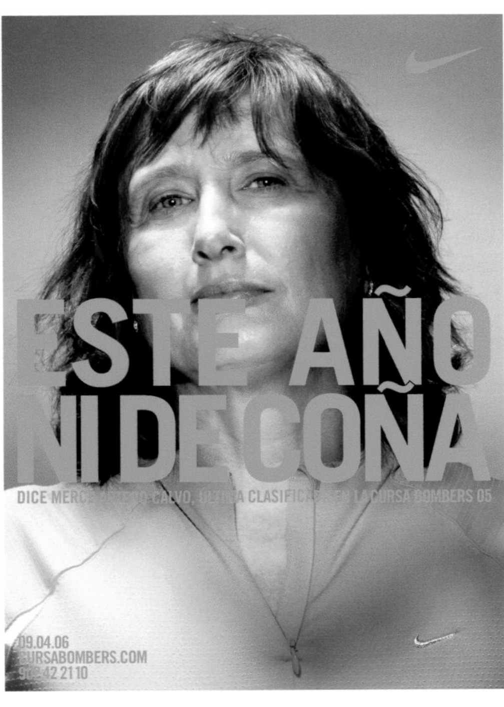

Mercè Artero
Spain

National Award
Silver
Agency
Villarrosàs
Client
American Nike
Creative Director
Oriol Villar,
Fernando Codina
Photographer
Ricardo Miras

Do you suffer
Spain

National Award
Silver
Agency
Villarrosàs
Client
American Nike
Creative Director
Oriol Villar,
Fernando Codina
Art Director
Marius Zorrilla,
Javier Gracia
Copywriter
Miguel Angel Elizalde
Photographer
Carlos Spottorno

Siamese Twins
Russia

National Award
Gold
Agency
Instinct
Client
Art Directors Club Russia
Creative Director
Yaroslav Orlov,
Roman Firainer
Art Director
Daniil Ostrovskyi
Copywriter
Igor Ivanov
Designer
Andrey Ivandikov

Madrunning
Spain

National Award
Silver
Agency
Villarrosàs
Client
American Nike
Creative Director
Oriol Villar
Art Director
Marius Zorrilla,
Javier Gracia
Photographer
Joan Garrigosa
Graphics
Ricardo Rousselot,
Vasava, Scott, Inocuo

Siamese Twins
ADCR Awards is exclusively an inter-professional contest, as the festival jury consists of professionals working in advertising. In general, we compete among ourselves.

Madrunning
MadRunning exhibit. 30 years of running in Madrid.

Mirror dance
"Michael Conrad dancing lessons". This poster was used to promote a creative academy hosted by Michael Conrad, named -Dancig with ideas- and held at the last Golden Drum Festival.

Vasco Rules!
"Take a photo with Vasco and go to the Oceanarium". Someone takes a photo of a child standing in front of the poster right next to Vasco. Then, the photo is shown at the Oceanarium ticket office and a free pass is given to the child.

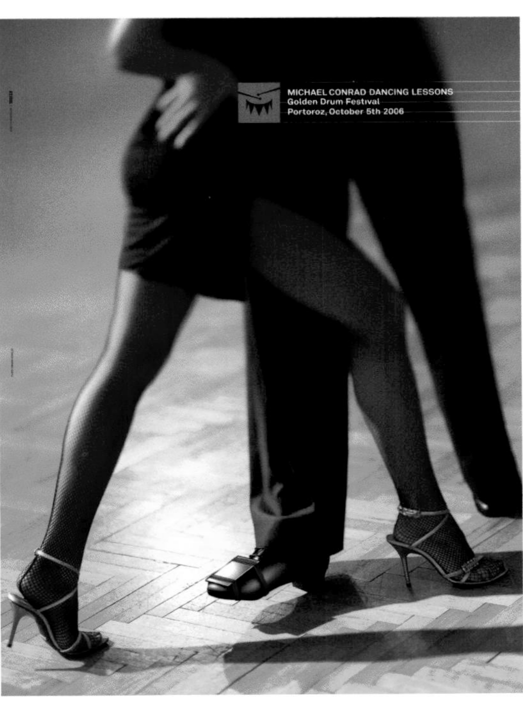

Mirror dance
Slovenia

National Award
Gold
Agency
Studio 360 d.o.o.
Client
Golden Drum Festival, Michael Conrad
Creative Director
Vladan Srdic
Art Director
Vladan Srdic
Copywriter
Vladan Srdic
Designer
Vladan Srdic
Photographer
Dragan Arrigler

Vasco Rules!
Portugal

National Award
Gold
Agency
Lowe & Partners Portugal
Client
Oceanario de Lisboa
Creative Director
Susana Albuquerque, Joao Coutinho
Art Director
Jose Gomes
Copywriter
Cesar Silva
Agency Producer
Ana Rondao

Advertising Print. Newspaper Advertising

Austria

Estonia

Italy

Ireland: 1 Nomination

Germany: 4 Nominations

Poland: Gold

Switzerland: 3 Nominations

Gold
Keso Door Locks
Poland

National Award
Silver
Agency
Saatchi & Saatchi Poland
Client
Freiberger
Creative Director
Max Olech
Art Director
Aneta Szeweluk
Copywriter
Piotr Skarbek
Agency Producer
Saatchi & Saatchi Poland
Photographer
Mejor Samrai/firstbase
Imaging London
Programmer
Mejor Samrai/firstbase
Imaging London

"Keso door locks". Swiss quality Keso door locks make your door as secure as a wall.

Nomination
Animals
Germany

National Award
Bronze
Agency
DDB Germany, Berlin
Client
Volkswagen AG
Creative Director
Amir Kassaei, Mathias Stiller, Wolfgang Schneider
Art Director
Kristoffer Heilemann
Copywriter
Ludwig Berndl
Designer
3D Design (Dummy-Bau)
Agency Producer
Elke Dilchert, Sandra Markus (Art Buying)
Photographer
Jan Steinhilber
Other
Planning: Jason Lusty, Wiebke Dreyer

Animals
Three extremely powerful animals: gorilla, bear and walrus; eat and drink from tiny toy plates and cups. They symbolize the extraordinary qualities of Volkswagen's new TSI-engine: Maximum power. Minimal consumption.

Love Life
"No action without protection". Dangerous sports without protection. The message being: you would not do this without protecting yourself, so why would you have sex without condoms?

Nomination
Love Life
Switzerland

National Award
Bronze
Agency
Euro RSCG Group Switzerland
Client
BAG / Stop Aids
Creative Director
Petra Bottignole
Art Director
Patrick Beeli
Copywriter
Serge Deville
Designer
Daniel Buergisser
Agency Producer
Novavista
Photographer
Finlay Mackay
Other
Account Director:
Marc van der Heijden

Nomination
Camera for Kids
Germany

National Award
Bronze
Agency
Jung von Matt AG
Client
Mattel Austria GmbH
Creative Director
M. Stiller, W. Schneider, D. Mously, J. Harbeck
Art Director
Martin Gruenhoff
Copywriter
Jan Hendrik Ott
Agency Producer
Andreas Reinhardt
Photographer
Michael Tewes
Other
Production:
Twentyfour-7

Nomination
Joy of writing
Germany

National Award
Shortlist
Agency
Jung von Matt AG
Client
BIC Deutschland GmbH & Co. OHG
Creative Director
M. Stiller, W. Schneider, J. Harbeck, D. Mously
Art Director
Michael Janke
Copywriter
Michael Haeussler
Designer
Leila El-Kayem, Kristina Pinkert
Agency Producer
Andreas Reinhardt
Photographer
Dan Zoubek
Other
Art Buying:
Huelya Corty,
Post Production:
PX1

Camera for Kids
The children's cameras from Fisher Price are to be positioned as creative toys.

Joy of writing
An ad campaign that communicates the "joy of writing" in an unusual and novel way. Especially with the right pen, the BIC Cristal, which makes writing a true joy, as using it is so much fun, even the most hurried note is jotted down with great passion.

Nomination
Terminator
Ireland

National Award
Silver
Agency
Leo Burnett, Dublin, Ireland
Client
Channel 6
Creative Director
John Flynn
Art Director
Fergal Hurley
Copywriter
Eoin Ryan
Photographer
Donal Moloney

IRTHS, MARRIAGES, DEATHS

33

DEATHS

CONNOR (Sarah, M) - 21st April, 2006 (accidental), shot herself five times during a hunting trip, darling mother of John. Service this morning, at 11 o'c. Internment at Cemetery at 2.20 o'c approx.

CONNOR (Mrs. S) - 21st April, 2006 (unexpectedly), ran into a concrete wall repeatedly while out jogging. May she rest in peace. Removal from Jim Jackson's Funeral Home, Pollontown this evening at 5.30 o'c. Private cremation.

CONNOR (Sarah) - 21st April, 2006 (accidental), tripped and fell through twenty plate glass windows, will be deeply missed by family, friends and those fighting the war against the machines. Her spirit of determination will always be celebrated. Removal at 2.00 o'c. Service tomorrow at 3 o'c. Family flowers only please. May she rest in peace.

CONNOR (Sarah, T) - 21st April, 2006 (unexpectedly), died at home when a table spontaneously leapt across the room and landed on top of her. Her good humour will be sadly missed. Removal this evening at 6.45. Reception at 7.30. Donations if any to Charity.

CONNOR (S. Murray) - 21st April, 2006 (unexpectedly), while buttering bread, accidentally stabbed herself in the back, rest in peace always. Reposing at Geherty's Funeral home, Perton Street. Removal this evening at 7.15 o'c. Service tomorrow at 12.30. Donations Charity c/o the family.

DEATHS

CONNOR (Sarah, O) - 21st April, 2006 (accidental), fell into a vat of molten liquid while out for a stroll through iron works, sadly missed by family and friends. Removal this evening to Letrahenna, arriving at 5 o'c. Service tomorrow after 10 o'c. 12 o'c to Crematorium.

CONNOR (Sarah, J) - 21st April, 2006 (accidental), fell up five flights of stairs and out through a concrete wall, deeply regretted by family and friends. May she rest in peace. Removal this evening, arriving at 4.30 o'c. Family flowers only please, donations if desired to Charity.

CONNOR (Ms. S) - 21st April, 2006 (unexpectedly), accidentally nailed herself to a wall while carrying out DIY, deeply mourned by brothers and sisters. Service today at 12 noon. Burial afterwards at Parklin Cemetery.

CONNOR (Ms. S, Hanson) - 21st April, 2006 (suddenly), collided with a helicopter while driving through a tunnel, dearly missed by Reese and members of the future resistance. Remembered for being a hard worker, dedicated mother of one and excellent field medic. Service at 12 noon today. Family flowers only please.

CONNOR (Sarah, G) - 21st April, 2006 (unexpectedly), decapitated herself with hedge clippers in unfortunate hedge trimming accident, deeply regretted by her loving sisters and brothers. Rest in peace. Removal tomorrow morning from house. Arrival at 11.15 o'c. Servic

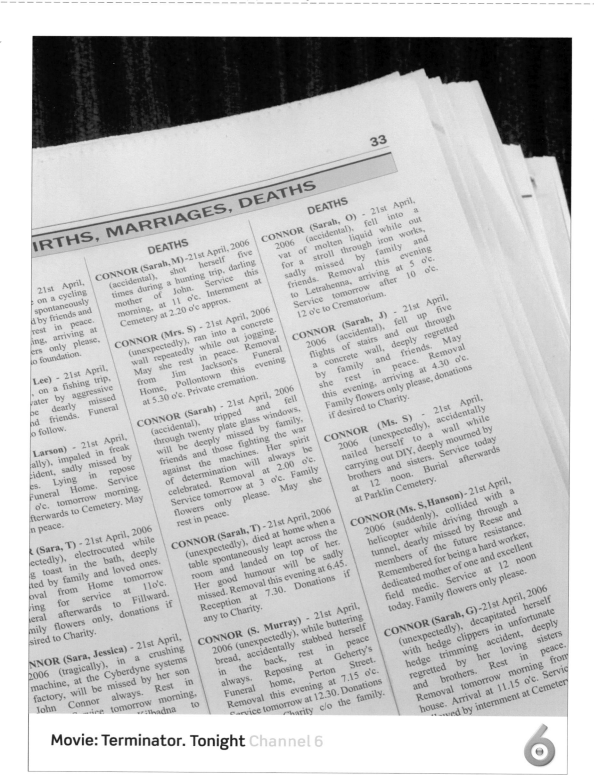

Movie: Terminator. Tonight Channel 6

6

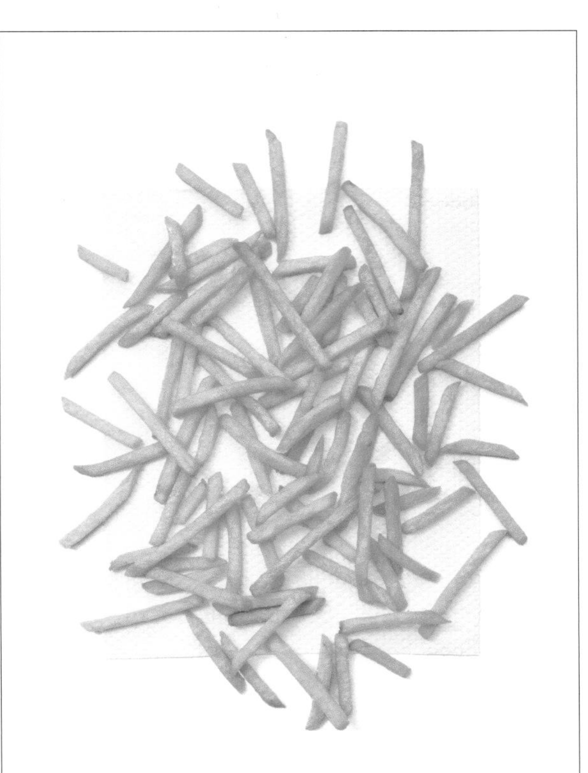

Nomination
French Fries
Switzerland

National Award
Silver
Agency
Spillmann/Felser/
Leo Burnett
Client
Kimberly-Clark
Creative Director
Martin Spillmann
Art Director
Cornelia Wenk
Copywriter
Stefan Ehrler
Agency Producer
Sebahat Derdiyok
Photographer
Walter+Spehr
Other
Account Director:
Pam Hügli

Terminator
"Terminator, tonight on 6". The obituaries page of a newspaper is full of deceased woman called Sarah Connor.

French Fries
The extra thick Tela Cucina kitchen roll is ultra absorbent.

Nomination
Builders of Tomorrow
Germany

National Award
Bronze
Agency
Jung von Matt AG
Client
Lego GmbH
Creative Director
Arno Lindemann,
Bernhard Lukas
Art Director
Szymon Rose
Copywriter
Daniel Schaefer
Photographer
Achim Lippoth
Other
Art Buying:
Martina Traut

Builders of Tomorrow
Lunchtime Atop a Skyscraper by Charles C. Ebbets is one of the most reprinted pictures in the world. Here the famous photograph of New York construction workers is re-created, replacing them with children as part of a LEGO structure.

Nomination
No Boundaries
Switzerland

National Award
Shortlist
Agency
Lowe
Client
BSW/Street Safety
Creative Director
Keith Loell
Art Director
Fernando Perez
Copywriter
Iris Alder
Designer
Keystone

Grime
Poland

National Award
Silver
Agency
Euro RSCG Warsaw
Client
Reckitt Benckiser
Creative Director
Jacek Szulecki
Art Director
Sylwia Rekawek
Copywriter
Justyna Nakielska
Photographer
Szymon Swietochowski

Broken teeth
Switzerland

National Award
Silver
Agency
Ruf Lanz Zurich
Client
Suva Accident prevention
Creative Director
Markus Ruf,
Danielle Lanz
Art Director
Katja Puccio
Copywriter
Markus Ruf
Photographer
Stefan Minder,
Felix Schregenberger

Grime
Dirt Surrenders.

Broken teeth
Wintersport accidents can have bad consequences.

Sopranos
"The early Days of The Sopranos"
A child's toy gun is used to emphasise the early days of the crime drama.

Eastgate Park
Eastgate Park. Where your business with the East will soon fly high. Eastgate Park. Where tireless workers do business with the East. Eastgate Park. Where the most industrious companies are finding new nourishment for their business with the East.

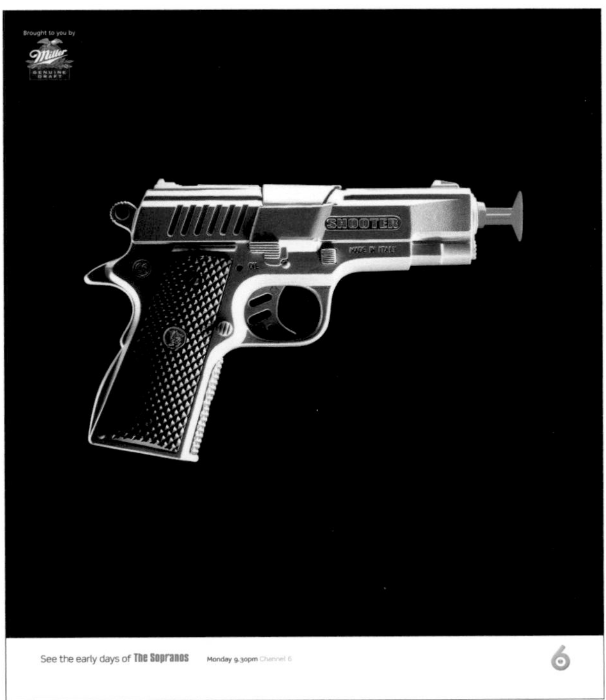

Sopranos
Ireland

National Award
Silver
Agency
Leo Burnett, Dublin, Ireland
Client
Channel 6
Creative Director
John Flynn
Art Director
Stephen Rodgers
Copywriter
Dara Daly

Eastgate Park
Italy

National Award
Gold
Agency
D 'Adda Lorenzini Vigorelli BBDO
Client
Pirelli RE
Creative Director
Luca Scotto di Carlo, Giuseppe Mastromatteo
Art Director
Serena Di Bruno
Copywriter
Giovanni Chiarelli
Photographer
LSD

Mother's Day Campaign
Switzerland

National Award
Gold
Agency
walker
Client
Fleurop Interflora
Creative Director
Pius Walker
Copywriter
Roger Beckett
Designer
Mieke Haase
Photographer
Uwe Duettmann
Graphics
Jan-Christoph Prilop, Ibrahim Zbat
Other
Art Buying:
David Haisch, Melanie Auerbach

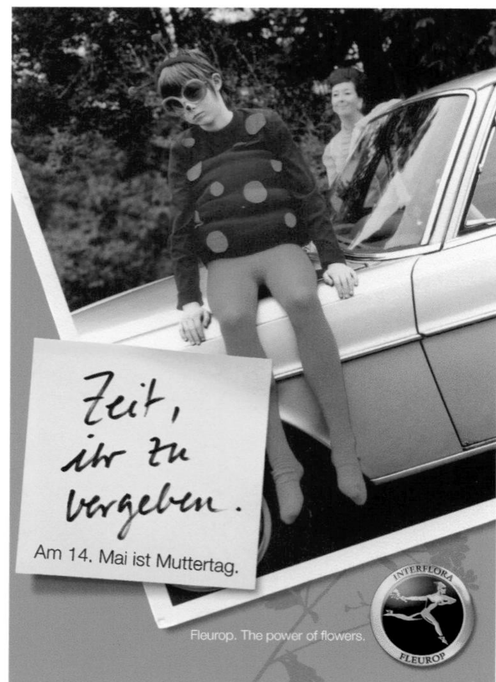

Mother's Day Campaign
Fleurop-Interflora's Mother's Day Campaign for once doesn't thank mothers. It far more recalls all the little sins with which they made us suffer, reminding us that mother's day is a good occasion to forgive her.

World Championship Flag
"You see the World Champion 2006". An ad for the online newspaper shown on the day of the WM finale at a point in time when it was still totally uncertain whether France or Italy would become World Champions. Thanks to the magenta CI, this ambiguous yet precise prediction was possible.

Ronaldinho
An ad for the online newspaper derStandard.at, published 2006 at the time of the World Football Championship.

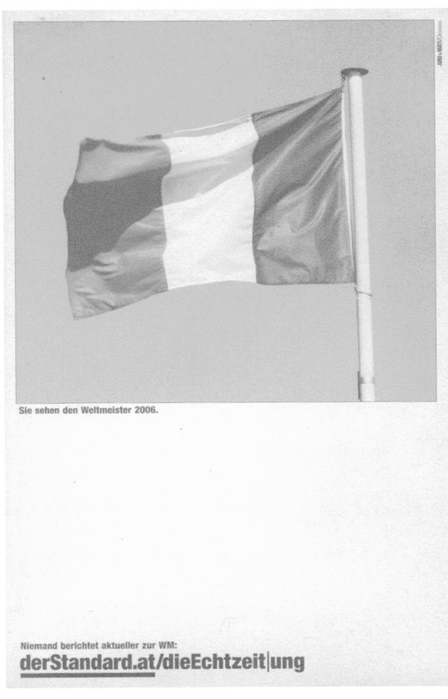

Sie sehen den Weltmeister 2006.
Niemand berichtet aktueller zur WM:
derStandard.at/dieEchtzeit|ung

World Championship Flag
Austria

National Award
Silver
Agency
Jung von Matt/Donau Werbeagentur GmbH
Client
Bronner Online AG
Creative Director
Andreas Putz, Volkmar Weiss
Art Director
Volkmar Weiss
Copywriter
Michael Haeussler
Graphics
Eva Jordan

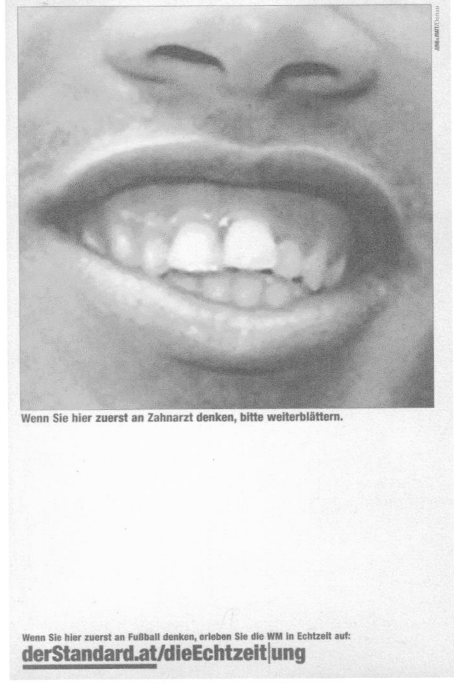

Wenn Sie hier zuerst an Zahnarzt denken, bitte weiterblättern.
Wenn Sie hier zuerst an Fußball denken, erleben Sie die WM in Echtzeit auf:
derStandard.at/dieEchtzeit|ung

Ronaldinho
Austria

National Award
Silver
Agency
Jung von Matt/Donau Werbeagentur GmbH
Client
Bronner Online AG
Creative Director
Andreas Putz, Volkmar Weiss
Art Director
Volkmar Weissl
Copywriter
Michael Haeussler
Graphics
Eva Jordan

Meinl Coffee Decaf
Austria

National Award
Gold
Agency
Demner, Merlicek & Bergmann
Client
Julius Meinl Austria GmbH
Creative Director
Francesco Bestagno
Art Director
Francesco Bestagno
Copywriter
Claus Gigler
Agency Producer
Norbert Rabenseifner, Daniela Kalmar
Graphics
Daniela Schabernak
Other
Digital Imaging: Siegfried Duft

Unimaginable combination
Estonia

National Award
Silver
Agency
Kontuur LB
Client
Rakvere Meatfactory
Creative Director
Urmas Villmann
Art Director
Andres Abe
Copywriter
Andrus Niit
Designer
Tarmo Talvik
Photographer
Tarmo Talvik, Viktor Kozhkin

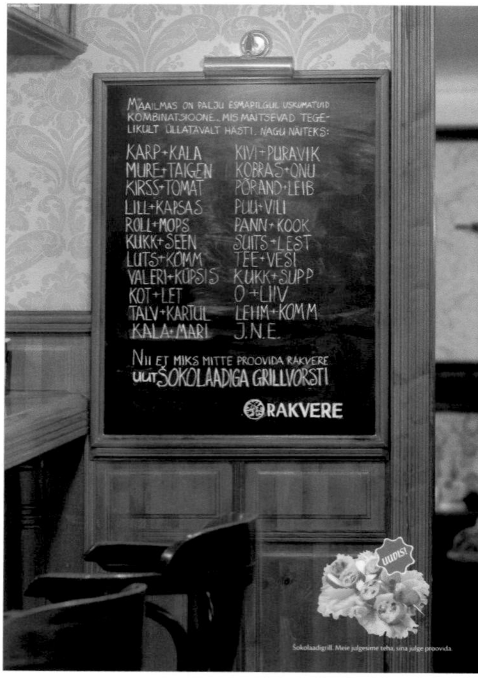

Meinl Coffee Decaf
An ad for the decaffeinated variation of Austria's famous Julius Meinl coffee where the Meinl logo, the North-African boy, was slightly altered to fit the new product.

Earphones
Earphones promotes the re-opening of the newly refurbished Hugh Lane Gallery and celebrates the return of 8 Impressionist paintings which haven't been displayed together in Ireland for nearly 100 years.

Sheeppower
If car power is measured in Horsepower, Lawnmowers' efficiency should be measured in Sheeppower.

Earphones
Ireland

National Award
Silver
Agency
Publicis QMP
Client
Hugh Lane Gallery
Creative Director
Ger Roe
Art Director
Ger Roe
Copywriter
Ted Barry
Photographer
Neil MacDougald

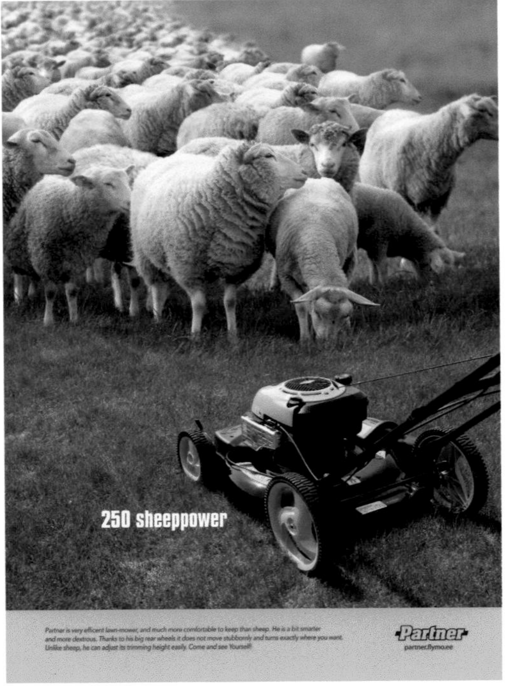

Sheeppower
Estonia

National Award
Gold
Agency
DDB Estonia
Client
Husqvarna Eesti Oü
Creative Director
Meelis Mikker
Art Director
Erik Teemägi
Copywriter
Peeter Sauter
Agency Producer
Reilika Mäekivi
Photographer
Toomas Tikenberg

Advertising Print. Magazine Advertising

Austria: 1 Nomination

Czech Republic

Bosnia & Herzegovina

Germany: 9 Nominations

Ireland

Italy

Poland: 1 Nomination

Portugal

Slovenia

Spain: Gold

Sweden

Switzerland: 1 Nomination

Gold
Emotions Campaign Tear-Nipple-Hair
Spain

National Award
Gold
Agency
DDB Barcelona
Client
V.A.E.S.A.
Creative Director
Alberto Astorga
Art Director
Jaume Badia
Copywriter
Alfredo Binefa
Graphics
David Ruiz

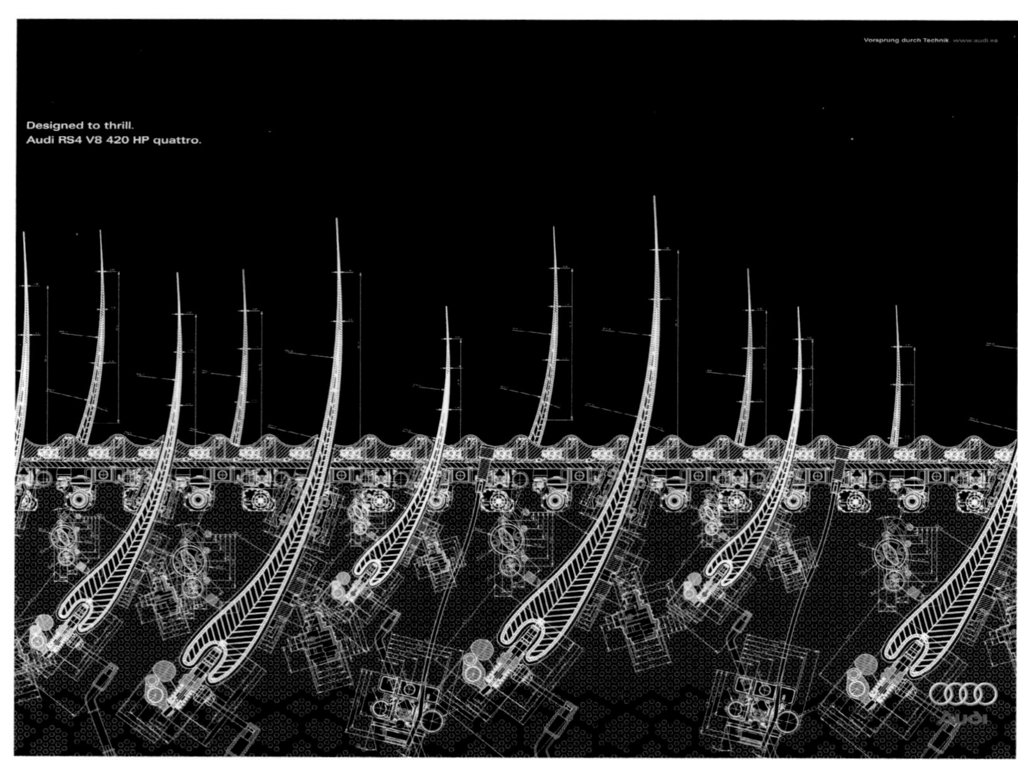

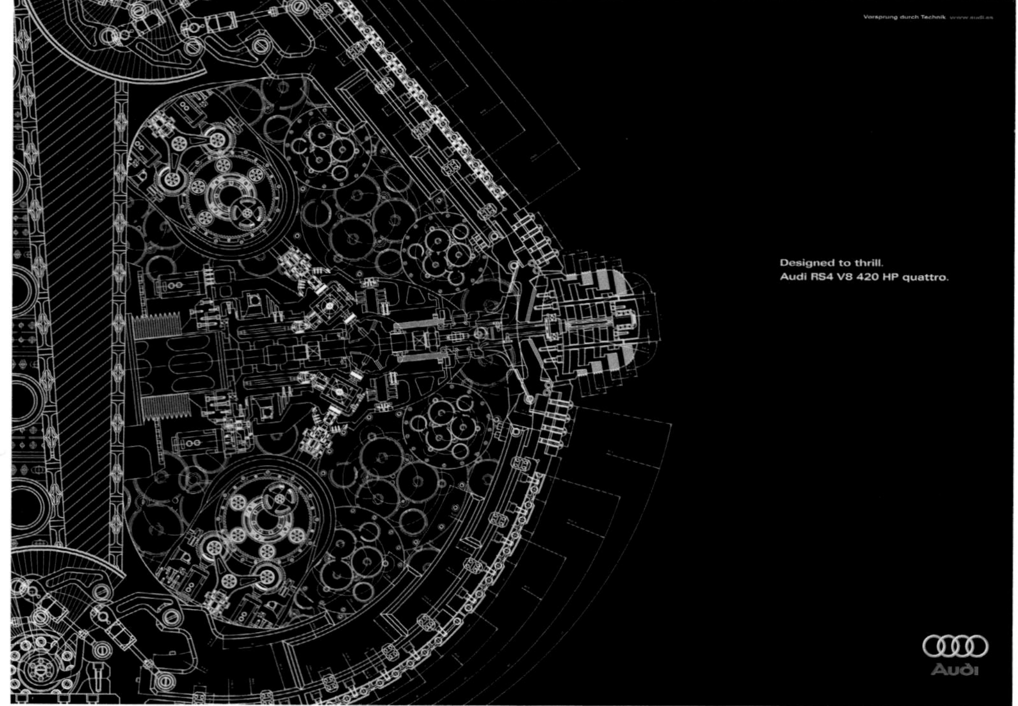

Designed to thrill. Human emotions expressed as if they were a technical drawing. Because this is the Audi RS4, a car designed for emotions.

Nomination
Rescue
Austria

National Award
Bronze
Agency
Draftfcb Kobza
Client
Unicef Austria
Creative Director
Patrik Partl
Art Director
Holger Friedrich
Copywriter
Eva Sommeregger,
Florian Schwab
Designer
Kerstin Schudo
Photographer
Corbis

Rescue
The objective was to draw attention to children in distress in poor regions of the world in a striking manner and show at the same time that even a small donation can have a big impact. A simple trick (whereby you pull out the card) demonstrates that.

Porsche
Two child seats. Up front.

Nomination
Porsche
Germany

National Award
Shorlist
Agency
UCA Geschke, Pufe GmbH
Client
Porsche Nord-West
Creative Director
Jan Geschke, Stefan Pufe
Art Director
Jonathan Blunk
Copywriter
Jan Geschke, Stefan Pufe
Photographer
Porsche/KEK

Two child seats.
Up front.

Porsche Zentrum
Hamburg Nord-West

Raffay Automobil-Handelsges.
Nord-West mbH & Co.
Nedderfeld 2 · 22529 Hamburg
Tel.: 040/55 77 68 0
Fax: 040/55 77 68 22
www.porsche-hamburgnordwest.de
servicenw@raffay.de

Nomination
The Post-it Campaign
Germany

National Award
Silver
Agency
Scholz & Friends
Client
Queisser Pharma GmbH & Co.KG
Creative Director
Suze Barrett, Matthias Schmidt, Stefan Setzkorn
Art Director
Marcin Baba
Copywriter
Dennis Lueck, Roman Jonsson
Photographer
Susanne Ludwig
Other
Postproduction:
Metagate GmbH, Hamburg

The Post-it Campaign
"If your memory needs help".
The task was to develop a striking and convincing campaign demonstrating that Doppelherz Lecithin pills strengthen the memory. The campaign shows people in normal everyday situations - except that absolutely everything is covered with post-its.

Giant Houses
"Find your way faster. Carminat 3 navigation system".
The ad focuses especially on the 3D-bird-view of the navigation system.

Nomination
Giant Houses
Germany

National Award
Shortlist
Agency
Publicis Frankfurt GmbH
Client
Renault Deutschland AG
Creative Director
Stephan Ganser, Joern Welle, Stefan Leick
Art Director
Lars Heberer
Copywriter
Stephen Quell
Agency Producer
Heide Hartwig
Other
Gerald Heinecke, Sebastian Mensing

Nomination
Idols
Germany

National Award
Shortlist
Agency
Springer & Jacoby Werbeagentur GmbH & Co. KG
Client
Medion AG
Creative Director
Dirk Haeusermann, Matthias Harbeck
Art Director
Myles Lord
Copywriter
Michael Benzinger
Agency Producer
Mini Kotzan
Graphics
Susanne Moebius

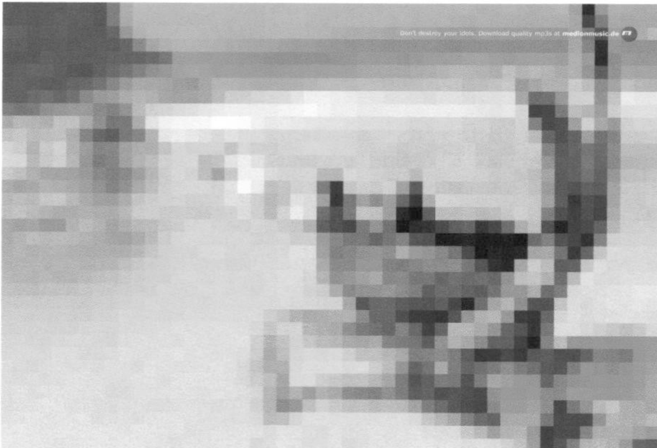

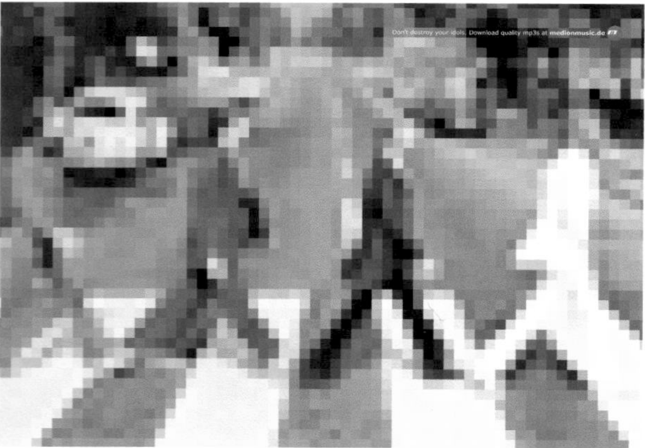

Idols
At medionmusic.de, Medion offers a download service, allowing users to buy their music online. In contrast to, often illegal, competitors, Medion guarantees a first-class product. The campaign's intention is to spotlight this advantage in an eye-catching and intense form.

Nomination
Comedy Central Launch Campaign
Germany

National Award
Bronze
Agency
kempertrautmann gmbh
Client
MTV Networks GmbH & Co. OHG
Creative Director
Frank Bannoehr, Daniel Ernsting
Art Director
Frank Bannoehr, Axel Schilling
Copywriter
Daniel Ernsting, Christian Soldatke
Photographer
Arthur Mebius
Graphics
Tim Belser, Marita Loecmele

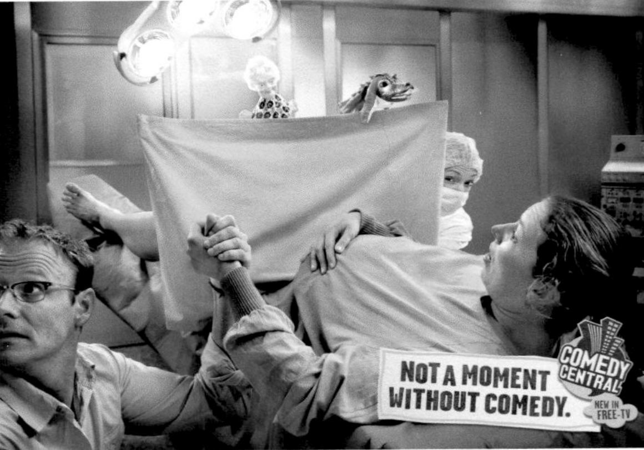

Comedy Central
Launch Campaign
MTV Comedy Central Launch Campaign. "Not a moment without comedy".

Nomination
Planning
Germany

National Award
Shortlist
Agency
Grabarz & Partner
Client
Gruner + Jahr AG & Co. KG
Creative Director
Patricia Paetzold,
Ralf Nolting,
CCO: Ralf Heuel
Art Director
Tomas Tulinius,
Djik Ouchiian,
Alexandra Marzoll
Copywriter
Martin Grass
Photographer
Sven Berghaeuser
c/o Kelly Kellerhoff

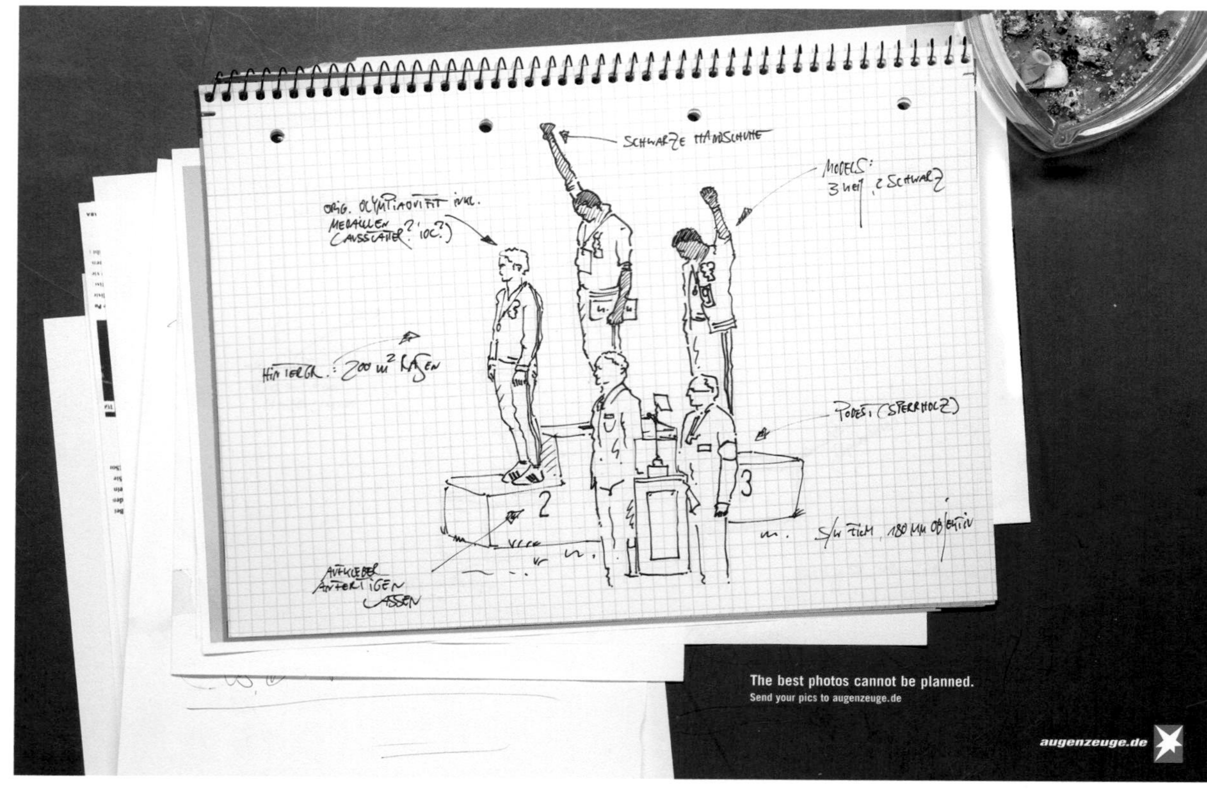

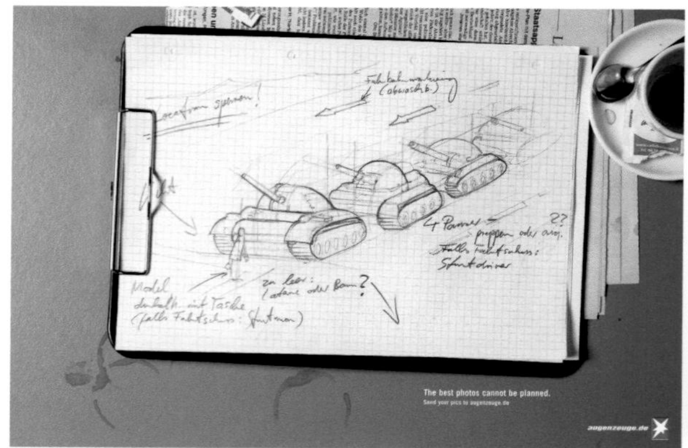

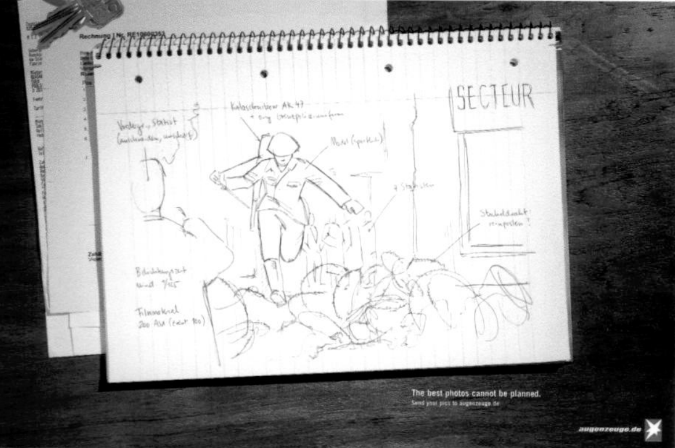

Planning
A world-changing photograph can't be planned because it doesn't depend on painstaking preparation and expensive equipment but more on pressing the shutter button at the right place at the right time. This is what our campaign for augenzeuge.de (eyewitness) dramatises. Augenzeuge is Stern magazine's photo agency for amateur photographers, which offers professional marketing for their pictures.

The Annual Ticket Campaign
The ads show what can happen if one visits the Zoo: the animals are hiding or sleeping in their burrows and just won't feel like posing in front of the visitors. So sometimes one has to be a little patient to experience all the animals in the zoo. With the annual ticket it is not a problem. One can come back and try again any time.

Nomination
The Annual Ticket Campaign
Germany

National Award
Shortlist
Agency
Scholz & Friends
Client
Zoologischer Garten Berlin AG
Creative Director
Matthias Spaetgens, Jan Leube, Martin Pross
Art Director
Mathias Rebmann
Copywriter
Florian Schwalme
Photographer
Matthias Koslik
Graphics
Heidrun Kleingries, Felix Pfannmueller
Other
Postproduction:
Futura Berlin GmbH

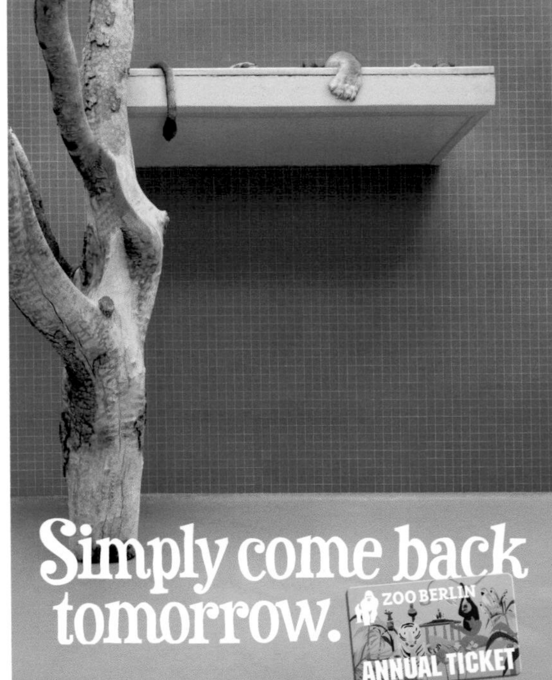

Nomination
Animals
Germany

National Award
Shortlist
Agency
DDB Germany, Berlin
Client
Volkswagen AG
Creative Director
Amir Kassaei, Mathias Stiller, Wolfgang Schneider
Art Director
Kristoffer Heilemann
Copywriter
Ludwig Berndl
Designer
3D Design (Dummy-Bau)
Agency Producer
Elke Dilchert, Sandra Markus (Art Buying)
Other
Planning: Jason Lusty, Wiebke Dreyer

Nomination
Head Jet
Switzerland

National Award
Bronze
Agency
Advico Young & Rubicam
Client
Head Snowboards
Creative Director
Urs Schrepfer
Art Director
Marietta Albinus
Copywriter
Martin Stulz
Agency Producer
Kathrin Gerber
Photographer
Markus Weber
Graphics
Diana Kaleicli

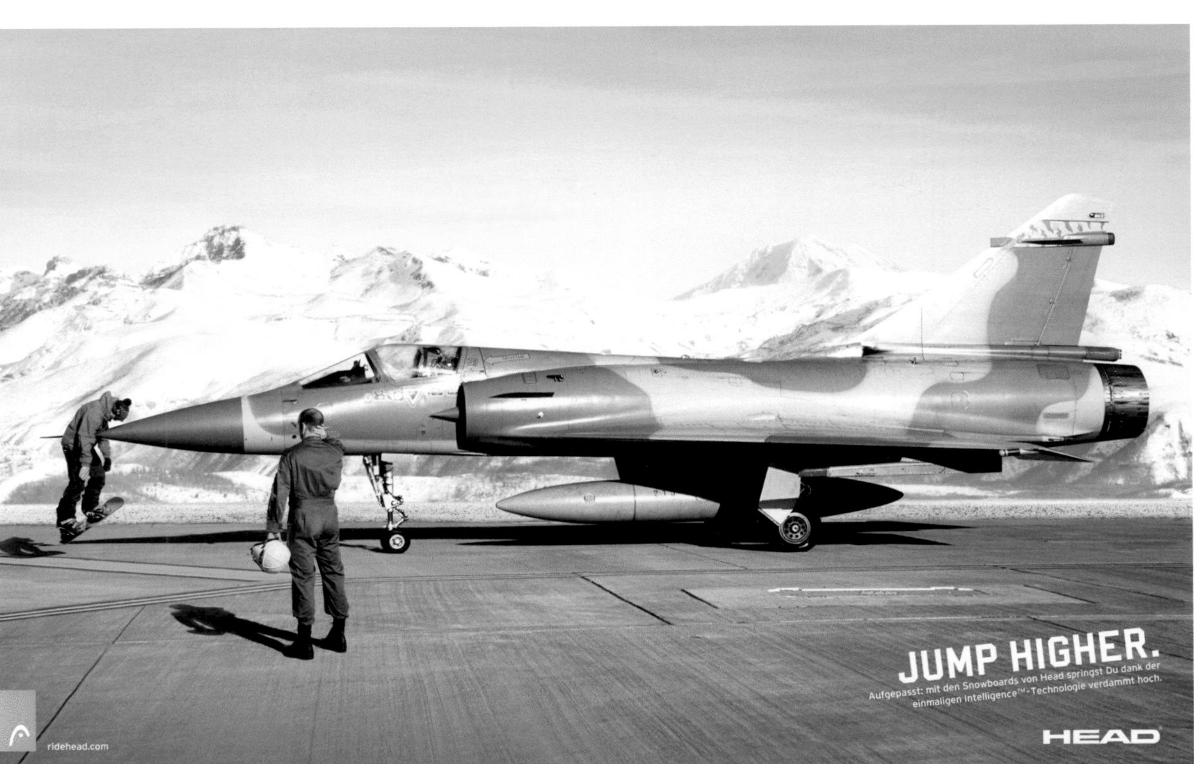

Animals
Three extremely powerful animals: gorilla, bear and walrus; eat and drink from tiny toy plates and cups. They symbolize the extraordinary qualities of Volkswagen's new TSI-engine: Maximum power. Minimal consumption.

Head Jet
"Jump higher". With the intelligence technology by Head Snowboards.

Nomination
Keso Door Locks
Poland

National Award
Silver
Agency
Saatchi & Saatchi Poland
Client
Freiberger
Creative Director
Max Olech
Art Director
Aneta Szeweluk
Copywriter
Piotr Skarbek
Agency Producer
Saatchi & Saatchi Poland
Photographer
Mejor Samrai/firstbase Imaging London

Keso Door Locks
Keso door locks. Swiss quality Keso door locks make your door as secure as a wall.

Lined Block of Paper
Three ads show notepads, the lines and holes of which were changed into prison bars, mouth tape and shots in the head respectively. The face of a mistreated journalist was depicted behind them. A brief copy informed the observer about his fate.

Nomination
Lined Block of Paper
Germany

National Award
Bronze
Agency
Grabarz & Partner
Client
Internationale Gesellschaft fur Menschenrechte
Creative Director
Ralf Heuel, Dirk Siebenhaar
Art Director
Sebastian Hahn
Copywriter
Heike Frank
Photographer
Imke Jansen
Graphics
Hannes von Doehren, Benjamin Busse

Decaffeinated Coffee
Austria

National Award
Silver
Agency
Draftfcb Kobza
Client
Naber Kaffee
Creative Director
Joachim Glawion
Art Director
Tolga Büyükdoganay
Copywriter
Jürgen Heel

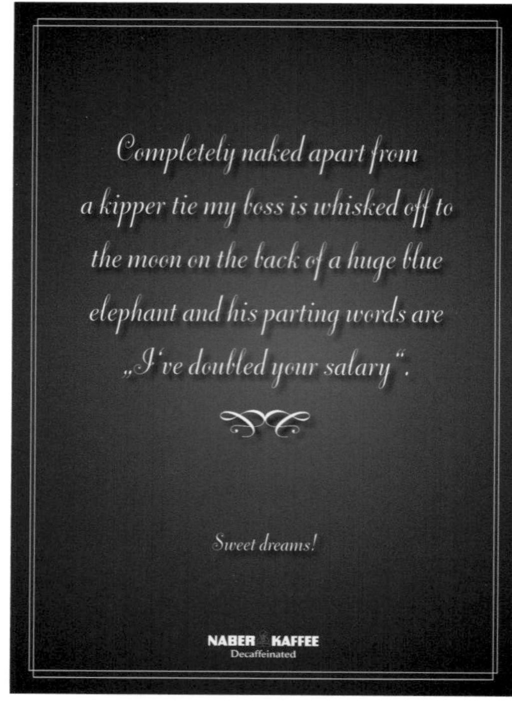

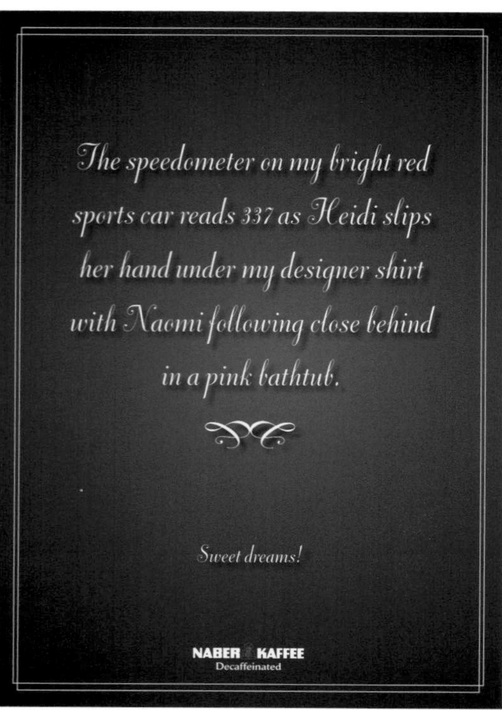

Fetish
Austria

National Award
Gold
Agency
Draftfcb Kobza
Client
Cosmos Elektrohandelsges. m.b.H & Co KG
Creative Director
Erich Falkner
Art Director
Andreas Gesierich
Designer
Daniel Senitschnig
Photographer
Wolfgang Zajc

Decaffeinated Coffee
Decaffeinated Coffee shows how well you sleep and dream after drinking decaffeinated Naber Coffee.

Fetish
"Electronic devices". The creative concept was to promote electronic devices by exaggerating their erotic attraction. This teaser print campaign was created to lure people to the website.

Ticketing - Stars, now cheaper/Madonna, Michael Jackson
In the middle of the star posters in a teenage magazine was an advertisement for the Ba-Ca Ticket Service under the logo "Cut-price stars". The posters showed cheap, star look-alikes.

Incredibly MINI
The new MINI is out! A worldwide campaign spreads the great. And tells the people that the new model of the legendary car is more driving fun than ever.

Ticketing - Stars, now cheaper/ Madonna, Michael Jackson
Austria

National Award
Silver
Agency
Jung von Matt/Donau Werbeagentur GmbH
Client
Bank Austria Creditanstalt
Creative Director
Andreas Putz, Gerd Schulte-Doeinghaus
Art Director
Eva Ortner, Christian Hummer-Koppendorfer
Copywriter
Helena Giokas
Agency Producer
Joerg Guenther, Lisa Ilchmann
Photographer
Joerg Reichardt
Graphics
Clemens Ascher
Other
Art Work: Albert Winkler/ Vienna Paint

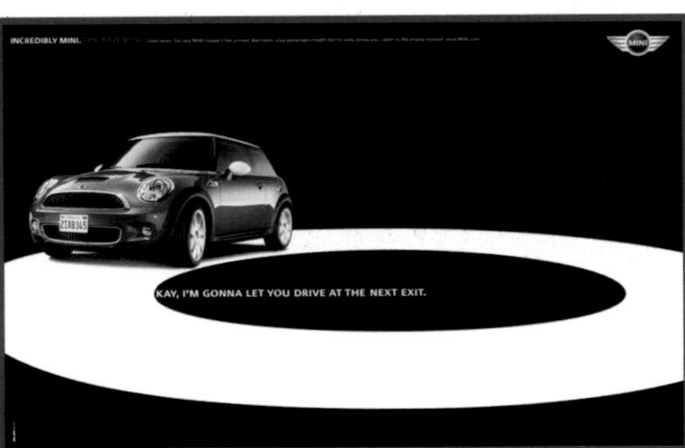

Incredibly MINI
Germany

National Award
Silver
Agency
Jung von Matt AG
Client
BMW AG
Creative Director
Oliver Voss, Goetz Ulmer
Art Director
Julia Ziegler
Copywriter
Baki Kieper, Dennis May, Fabian Frese
Photographer
Uwe Duettmann
Graphics
Javier Suarez Argueta, Simon Hiebl, Florian Zwinge
Other
Graphics: Michael Wilk

Lowe GGK
Austria

National Award
Silver
Agency
Lowe GGK
Client
Lowe GGK
Creative Director
Alexander Zelmanovics,
Dieter Pivrnec
Art Director
Hannes Böker
Copywriter
Werner Bühringer
Designer
Justin Nickerl
Photographer
Hannes Böker

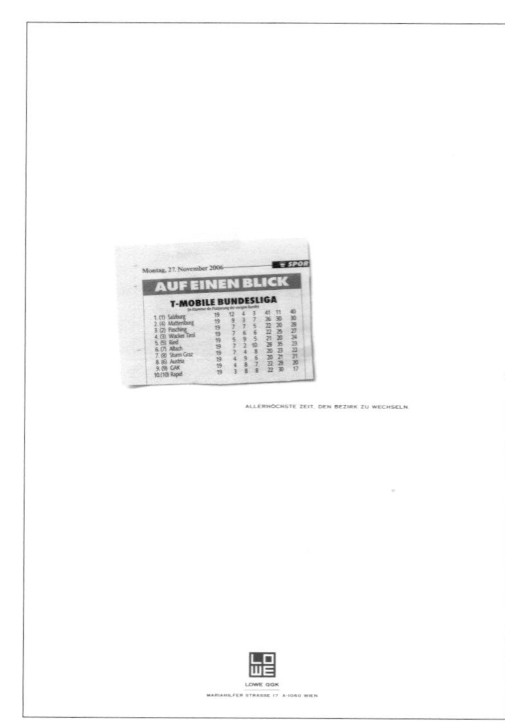

Premium seat meat
Austria

National Award
Silver
Agency
CCP, Heye Werbeagentur GmbH
Client
Bene AG
Creative Director
Michael Huber,
Gerhard Plakolm
Art Director
Thomas Riegler
Copywriter
Avin Fathulla
Photographer
Bernhard Angerer
Graphics
Lisbeth Schneider

Lowe GGK
"It's high time to change the district". On Monday November 27th 2006 the Rapid soccer team played so badly that the Lowe GGK changed district.

Premium seat meat
The trade advertisement for Bene's multimedia office chair was developed for an Austrian magazine with the title Fleisch ("Flesh").The idea was tailor-made for this magazine, so all product features were represented as beef specialities from a steer.

Bestseller
Savings book was inserted as an info booklet in magazines, glued over the ad, with a red paper ribbon placed around the savings book like bestseller books. Under the savings book is a text about this new product, in the form of a book review: "Loud and adorable magazine seller, well-known for creative and witty comments on the papers contents, yelling out the name of the product, text and punch lines on the main square. Hard to miss if walking by, witty comments catching your attention".

Lungs
The new technology of the Samsung vacuum cleaner prevents dust from being stirred up in the air.

Bestseller
Germany

National Award
Gold
Agency
Communis - ADC
Client
Raiffeisen Bank BiH
Creative Director
Anur Hadziomerspahic
Art Director
Ajna Zlatar
Copywriter
Anur Hadziomerspahic, Ajna Zlatar
Designer
Anur Hadziomerspahic, Ajna Zlatar
Agency Producer
Tarik Zahirovic
Graphics
Anur Hadziomerspahic, Ajna Zlatar
Other
Account manager: Arif Avdic, Nevena Sijercic

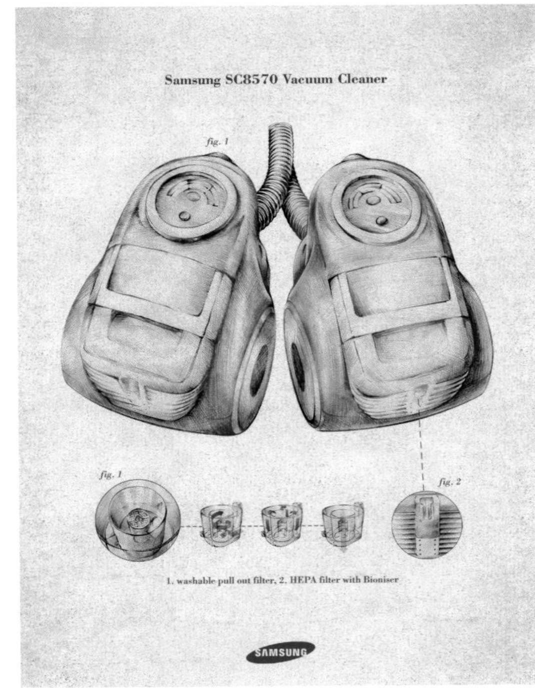

Lungs
Czech Republic

National Award
Silver
Agency
Leo Burnett Advertising
Client
Samsung Electronics
Creative Director
Jiri Langpaul
Art Director
Jakub Rendla
Copywriter
Vit Hradec, Daniel Prokes
Agency Producer
Simona Tomanova
Illustrator
Lubomir Czaban

Blocks
Switzerland

National Award
Silver
Agency
Publicis Werbeagentur AG
Client
Pastorini
Creative Director
Philipp Skrabal
Art Director
Simon Staub
Copywriter
Livio Dainese
Photographer
Felix Streuli
Graphics
Moritz Stillhard
Other
Account Executive:
Claudia Camenisch

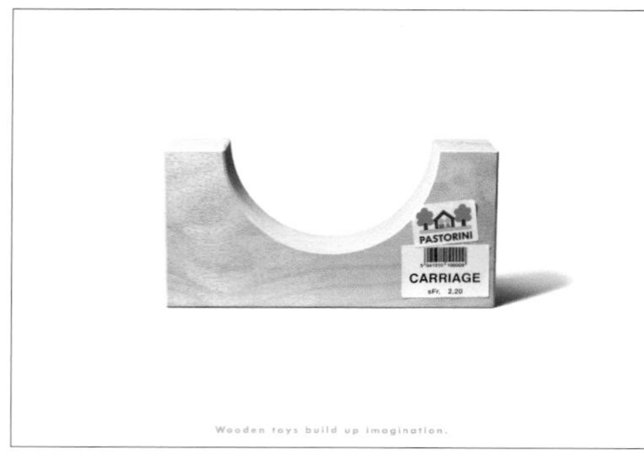

WWF Donations Campaign
Austria

National Award
Silver
Agency
Jung von Matt/Donau Werbeagentur GmbH
Client
WWF Austria
Creative Director
Andreas Putz, Gerd Schulte-Doeinghaus
Art Director
Eva Ortner
Copywriter
Helena Giokas
Photographer
Graham Westmoreland/ www.enste-jaspers.de, Pim Vuik
Graphics
Eva Ortner
Other
Illustrator: Hannes Kosina, Friendly Fire Comm.

Blocks
Wooden toys fully come to life in the imagination of children and do not dictate how they should be used. To dramatize this quality, simple wooden blocks that Pastorini sells are labelled with a price tag and a possible use.

WWF Donations Campaign
Save the world with a few coins. Become a partner of the WWF. Donate at www.wwf

Eastgate Park
Eastgate Park. Where your business with the East will soon fly high. Eastgate Park. Where tireless workers do business with the East. Eastgate Park. Where the most industrious companies are finding new nourishment for their business with the East.

White PSP
Last year Sony launched the new PlayStation Portable. The launch-color was black. After almost one year of being a hot seller, PSP expanded its target audience. They introduced the white PSP. The campaign was simple: White is the new black. And big emotions now come in white as well. PlayStation Portable now available in white.

Eastgate Park
Italy

National Award
Gold
Agency
D 'Adda Lorenzini Vigorelli BBDO
Client
Pirelli RE
Creative Director
Luca Scotto di Carlo, Giuseppe Mastromatteo
Art Director
Serena Di Bruno
Copywriter
Giovanni Chiarelli
Photographer
LSD

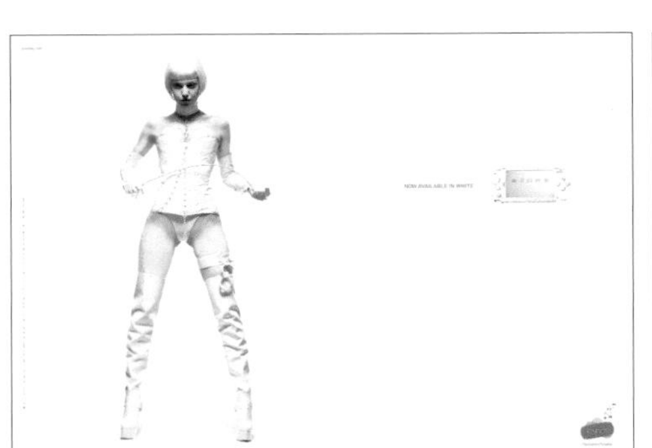

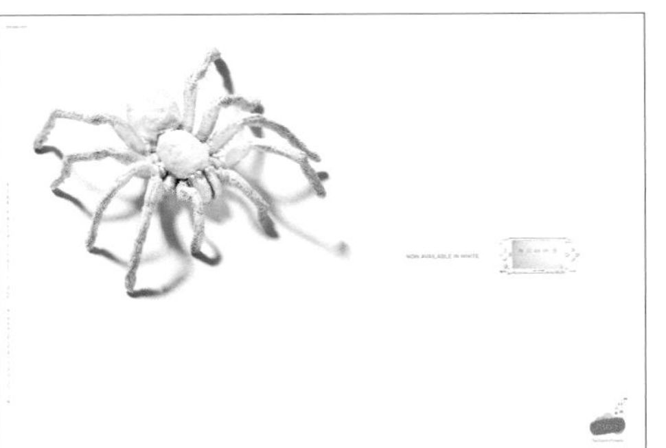

White PSP
Germany

National Award
Silver
Agency
TBWA Germany, Berlin
Client
Sony Computer Entertainment Deutschland GmbH
Creative Director
Philip Borchardt, Dirk Henkelmann
Designer
Arnaud Loix van Hooff
Agency Producer
Katrin Dettmann
Photographer
Alexander Gnaedinger
Graphics
Verena Panholzer, Jutta Kuss

Colestrol, lego; colestrol, peluche
Portugal

National Award
Silver
Agency
McCann Erickson
Client
Ministerio da Saude
Creative Director
Diogo Anahory,
José Bomtempo
Art Director
Diogo Mello
Copywriter
Fabio Seidl
Photographer
Léo Vilela

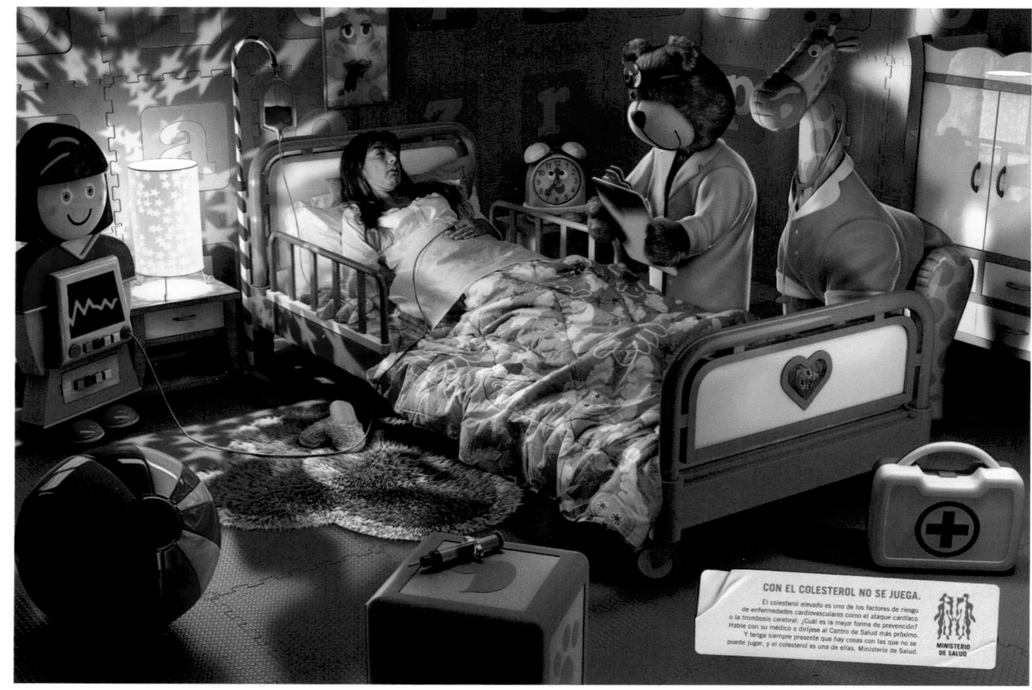

Animals
Italy

National Award
Silver
Agency
Lowe Pirella
Client
Arena Italia
Creative Director
Francesco Bozza,
Umberto Casagrande
Art Director
Ferdinando Galletti
Copywriter
Paolo Platania
Photographer
Moreno Monti
Other
Post Production:
Matteo Tranchellini

ABBIAMO SOLUZIONI COSÌ MIRATE DA FARLI SENTIRE UNA SPECIE PROTETTA.
Pfizer Animal Health

Endangered Species
Italy

National Award
Silver
Agency
D'Adda Lorenzini Vigorelli BBDO
Client
Pfizer
Creative Director
Luca Scotto di Carlo
Art Director
Sara Portello
Copywriter
Alessandro Fruscella
Photographer
LSD

Animals
Dragonflies/ Barracuda

Endangered Species
We have solutions, so targeted they will feel like an endangered species.

Planets
With this ad the jeep is to be represented as the ultimative Offroad vehicle.

Planets
Germany

National Award
Silver
Agency
KNSK Werbeagentur GmbH
Client
DaimlerChrysler AG
Creative Director
Tim Krink, Niels Holle
Art Director
Oliver Fermer
Copywriter
Berend Bruedgam, Steffen Steffens
Agency Producer
Heinz-Rudi Junge
Graphics
Thomas Thiele, Boris Schatte, Steffen Koenig

Panda, Mummy, Indian
Poland

National Award
Silver
Agency
DDB Warszawa
Client
Nobody's Children Foundation
Creative Director
Marcin Mroszczak, Jacek Pawlak, Dariusz Szubiak
Art Director
Maciej Waligora, Filip Berendt
Copywriter
Maciej Waligora, Filip Berendt
Agency Producer
DDB Warszawa
Photographer
Adam Wlazly

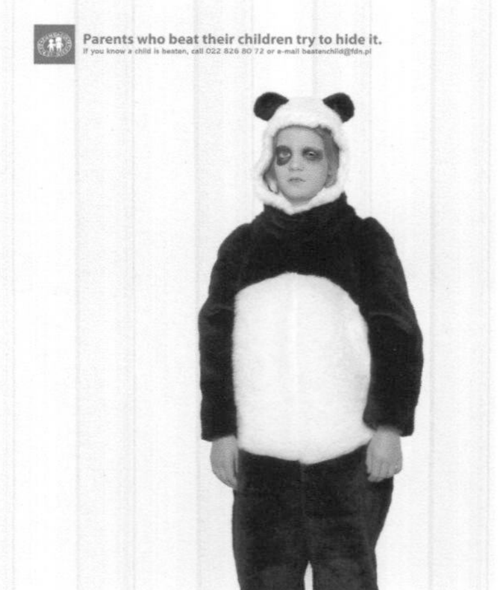

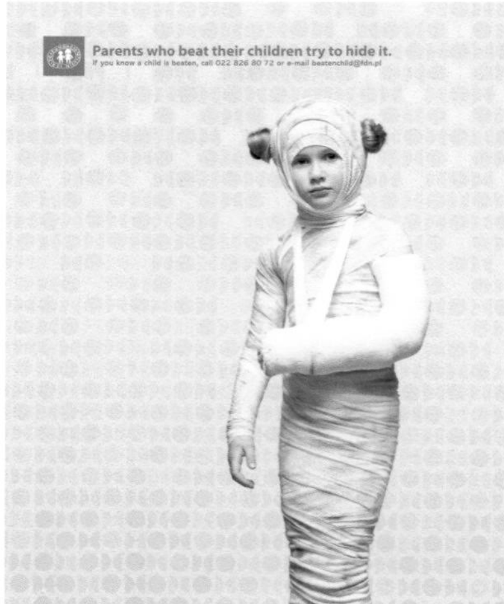

Mini Cinema
Italy

National Award
Silver
Agency
D'Adda Lorenzini Vigorelli BBDO
Client
Mini
Creative Director
Luca Scotto di Carlo, Giuseppe Mastromatteo
Art Director
Anselmo Tumpic
Copywriter
Marco Venturelli
Photographer
Piero Perfetto

Campanya Maria USB
Spain

National Award
Silver
Agency
Porcuatro
Client
Abr.
Art Director
Marcel Juan
Copywriter
Luis Eslava
Designer
Marcel Juan
Photographer
Artur Muñoz
Graphics
Gratapeus

Panda, Mummy, Indian
Parents who beat their children try to hide it.

Mini Cinema
Mini. Sponsor of "Cinema. Rome International Festival"

Campanya Maria USB
"Advertising campaign for Maria USB". Advertising campaign to promote the Virgin shape Pen drive Maria USB of Abr. creating a mental image of the digital memory that people wish to store in the USB

Strays
When it is so hard to find the right way home just dial 9191.

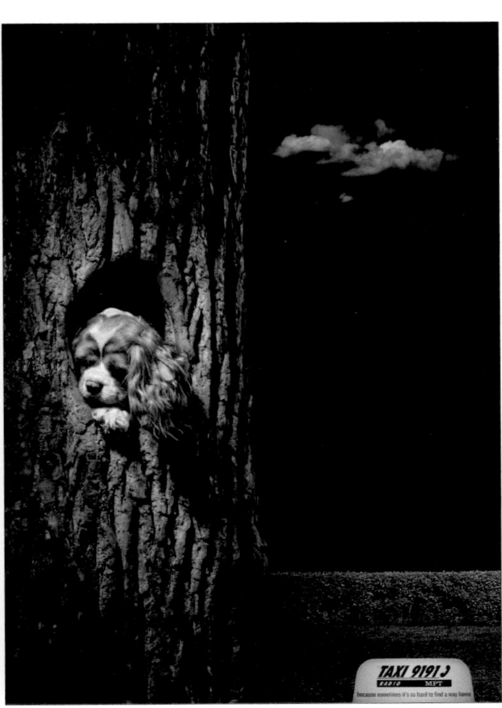

Strays
Poland

National Award
Gold
Agency
McCann Erickson
Client
MPT Warsaw taxi service
Creative Director
Iwona Kluszczynska, Wojciech Dagiel
Art Director
Lukasz Kotlinski, Iza Przepiorska-kotlinska
Copywriter
Iza Przepiorska-kotlinska, lukasz Kotlinski
Agency Producer
McCann Erickson: Monika Dagiel, Karolina Czplarska
Photographer
Lukasz Murgrabia
Other
Iza Zambrzuska (Tomograf), Marek Lesniak

Sopranos
Ireland

National Award
Silver
Agency
Leo Burnett,
Dublin, Ireland
Client
Channel 6
Creative Director
John Flynn
Art Director
Stephen Rodgers
Copywriter
Dara Daly

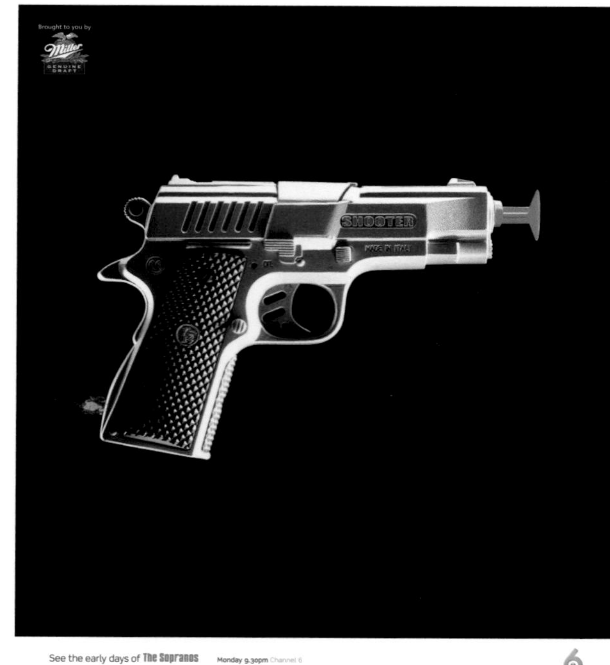

See the early days of The Sopranos Monday 9.30pm Channel 6

Now Together
Portugal

National Award
Gold
Agency
Touch Me Wunderman
Client
Touch Me Wunderman
Creative Director
Miguel Pate,
Nuno Duarte
Art Director
Rui Saraiva
Copywriter
Andre Freitas
Other
Luis Segadaes

Now Together
Given that it was a merger we are talking about, we decided to merge two press ads into one.

Sopranos
A toy gun that shoots sucker darts is used to convey the beginnings of a life of crime. See the early days of The Sopranos.

Sushimama
Sushimama is a fine Japanese sushi-restaurant.

Mirror Dance
"Michael Conrad Dancing Lessons". This poster was used to promote a creative academy hosted by Michael Conrad, named –Dancing with ideas– and held during the last Golden Drum Festival.

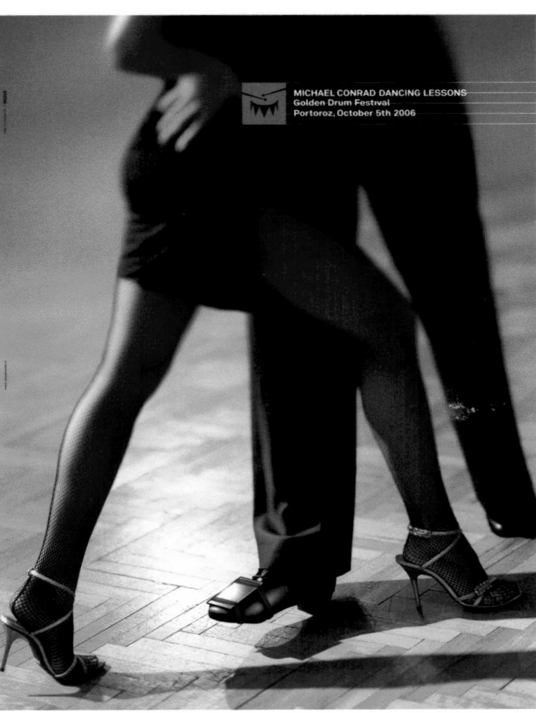

Mirror dance
Slovenia

National Award
Gold
Agency
Studio 360 d.o.o.
Client
Golden Drum Festival, Michael Conrad
Creative Director
Vladan Srdic
Art Director
Vladan Srdic
Copywriter
Vladan Srdic
Designer
Vladan Srdic
Photographer
Dragan Arrigler

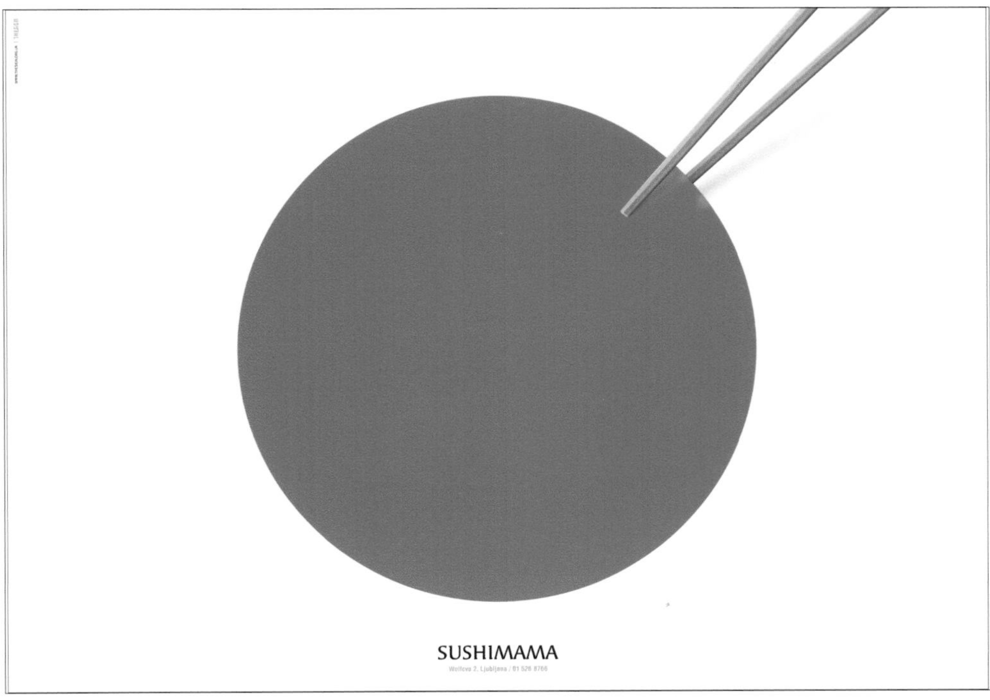

Sushimama
Slovenia

National Award
Gold
Agency
Studio 360 d.o.o.
Client
Sushimama Sushi restaurant
Creative Director
Vladan Srdic
Art Director
Vladan Srdic
Designer
Vladan Srdic
Photographer
Uros Potocnik

Do you suffer
Spain

National Award
Silver
Agency
Villarrosàs
Client
American Nike
Creative Director
Oriol Villar,
Fernando Codina
Art Director
Marius Zorrilla,
Javier Gracia
Copywriter
Miguel Angel Elizalde
Photographer
Carlos Spottorno

Shining
Czech Republic

National Award
Silver
Agency
Mark BBDO
Client
Wrigley
Creative Director
Leon Sverdlin,
Martin Charvat
Art Director
Jan Tamchyna
Copywriter
Pavel Brazda
Agency Producer
Pavel Jankovsky
Graphics
Retouching: Drawetc

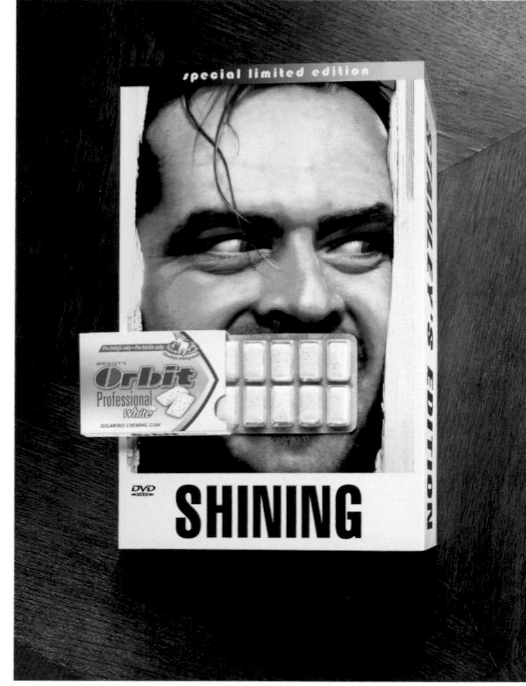

Do you suffer
"Do you suffer more when you run or when you don't?" Campaign aimed at regular runners, showing the runners at their limit.

Shining
"Orbit Professional White chewing gum". Orbit White gives you shining white teeth.

Madrunning
"MadRunning Exhibition". Posters were created in the style of the 70s, 80s, 90s and 00s, inviting people to the MadRunning footwear exhibition. 30 years of running in Madrid.

Broken teeth
Wintersport accidents can have bad consequences.

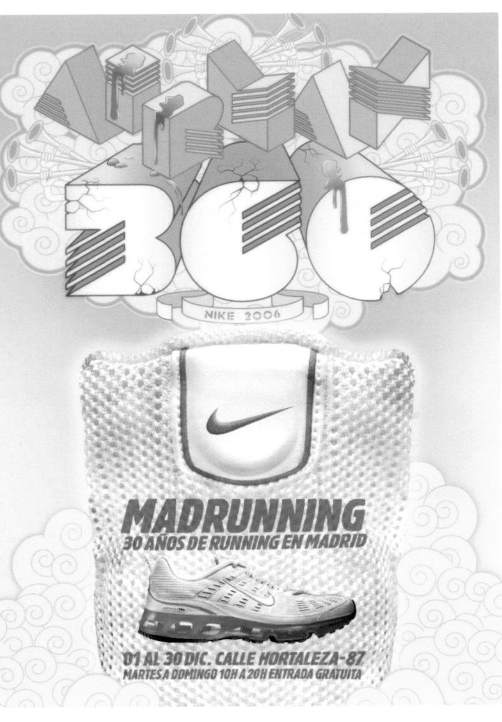

Madrunning
Spain

National Award
Silver
Agency
Villarrosàs
Client
American Nike
Creative Director
Oriol Villar
Art Director
Marius Zorrilla, Javier Gracia
Photographer
Joan Garrigosa
Graphics
Ricardo Rousselot, Vasava, Scott, Inocuo

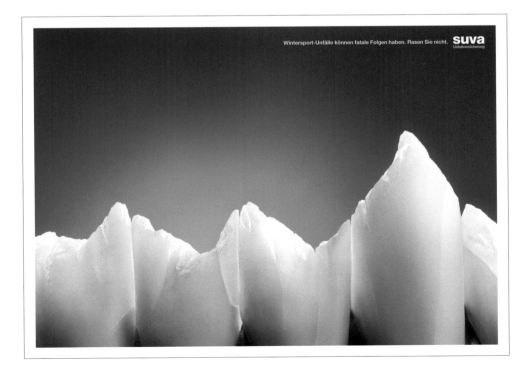

Wintersport-Unfälle können fatale Folgen haben. Rasen Sie nicht. suva Unfallversicherung

Broken teeth
Switzerland

National Award
Silver
Agency
Ruf Lanz Zurich
Client
Suva Accident prevention
Creative Director
Markus Ruf, Danielle Lanz
Art Director
Katja Puccio
Copywriter
Markus Ruf
Photographer
Stefan Minder, Felix Schregenberger
Other
Account Manager:
Chantal Baur

Is your diet sufficiently varied?
Sweden

National Award
Gold
Agency
Ogilvy Group Sweden
Client
Delicato
Creative Director
Björn Ståhl
Art Director
Hans Elander
Copywriter
Mikael Strom
Designer
Kerstin Engberg
Photographer
Henrik Bonnevier
Other
Jenny Raspe,
Karin Lönnberg

May contain traces of vitamins and minerals
Sweden

National Award
Gold
Agency
Ogilvy Group Sweden
Client
Delicato
Creative Director
Björn Ståhl
Art Director
Hans Elander
Copywriter
Mikael Strom
Designer
Kerstin Engberg
Photographer
Henrik Bonnevier
Other
Jenny Raspe,
Karin Lönnberg

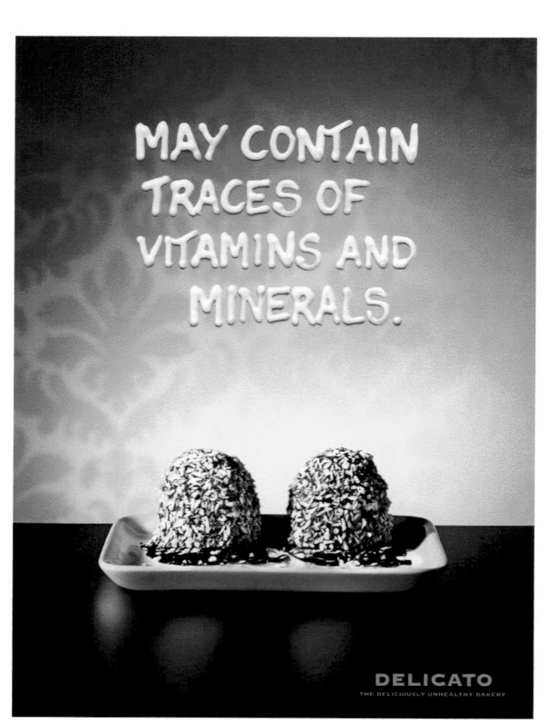

Definitely no whole grain
In these times of a hysterical emphasis on health, when even hotdog buns should be whole-grain, how does Delicato go against the flow and say it is all right to sin a little now and then? While others talk about health fads and whole-grain, Delicato says "Definitely no whole-grain" and goes against the whole health-trend hysteria.

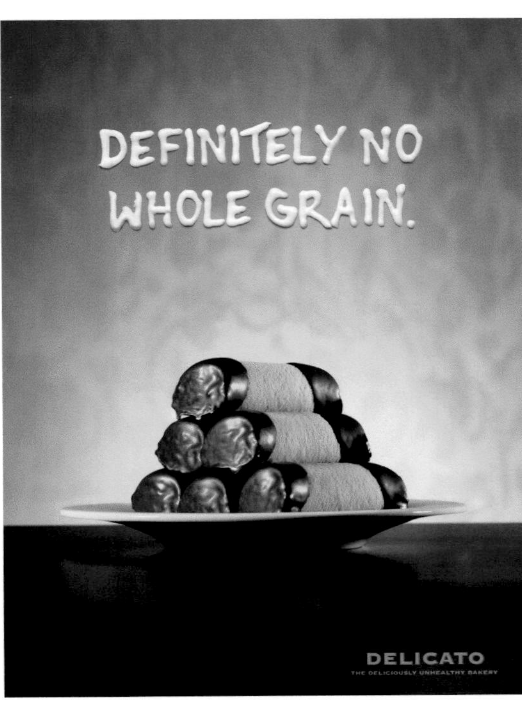

Definitely no whole grain
Sweden

National Award
Gold
Agency
Ogilvy Group Sweden
Client
Delicato
Creative Director
Björn Ståhl
Art Director
Hans Elander
Copywriter
Mikael Strom
Designer
Kerstin Engberg
Photographer
Henrik Bonnevier
Other
Jenny Raspe,
Karin Lönnberg

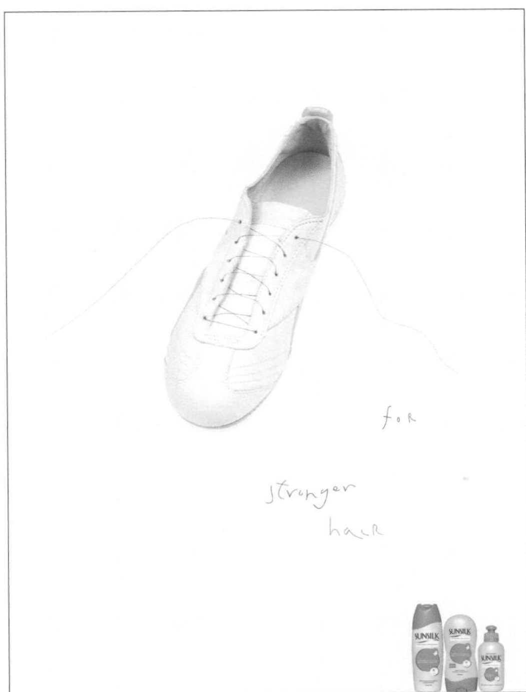

Shoe
Poland

National Award
Gold
Agency
J. Walter Thompson
Client
Unilever HPC
Creative Director
Darek Zatorski
Art Director
Karolina Czarnota
Copywriter
Monika Kaminska
Agency Producer
Jwt Poland
Photographer
Darek Zatorski

Advertising Print. Trade Advertising

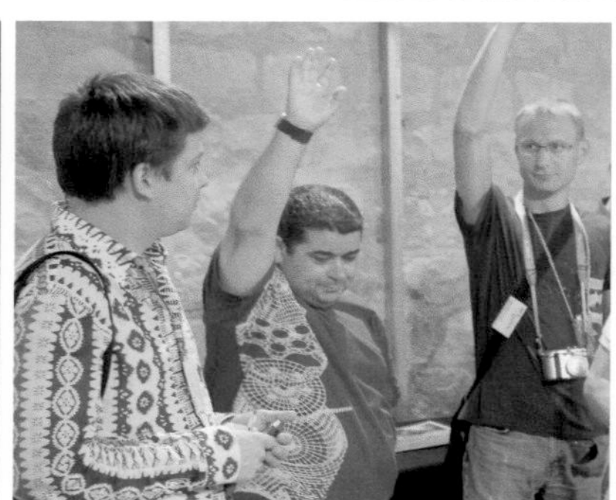

Germany: 1 Nomination

Austria

Russia

Spain

Switzerland: 1 Nomination

Nomination
Letters of application
Switzerland

National Award
Bronze
Agency
Ruf Lanz, Zurich
Client
Radio Energy Zurich
Creative Director
Markus Ruf, Danielle Lanz
Art Director
Marcel Schlaefle
Copywriter
Thomas Schöb
Other
Nicole Sommermeyer

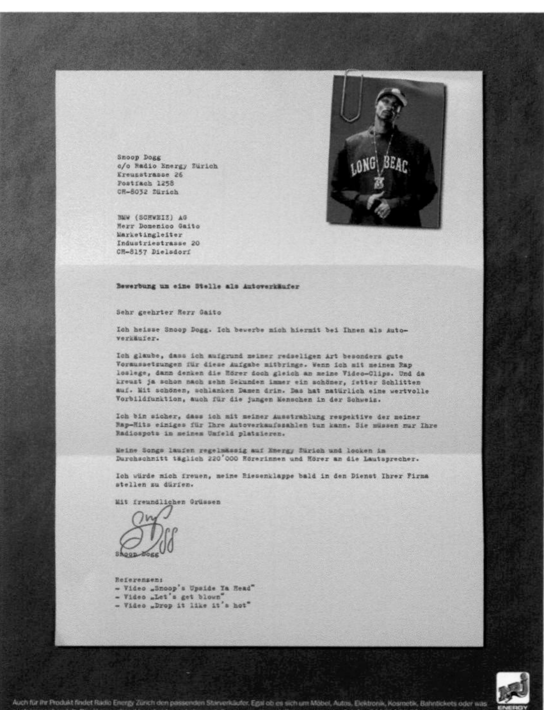

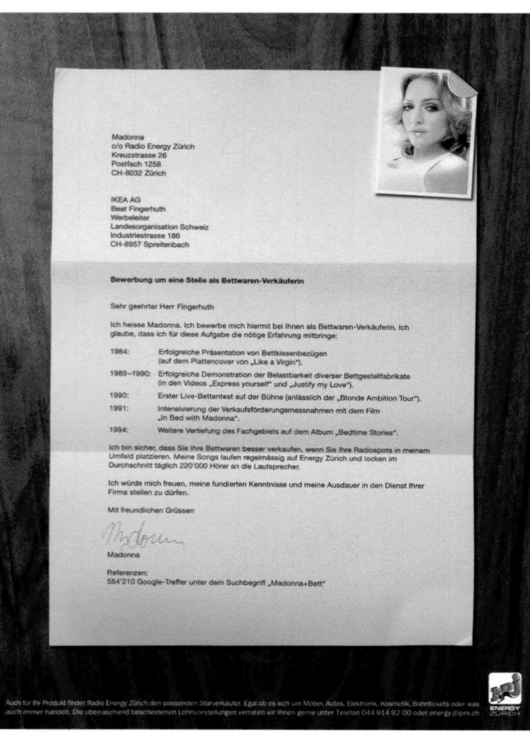

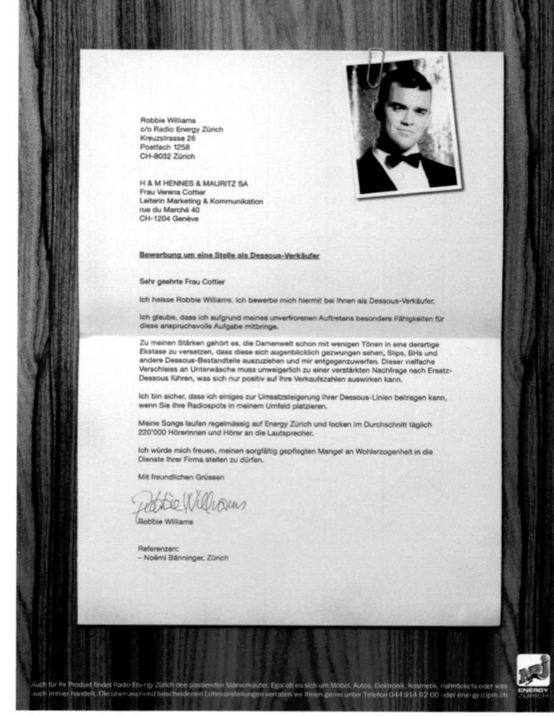

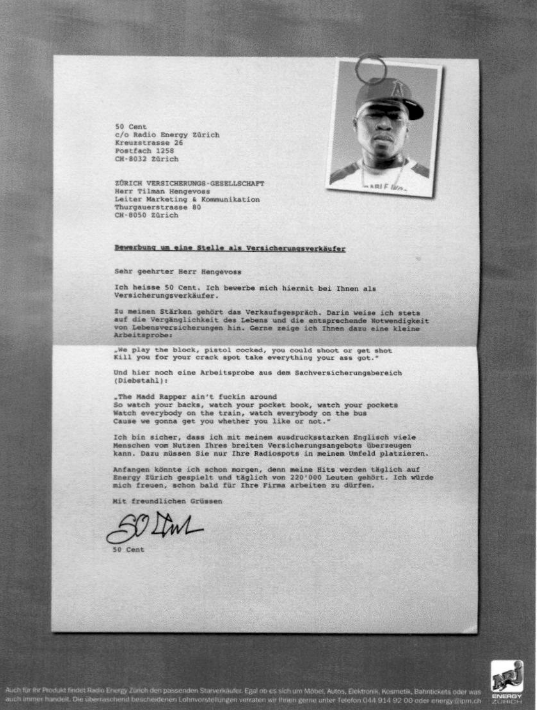

Nomination
Ups
Germany

National Award
Shortlist
Agency
Jung von Matt AG
Client
DPWN
Creative Director
W. Schneider,
M. Stiller,
D. Mously,
J. Harbeck
Art Director
David Mously
Copywriter
Jan Harbeck
Designer
Marius Lohmann
Agency Producer
Andreas Reinhardt
Other
Post Production:
PX! Berlin

Letters of application
"No Headlines. Letters of application in a typical commercial style". Daily 220,000 people listen to Radio Energy. Companies from all kind of industries can benefit from that, by broadcasting their radio spots.To communicate this benefit, superstars like Robbie Williams apply for a position as salesperson at the companies.

Ups
Scoring for DHL with respect to reliability and safety of transport compared to its competition.

Bookmark
Russia

National Award
Silver
Agency
Leo Burnett Moscow
Client
P&G
Creative Director
Mikhail Kudashkin
Art Director
Arina Avdeeva
Copywriter
Vera Karpova

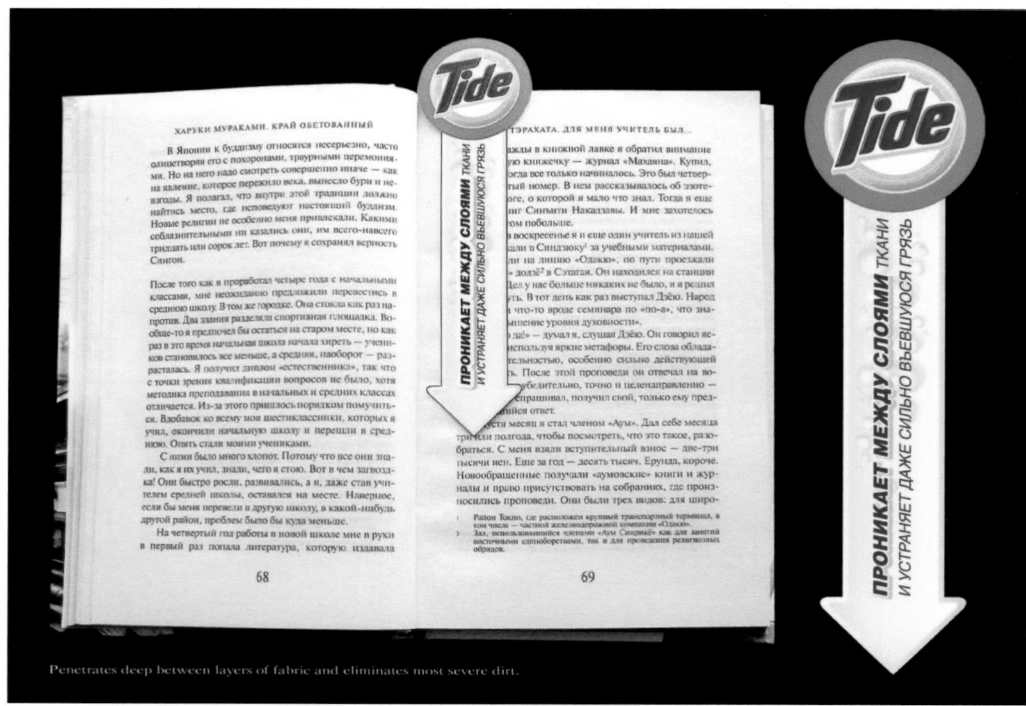

Posters Power of dreams
Spain

National Award
Gold
Agency
Villarrosàs
Client
Honda
Creative Director
Oriol Villar,
Fernando Codina
Copywriter
Miguel Angel Elizalde

Bookmark
Ambient item for women's books sections in bookstores. Text: "Deeply penetrates between the layers of tissue and removes even deeply soaked mud".

Posters Power of dreams
Posters explaining the technological advances and philosophy of Honda via the dreams of its engineers.

Media1 - More efficient media planning
Media 1 is Austria's most creative Media Agency and is known for its creative, individual placements.

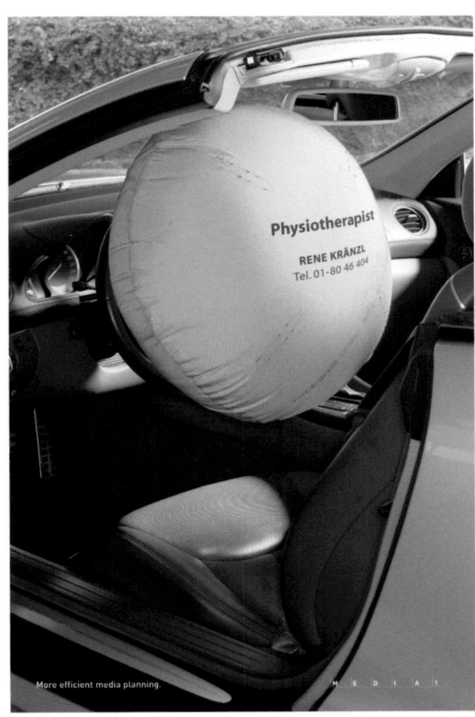

Media1 More efficient media planning
Austria

National Award
Silver
Agencya
Demner, Merlicek & Bergmann
Client
Media 1 - Mediaplanning and -buying
Creative Director
Francesco Bestagno
Art Director
Francesco Bestagno
Copywriter
Alexander Hofmann, Antonia Kiefhaber
Agency Producer
Norbert Rabenseifner
Photographer
Staudinger + Franke
Graphics
Daniela Schabernak
Other
Art Buying:
Ilona Urikow

Q: Are non professionals - in the web - changing the rules of communication?

Q: Will privacy be possible in the future?

Q: Copyright or copyleft?

3

New & Mixed Media

Q: Has Capitalism survived because it has adapted to the media?

New & Mixed Media jury

"For the times they are a-changin'" *Bob Dylan*

My tribute goes to the passion, dedication and professionalism of:
Erich from Austria,
Jan from Czech Republic,
Tiia from Estonia,
Hans-Joachim from Germany,
Adalgeir from Iceland,
Mick from Ireland,
Paolo Cesano from Italy,
Armands from Latvia,
Miguel from Portugal,
Dmitri from Russia,
Olivier from Spain,
and Thomas from Switzerland.
Our tribute goes to the work we had the privilege to judge which made our session an enlightening experience.
Is the New and Mixed Media the future?
Not really, it is the present.
Let the Grand Prix in this book be the answer.

So what about the future?

Franco Moretti
Chairman
Chief Creative Officer
Leo Burnett
Italy

He studied architecture in Italy. He began his career as an illustrator in Australia, and worked in three agencies, from Assistant Art Director to Creative Director. In 1970 he moved to London as Creative Group Head in Brunnings. In 1973 he joined McCann-Erickson in Milan as Senior Art Director Group Head. In 1979 he moved to NY to found the creative international team for Coca-Cola campaigns. In 1984, he became Exec. Creative Dir. Vice President of Italian McCann offices, and in 1990 he was named Senior Vice President of McCann Worldwide and European Creative Director. In 1996 he joined Leo Burnett Italy as Chief Creative Officer, and in 2001 he was named Group Vice Chairman. President of the ADCI from 1995 to 1999, today he is on board of ADCE, Pubblicità Progresso Foundation, and an active member of TP and IAA.

Erich Falkner
Chief Creative Officer, DRAFTFCB Kobza
Austria

He began his career as an Assistant to Henry F. Porsche in the Advertising Bureau of General Motors Austria. In 1981, he began his self-educated career with Gunther O. Lebisch. After 3 years with Demner&Merlicek, he switched to Schretter & Comp, where he worked as an Art director and afterwards as Creative Director for Lowe GGK. In 1995, he joined the Management Board at Lowe in the newly founded Lowe Lintas GGK Unit. During his career, Erich worked with important brands and his work has been rewarded with all significant Austrian Advertising Awards and on Shortlist place in Cannes.
At present, Erich manages FCB Retail, together with CEO Manfred F. Berger.

Jan Rídl
Copywriter
McCann Erickson Prague
Czech Republic

He has a Master of Philosophy at Charles University in Prague, Branch Film Studies. From 2001 to 2005, he worked as a Copywriter for Mark/BBDO and also worked as a Copywriter for Dorland since 2001. Since 2006, he has been a Copywriter at McCann Erickson.

Tiia Nömm
Managing Director
Korpus
Estonia

After graduating with a Bachelor's degree in Fine Arts in 1996 Tiia has successfully worked in Estonian creative business. Her areas of interest have developed from Fine Arts to communication design and from there to interactive advertising. Forever curious, she currently elaborates the perfect formula of simultaneously leading 5-year-old creative agency, bringing up 5-year-old son and combining several other ingredients of great importance (including ADC Estonia).

Hans-Joachim Berndt
Director Chairman, House of Packshots Film- und Fernsehproduktion GmbH
Germany

Born in Hamburg in 1949, he studied business management and psychology in Hamburg and Kie. In 1975, he started as a production manager in Dr. Brandau's film production co., and then became partner and managing director. Berndt founded what later became Neue Constantin Film München, and in 1979 began building up the FILMHAUS. He has won 380 prizes in Cannes, NYC and London, around 60 ADC awards, over 50 Klappe awards and 2 honorary prizes from the Government of Berlin. He held until 2002 the professorship in audiovisual graphic design at the Academy of Arts in Nuremberg. His latest initiative is the European CHAINSAW ACADEMY, in association with YALE University and the Art Center Pasadena. He has been an ADC Board member since 1982.

Adalgeir Arnar Jonsson
Art Director
Metall Design Studio
Iceland

He graduated from the Iceland Academy of the Arts in 2005 with a BA in Graphic Design. He has worked in both large and small agencies in Iceland since 1997. Today he runs his own multi-disciplinary design studio. Adalgeir thinks it is crucial for a graphic designer to be able to design both for print and for the web.

Mick O'Dwyer
Creative Director
Nexus 451
Ireland

Mick graduated in Visual Communications at the College of Marketing & Design in the 80s. He began and worked for 7 years as a freelance photographer and graphic designer and then took time out to write a novel before joining BBC Advertising as Creative Director for 4 years. After that he worked as Senior Designer with a large Dublin based Internet agency and in 2001 he set co-founded Nexus451, a web design and development company with his business partner, Niall Curran. Based in Dublin, Nexus451 employs 10 people developing integrated solutions and products for a broad range of clients across different industry sectors both in Ireland and abroad.

Paolo Cesano
Associate Creative Director
JWT Italia
Italy

He is an Associate Creative Director at JWT Milan. His talent was awarded at D&AD (Silver nomination), ADCE (gold), EPICA (gold), New York Festivals (silver), Italian Art Directors Club (silver), Effie Awards (gold), Communication arts, and LIAA.

Armands Zelcs
DDB, Latvia
Latvia

Art Director of DDB Latvia, core organizer of worldwide short film festival Future Shorts in Riga, but foremost - one of the most promising young artists on the Latvian contemporary arts scene. Being renowned for his exclusively academic upbringing, striking spectre of knowledge, fine taste in absurdities and sharp sense of humour, Armands has been the author of some of the most awarded campaigns.
Armands graduated with distinction from Latvian Arts Academy and is currently undertaking his Master studies. His exhibition list so far covers Riga (BooM) and Berlin (Riga Review) with many more to come in year 2008.

Miguel Paté
Creative Director
TouchMe Wunderman
Portugal

Since January 15th, Miguel Pate is the Wunderman Lisbon's Creative Director.

He studied Advertising and Marketing in Lisbon and Barcelona, and, in 1993, he joined Quartzo Advertising as a trainee Copywriter. In 1994, he moved to Novo Design and, in 1995, he entered Wunderman Cato Johnson Lisbon. After almost 5 years in WCJ, he was invited to lead the creative department of CP Communication in Portugal, which later became CP Proximity.

In 2004, Miguel started at Olgivy One Portugal, and, in 2005, he joined TouchMe Redcell.
In addition, he was a member of the DMA Echo Awards Jury in 2003 and the Caples Awards in 2006.

Dmitri A. Belkov
Executive Creative Director
Two Signs Production
Russia

Dmitri was born in Leningrad - a city built on the peat-bog. And as one Russian poet said "every Leningrad citizen must have wings to fly over that bog." Started flying as a copywriter in a small agency. Dmitri is now leading the Russian new media company, TwoSigns, as a Creative Director. With his BA in Linguistics and MA in Psychology, Dmitri is managing a small laboratory researching the aspects of colour perception.

Q: Is erudition an obsolete concept?

Olivier Grau
Art Director
Vis-tek
Spain

Thomas Schöb
Copywriter
Ruf Lanz
Werbeagentur AG
Switzerland

After taking his degree in Advertising at the Autonomous University of Barcelona, he started his career in the interactive advertising field with Ogilvy Interactive Barcelona. In 2002, he founded the Vis-Tek studio, and he has been working in on-line and off-line communication projects for clients such as Volkswagen, Grup Agbar, the City Council of Barcelona, etc.

He was born in Zurich in 1965 and obtained his Master's degree in the Arts (German Language and literature, Italian Literature, and Mass Media Science) at the University of Zurich in 1994. He took his first steps at several agencies, and from 1995 to 2005 he worked as a Freelance Copywriter in Zurich. Since 2005 he works at advertising agency Ruf Lanz in Zurich.

New & Mixed Media. Interactive Media: Websites & DVDs

Austria

Germany: 2 Nominations

Ireland

Italy

Latvia

Norway: 1 Nomination

Poland: 1 Nomination

Portugal

Russia

Spain: Gold

Sweden: 1 Nomination

Switzerland: 1 Nomination

Gold

Página en construcción

(In DVD)
Spain

National Award
Gold
Agency
HTTP Comunicació
Client
HTTP Comunicació
Creative Director
Vicente Reyes
Art Director
Álex Catalán,
Joaquim Salat,
Isaac León
Copywriter
Adriano Latorre
Programmer
Adriano Latorre
Url
www.httpcomunicacio.com/piezas/teaser/

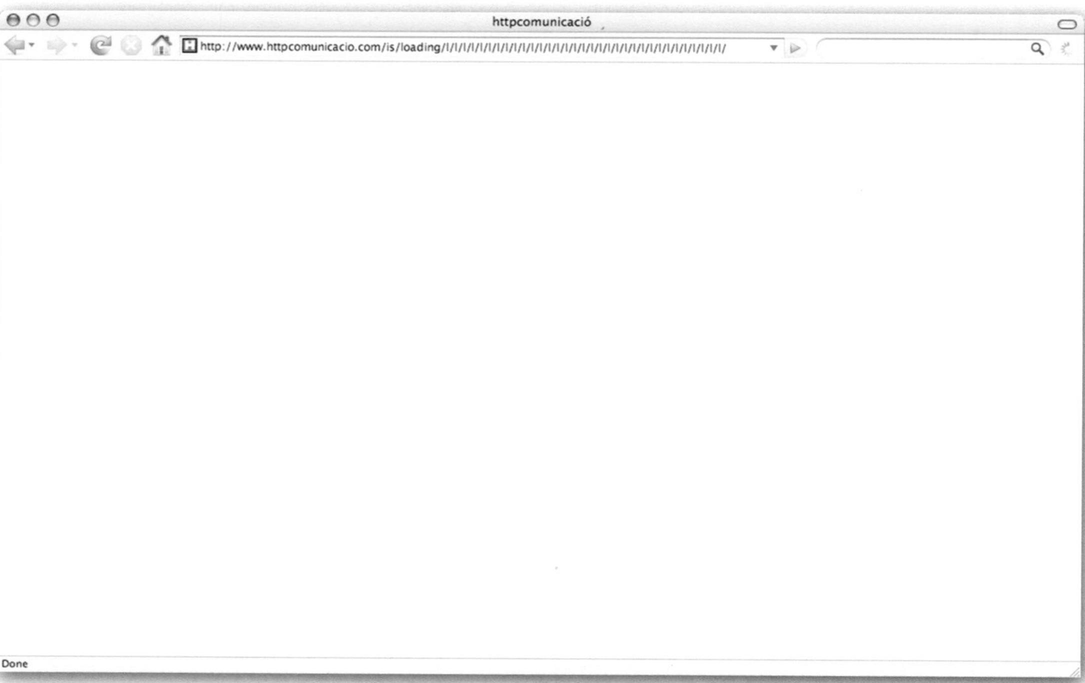

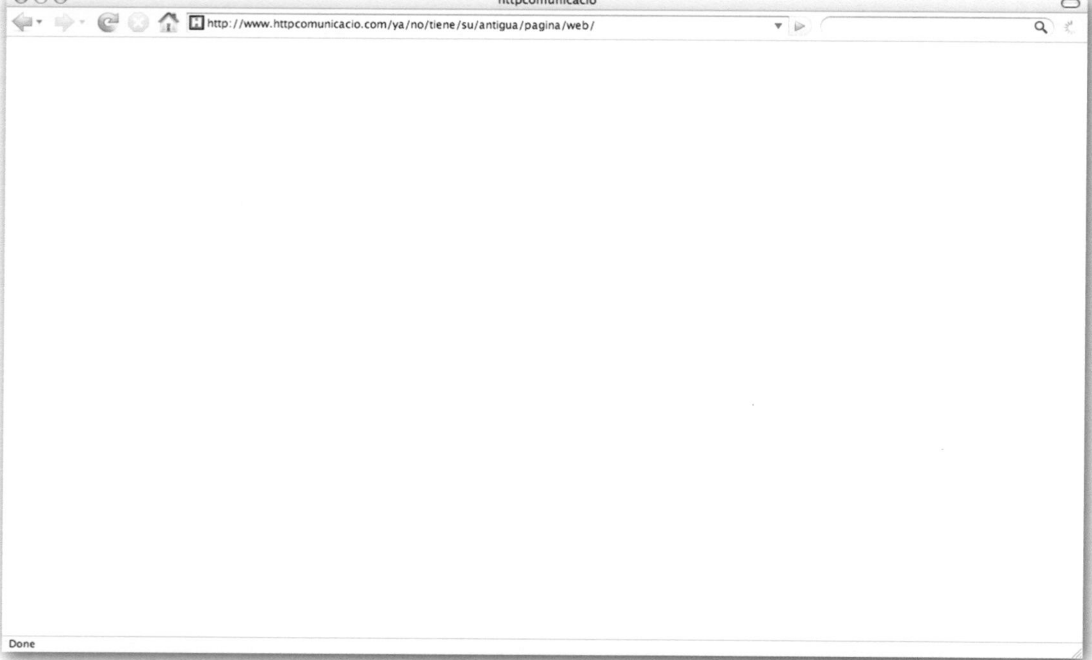

During a short period, this piece of creativity replaced the old agency website while the new one was being completed. It was a bold move, because the website was left literally blank and only the address bar of the browser was used to communicate with the user.

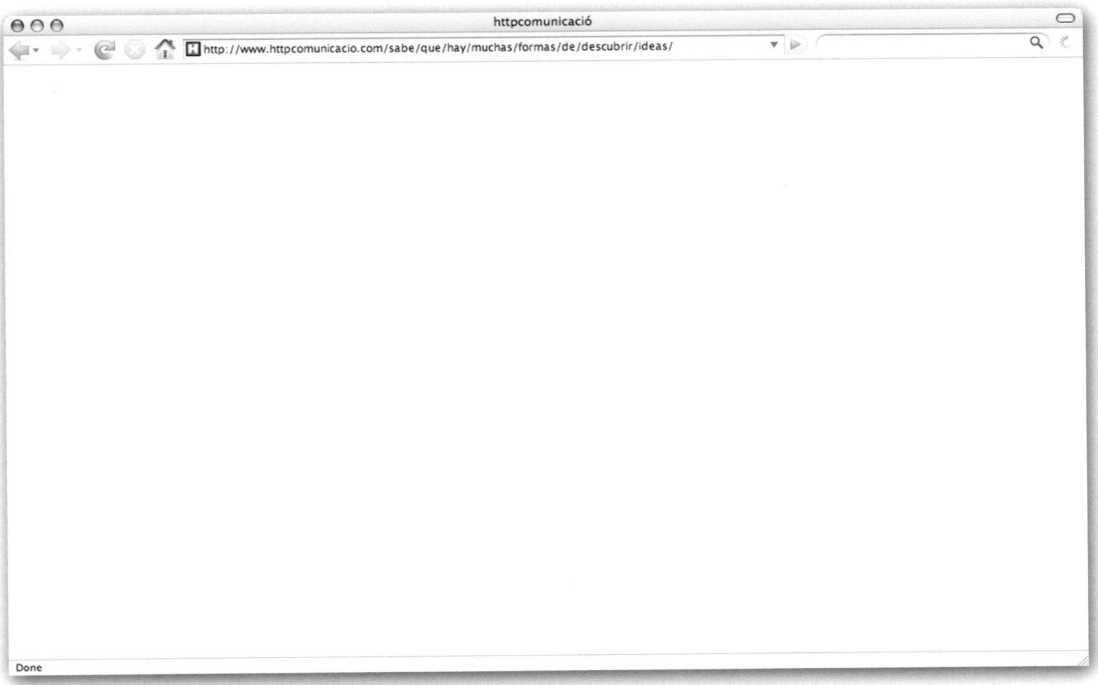

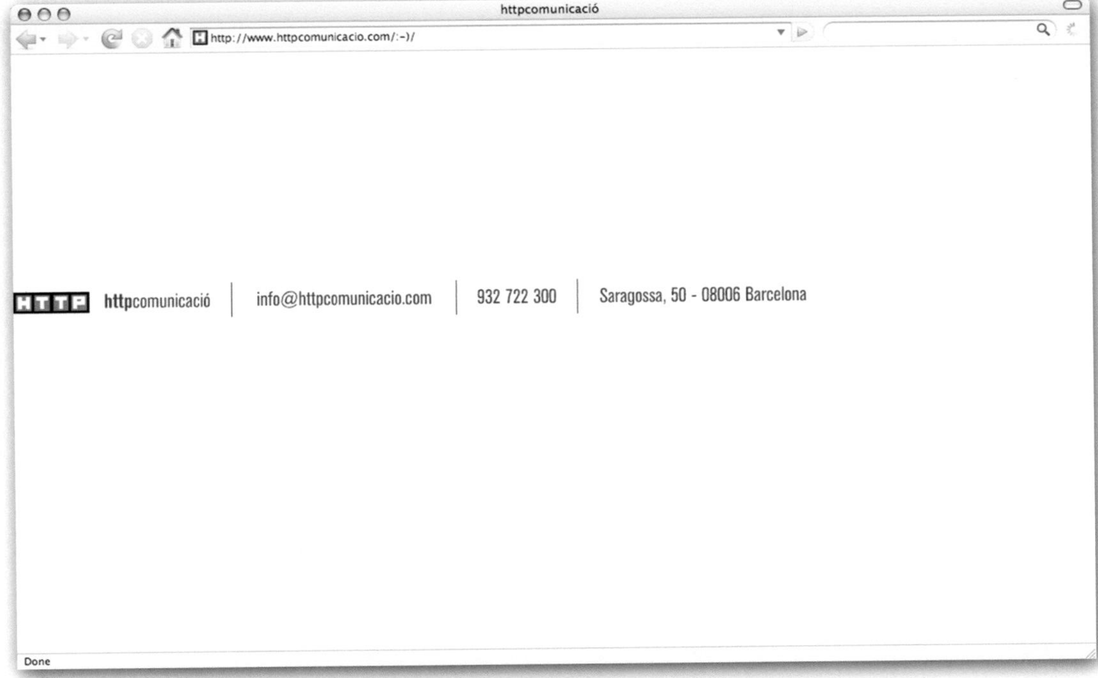

Nomination
Adidas Y-3 Reflections
(In DVD)
Germany

National Award
Bronze
Agency
Neue Digital GmbH
Client
Adidas Group
Creative Director
Elke Klinkhammer
Art Director
Bejadin Selimi
Designer
Andrè Bourguignon
Production Company
Effekt-Etage, Berlin
Programmer
Heiko Schweickhardt,
Thomas Junk
Url
www.neue-digitale.de/projects/y-3_fw2006

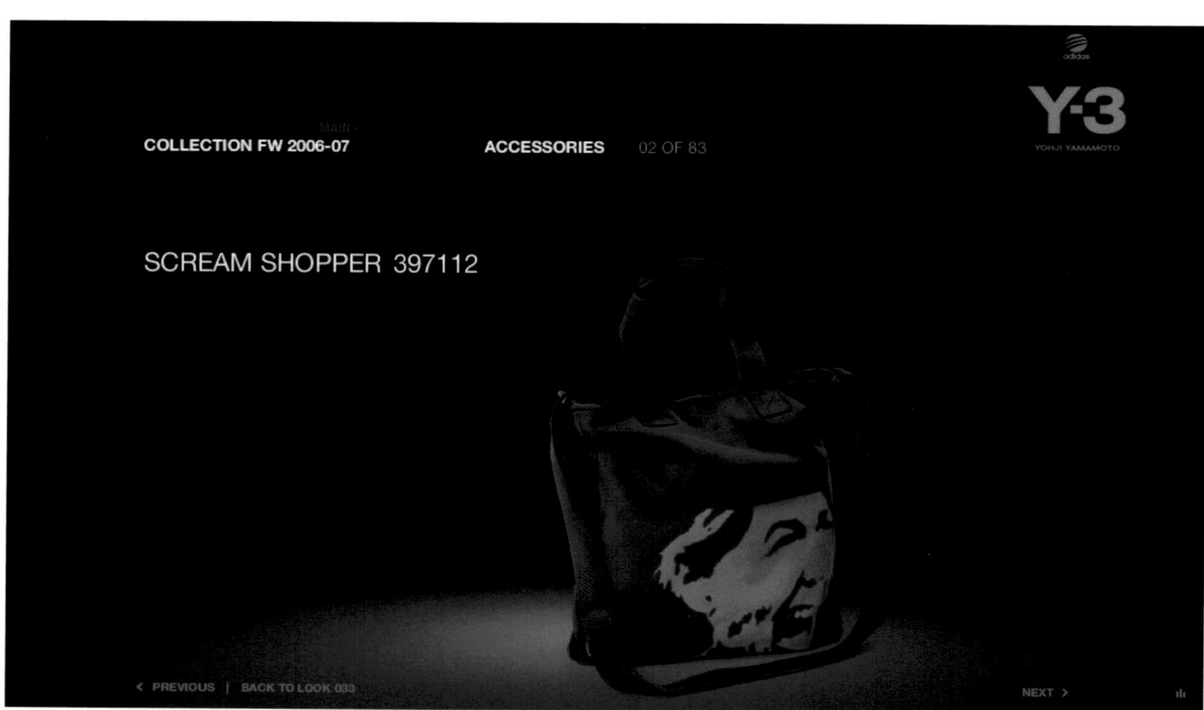

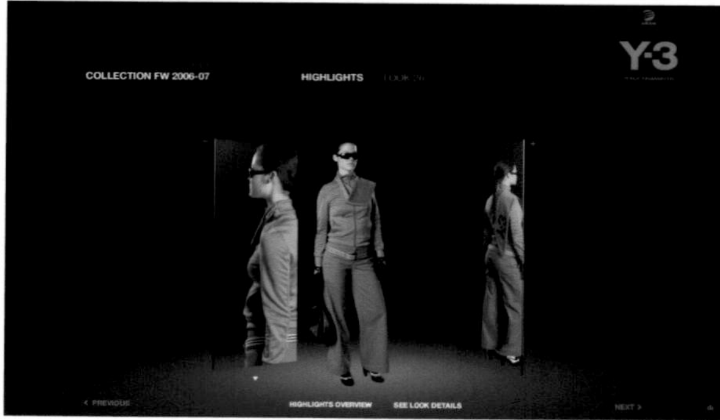

Nomination
Nastuh Abootalebi
(In DVD)
Germany

National Award
Bronze
Agency
Scholz & Volkmer
Client
Nastuh Visual Effects
Creative Director
Heike Brockmann
Art Director
Tobias Kreutzer
Copywriter
Tim Sobczak
Designer
Christoph Noe
Programmer
Peter Reichard
Url
www.s-v.de/projects/nastuh
Other
Project Manager:
Pia Tannenberger

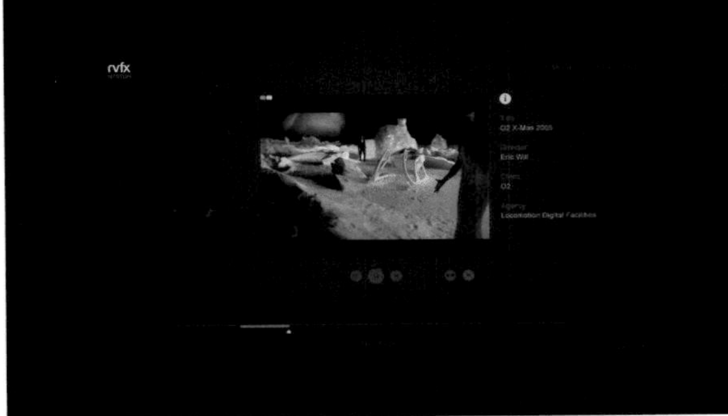

Adidas Y-3 Reflections
The Y-3 Reflections website arouses the users' curiosity and provokes irritation simultaneously. The presentation of the models in the mirrors blurs the border between reflection and reality.

Nastuh Abootalebi
Corporate website for visual effects artist Nastuh Abootalebi. The website will present the portfolio of the visual effects artist, and appeals to existing and potential customers such as post-production companies, directors and agencies. Concept: Making the actual service of visual effects visible.

Nomination
Try Drugs
(In DVD)
Norway

National Award
Gold
Agency
Kitchen Leo Burnett
Client
Rusmiddeletaten
Department of Health
Art Director
Anne Gravingen,
Tom Rainer Thuv
Copywriter
Benedik Romstd
Designer
Severre Stabel- Mediafront
Programmer
Martin KG
Berggren- Mediafront
Url
www.trydrugs.net
Other
Mikael Eriksson- Project
Manager for Mediafront

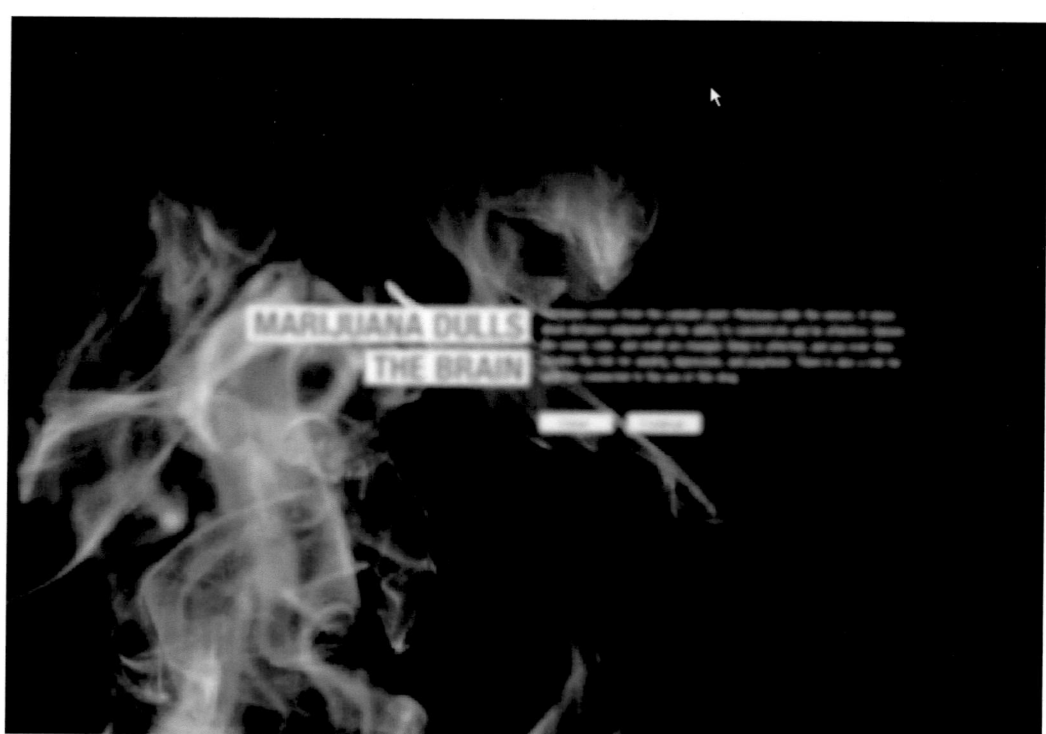

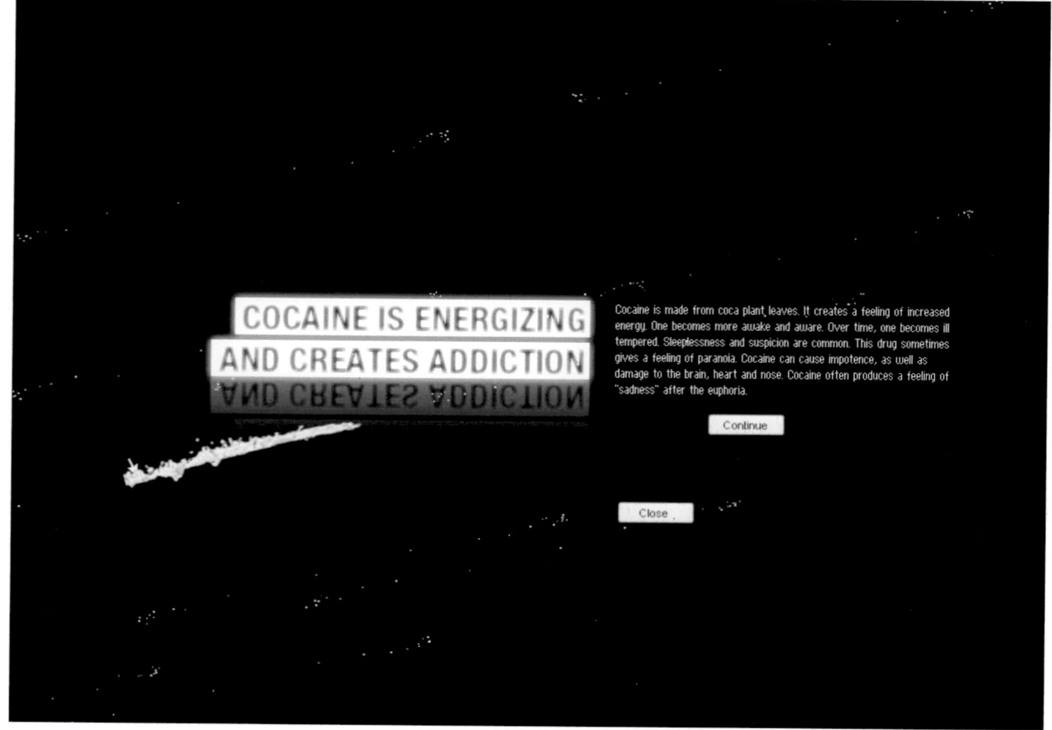

Try Drugs
"Drug prevention".
A website that shows the effects of drugs and tells people where they can find help for substance abuse if they need it.

Helping Makes You Stronger
A pop-up of World Strongman Champion Mariusz Pudzianowski appears. On either side of him are two little dog pop-ups he's got on leashes. On the left dog, visitors can sign up to volunteer, on the right one people seeking help can locate volunteers.

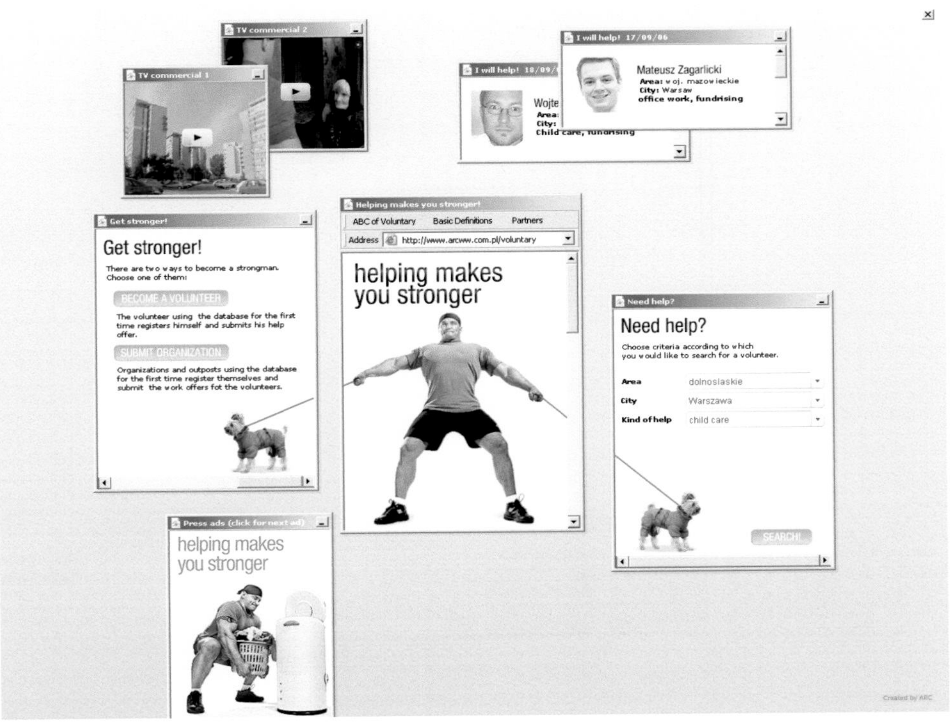

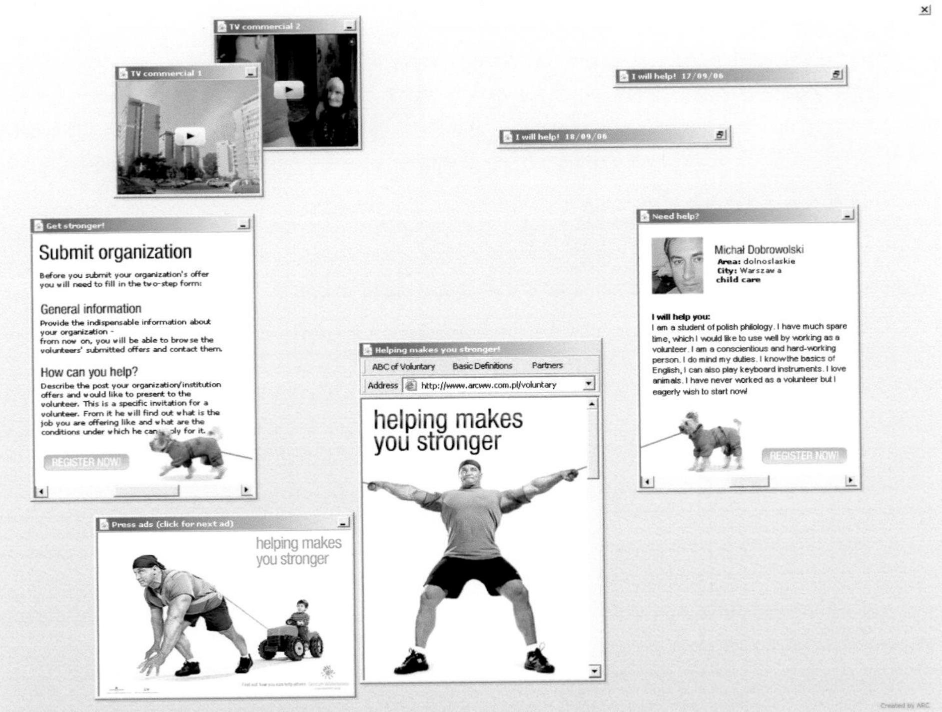

Nomination
Helping Makes You Stronger
(In DVD)
Poland

National Award
Silver
Agency
Leo Burnett Warsaw
Client
Centrum Wolontariatu
Creative Director
Martin Winther
Art Director
Marcin Serafin, Jakub Zielecki, Adam Smereczynski
Copywriter
Michael Lars, Maciej Porebski
Designer
Konrad Grzegorzewicz (Arc Warsaw)
Production Company
Leo Burnett Warsaw
Url
www.arcww.com.pl/voluntary/

Nomination

The 100 Absolutes

(In DVD)
Sweden

National Award
Gold
Agency
Great Works
Client
V&S Absolut Spirits,
Patric Blixt
Creative Director
Ted Persson
Art Director
Jacob Astrom
Copywriter
Kristoffer Triumf
Designer
Jacob Astrom,
Bjorn Wissing,
Jens Eriksson,
Fredrik Karlsson
Agency Producer
Eva Nilsson
Programmer
Jocke Wissing,
Fredrik Karlsson
Url
http://absolut.com/100absolutes_campaign
Other
Account Director: Magnus Walsten;
Music: DNM/Jonas Quant;
Animation: Wreck

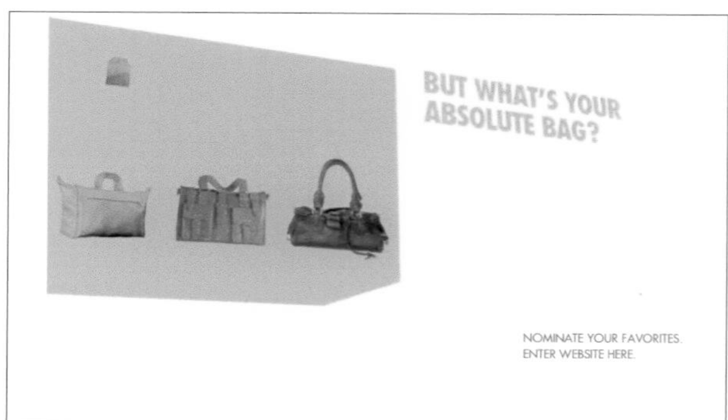

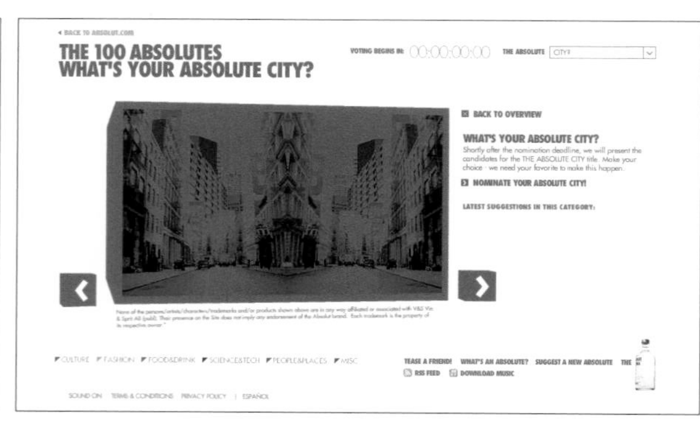

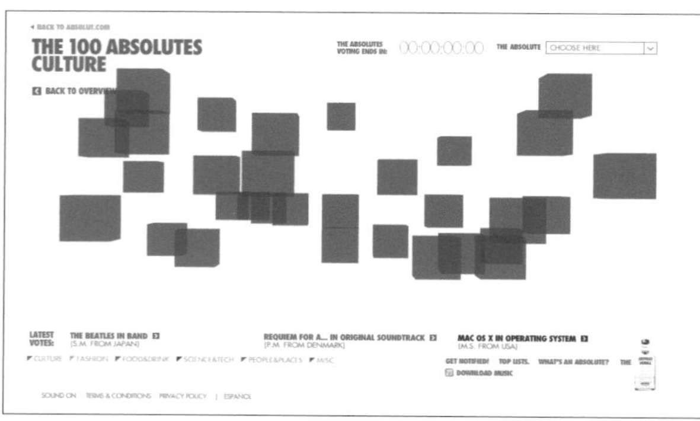

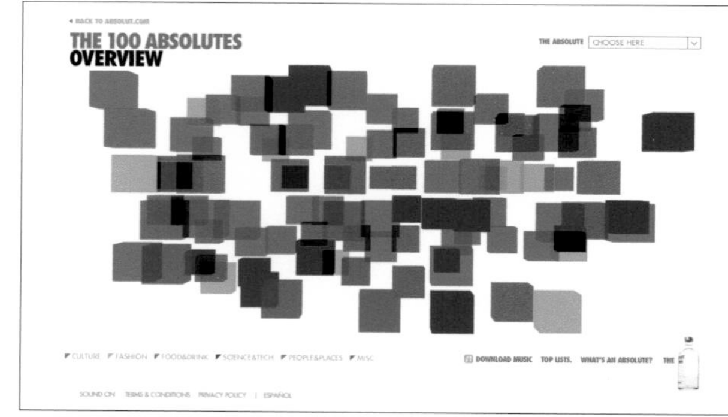

The 100 Absolutes
The objective with the campaign is to make people think about the meaning of the word ABSOLUT again. In the first phase, people upload their own favourites within the given categories. In the second phase, two to ten nominees are selected for the final vote. At the end of the 2006, THE 100 ABSOLUTES list was completed.

Mary Woodbridge
Mary Woodbridge: a perfectly normal 85-year-old Brit who takes her dachshund Daisy for a walk every day. To protect herself against the elements, she buys herself a Mammut jacket in December of 2005. And suddenly the old lady gets an idea: she's going to climb Everest.

Nomination
Mary Woodbridge
(In DVD)
Switzerland
National Award
Bronze
Agency
Spillmann/Felser/ Leo Burnett
Client
Mammut Sports Group
Creative Director
Martin Spillmann
Art Director
Raul Serrat
Copywriter
Peter Brönnimann
Production Company
Plan B Film
Graphics
Ricco Pachera
Url
www.snipurl.com/ mary_woodbridge

Bank Austria Creditanstalt
Austria

National Award
Silver
Agency
DRAFTFCBi Directmarketing & Interactive GmbH
Client
Bank Austria Creditanstalt
Creative Director
Dieter Weidhofer, Julia Zemann
Art Director
Marko Malle
Copywriter
Martin Gessoni, Petra Hauer
Designer
Marko Malle
Graphics
Marko Malle
Programmer
Simone Haider, Sebastian Mayrhuber
Url
www.fcb.at/projects/baca/bleigiessen/
Other
Concept: Martin Gessoni, Petra Hauer

Bank Austria Creditanstalt
Lead-pouring is an Austrian tradition that is done on New Year's Eve to know what the future will bring. Bank Austria Creditanstalt requested a tool where every result shows the bank as the perfect partner in the focus. "Your choice! Use your mouse to put a lead-figure on the spoon. Careful! It's getting hot. Put the spoon over the candle and click the left mouse button until the figure melts. A quick cold shower! Pour the melted lead into the glass!".

Change of number
Change your number whenever you want. Zero rubles, zero hassle.

500 Faces
500 Wants you

www.airport.lv
A creation of a henhouse environment on the web page, but since the client refused to rename the company Airport to Chicken Farm, they were forced to make an airport…

Change of number
Russia

National Award
Silver
Agency
BBDO Interactive
Client
Vympelcom
Art Director
Paul Solovyev
Designer
Dmitriy Krasnikov
Illustrator
Vladimir Danilov

Меняй свой номер когда захочешь

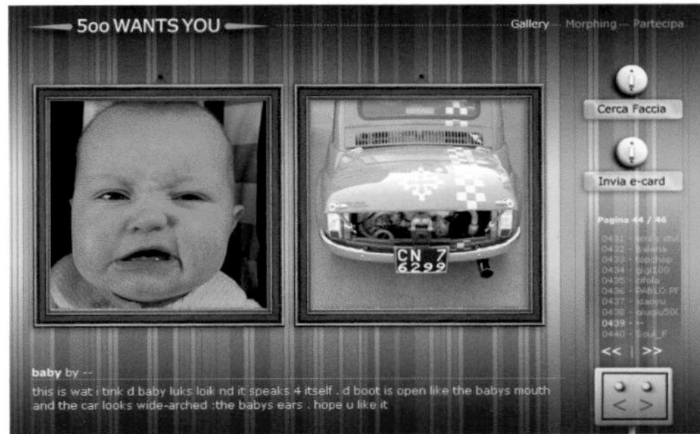

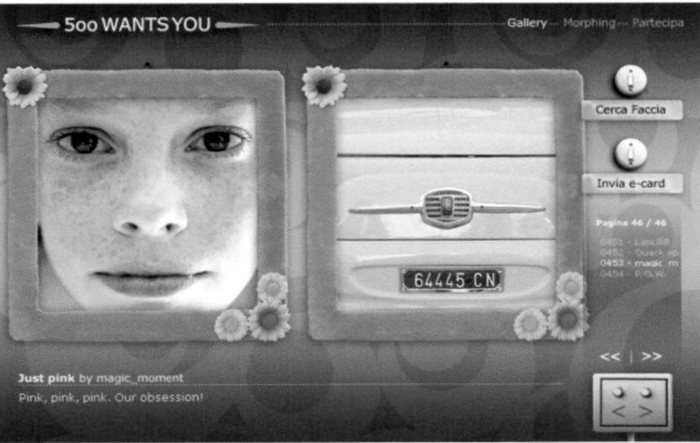

500 Faces
Italy

National Award
Silver
Agency
ARC/Leo Burnett
Client
Fiat Automobiles
Creative Director
Riccardo Robiglio, Paolo Dematteis
Art Director
Gaetano Musto
Copywriter
L. Marucco, R.Ramondetti, B.Berardi
Designer
Paolo Medda
Graphics
P. Medda, R. Agagliate, M. Righi, T. Allemand
Programmer
G. Mori, P. Faccini, M. Carrodano, E. Marquez
Url
www.fiat500.com/faces/
Other
Internet Creative Director:
Matteo Righi

www.airport.lv
Latvia

National Award
Silver
Agency
E950
Client
Advertising agency-Airport
Creative Director
Janis Nigals
Art Director
Otto Zitmanis

Mono-No-Aware
Italy

National Award
Silver
Agency
DDB
Client
Ryuchi Sakamoto
Creative Director
Vicky Gitto
Art Director
Giuseppe La Spada
Photographer
Giuseppe La Spada
Url
www.mono-no-aware.org

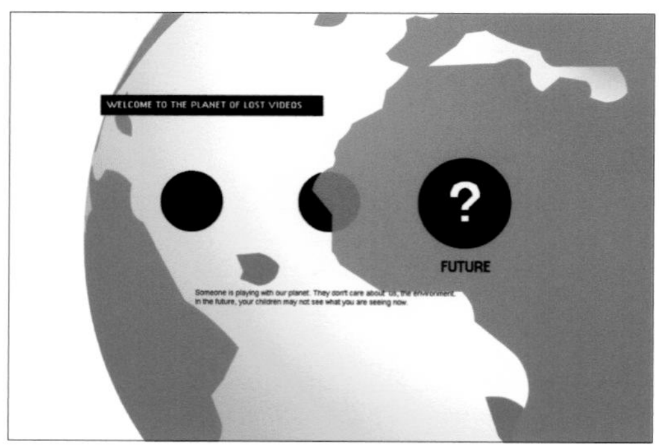

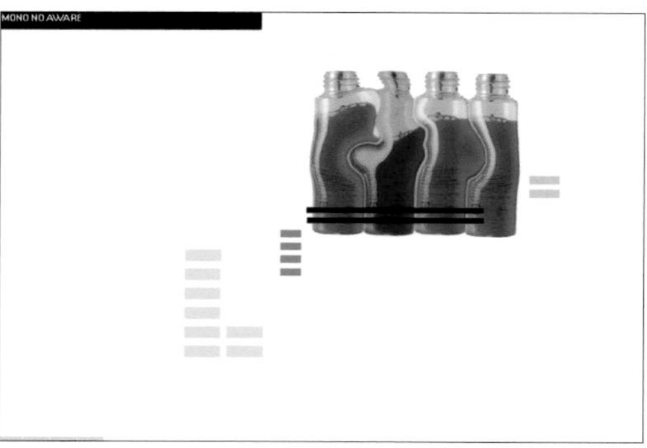

Explosion
Portugal

National Award
Silver
Agency
BBDO Portugal
Client
BBDO Portugal
Creative Director
Pedro Bidarra
Art Director
André Moreira
Copywriter
Nuno Jerônimo,
Pedro Bidarra,
Nuno Cardoso
Url
www.youtube.com/watch?v=3RspNOL_PQs

Mono-No-Aware
The site is divided into three distinct synergic phases generated by the need to support a non-profit project promoting social awareness through the use of metaphors and sophisticated technology to trigger user interactivity.

Explosion
BBDO Lab was born of the conviction that an ad agency's artistic and creative potential is much greater than its immediate achievements. It therefore constitutes an Ideas Lab, a creative space attempting to exploit this potential to the utmost.

www.dancesisterdance.com
An interactive website promoting the Scissor Sisters' single "I Don't Feel Like Dancing". Users upload photos of their faces, choose outfits and wigs, then watch themselves star in a music video. Current views: 10 million.

Bravo Deserves Applause!
Internet game where you give applause to the new Fiat BRAVO. Move the car forward by clapping your hands to the microphone plugged into the computer. Whoever makes the new BRAVO go the furthest wins 1000$.

www.dancesister-dance.com
Ireland

National Award
Silver
Agency
ICAN
Client
Universal Music
Creative Director
Flick Henderson
Art Director
Ian McFarlane
Copywriter
Lizzie Kinross
Designer
Ian McFarlane
Production Company
IceBubble
Graphics
Ian McFarlane
Illustrator
Ian McFarlane
Programmer
Torlogh O'Boyle
Url
ican.ie/campaigns/universalmusic/dancesisterdance

Bravo Deserves Applause!
Poland

National Award
Silver
Agency
Arc Warsaw,
Leo Burnett Group
Client
Fiat Auto Poland
Creative Director
Rafal Górski
Art Director
Adam Smereczynski
Copywriter
Rafal Gorski
Designer
Adam Smereczynski
Programmer
Konrad Grzegorzewicz
Url
www.arcww.com.pl/bravo1000_en
Other
Flash Developer:
Konrad Grzegorzewicz

Ojars Vacietis. Multimedia.
Latvia

National Award
Silver
Agency
Dd Studio
Client
The Memorial Museum of Ojars Vacietis
Creative Director
Janis Mitrevics
Art Director
Miks Mitrevics

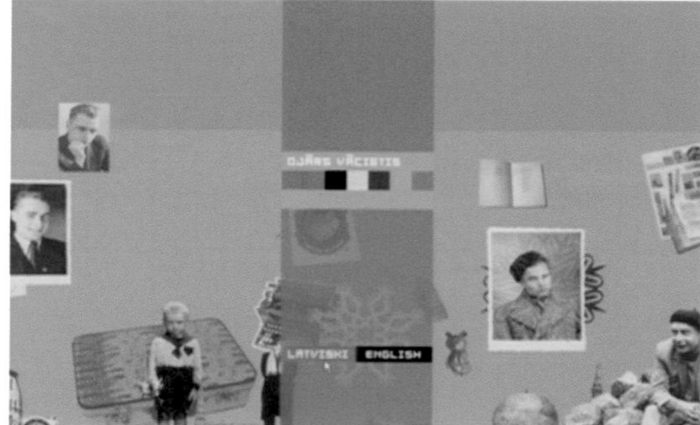

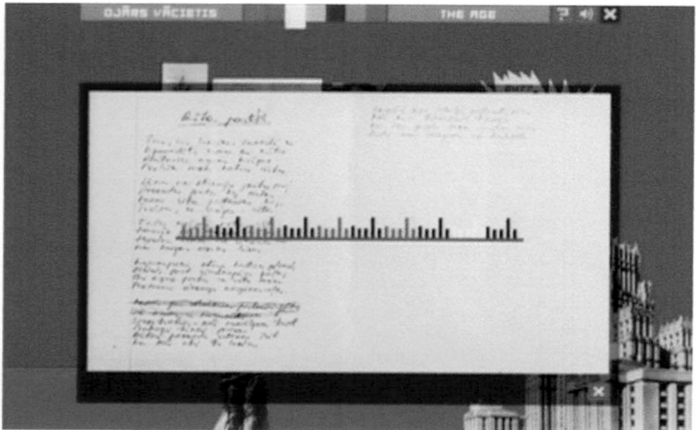

iCat FM
Spain

National Award
Silver
Agency
CCRTV Interactiva
Client
Catalunya Ràdio
Creative Director
La Mosca
Art Director
Aleix Fernández
Copywriter
Josep Maria Escofet
Designer
Stefano Mazza
Production company
La Mosca
Programmer
Alberto Alejo
Url
www.icatfm.cat

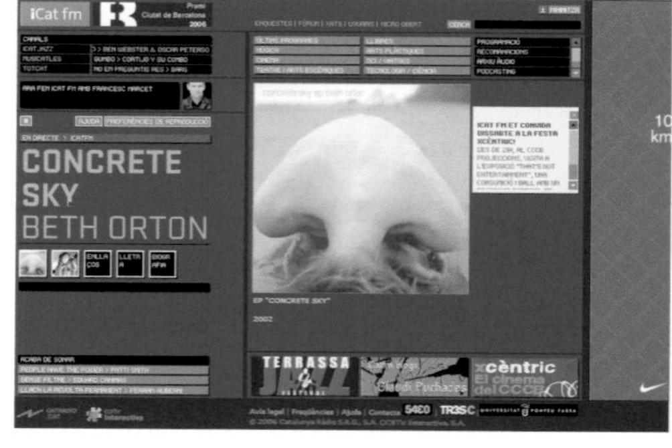

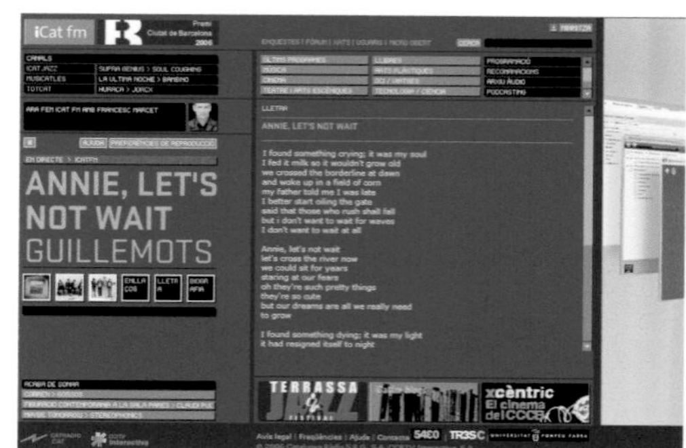

Ojars Vacietis. Multimedia.
This webpage was made for the Ojars Vacietis Memorial Museum

iCat FM
It is a new concept of a music radio station that features complete integration of radio and Internet. iCat fm is synchronized with radio broadcasts, showing in real time what is being played on the radio and providing additional information that enhances traditional radio broadcasts. It also provides participation tools and virtual communities.

MTV Movie Awards 2007 website
The task set for us by the MTV Russian Movie Awards was to create something original, interesting and impressive. The corporate identity had to be fully developed for the award including the logo. The concept of the website design was in line with it.

Help Mexicans to get to Russia
Help Pedro, Julio and Juan to cross the border and reach Russia — the only place they can get Orbit Lime, a 100% Mexican pleasure. It's just like lime, but better! Use a butting cow for a take off. Don't miss out on the bonuses and your instrument. And get ready to land in Red Square!

"MTV Movie Awards 2007" website
Russia

National Award
Silver
Agency
Nile Studio
Client
MTV Russia
Creative Director
Yura Alexeev, Ilya Shekurov
Art Director
Yura Alexeev, Ilya Shekurov
Copywriter
Vladimir Zhidkov
Designer
Sonya Chirta, Kiryll Golyshev
Production Company
Nile Studio
Photographer
Vera Shvartzer
Illustrator
Victor Melamed
Url
http://kino.mtv.ru

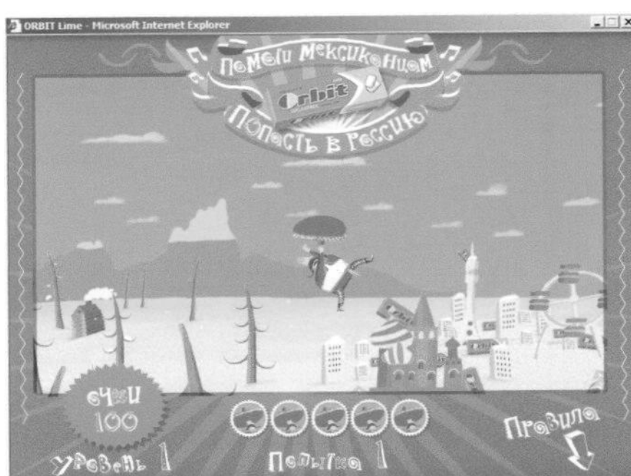

Help Mexicans to get to Russia
Russia

National Award
Silver
Agency
BBDO Interactive
Client
Wrigley
Art Director
Paul Solovyev
Copywriter
Elena Zaritovskaya
Designer
Ilya Ovchinnikov
Photographer
Sergey Burtsev
Illustrator
Vladimir Danilov
Url
www.orbitlime.ru/game/lime.html

iam studios
Spain

National Award
Silver
Agency
Fat-Man Colectivo SL / Fat-Bitch
Client
iam studios
Creative Director
David Okuniev
Art Director
Andrés Felipe Hernandez, David Okuniev
Copywriter
Barnier Geerling
Designer
Andrés Felipe Hernandez, David Okuniev, Iván Alviar
Production company
Fat-Man Colectivo SL / Fat-Bitch
Graphics
David Okuniev
Illustrator
n/a
Programmer
David Okuniev, Iván Alviar
Url
www.iam-studios.nl

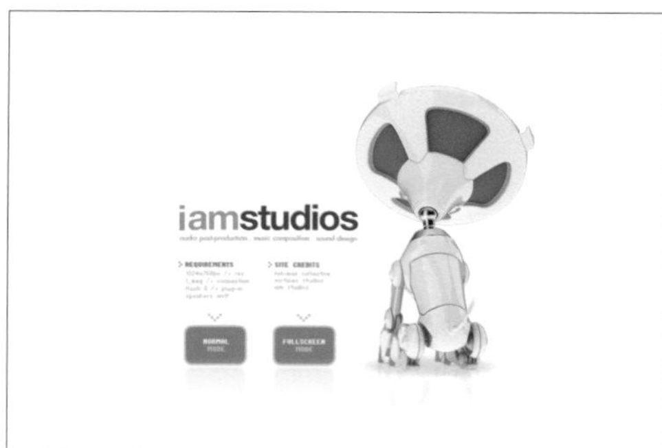

Nuevo Renault Mégane - Recupera El Control
Spain

National Award
Gold
Agency
Orbital Grupo de comunicación, S.L.
Client
Renault
Creative Director
Eduardo De La Herrán
Art Director
Miguel Ángel Salcedo, Alicia Manero
Copywriter
Dan Manasés Perales, Munia Bilbao
Designer
Javier González, Víctor Madueño, Fernando García
Programmer
Juan Manuel Marín, Susana Tamarit
Url
www.nuevomegane.com/en

iam studios
Investigation into a new logo produced. Hybrid Flash site with extensive use of 3D, for a music production company in Holland.

Nuevo Renault Mégane
"Regain Control". Inhabitants of Little Village have lost their heads and the control of their lives. Through the site of New Renault Mégane, the user interacts with the inhabitants in a film and helps them regain control while discovering the car equipment.

Ovip Lokos
The site was launched to grant every one of our consumers instant access to the virtual world of Ovip Lokos. Travel into a world where our products live and breathe and where every zone is full of hidden ways. Every step is a discovery and every click reveals the Ovip Lokos philosophy – that is our goal. So that everyone can see that Ovip Lokos stands for freedom of individuality and creativity itself; it is shown through the unique art-direction style and music...

Dexter
"Dexter" is the first Russian air taxi. It carries out express flights to a distance up to 800 km between any Russian cities having working airports. Dexter has a proprietary repair and maintenance depot it Bykovo airport, Moscow. Its project general investors are "Industrial Investors" group (www.prominvestors.com) and "Kaskol" aerospace holding (www.kaskol.ru), which have undertaken a number of major transport and infrastructure projects in the state.

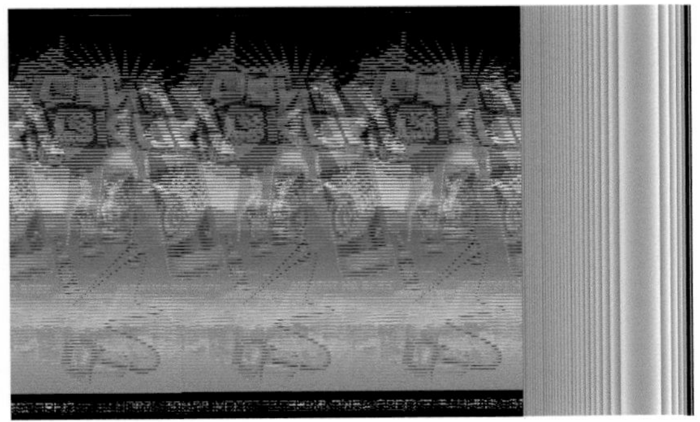

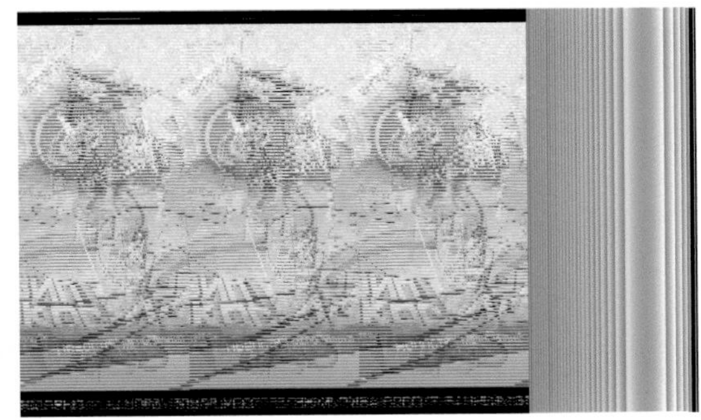

Ovip Lokos
Russia

National Award
Silver
Agency
Rodnaya Rech
Client
EFES
Creative Director
Ilya Olenev
Art Director
Julia Chernyshova
Copywriter
Valentin Vlasov
Url
www.oviplokos.ru

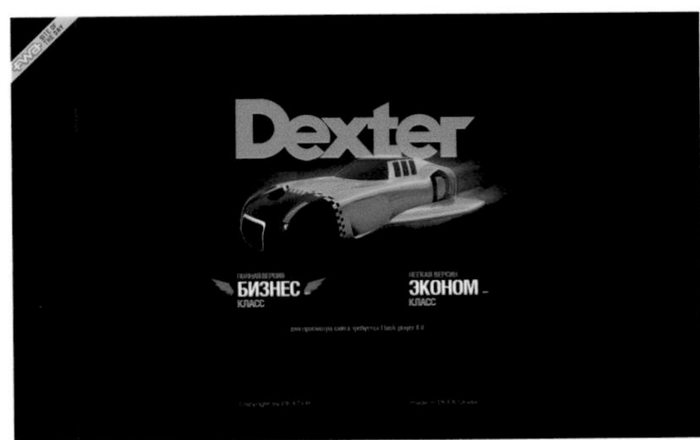

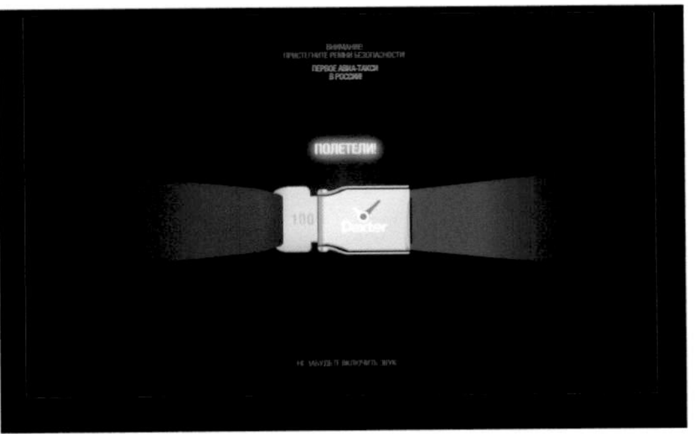

Dexter
Russia

National Award
Gold
Agency
DEFA Studie
Client
Dexter
Art Director
Grisha Sorokin
Designer
Igor Dolgov,
Michail Konovalov,
Vladimir Vashnev,
Ivan Yashukov,
Timur Gubaydullin
Agency Producer
Alexey Glazkov
Url
www.dexter.ru

www's
Spain

National Award
Silver
Agency
minnim
Client
women's secret
Creative Director
Andreu Colomer,
Sergi Mula, Carles Sanz
Art Director
Andreu Colomer,
Sergi Mula
Copywriter
Andreu Colomer
Designer
Andreu Colomer,
Sergi Mula
Graphics
Andreu Colomer,
Sergi Mula
Programmer
Javier Álvarez
Url
www.minnim.tv/
festivales/wwws
Other
Music: Sergi Mula

Friendly Fire
Austria

National Award
Gold
Agency
Friendly Fire
Client
Friendly Fire
Creative Director
Thomas Schmid,
Roman Saravia
Art Director
Norbert Horvath,
Roman Saravia
Copywriter
Thomas Schmid,
Klaus Fekesa
Designer
Manuel Godetz, Hannes
Kosina, Martin Stegmayer
Graphics
Manuel Godetz, Hannes
Kosina, Martin Stegmayer
Illustrator
Roman Saravia, Manuel
Godetz, Hannes Kosina
Programmer
Peter Rieder
Url
www.friendlyfire.at

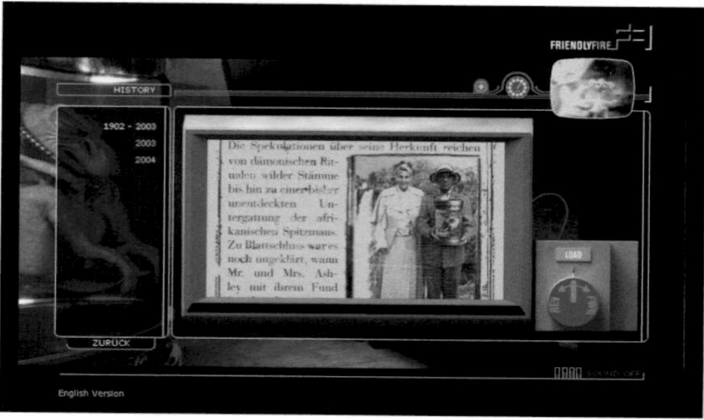

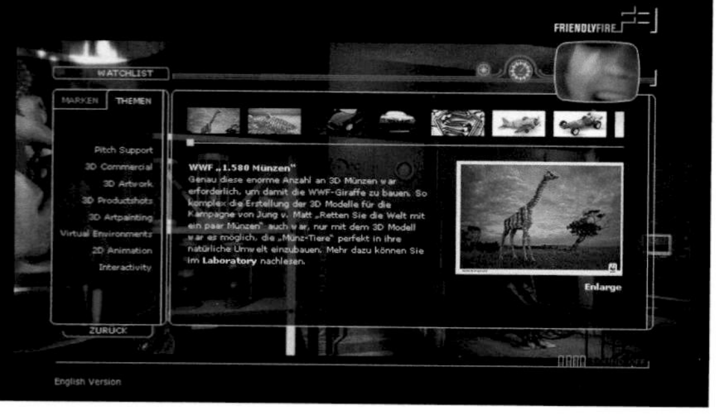

www's
"www's : world wide women's secret". Women's secret new website, where to move around, you have to be as lightweight as the air: that is the only way you will be able to find our new sensations.

Friendly Fire
A journey to the dark and mysterious cellars of Friendly Fire Homepage. In the centre of the homepage there is the beast. It symbolizes the complexity of Friendly Fire: All the questions, doubts, dreams and visions.

Trucco
Autumn-Winter 06-07
In order to design a site that is a mixture of textures and styles characteristic of a painting, Trucco's new collection was put in the context of a simulated space that welcomes the users as if they were in a warm and comfortable old country house.

SeCond Nature
Tying your shoes, riding a bike, dancing, writing… Life is full of actions that we perform without thinking; behaviour acquired that have been naturally internalised. Using a Nokia is just another example.

Trucco Autumn-Winter 06-07
Spain

National Award
Silver
Agency
Wysiwyg Comunicación Interactiva
Client
Trucco
Creative Director
Marga Castaño, Nuria Martínez
Art Director
Pablo García
Copywriter
Elena Baños
Programmer
Carlos Martínez, Ricardo Sánchez
Url
www.wysiwyg.net/fest07/laus/trucco/
Other
Planner: Patricia Cavada

SeCond Nature
Spain

National Award
Silver
Agency
Wysiwyg Comunicación Interactiva
Client
Nokia España
Creative Director
Marga Castaño, Nuria Martínez
Art Director
Pablo García, Kike Besada
Copywriter
Elena Baños
Programmer
Carlos Martínez, Ricardo Sánchez
Url
www.wysiwyg.net/fest07/oneshow/nokia/
Other
Planner: Patricia Cavada

Juicymania
Russia

National Award
Silver
Agency
BBDO Interactive
Client
Wrigley
Art Director
Paul Solovyev
Designer
Ilya Ovchinnikov
Photographer
Sergey Burtsev
Illustrator
Vladimir Danilov

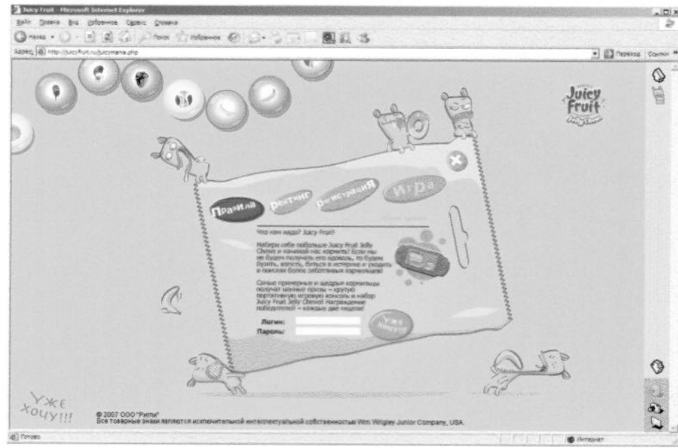

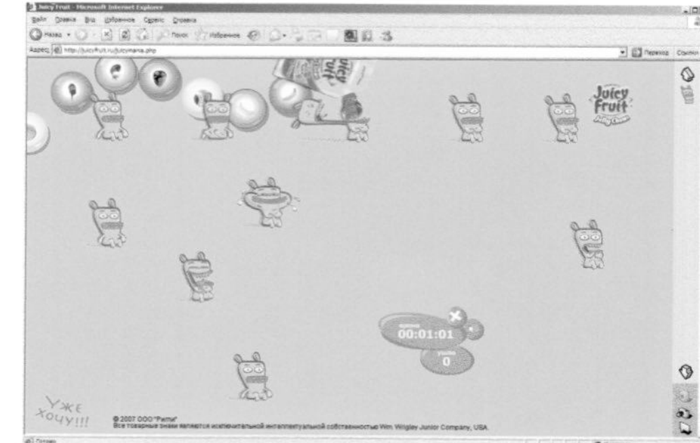

Mobile payment
Tired of wasting time on mobile phone payments? Just take a coin. Now your cellphone is able to pay for itself. It's really simple and easy to use!

Juicymania
To attract our users to the product a charismatic hooligan was produced - onscreen tamagochi, a real Juicy Fruit addict. And then he becomes the centre of two online activities: JuicyMania game and a screenmate. "You will love to play. Pick a bunch of a JF packs and feed a yellowhead! Just be generous and you'll be rewarded with a real Sony PSP. But if you lose five "Y"s you'll be damned for sure!"

50
Пополняйте счет прямо с мобильного телефона!

Mobile payment
Russia

National Award
Gold
Agency
BBDO Interactive
Client
Vympelcom
Art Director
Paul Solovyev
Designer
Dmitriy Krasnikov
Illustrator
Vladimir Danilov

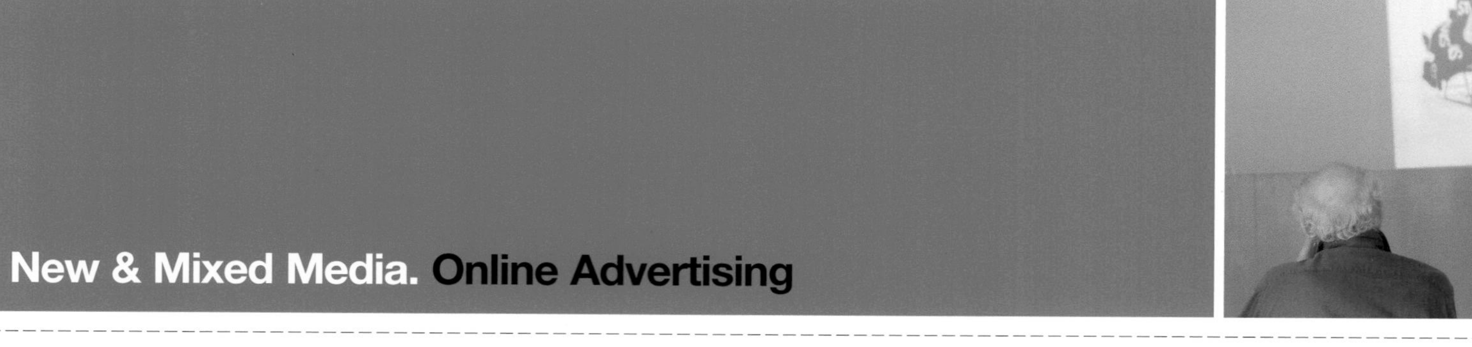

New & Mixed Media. Online Advertising

Czech Republic

Poland: Gold 1 Nomination

Germany: 2 Nominations

Austria

Ireland

Portugal

Italy

Gold
Aids Search Engine Protection

(In DVD)
Poland

National Award
Gold
Agency
ARC Warsaw
Leo Burnett Group
Client
National Aids Centre
Creative Director
Rafal Górski
Art Director
Adam Smereczynski,
Konrad Grzegorzewicz,
Rafal Górski
Copywriter
Rafal Górski
Designer
Rafal Górski
Url
www.arcww.com.pl/
searchengine

AIDS search engine protection
http://www.arcww.com.pl/searchengine/sex_results.html
Inquisitor
AIDS search engine protect...
Homepage
Help | Send to a friend
WWW | Images | News | Video | Encyclopedia | Dictionaries
netsprint
sex
10
Search
Advanced Search
Preferences
Add site i phone number | Advertise here | Find the answer. The festest.
WWW: **sex**
Search results 1 - 10 z **1200000** Family filter

Free Pic Series - Free sex Pictures Hardcore and Free sex pics
WorldSex Daily Updated Free Links to sex Pictures, Movies, Free Porn Videos sex links and XXX Live sex Cams.
sex-randka.com cached - similar pages

sex Links To Quality Adult Sites Free porno pictures
sex-zakupy.pl

sex Shop(sex-Shop) RED LIGHT
Hard Quickie sex Pictures Of A Couple Making Love. sex Party porn pictures sites by a complete smut pervert iust for you. Massive titted mommy Harley Rain in hot interracial Two guys fuck blonde original sex com is one of the oldest and baddest porno sites ...
redlight.abc24.pl

Amateur Community: Blowjob sex Voyeur
Oral sex Game How To: In this sexy minigame you have to click the arrows to ... Oral sex Game game is copyrighted or trademarked by its respective owner or ...
erotex.pl

Angelina Jolie and Brad Pitt rough sex and facial
Angelina Jolie and Brad Pitt rough **sex** and facial cumshot on stolen sex tape orrent torrent.
sex-city.pl

sex Shop(sex-Shop) RED LIGHT
Hard Quickie sex Pictures Of A Couple Making Love. sex Party porn pictures sites by a complete smut pervert iust for you. Massive titted mommy Harley Rain in hot interracial Two guys fuck blonde original sex com is one of the oldest and baddest porno sites ...
redlight.abc24.pl

Advertisement Add box
before you enter
AIDS
aids - don't give it a chance

EroPowerLINK – LinkERO
Get hundreds erotic links for free! Amazing library of free videos!!
www.eropowerlink.pl

How to enlarge your penis?
It can be even twice bigger! Don't believe in it? Click here.
www.magna-rx.pl

Page 1 - 2 - 3 - 4 - 5 - 6 - 7 - 8 - 9 - 10 Next

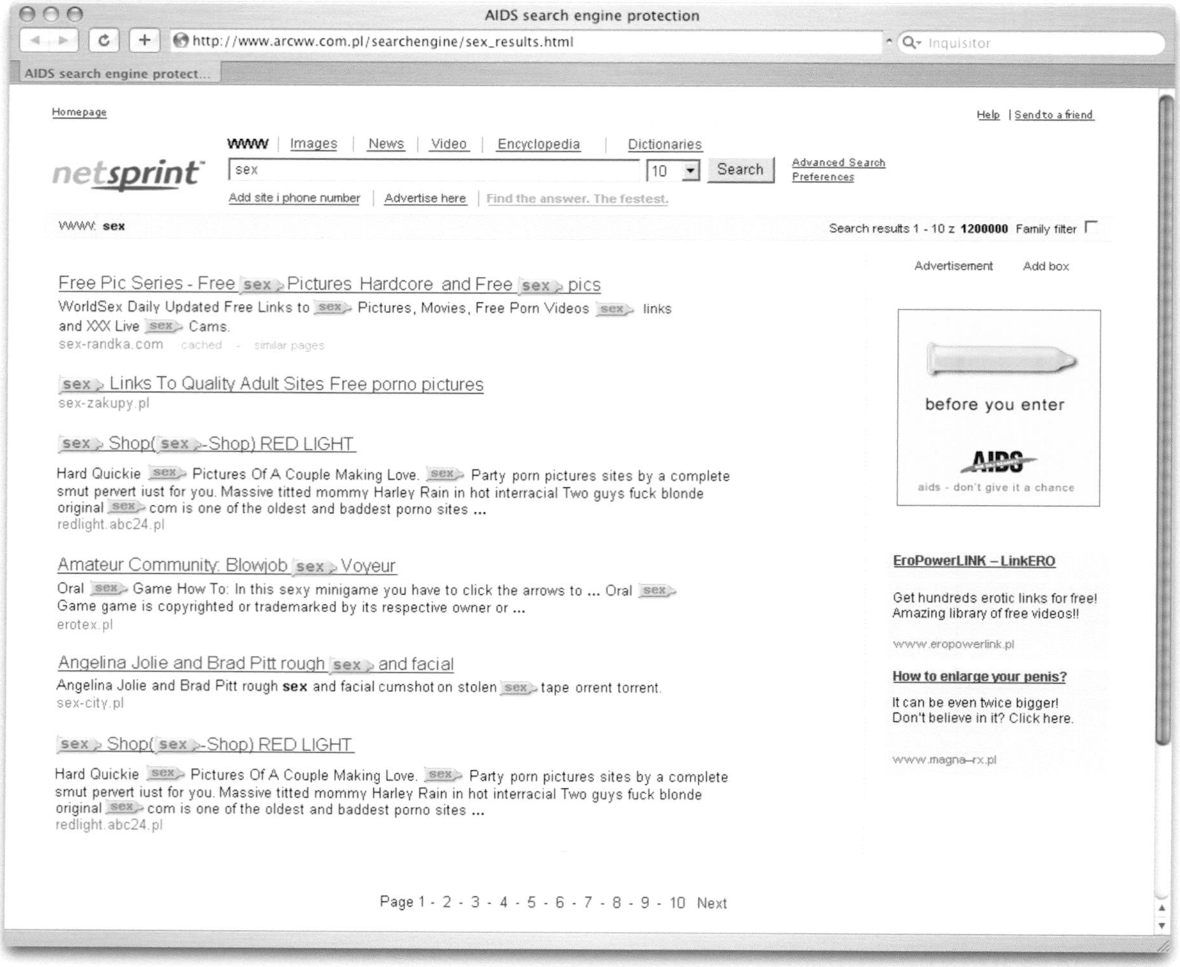

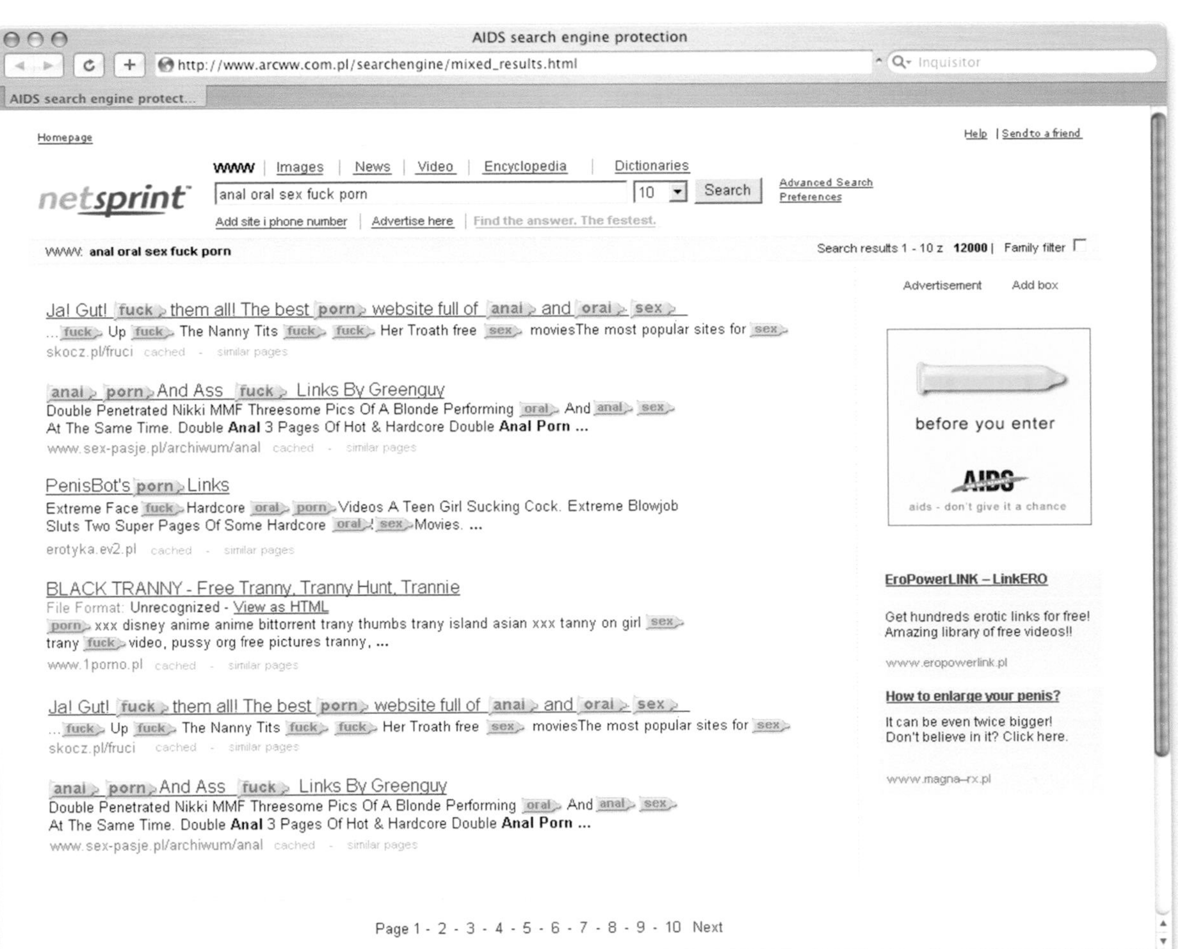

Campaign against AIDS. All sites with erotic content are protected. If a user of the search engine looks for "sex", "anal", "oral", "porno" or "fuck" all these words are packed in small condoms and a banner "Before you enter" appears.

Nomination
Search errors
(In DVD)
Germany

National Award
Bronze
Agency
Kolle Rebbe Werbeagentur GmbH
Client
Bibliographisches Institut & F. A. Brockhaus AG
Creative Director
Sven Klohk, Lorenz Ritter
Art Director
Kay-Owe Tiedemann
Copywriter
Constantin Sossidi
Programmer
Tobias Boehning
Url
http://cannes.kolle-rebbe.de/duden
Other
Account manager:
Birgit Heikamp

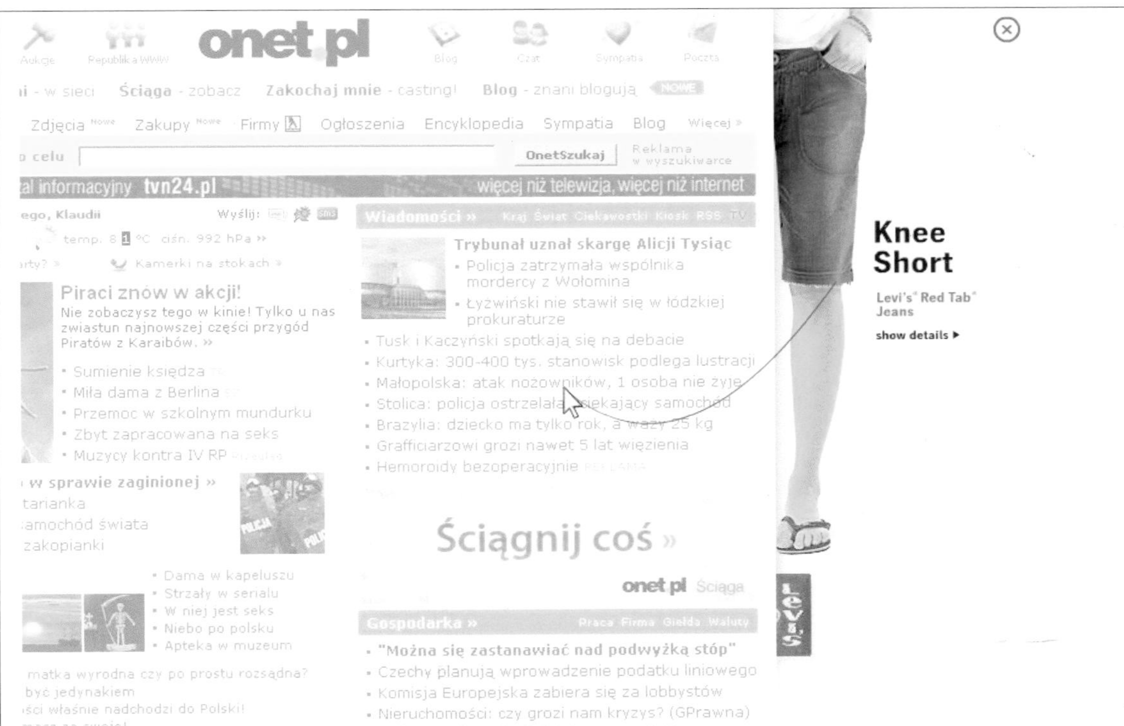

Nomination
Levi's One Thread Fits All
(In DVD)
Poland

National Award
Silver
Agency
ARC Warsaw
Leo Burnett Group
Client
Levi's Poland
Creative Director
Rafal Górski
Art Director
Adam Smereczynski,
Rafal Górski
Copywriter
Rafal Górski
Designer
Adam Smereczynski,
Konrad Grzegorzewicz,
Rafal Górski
Url
www.arcww.com.pl/levis_thread
Other
Flash Developer:
Konrad Grzegorzewicz

Search errors
The brief was to promote the new edition of the Duden, the official reference guide to the German language, using a low-cost online campaign. Google was chosen as the ideal medium, as it checks 280 million searches for spelling mistakes every day. If search terms are spelt incorrectly, Google asks "Did you mean…?" The perfect place for the advertisement! We adopted our own version of this Google function using Google AdWords. This involves linking search terms with advertisements, which then appear with the search results. We registered our ads with the most common spelling mistakes, thus imitating the Google spelling function. Now, if the user types "bicycel", the following message appears: Did you mean: bicycle? www.duden.de/rechtschreibung. Did you spell bicycle incorrectly? Duden - the official guide to German spelling.

Levi's - One Thread Fits All
A banner presenting the freshest models of Levi's Girls Bottoms. Move the mouse to the left, pull the thread and rip the jeans.

Nomination
WDCS life size whale
(In DVD)
Germany

National Award
Shortlist
Agency
Jung von Matt AG
Client
WDCS Deutschland
Creative Director
Jan Rexhausen, Doerte Spengler-Ahrens
Art Director
Pablo Schencke
Copywriter
Sergio Penzo
Designer
Sound Designer: Hastings Hamburg
Production company
Animation: www.soulpix.de
Graphics
Philip Bartsch
Programmer
Benjamin Herholz
Url
http://award.jvm.de/wdcs/index_en.php
Other
Webproducer: Sven Loskill
Account Manager: Nic Heimann, Matthias Lauten

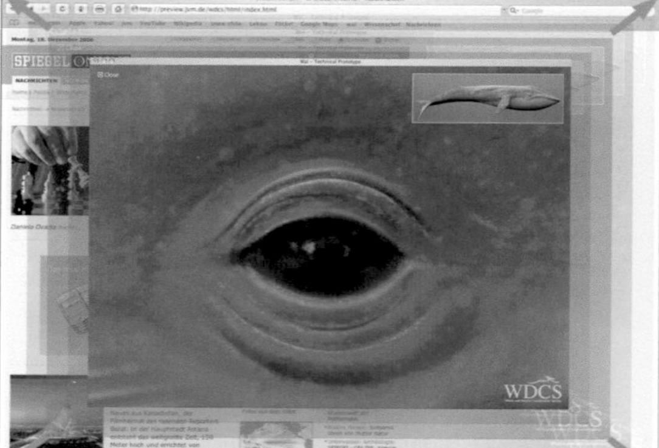

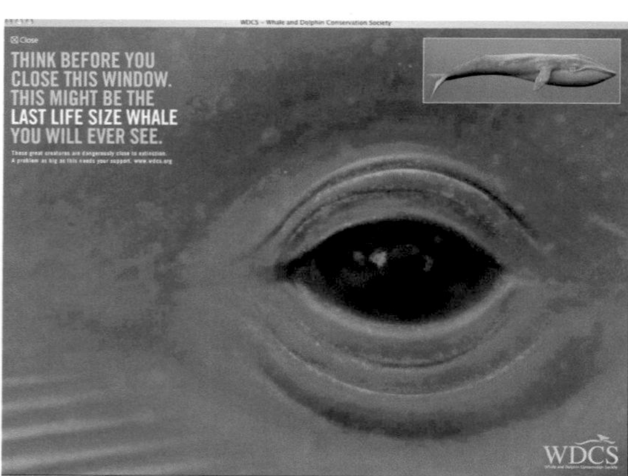

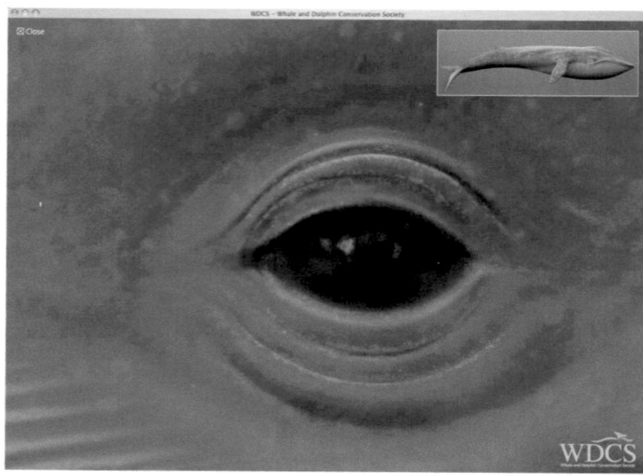

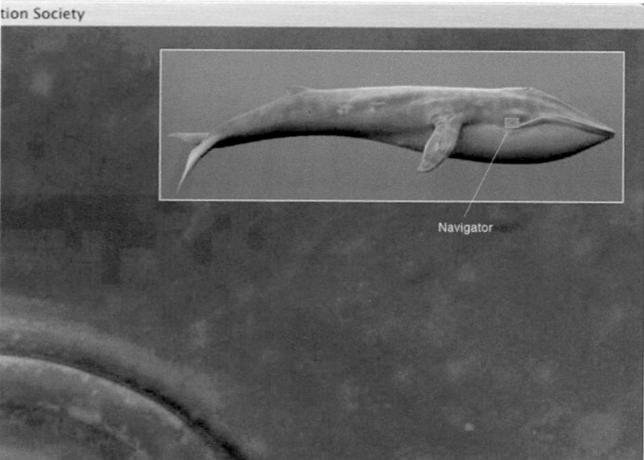

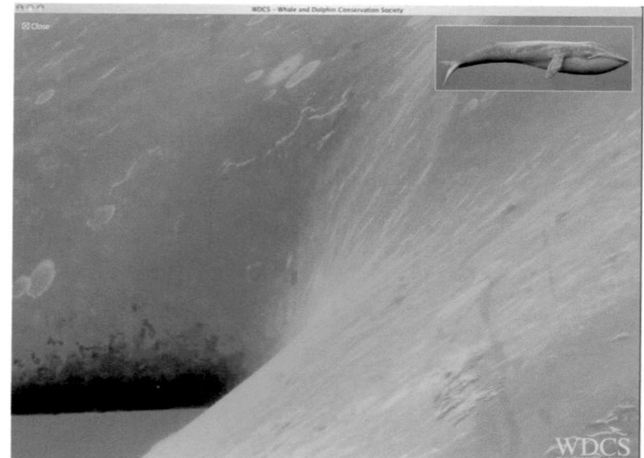

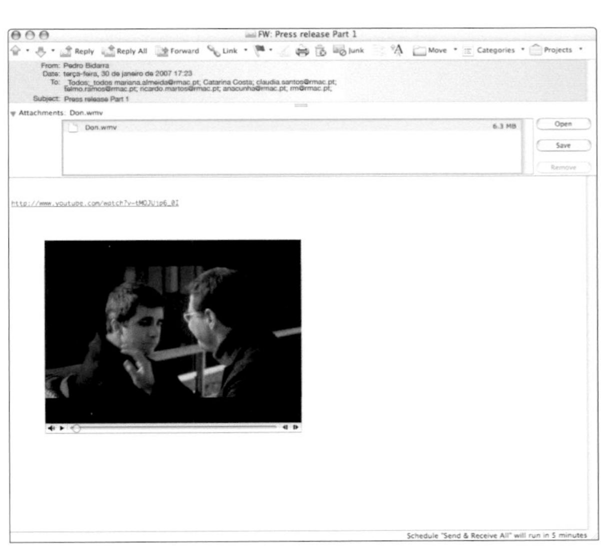

FW: Part 2

From: Pedro Bidarra
Date: terça-feira, 30 de janeiro de 2007 17:31
To: _Todos;_todos mariana.almeida@rmac.pt; Catarina Costa; claudia.santos@rmac.pt; telmo.ramos@rmac.pt; ricardo.martos@rmac.pt; anacunha@rmac.pt; rm@rmac.pt; Mafalda.rocha@olhoazul.com; cnunes@mailexpresso.pt; lcrespo@mediafiln.pt; cbrito@economicasgps.com; romarques@meiosepublicidade.workmedia.pt; cbferreira@meiosepublicidade.workmedia.pt; btrindade@mce.iol.pt
Subject: Press release Part 2

I know that, after seeing the film, everyone was left with a puzzling question - that I'll answer at the end of this mail.
First and foremost let's get down to brass tacks: Nuno Jeronimo.
February 5 was the official start of a situation that actually commenced when the New BBDO was relaunched: Nuno Jerónimo, aka Don Jerónimo, is officially the new director of creative department.
We're all familiar with Nuno's curriculum. A footballer, excelling in mental agility and a sense of humour - two absolutely unnecessary ingredients for practise of the sport - Jerónimo decided to abandon a career that would undoubtedly have taken him to Leiria, Faro or even Chaves if it hadn't been for his mother who said peremptorily "Footer - you must be nuts".
So the young Nuno, after completing his studies (which he did successfully) at the Universidade Nova in Lisbon, and having spent brief stints in two small agencies - Ogilvy and Publicis - arrived at agency in 2000.
Seven years later, he knows the agency and its clients like the back of his hand, but above all he understands, better than anyone, our quality threshold. He was the one of the key creatives involved in works such as "Less Sighs" for GALP, "Woody Allen" for Público, and countless campaigns for BES "If you haven't got rich parents ..." amongst others.
As a result, 7 years later, in return for his dedication and in order to ensure that our quality threshold continues to rise, Nuno is being naturally rewarded with the task of managing the agency's creative department - that has been elected Agency of the Year on five occasions over the last decade.
A task that I'm thereby liberated from, enabling me to dedicate more time and energy to the Group's Total Work and for any projects where Nuno considers I can provide a valuable contribution.
And now the question lingering in everyone's mind.
Who's Barzini?
The answer is far from simple, because Barzinis aren't exactly few and far between...

Pedro Bidarra (consiglieri)

P.S.: Nuno Jerónimo's first task will be to leave our offices for a month, on a tour around the best agencies in the world. Only afterwards will he be available for formal presentations to clients and press interviews. If you have any doubts in the meantime or would like to send him a message:
nuno.jeronimo@bbdo.pt

Godfather
Portugal

National Award
Silver
Agency
BBDO Portugal
Client
BBDO Portugal
Creative Director
Pedro Bidarra
Copywriter
Pedro Bidarra,
Nuno Jerônimo

WDCS life size whale, the biggest internet banner in the world
"To draw attention to the whale's dramatic struggle for survival, the world's biggest Internet banner was created: a life-size whale – 16 by 5 meters! Text: "Think before you close this window. This might be the last life size whale you ever see". It's a new dimension of online-marketing, an international organization called WDCS – the Whale and Dolphin Conservation Society."

Godfather
There was about to be a transfer of leadership in BBDO's creative department and it was necessary to communicate this fact to the entire advertising market in a surprising manner. Send a small, intriguing film via e-mail.

Cursor Costume
The fancy dress shop Kostümverleih Kostümwerkstätte is one of the biggest costume-making workshops in Austria. It has a suitable costume for everyone - even for the cursor hand when it passes over the banner.

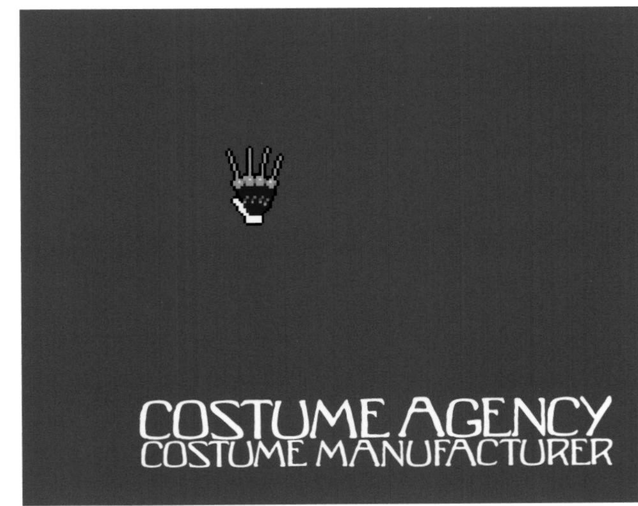

Cursor Costume
Austria

National Award
Gold
Agency
Demner, Merlicek & Bergmann
Client
Kostümverleih Kostümwerkstätte
Creative Director
Gerda Reichl-Schebesta
Art Director
Bernhard Grafl
Copywriter
Arno Reisenbüchler
Graphics
Marion Schlipfinger
Illustrator
Marion Schlipfinger
Programmer
Tim Jost
Url
www.dmb.at/einreichung/costume_agency/index

Jingle Box 500 Playable overlay
Italy

National Award
Silver
Agency
ARC/Leo Burnett
Client
Fiat Automobiles
Creative Director
R. Robiglio, P. Dematteis
Art Director
G. Musto
Copywriter
L. Marucco, R. Ramondetti, B. Berardi
Designer
P. Medda
Graphics
P. Medda, R. Agagliate, M. Righi, T. Allemand
Programmer
G. Mori, P. Faccini, M. Carrodano, E. Marquez
Url
www.fiat500.com/awards/banner/Plectrum.html
Other
Internet Creative Director: M. Righi
Music: T. Lamberti

Bobiks ending
Czech Republic

National Award
Gold
Agency
Kaspen
Client
NetCentrum
Creative Director
Lester Tullett
Art Director
Miro Minarovych, Pavel Fuksa
Copywriter
Petr Hanousek
Designer
Miro Minarovych, Pavel Fuksa
Production company
Putsch Films, Stillking Films
Graphics
Krystal Creative, Abdelar Smokvoj, Premek Ponahly
Programmer
WDF
Url
www.centrum.cz

Jingle Box 500
Playable overlay
"500 wants you"
Interactive overlays promote the Jingle Box 500 minisite.

Bobiks ending
"Centrum. A place too lively for some". This on line campaign for a big CZ portal uses a TV commercial of a popular character being killed, but ends before the action. It tells people to see the ending on the portal, where the story ends in 30 different twisted and surprising ways.

Sperm dodge
Use your mouse to move the egg to try and dodge the sperm. You have 350,000,000 chances of getting pregnant after unprotected sex.

Christmas Card for Genetix Sound Studio
A Christmas card for Genetix, a sound design/recording studio. Users receive email containing a Christmas tree made from someone's voice recording. Then user can record their own voice to make a Christmas tree card and add to a gallery of trees.

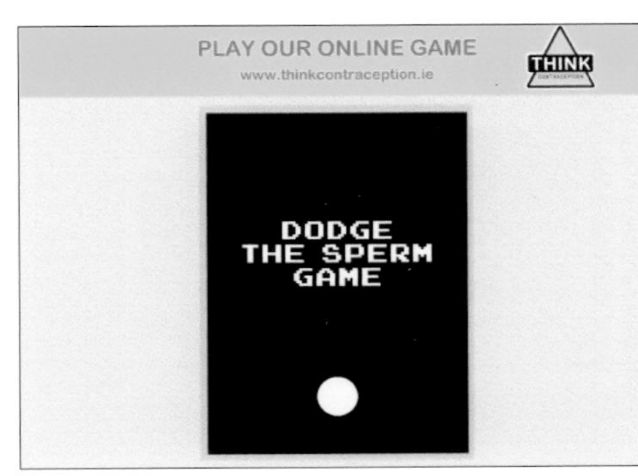

Sperm dodge
Ireland

National Award
Silver
Agency
Leo Burnett, Dublin, Ireland
Client
Crisis Pregnancy Agency
Creative Director
John Flynn
Art Director
Stephen Rodgers
Copywriter
Dara Daly

Christmas Card for Genetix Sound Studio
Poland

National Award
Silver
Agency
Leo Burnett Warsaw
Client
Genetix
Creative Director
Martin Winther, Rafal Gorski (Arc Warsaw)
Art Director
Leszek Ziniewicz, Adam Smereczynski (Arc Warsaw)
Copywriter
Konrad Grzegorzewicz (Arc Warsaw)
Designer
Konrad Grzegorzewicz (Arc Warsaw)
Production company
Leo Burnett Warsaw

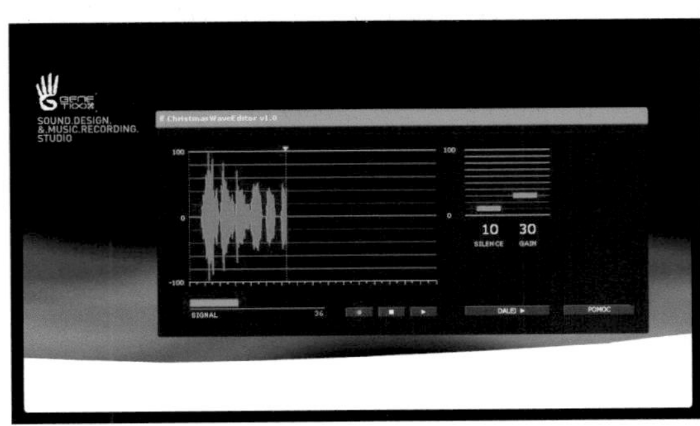

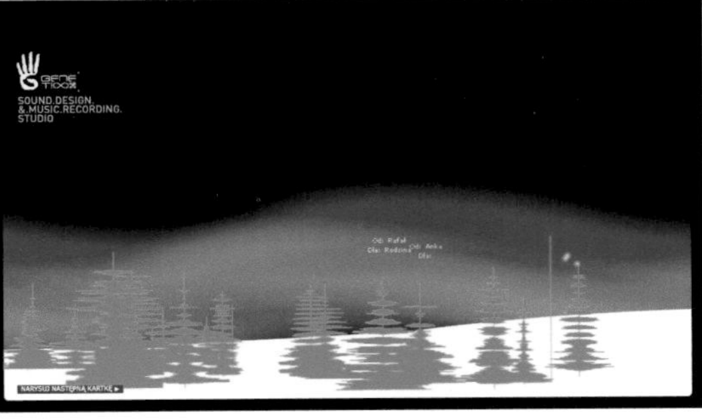

Def Mini Records
Germany

National Award
Silver
Agency
Interone Worldwide / .start GmbH
Client
BMW AG
Creative Director
Marco Mehrwald, Shin Oh, Andreas Teigeler
Copywriter
G. Immisch, U. Dreyheller, B. Pfarr, N. Treutlein
Designer
Michael Fuesslin
Production company
Florian Seidel, Christian Belej
Graphics
Verena Janzik, Kathrin Flake
Programmer
Klaus Neher, Florian Schleuppner
Url
www.4thejury.com/sites/interone/projects/mini/defMINIrecords

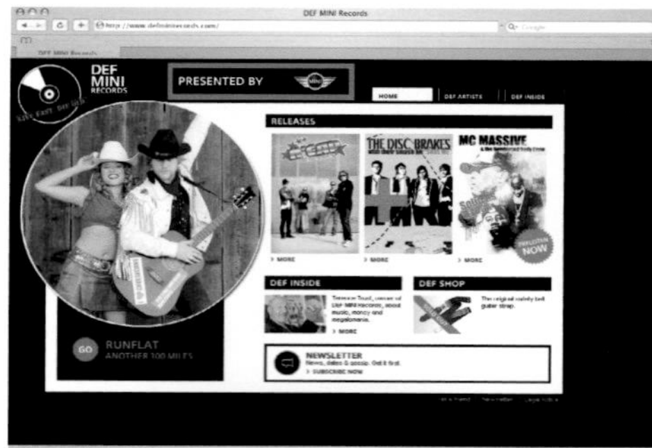

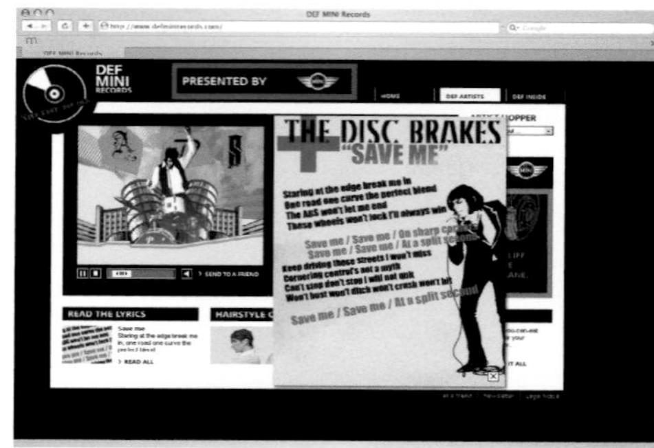

Def Mini Records
An integrated campaign to promote the MINI safety topics (Runflat tyres, excellent NCAP crash test ratings): DEF MINI Records. It's all about safety. THE DISC BRAKES sing "Save me", RUNFLAT perform "Another 100 miles" and NCAP "Save me".

Time to fight back
"Easydriver car insurance". There's a way to get a double win: first by playing, with the extreme and innovative creativity of the banner; second, obviously by picking up on the suggestion to switch to Easydriver.

Cisco boooming
Call a website,shout.

Enel Ambient
The true revolution is not to change the world.

Cisco boooming
Germany

National Award
Gold
Agency
OgilvyOne world wide GmbH
Client
Cisco Germany
Creative Director
Michael Kutschinski, Ulf Schmidt
Art Director
Uwe Jakob
Copywriter
Ulf Schmidt
Designer
Serena Stoerlein, Nicole Holzenkamp
Url
www.ourwork.de/cisco/boooming
Other
Sound Sinus AV Studio

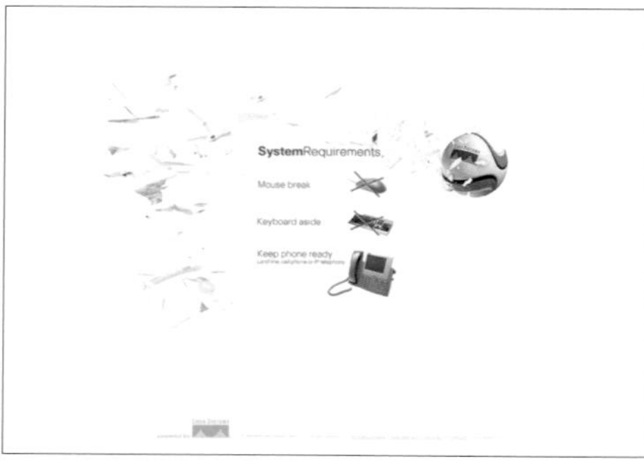

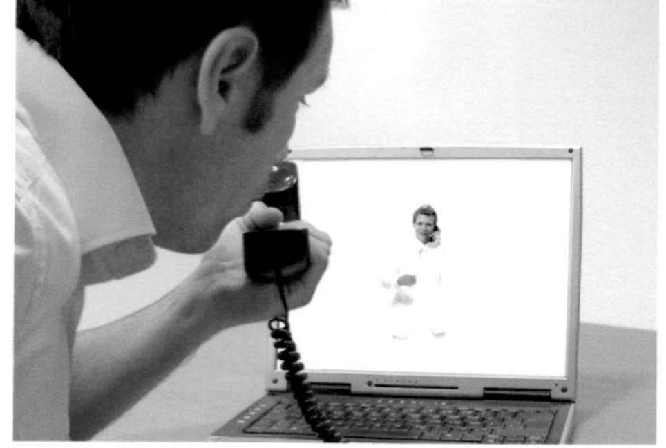

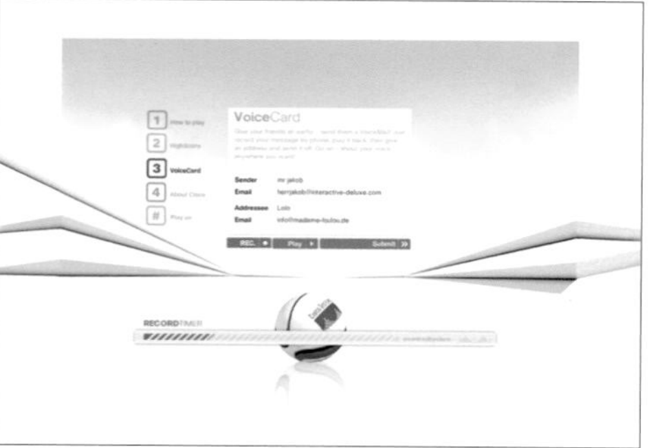

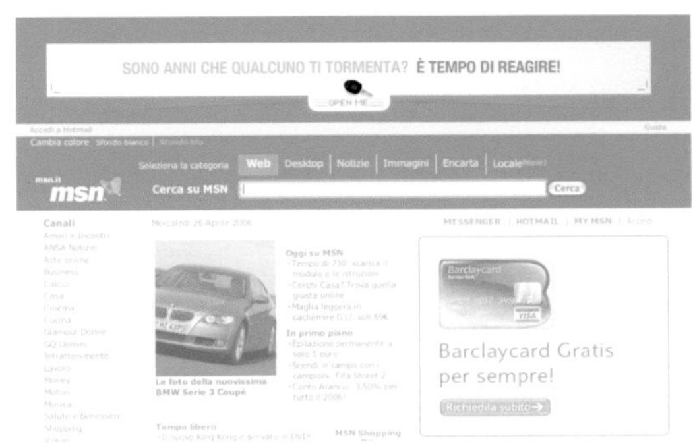

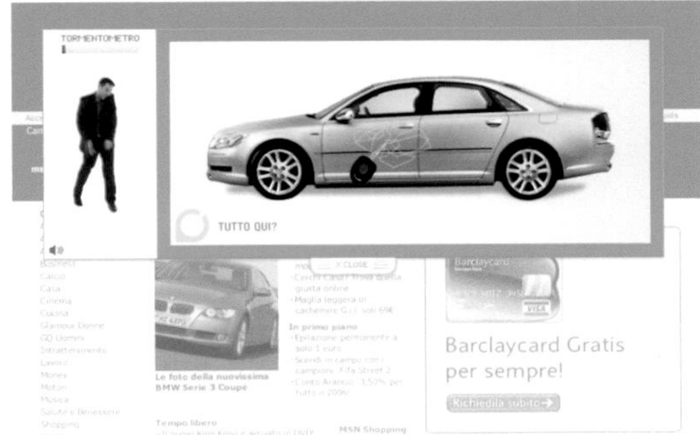

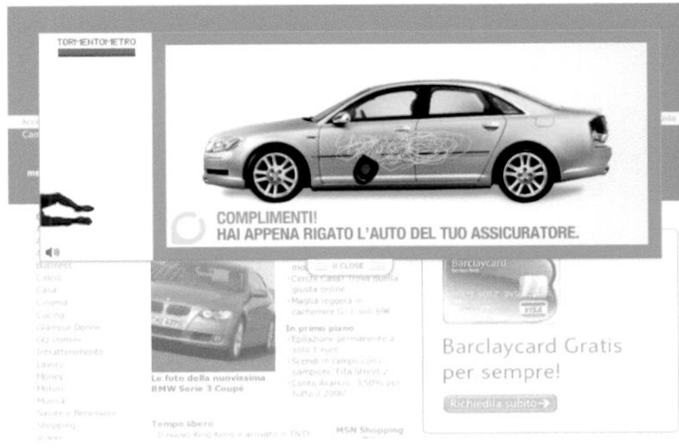

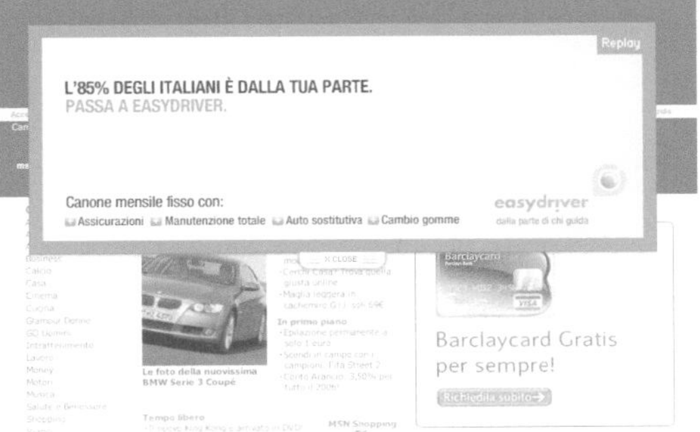

Time to fight back

Italy

National Award
Gold
Agency
FullSIX
Client
Easydriver
Creative Director
Simonetta De Brumatti
Art Director
Giuseppe Bizzarro
Copywriter
Luca Comino
Programmer
Piero Orlandi
Other
Post Production Programmer:
Cow and Boys

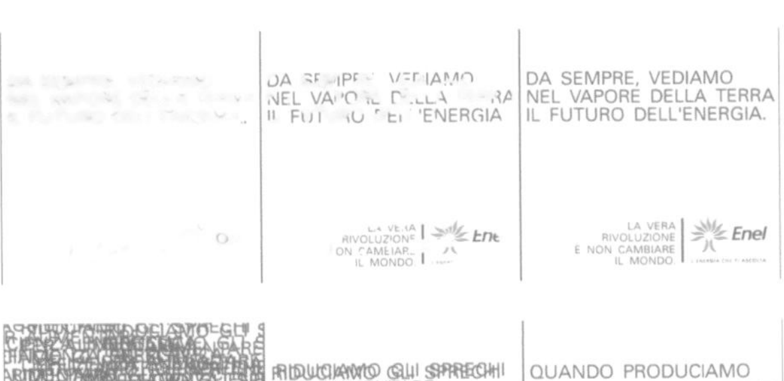

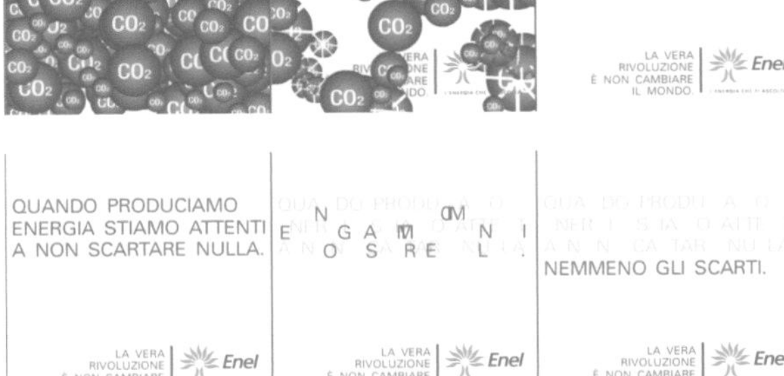

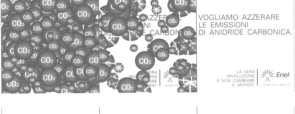

Enel Ambient

Italy

National Award
Silver
Agency
Saatchi & Saatchi
Client
Enel
Creative Director
Alessandro Orlandi
Art Director
Gianluigi Bellini
Copywriter
Laura Sordi
Designer
Gianluigi Bellini
Url
www.vision.saatchi-saatchi.it/work/onlineadv/enelAmbiente/

Austria

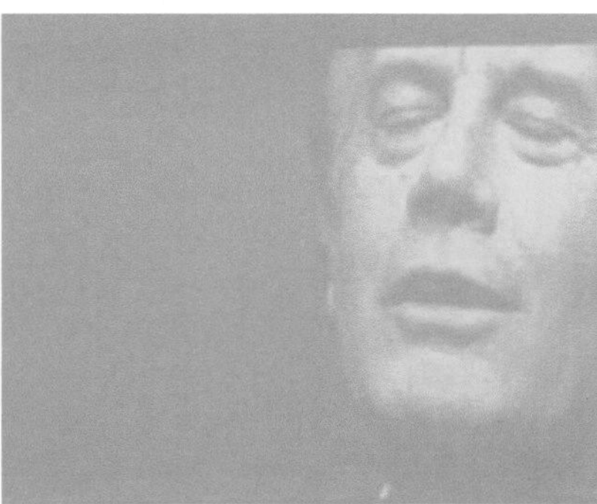

Germany: ★ Grand Prix 1 Nomination

Czech Republic

Ireland

Italy: 1 Nomination

Latvia

Russia

Switzerland: 1 Nomination

Grand Prix

The Make-Believe Story of Ron Hammer

(In DVD)
Germany

National Award
Gold
Agency
Heimat, Berlin
Client
Hornbach AG
Creative Director
Guido Heffels, Juergen Vossen
Art Director
Tim Schneider
Copywriter
Till Eckel
Designer
Jan Wentz, Michael Mackens, Proximity Germany GmbH
Film Director
Jan Wentz
Director of photography
Jo Molitoris
Agency Producer
Kerstin Breuer
Production Company
Markenfilm Berlin / Treibstoff Pictures
Post production
nhb Berlin / Niko Papoutsis
Graphics
Sound Design: Nima Gholiagha, nhb Berlin
Web Producer
Proximity Germany GmbH
Other
Executive Producer: Lutz Müller / Editor: Piet Schmelz Account Management: Yves Krämer, Mark Hassan, Sammy

The Legend of Ron Hammer. In the run up to a V.A.T. increase, the job was to communicate to D.I.Y. enthusiasts the size of Hornbach Superstores. So we used a yet unknown motorbike stuntman to communicate the size of Hornbach by letting him try to jump over one. An amateur video captured the crash. Usually a campaign like that ends here but this was where the RON HAMMER campaign started to take off. Step by step the media, both on and offline were brought on board to increase the credibility and, gradually, even the non-believers became believers.

Nomination
Def Mini Records
(In DVD)
Germany

National Award
Bronze
Agency
Interone Worldwide / Start GmbH
Client
BMW AG
Creative Director
Marco Mehrwald, Shin Oh, Andreas Teigeler
Copywriter
G. Immisch, U. Dreyheller, B. Pfarr, N. Treutlein
Designer
Michael Fuesslin
Production company
Florian Seidel, Christian Belej
Graphics
Verena Janzik, Kathrin Flake
Programmer
Klaus Neher, Florian Schleuppner
Url
www.4thejury.com/sites/interone/projects/mini/def MINI records/index.html

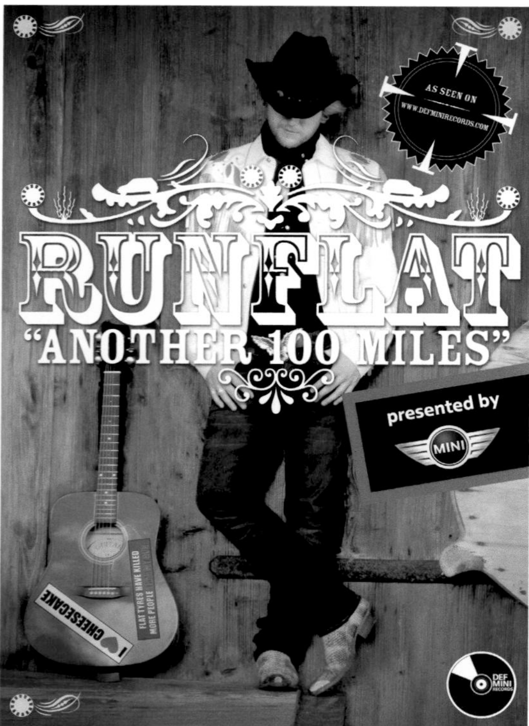

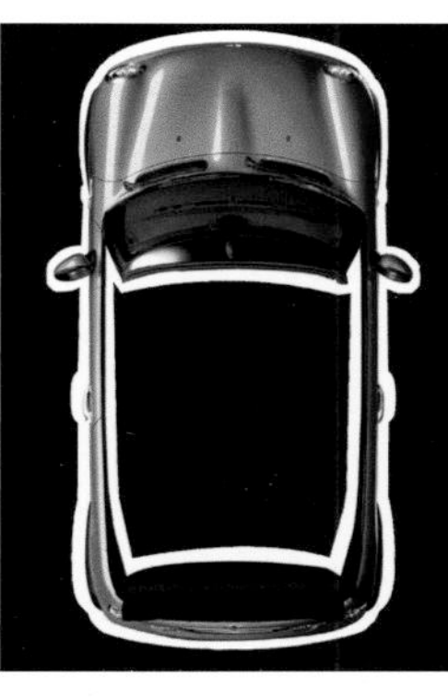

Nomination
Mini Cabrio
Italy

National Award
Gold
Agency
D'Adda Lorenzini Vigorelli BBDO
Client
Mini
Creative Director
Giuseppe Mastromatteo, Luca Scotto di Carlo
Art Director
Dario Agnello
Copywriter
Cristino Battista

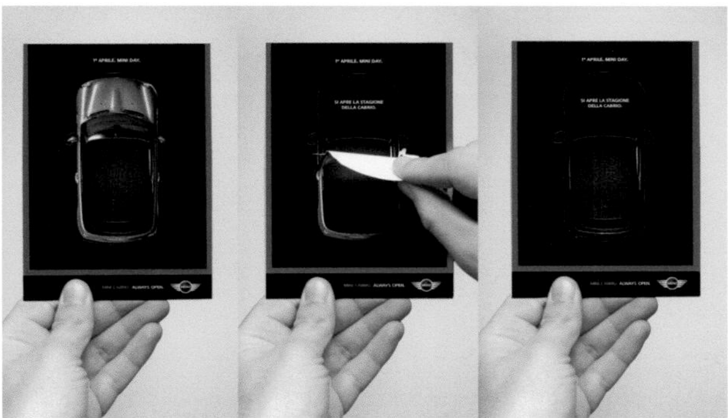

Def Mini Records
An integrated campaign to promote the MINI safety topics (Runflat tyres, excellent NCAP crash test ratings): DEF MINI Records. It's all about safety. THE DISC BRAKES sing "Save me", RUNFLAT perform "Another 100 miles" and NCAP "Save me".

Mini Cabrio
Mini Convertible "Always Open"

Nomination
Mary Woodbridge
(In DVD)
Switzerland

National Award
Gold
Agency
Spillmann/Felser/
Leo Burnett
Client
Mammut Sports Group
Creative Director
Martin Spillmann
Art Director
Raul Serrat
Copywriter
Peter Brönnimann
Graphics
Ricco Pachera
Url
www.snipurl.com/
mary_woodbridge

20 Years Lotto
Austria

National Award
Silver
Agency
Lowe GGK
Client
Österreichische Lotterien Ges.m.b.H.
Creative Director
Alexander Zelmanovics, Dieter Pivrnec
Art Director
Johannes Niedermaier
Copywriter
Nikolaus Leischko
Designer
Lisi Laggner
Production company
Sabotage Filmproduktion Ges.m.b.H.
Photographer
Stockmaterial
Other
Music: MG-Sound

Mary Woodbridge
Mary Woodbridge: a perfectly normal 85-year-old Brit who takes her dachshund Daisy for a walk every day. To protect herself against the elements, she buys herself a Mammut jacket in December of 2005. And suddenly the old lady gets an idea: she's going to climb Everest.

20 Years Lotto
Everything is possible! Lotto. 4 tv-spots, 3 free cards, 3 ads, 3 outdoor posters.

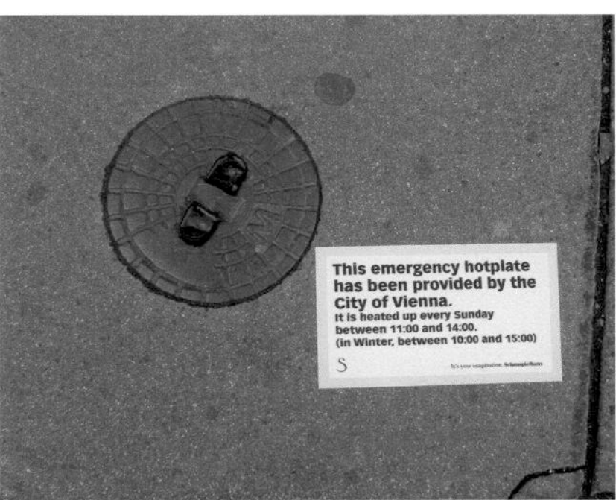

It's your imagination
Austria

National Award
Silver
Agency
Jung von Matt/Donau Werbeagentur GmbH
Client
Schauspielhaus Wien
Creative Director
Andreas Putz
Art Director
Eva Ortner
Copywriter
Andreas Putz, Valerie Gudenus
Sound
Tonstudio Holly
Photographer
Jork Weismann
Graphics
Philipp Glück
Other
Speaker: Andreas Putz

One loves Music
Austria

National Award
Gold
Agency
Jung von Matt/Donau
Werbeagentur GmbH
Client
One GmbH
Creative Director
Andreas Putz,
Christoph Gaunersdorfer
Art Director
Georg Feichtinger
Copywriter
Christoph Gaunersdorfer,
Bernd Wilfinger
Production company
Neue Sentimental Film Wien
Photographer
Maria Ziegelböck
Graphics
Max Luczynski,
Christian Begusch
Url
www.onelovesmusic.at
Other
Concept: Christian Begusch
Director: Niklas Weise

Fake Reindeer
Czech Republic

National Award
Silver
Agency
Vodafone Czech Republic,
The Farm, Mods
Client
Vodafone Czech Republic
Creative Director
Vodafone Czech Republic,
The Farm, Mods
Copywriter
Vodafone Czech Republic,
The Farm, Mods
Production company
Bistro Films, Colorbox
Photographer
Bohous Pospisil

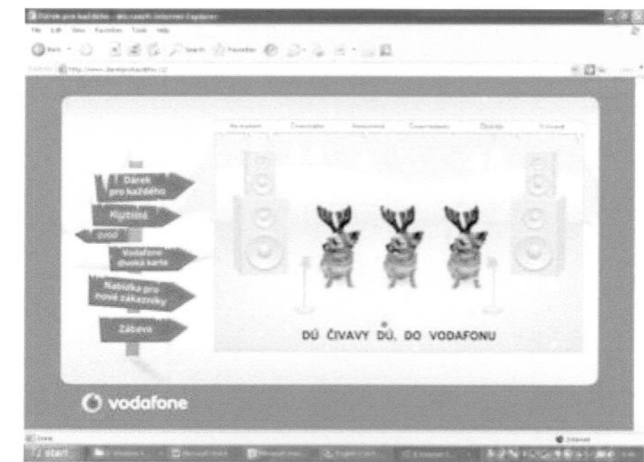

Fake Reindeer
Gifts for everyone. Vodafone offers free weekend SMS for all existing and new customers.

Dublin Coastal Development
This capitalises on Ireland's property obsession by creating a hoax property developer, who was applying for planning permission, with a viral video, a website, planning permission notices posted along the well-trod paths of Dublin Bay and in press. When they build it, it will be on Ireland's newest property website, www.Funda.ie

Head & Shoulders "White Man"
The idea here is to portray dandruff as a physical entity, an annoying guy dressed all in white who is with you wherever you go and crops up at the least appropriate moments. Dandruff spoils life, even if the carrier doesn't notice it.

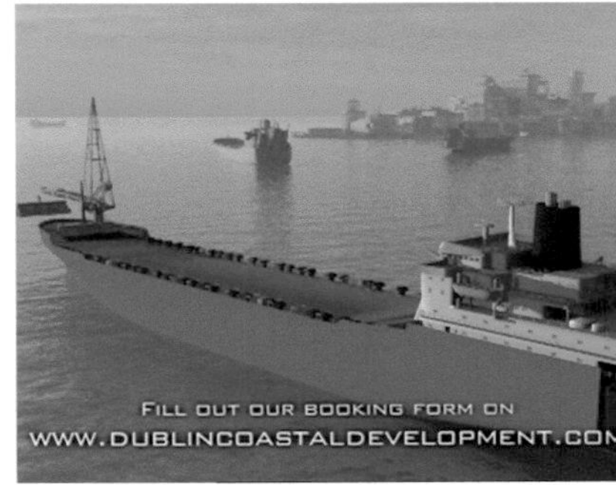

Dublin Coastal Development
Ireland

National Award
Silver
Agency
Chemistry
Client
Funda
Creative Director
Mike Garner
Art Director
Nicole Sykes
Copywriter
Anne Fleming
Production company
The Farm
Url
www.dublincoastal-development.com
Other
Concept: Fitz-Simon, Fleming, O'Beirne & Sykes

Head & Shoulders "White Man"
Russia

National Award
Gold
Agency
Saatchi & Saatchi Moscow
Client
Procter & Gamble
Creative Director
Stuart Robinson
Art Director
Yuri Polonski
Copywriter
Irina Gorshkova

Drink. Drive. Join.2
Latvia

National Award
Gold
Agency
ZOOM!
Client
Road traffic,
safety directorate
Creative Director
Eriks Stendzenieks
Art Director
Maris Upenieks
Peteris Lidaka

Close vacancies. Open opportunities
Russia

National Award
Silver
Agency
Bazina.sass+
Client
Kelly Services
Creative Director
Natalia Bazina
Art Director
Natalia Bazina
Copywriter
Svetlana Maybrodskaya
Designer
Natalia Bazina

Drink. Drive. Join.2
Drink.Drive.Join. Campaign prepares potential drink-and-drivers for life in prison. It informs how to behave in prison, what rules to obey, meaning of tatoos etc. It also shows prision life.

Close vacancies. Open opportunities
The Slogan: Development of a slogan which reflects the new positioning in a bright sentence: "Kelly Services. Close Vacancies - Open Opportunities". Creative Concept: Visualisation of personal "limits" and the opportunities. Strong focus on non-standard vehicles and ambient media (together with classical media).

Missing beef
"Missing Beef". To communicate the brand to a young public, an integrated campaign was created using unconventional media to tell the story of the search by Argentine rancher, Pedro Gomez, for his favourite bull, Alvaro, kidnapped one night by Martians.

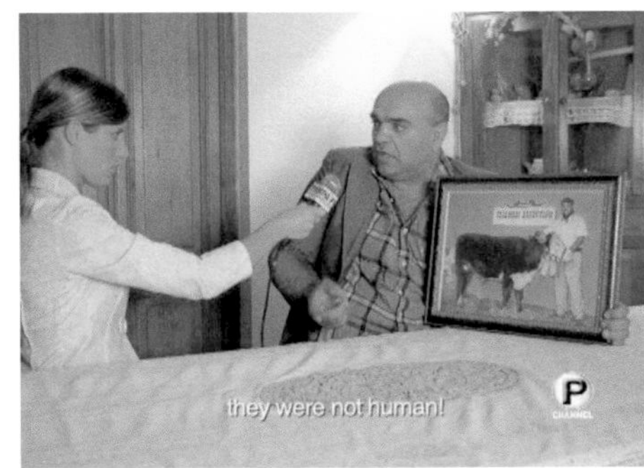

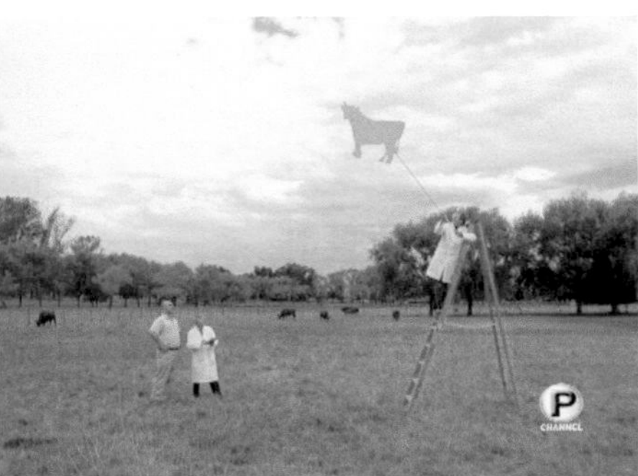

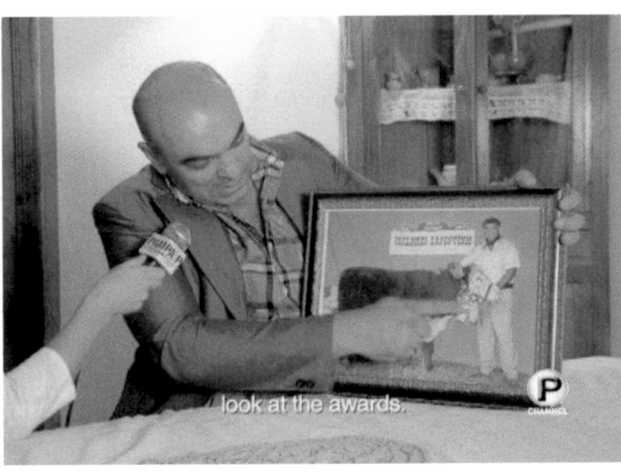

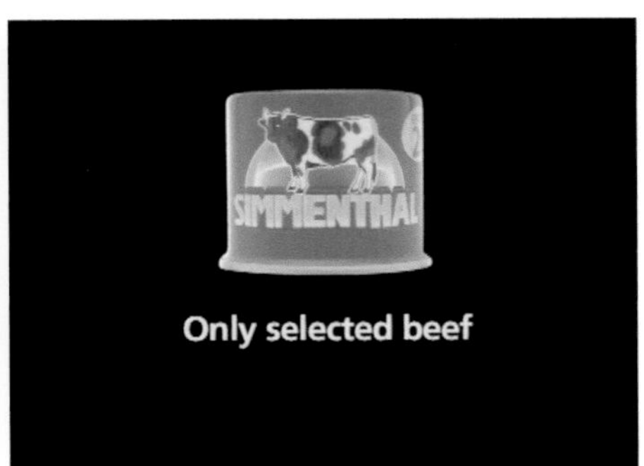

Missing beef
Italy

National Award
Silver
Agency
JWT
Client
Kraft Foods Italy
Creative Director
Pietro Maestri, Alex Brunori
Art Director
Fabio Anzani
Copywriter
Alex Brunori
Url
www.manzoscomparso.com

New & Mixed Media. Promotions and Mailings

Austria

Estonia

Ireland

Germany: 7 Nominations

Italy

Latvia

Portugal

Russia

Spain: Gold

Switzerland: 2 Nominations

Gold
San Sebastian's Film Festival Event
(In DVD)
Spain

National Award
Shortlist
Agency
Vitruvio Leo Burnett
Client
Aol. Time Warner
Creative Director
Rafa Antón
Art Director
Ricardo Sáez,
Javier Álvarez
Copywriter
Francisco Cassis,
Santiago Saiegh

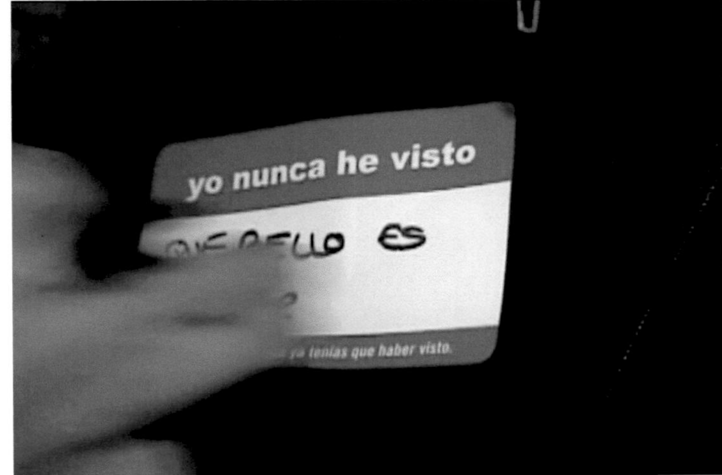

The films you should have seen by now.

Nomination
Bowling lane
Germany

National Award
Shortlist
Agency
Jung von Matt AG
Client
KarstadtQuelle Insurance
Creative Director
Deneke von Weltzien,
Fabian Frese,
Thimoteus Wagner
Art Director
Anke Borchers,
Jan Knauss,
Sina Gieselmann
Copywriter
Thies Schuster,
Max Biedermann
Graphics
Anke Borchers

Nomination
Ghost Photos
Germany

National Award
Shortlist
Agency
TBWA Germany, Berlin
Client
Sony Computer Entertainment Deutschland GmbH
Creative Director
Dirk Henkelmann, Philip Borchardt
Art Director
Leila El-Kayem
Copywriter
Friedrich Tromm
Designer
Arnaud Loix van Hooff
Agency Producer
Katrin Dettmann

Bowling lane
"Dental implant insurance from Euro 9.90 per month". KarstadtQuelle Insurance is making the best use of bowling lanes by advertising dental implant coverage. Banners with faces printed on were attached to the wall at the end of the lanes. When a bowling ball hits the pins it looks like teeth being knocked out.

Ghost Photos
"Snap shot cameras were developed for the Games Convention and distributed by hostesses. From the outside the camera was only branded with the PlayStation Logo, but the film inside the camera made this promotion an action to remember. On every picture taken, ghosts and frightening faces appeared on the pre-exposed film. The last picture revealed the mystery with the line: 'The Horror is closer than you think'. Forbidden Siren II. Out now for PlayStation2. The click rate on the Forbidden Siren II Homepage tripled only a few days after the event. Photos from the cameras started to appear on the web. Some cameras made it onto eBay auctions as cult objects. The press reported the 'new advertising medium' in detail."

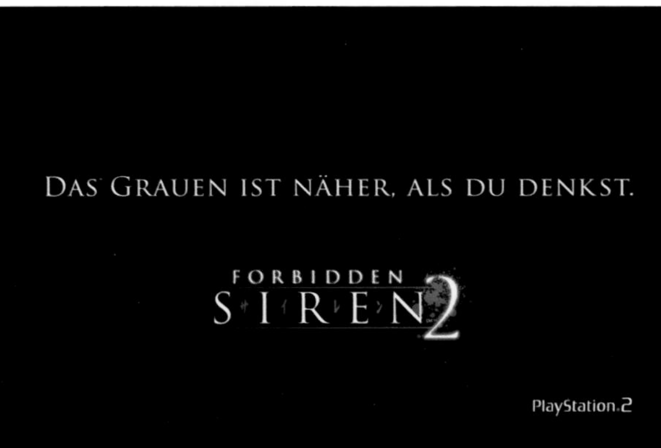

DAS GRAUEN IST NÄHER, ALS DU DENKST.
FORBIDDEN
SIREN 2
PlayStation.2

Nomination
Globus Crown Caps Promotion
Germany

National Award
Silver
Agency
Ogilvy Frankfurt
Client
Globus Supermarket Germany
Creative Director
Pit Kho
Art Director
Georg Fischboeck, Irina Schestakoff
Copywriter
Pit Kho, Kai-Oliver Sass
illustrator
Georg Fischboeck

Globus Crown Caps Promotion
All the stuff that men love most. In our beverage center.

Nomination
Living Video
(In DVD)
Germany
National Award
Bronze
Agency
Kolle Rebbe Werbeagentur GmbH
Client
Google Germany GmbH
Creative Director
Lorenz Ritter, Sven Klohk, Ulrich Zuenkeler
Art Director
Nina Zimmermann
Copywriter
Sebastian Oehme
Other
Account manager: Katharina Lechelt, Silke Schilling

Nomination
Pattex 3D Vase
Germany

National Award
Silver
Agency
DDB Germany, Duesseldorf
Client
Henkel KGaA
Creative Director
Heiko Freyland, Raphael Milczarek
Art Director
Fabian Kirner, Michael Kittel
Copywriter
Felix Lemcke, Jan Propach
Production Company
Display Modellbau Kueppers
Other
Chief Creative Officer:
Amir Kassaei

Short Message Headline
A recruitment ad written in numbers. The T9-mobilephone-function will translate the headline.

336578_
38_
8237_
343_
5527745_
446287?

Dann bewirb Dich bei uns. JUNG v. MATT

NOKIA
127/1
Denkst du über die klassik hinaus?
Option. Senden Löschen

A recruitment ad, written in numbers. You enter the "headline" as a short message, the mobile phone's T9 function translates: "Do you think beyond print?" If you get this far, you obviously do! The copy invites you to send an SMS. The human resources staff answers and a personal dialogue begins.

Nomination
Short Message Headline
Germany

National Award
Shortlist
Agency
Jung von Matt AG
Client
Jung von Matt AG
Creative Director
Till Hohmann, Tobias Eichinger
Art Director
Brian Piper
Copywriter
Philipp Mayer, Till Hohmann
Graphics
Daniel Bretzmann

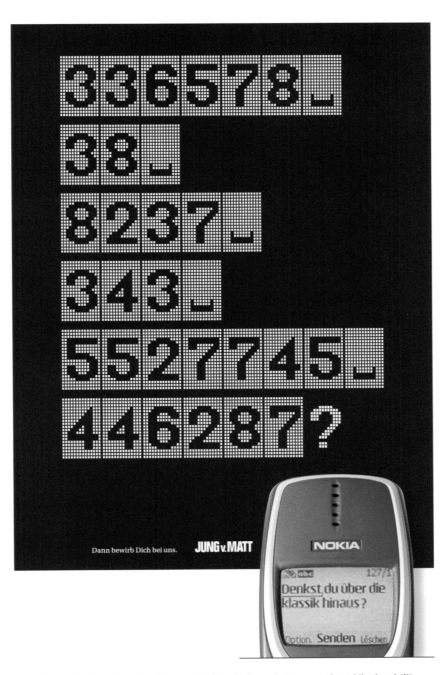

Nomination
Staff Distance Driver-Golfball Scattering action

Switzerland

National Award
Bronze
Agency
Publicis Werbeagentur AG
Client
Wilson
Creative Director
Philipp Skrabal
Art Director
Corinne Bresch
Graphics
Roy Spring

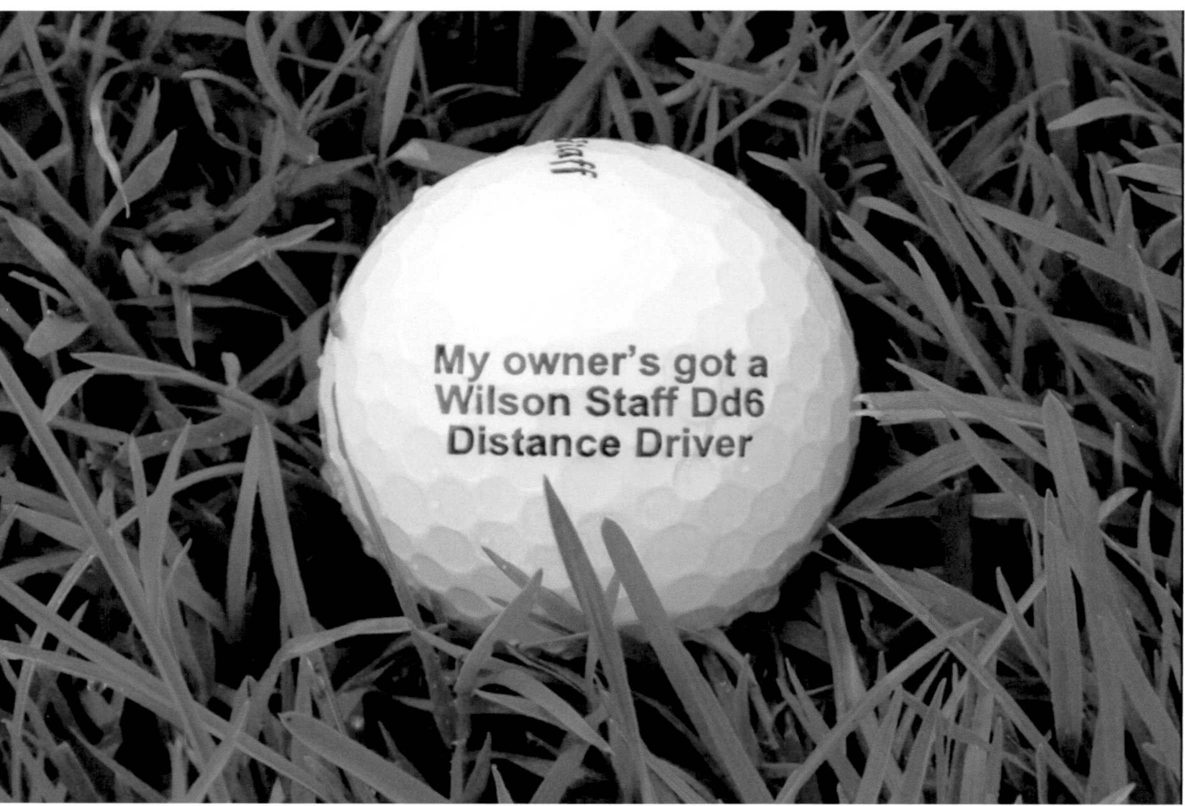

Staff Distance Driver - Give Away Golfballs
"The new Dd6 Distance Driver sets new distance standards for a golf club. To communicate its innovation and create maximum awareness, we turned golf balls into message carriers. Golf balls were scattered far from courses in up-market living environments, where target group would find them: in gardens, on walkways in front of homes, in convertibles or boats. We made the ball into a flyer with a printed message on it that spoke of the unique power of the club: 'My owner's got a Wilson Staff Dd6 Distance Driver.'"

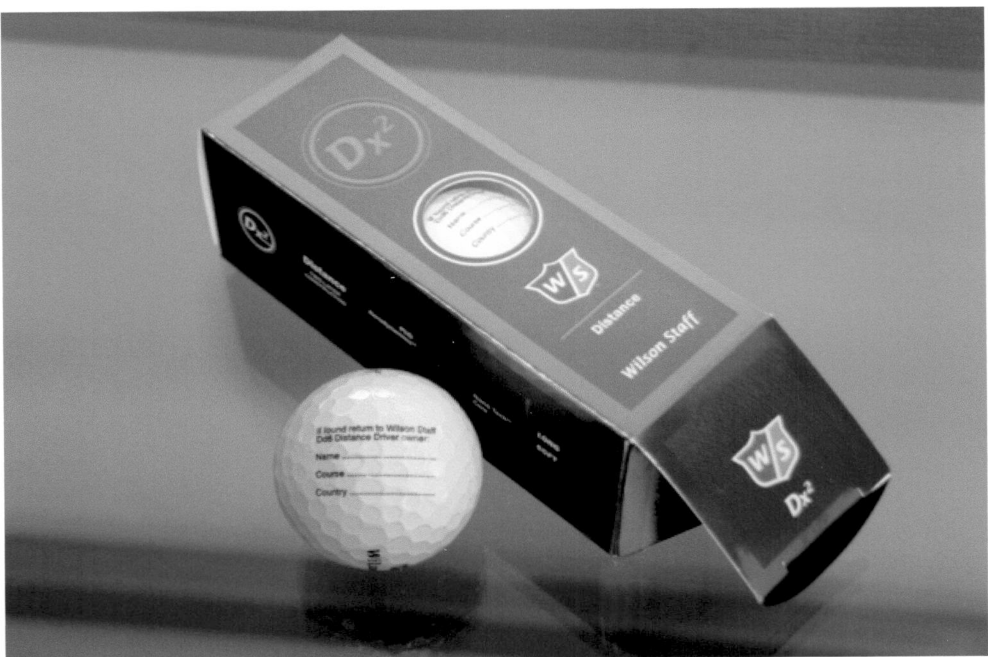

Nomination
Staff Distance Driver - Give Away Golfballs
Switzerland

National Award
Bronze
Agency
Publicis Werbeagentur AG
Client
Wilson
Creative Director
Philipp Skrabal
Art Director
Corinne Bresch
Graphics
Roy Spring

Nomination
Torture meets Modern Art
Germany

National Award
Silver
Agency
Ogilvy Frankfurt
Client
Amnesty International, Section Mannheim
Creative Director
Dr. Stephan Vogel, Christian Mommertz
Art Director
Christian Mommertz
Copywriter
Dr. Stephan Vogel
Photographer
Aziz Wakim
Graphics
Friedrich Detering
Other
Artist of sculpture:
Christian Schoenwaelder

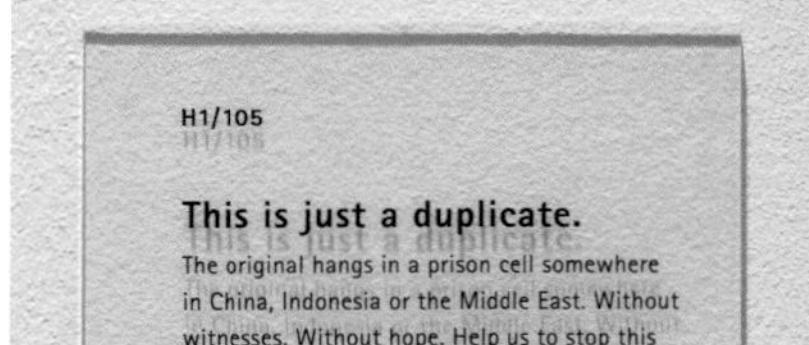

H1/105
This is just a duplicate.
The original hangs in a prison cell somewhere in China, Indonesia or the Middle East. Without witnesses. Without hope. Help us to stop this happening: www.amnesty-international.com

Torture Meets Modern Art
The Amnesty International Section of Mannheim (Germany) wanted to create new and strong public interest in their town. Because people often avoid the traditional Amnesty information stalls in pedestrian zones and shopping malls. Torture was disguised as a modern art sculpture and exhibited it in the most unusual context, the big local Art Museum (Kunsthalle Mannheim). The artist Christian Schönwälder created the sculpture.

Running Sushi
Austria

National Award
Silver
Agency
Draftfcb Kobza
Client
Sushi King
Creative Director
Erich Falkner
Art Director
Andreas Gesierich
Graphics
Daniel Senitschnig

Burned Clothes
Austria

National Award
Silver
Agency
Saatchi & Saatchi
WerbegesellschaftmbH
Client
Generali Versicherung AG
Creative Director
Marcus Hartmann
Art Director
Marcus Hartmann,
Ulf Ryberg
Copywriter
Karlheinz Wasserbacher

Ultra Sony Ericsson
Estonia

National Award
Silver
Agency
Age McCann
Client
Tele 2
Creative Director
Kaarel Grepp
Art Director
Maksim Loginov, Martin Algus
Copywriter
Martin Algus
Designer
Maksim Loginov
Production Company
Age McCann
Graphics
Maksim Loginov
Illustrator
Maksim Loginov
Programmer
Maksim Loginov
Url
www.loweage.com/klient/kuldmuna/ultra/

Scratch
Italy

National Award
Silver
Agency
D'Adda, Lorenzini Vigorelli, BBDO
Client
BMW Italy
Creative Director
Giuseppe Mastromatteo, Luca Scotto di Carlo
Art Director
Dario Agnello
Copywriter
Cristino Battista

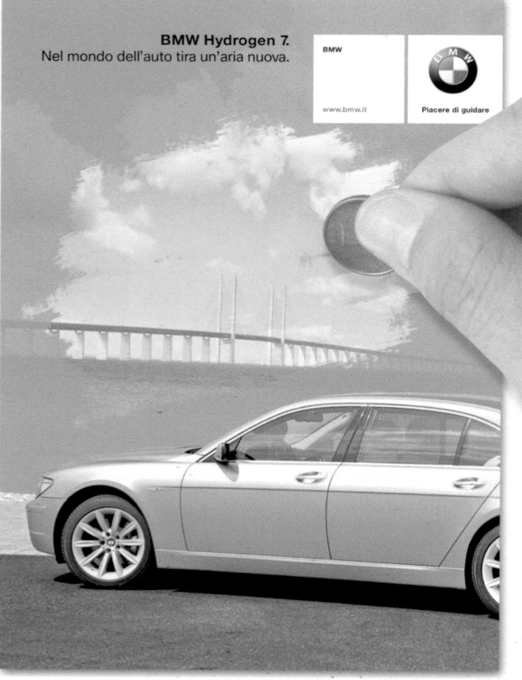

Ultra Sony Ericsson
"Lucky crash!" Now there's a mobile phone with a Walkman player! Join Ultra phone card Student package and get one at a good price!

Scratch
The BMW Hydrogen 7 is shown on a scratch card; when scratched, it reveals a clear sky in the background behind the car.

Cat Magazine
Envelope: Meeow prepares your cat for a new experience. Magazine cover: Meeow. Glamorous cats Articles: Bianca. Purrfect seduction. Well being. Tips for 9 better lives. Health. Get out of the couch.

Man Po
"Postcard" The aim: to attract attention with a provocative slogan-MAN PO (I don't give a shit) and plays with the P road sign that identifies parking. Feeling: I don't give a shit about penalties, parking cashiers and lack of coins in my pocket because I pay by SMS.

Cat Magazine
Portugal

National Award
Gold
Agency
OgilvyOne Lisboa
Client
Masterfoods
Creative Director
Jorge Coelho
Art Director
Catarina King
Copywriter
Pedro Aguiar
Photographer
Image Bank

Es maksāju ar
CiTYCREDiT

www.CiTYCREDiT.lv

BAD DOG POSTCARDS 2006 pastkaršu reklāma
Pārdot aizliegts. Not for sale. tel.7288871 www.baddog.lv
#387

Maksā ar SMS
par stāvvietu Rīgā un Vecākos!
Sāc lietot pakalpojumu līdz 1. jūlijam
un stāvi stundu bez maksas!

Man Po
Latvia

National Award
Silver
Agency
BADDOG
Client
CityCredit
Creative Director
BADDOG
Art Director
BADDOG

Envelope Scheme
Portugal

National Award
Silver
Agency
Touch_Me Wunderman
Client
Microsoft Portugal
Creative Director
Miguel Pate
Art Director
Rui Domingos
Copywriter
José Castelo
Other
Rodrigo Gralheiro,
Miguel Figueiredo

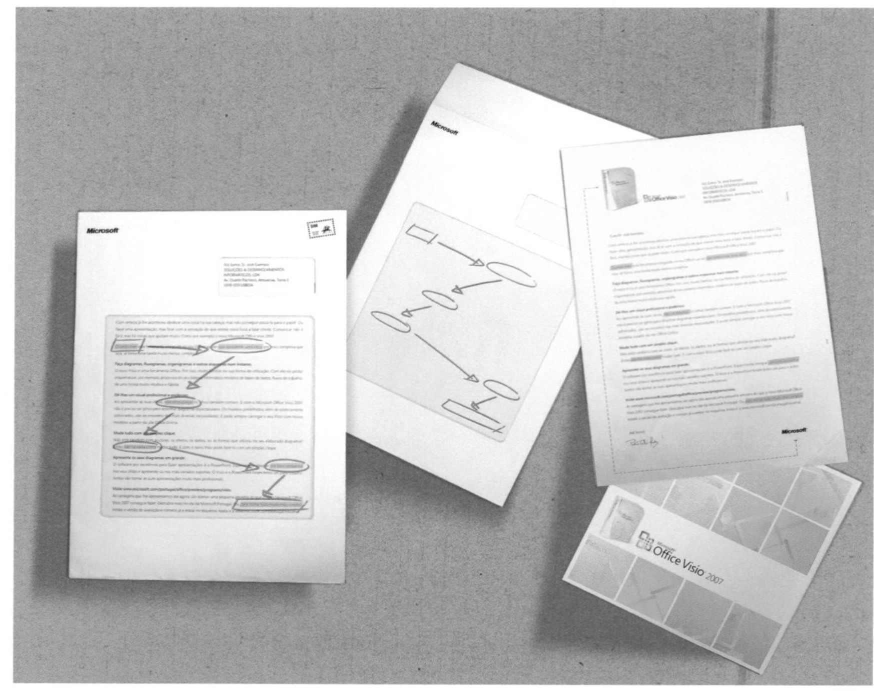

Milupa
Portugal

National Award
Silver
Agency
Touch_Me Wunderman
Client
Milupa
Creative Director
Miguel Pate
Art Director
Andreia Constantino
Copywriter
Luis Coelho
Other
Olga Orfao,
Monica Januario,
Miguel Figueiredo

Envelope Scheme
When you have to present an idea don't forget: there's nothing like a good scheme to make everything simpler.

Milupa
Dear Mr. Samples: this baby is also yours.

Soap Bar
"On the 7th, take the opportunity to wash your dirty laundry. The Client/Agency Relationship Seminar".

Virtual Watch
One is a local watch brand that asked us to develop a new way of presenting their catalogue to retailers. We've created a mailing that beside showing watches, allowed recipients to try them. The concept was: "One. For every moment".

Soap Bar
Portugal

National Award
Gold
Agency
Touch_Me Wunderman
Client
Touch_Me Wunderman
Creative Director
Miguel Pate and Nuno Duarte
Art Director
Nuno Duarte
Copywriter
Miguel Pate
Other
Luis Segadâes

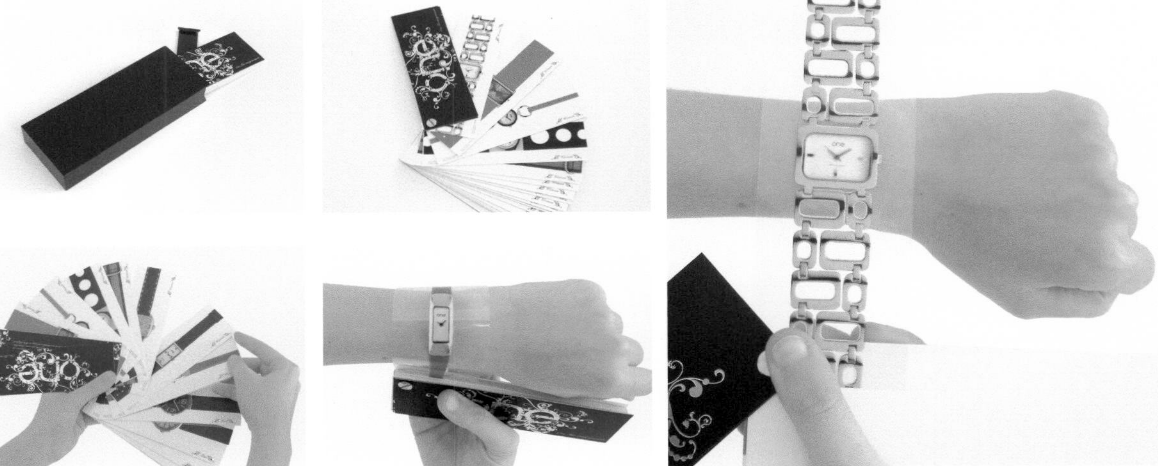

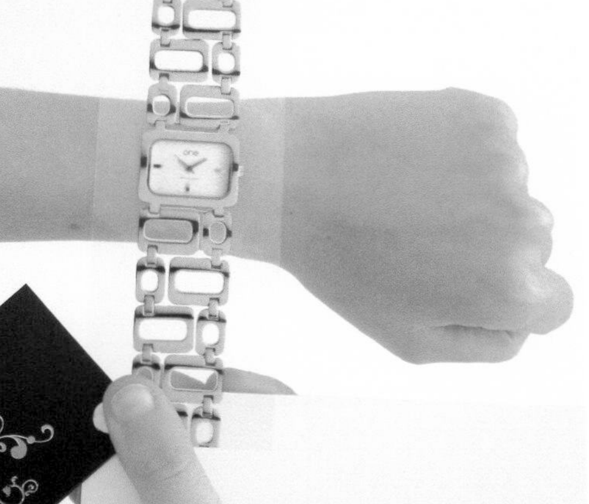

Virtual Watch
Portugal

National Award
Silver
Agency
Leo Burnett
Client
Planet One
Creative Director
Joâo Roque, Chacho Puebla
Copywriter
Pedro Ribeiro
Designer
Pedro Roque, Ana Ventura

Letters of application
Switzerland

National Award
Silver
Agency
Ruf Lanz, Zurich
Client
Radio Energy Zurich
Creative Director
Markus Ruf,
Danielle Lanz
Art Director
Marcel Schlaefle
Copywriter
Thomas Schoeb
Account Manager
Nicole Sommemeyer

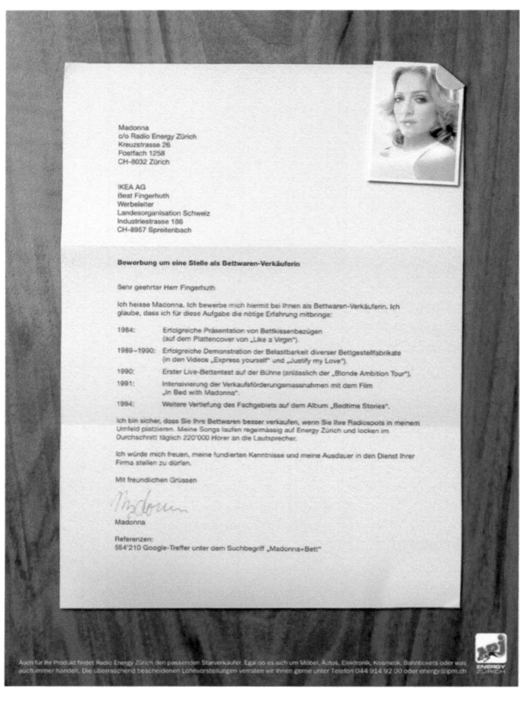

Madonna
c/o Radio Energy Zürich
Kreuzstrasse 26
Postfach 1258
CH-8032 Zürich

IKEA AG
Beat Fingerhuth
Werbeleiter
Landesorganisation Schweiz
Industriestrasse 186
CH-8957 Spreitenbach

Bewerbung um eine Stelle als Bettwaren-Verkäuferin

Sehr geehrter Herr Fingerhuth

Ich heisse Madonna. Ich bewerbe mich hiermit bei Ihnen als Bettwaren-Verkäuferin. Ich glaube, dass ich für diese Aufgabe die nötige Erfahrung mitbringe:

1984: Erfolgreiche Präsentation von Bettkissenbezügen (auf dem Plattencover von „Like a Virgin").
1989–1990: Erfolgreiche Demonstration der Belastbarkeit diverser Bettgestellfabrikate (in den Videos „Express yourself" und „Justify my Love").
1990: Erster Live-Bettentest auf der Bühne (anlässlich der „Blonde Ambition Tour").
1991: Intensivierung der Verkaufsförderungsmassnahmen mit dem Film „In Bed with Madonna".
1994: Weitere Vertiefung des Fachgebiets auf dem Album „Bedtime Stories".

Ich bin sicher, dass Sie Ihre Bettwaren besser verkaufen, wenn Sie Ihre Radiospots in meinem Umfeld platzieren. Meine Songs laufen regelmässig auf Energy Zürich und locken im Durchschnitt täglich 220'000 Hörer an die Lautsprecher.

Ich würde mich freuen, meine fundierten Kenntnisse und meine Ausdauer in den Dienst Ihrer Firma stellen zu dürfen.

Mit freundlichen Grüssen

Madonna

Referenzen:
554'210 Google-Treffer unter dem Suchbegriff „Madonna+Bett"

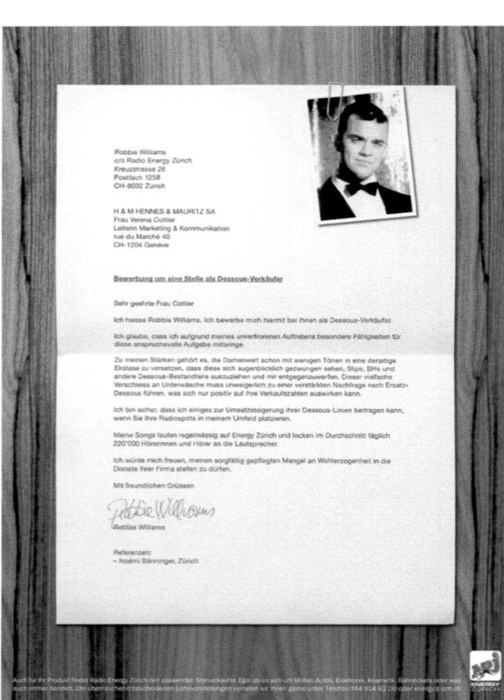

Robbie Williams
c/o Radio Energy Zürich
Kreuzstrasse 26
Postfach 1258
CH-8032 Zürich

H & M HENNES & MAURITZ SA
Frau Verena Cottier
Leiterin Marketing & Kommunikation
rue du Marché 40
CH-1204 Genève

Bewerbung um eine Stelle als Dessous-Verkäufer

Sehr geehrte Frau Cottier

Ich heisse Robbie Williams. Ich bewerbe mich hiermit bei Ihnen als Dessous-Verkäufer.

Ich glaube, dass ich aufgrund meines unverfrorenen Auftretens besondere Fähigkeiten für diese anspruchsvolle Aufgabe mitbringe.

Zu meinen Stärken gehört es, die Damenwelt schon mit wenigen Tönen in eine derartige Ekstase zu versetzen, dass diese sich augenblicklich gezwungen sehen, Slips, BHs und andere Dessous-Bestandteile auszuziehen und mir entgegenzuwerfen. Dieser vielfache Verschleiss an Unterwäsche muss unweigerlich zu einer verstärkten Nachfrage nach Ersatz-Dessous führen, was sich nur positiv auf Ihre Verkaufszahlen auswirken kann.

Ich bin sicher, dass ich einiges zur Umsatzsteigerung Ihrer Dessous-Linien beitragen kann, wenn Sie Ihre Radiospots in meinem Umfeld platzieren.

Meine Songs laufen regelmässig auf Energy Zürich und locken im Durchschnitt täglich 220'000 Hörerinnen und Hörer an die Lautsprecher.

Ich würde mich freuen, meinen sorgfältig gepflegten Mangel an Wohlerzogenheit in die Dienste Ihrer Firma stellen zu dürfen.

Mit freundlichen Grüssen

Robbie Williams

Referenzen:
– Noëmi Bänninger, Zürich

Waistline
Portugal

National Award
Silver
Agency
Touch_Me Wunderman
Client
Camara Municipal
de Santarém
Creative Director
Miguel Paté and Nuno
Duarte
Art Director
Rui Saraiva
Copywriter
Andre Freitas
Other
Camila Camargo,
Miguel Figueiredo

Waistline
National Gastronomy Festival. October the 21st, there is one thing you don't need to worry about: your waist line.

Letters of application
"No Headlines. Letters of application in a typical commercial style."

Calendar of creative recrudescences
Russia

National Award
Gold
Agency
LLC
Client
LLC DesignDepot
Creative Director
Bankov Piter
Art Director
Malyshev Evgeny
Copywriter
Pozharsky Denis
Designer
Malyshev Evgeny
Production Company
Evstyukhin Mikhail

New & Mixed Media. Ambient Media

Austria: Gold 1 Nomination

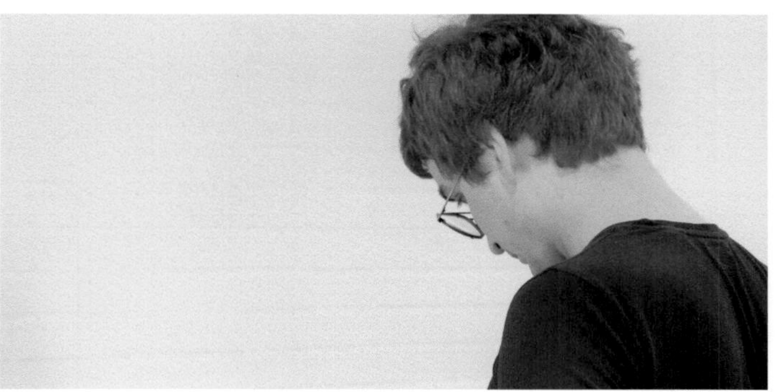

Bosnia & Herzegovina	**Germany:** 5 Nominations	**Portugal:** 1 Nomination
Czech Republic	**Italy:** 1 Nomination	**Spain**
Estonia	**Latvia**	**Switzerland:** 1 Nomination

Gold
Ramp
(In DVD)
Austria

National Award
Bronze
Agency
Draftfcb Kobza
Client
ÖZIV
Creative Director
Erich Falkner,
Ronni Ronniger
Art Director
Hannes Glantschnig
Copywriter
Dominik Niebauer,
Christoph Reicher
Graphics
Tanja Promitzer

2

3

4
FÜR EINE BARRIERE-
FREIE GESELLSCHAFT.
öziv
TÄGLICH.
GESELLSCHAFT.

Nomination
Running Sushi
Austria

National Award
Bronze
Agency
Draftfcb Kobza
Client
Sushi King
Creative Director
Erich Falkner
Art Director
Andreas Gesierich
Graphics
Daniel Senitschnig

Running Sushi
Oversized sushis were placed at Salzburg airport on the luggage conveyor belt in the arrival hall. While waiting for their luggage, the tourists' attention was attracted to moving sushis bearing the message "Greatest Running Sushi in Town".

Nomination
Together at last
Germany

National Award
Shortlist
Agency
Serviceplan Munchen/
Hamburg
Client
FriendScout24 GmbH
Creative Director
Ekki Frenkler
Art Director
Daniela Bardini
Copywriter
Christine Deinhart
Graphics
Daniela Bardini
Other
Account Executive:
Kristina Peters,
Monika Hornung

Nomination
Commercial break
(In DVD)
Germany

National Award
Silver
Agency
Jung von Matt AG
Client
DPWN
Creative Director
W. Schneider,
M. Stiller, D. Mously,
J. Harbeck
Art Director
David Mously
Copywriter
Jan Harbeck
Producer
Nicolai Niemann
Production company
Entspannt Film
Postproduction
Sascha Haber,
Sabine Weinreiss
Graphics
Kristin Brause
Programmer
Director: Nicolai Niemann
Other
Cinematographer: Klara Niemann

Commercial break
"Anywhere in record time". In cooperation with other brands, a truly innovative media idea was developed: a DHL van that drives through all ads in a TV advertising break to deliver a package. All the ads the van cross are existing and well-known commercials. They just added the car.

+10 Fresco
Football stars like Beckham, Zidane, Raul, Messi, Kaka or Ballack are considered to be real football gods by their fans. They are simply elevated to where they belong anyway - into football heaven.. The world's largest football fresco was created in the main lobby of the Cologne central train station, which happens to be right next to the stunning Cologne Cathedral.

Nomination
+10 Fresco
Germany

National Award
Gold
Agency
TBWA Germany (180/TBWA), Berlin
Client
Adidas AG
Creative Director
Kurt Georg Dieckert, Stefan Schmidt
Art Director
Boris Schwiedrzik
Copywriter
Helge Bloeck
Production company
Methodik Management & Partner
Illustrator
Felix Reidenbach
Other
Media Agency: Carat

Nomination
MINI. Wake the BULL!
Germany

National Award
Shortlist
Agency
Serviceplan
Munchen,Hamburg/
Mediaplus
Client
BMW AG
Creative Director
Jung von Matt,
Alster (Kreative Adaption),
BBDO DLV
Copywriter
Susanne Attmannspacher,
Cornelia Schmid
(Mediaplus)
Other
Florian Gmeinwieser
(Plan.Net)

MINI. Wake the BULL!
"Designed in Milan, the campaign's motif was originally intended for the print media. It shows the MINI Cooper S and visualizes its power and driving pleasure by comparing the car to a snorting bull.
By interacting via mobile phone, passers-by cause the bull to snort real smoke. Thereby the strict division of advertisement and reality is broken up and the visualization of power and driving pleasure can be experienced. The MINI on the poster awakens and its power becomes visible for everyone with real smoke representing the bull's snort."

Torture Meets Modern Art
The Amnesty International Section of Mannheim (Germany) wanted to create new and strong public interest in their town. Because people often avoid the traditional Amnesty information stalls in pedestrian zones and shopping malls. Torture was disguised as a modern art sculpture and exhibited it in the most unusual context, the big local Art Museum (Kunsthalle Mannheim). The artist Christian Schönwälder created the sculpture.

H1/105
This is just a duplicate.
The original hangs in a prison cell somewhere in China, Indonesia or the Middle East. Without witnesses. Without hope. Help us to stop this happening: www.amnesty-international.com

Nomination
Torture meets Modern Art
Germany

National Award
Shortlist
Agency
Ogilvy Frankfurt
Client
Amnesty International, Section Mannheim
Creative Director
Dr. Stephan Vogel, Christian Mommertz
Art Director
Christian Mommertz
Copywriter
Dr. Stephan Vogel
Photographer
Aziz Wakim
Graphics
Friedrich Detering
Other
Artist of sculpture:
Christian Schoenwaelder

Nomination
Not here but now
Switzerland

National Award
Gold
Agency
walker
Client
Amnesty International
Creative Director
Pius Walker
Copywriter
Roger Beckett
Designer
Marianne Friedli
Photographer
Federico Naef
Graphics
Florian Fröhlich, Carolina Gurtner

Not here but now Human Rights Campaign. This campaign shows how human rights are abused each and every day - within only a few hours flying distance of us. Two worlds collide on 200 posters, each one adapted to match its surroundings. So brutal scenes take place in the middle of Zürich.

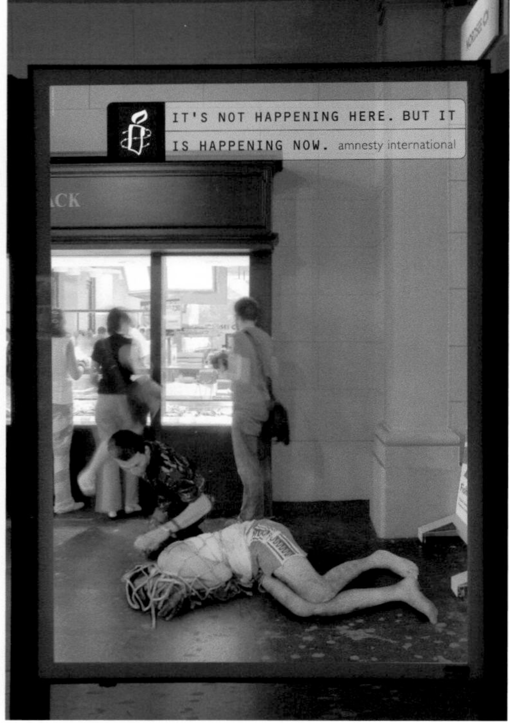

Nomination
Caixotes
Portugal

National Award
Bronze
Agency
McCann Erickson
Client
Associaçâo Vitae
Creative Director
Diogo Anahory,
José Bomtempo
Art Director
Diogo Mello
Copywriter
Fabio Seidl

Nomination
Roulette
Italy

National Award
Gold
Agency
ADMCOM
Client
Casino of Venice
Creative Director
Maurizio Cinti
Art Director
Maurizio Cinti
Copywriter
S. Fedrigo, R. Rossi, M. Cinti
Graphics
Sergio Lelli, Andrea Ligi

Roulette
Spinning roulette wheel proposed as an airport luggage carousel. Roulette "Keep Playing"

Bestseller
Loud and adorable magazine seller, well-known for creative and witty comments on the papers contents, yelling out the name of the product, text and punch lines on the main square. Hard to miss if walking by, witty comments catching your attention.

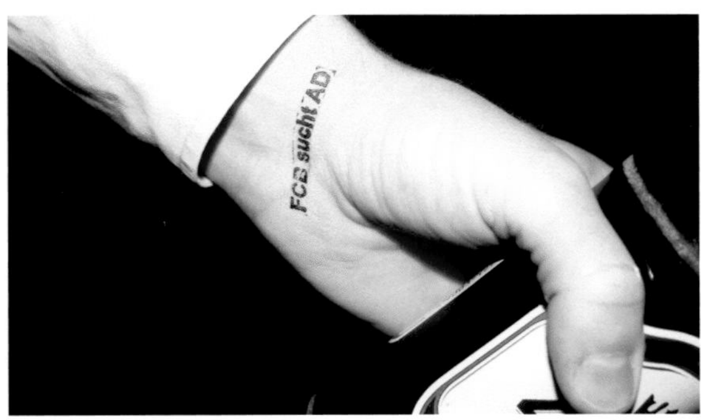

FCB Postmarks Creatives
Austria

National Award
Silver
Agency
Draftfcb Kobza
Client
Draftfcb Kobza
Creative Director
Joachim Glawion
Designer
Tanja Bug,
Renee Reust

Bestseller
Bosnia and Herzegovina

National Award
Gold
Agency
Communis - ADC
Client
Raiffeisen Bank BiH
Creative Director
Anur Hadziomerspahic
Art Director
Ajna Zlatar
Copywriter
Anur Hadziomerspahic,
Ajna Zlatar
Designer
Anur Hadziomerspahic,
Ajna Zlatar
Photographer
Tarik Zahirovic
Graphics
Anur Hadziomerspahic,
Ajna Zlatar
Url
www.communis.ba
Other
Medium, Zulejha

Don't Drive, Run! (On Air)
Czech Republic

National Award
Silver
Agency
Kaspen
Client
Nike Czech Republic
Creative Director
Lester Tullett
Art Director
Michal Sloboda
Copywriter
Petr Cech
Agency Producer
Alena Kondasova

UPOZORNĚNÍ PRO ŘIDIČE

Vážená paní, vážený pane,
vaše vozidlo je dle ustanovení § 17a, odst. 21, zákona č. 518/2007 o čerstvém vzduchu, ve znění pozdějších předpisů, zašlápnuto technickým prostředkem zabraňujícím jeho odjezdu. Netelefonujte nikam! Běžte se radši proběhnout na vzduch! Až tak učiníte, nasaďte technický prostředek někomu jinému.

POŠKOZENÍ UVEDENÉHO TECHNICKÉHO PROSTŘEDKU NENÍ TRESTNÉ, ALE ZCESTNÉ!

HINWEIS FÜR DIE KRAFTFAHRER

Sehr geehrte Kraftfahrerin, sehr geehrter Kraftfahrer,
Ihr Fahrzeug wurde laut Verfügung des § 17a, Abs. 21, des Frischluftgesetzes Nr. 518/2007 Slg. in der Fassung der späteren Vorschriften mit einer Parkkralle blockiert, die dessen Wegfahren verhindert. Telefonieren Sie nirgendhin! Üben Sie sich lieber ein wenig im Laufen in frischer Luft! Nachdem Sie das getan haben, machen Sie die Parkkralle jemanden anderen dran.

DIE BESCHÄDIGUNG DES ERWÄHNTEN TECHNISCHEN MITTELS IST NICHT STRAFBAR, IST JEDOCH ABSURD!

NOTICE TO DRIVERS

Dear Sir, dear Madam:
Pursuant to Regulation § 17a, Section 21 of the Air Protection Act No. 518/2007 as amended, your vehicle has been blocked by technical device preventing its movement. Do not call anywhere! You'll be better off to take a quick run somewhere in the fresh air! After you do that, place this technical device on somebody else's car.

TO DAMAGE THIS TECHNICAL DEVICE IS NOT PUNISHABLE BY LAW, BUT IT IS NOT A WISE MOVE!

Kahn
Germany

National Award
Gold
Agency
TBWA Germany (180/TBWA), Berlin
Client
adidas AG
Creative Director
Stefan Schmidt, Kurt Georg Dieckert
Art Director
Boris Schwiedrzik
Production company
Kinetic World Wide, Hi-Resolution
Photographer
Joerg Reichardt
Other
Media Agency: Carat

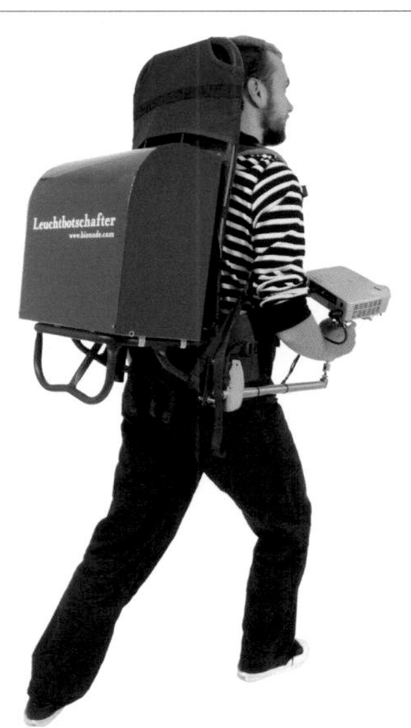

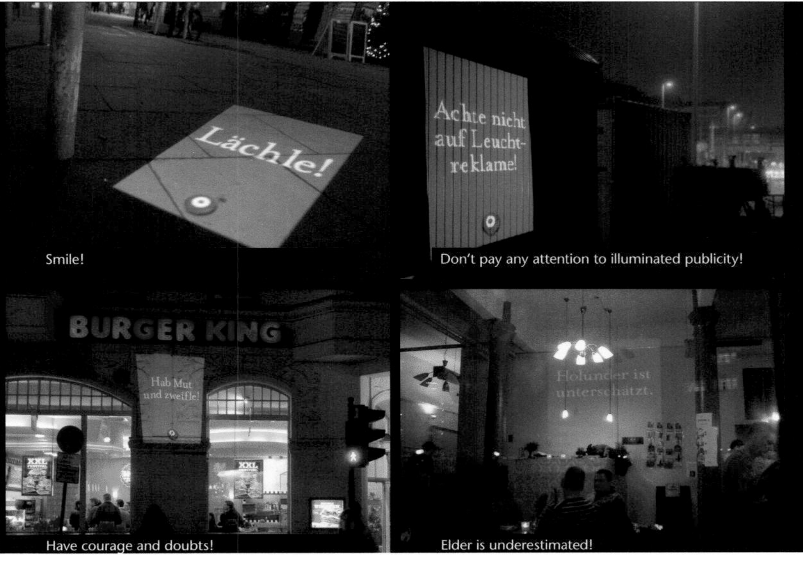

Bionade
Germany

National Award
Silver
Agency
Kolle Rebbe Werbeagentur GmbH
Client
BIONADE GmbH
Creative Director
Katrin Oeding
Art Director
Reginald Wagner, Lisa Kirchner
Copywriter
Alex Baron, Ingo Mueller, Florian Ludwig, Stefan Wuebbe
Designer
Reginald Wagner
Other
Idea: Olaf Oldigs

Bionade
The mobile messenger.

Gauloises
'The Liberty mobile'
Develop a new promotion that communicates the freedom brand value for the traditional French brand Gauloises. Something completely new was developed for the first time in the history of Gauloises: the Liberté mobile, a remote-controlled megaphone that can be driven via radio control and speaks to the target group directly. The ideas behind the Liberté toujours claim were perfectly embodied: with lots of charm, spontaneity, humour and a touch of mischievousness. The laughs and brand trust were on our side. The Gauloises Liberté mobile was the talk of the town for days in the major German cities Hamburg and Berlin.

Gauloises 'The Liberty mobile'
Germany

National Award
Silver
Agency
Kolle Rebbe Werbeagentur GmbH
Client
British American Tobacco (Deutschland) GmbH
Creative Director
Katrin Oeding, Ulrich Zuenkeler
Art Director
Reginald Wagner, Lisa Kirchner
Copywriter
Alexander Baron, Florian Ludwig, Stefan Wuebbe
Designer
Reginald Wagner
Other
Idea: Olaf Oldigs

Sculptures talk
Estonia

National Award
Gold
Agency
Division
Client
KUMU - Estonian Art Museum
Creative Director
Alvar Jaakson, Kristian Kirsfeldt
Art Director
Kristian Kirsfeldt
Copywriter
Alvar Jaakson, Kristian Kirsfeldt
Designer
Marje Essenson

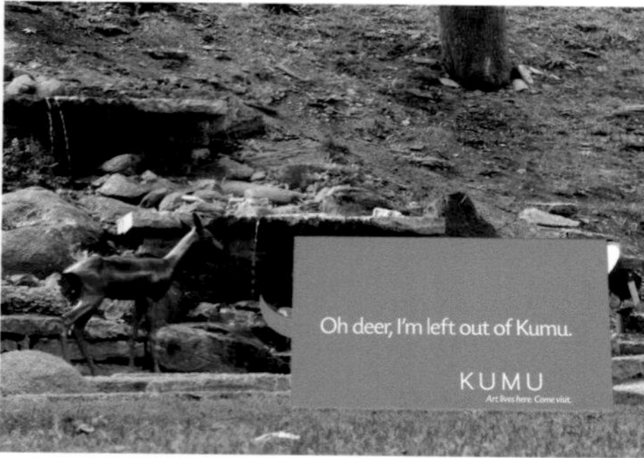

ZZ tram-apartment
Latvia

National Award
Silver
Agency
DDB Worldwide Latvia
Client
Ltd. TELE 2
Creative Director
Edgars Subrovskis
Art Director
Armands Zeles

Sculptures talk
Art lives here.

ZZ tram-apartment
Probably the first tram-apartment in the world! In 2005 Zelta Zivtina launched new advertising sitcom series about the relationship and adventures of four friends, who share an apartment. In 2006 anyone can visit their apartment and get the feeling of TV sitcom series by simply entering the city tram. The exterior of the tram represents the brand by pictures of Zelta Zivtina heroes, while the interior does it using the details from sitcom apartment.

Optimus Experience
Portugal

National Award
Gold
Agency
BBDO Portugal
Client
Optimus
Creative Director
Nuno Cardoso

Try it
Portugal

National Award
Gold
Agency
BBDO Portugal
Client
Optimus
Creative Director
Nuno Cardoso

Opel Corsa C'MON!
Spain

National Award
Silver
Agency
Cuatic
Client
General Motors
Creative Director
Natalia Rojas,
Alejandro Bica,
Jordi Puig
Art Director
Alejandro Bica
Production company
Esfera Comunicación
Programmer
Natalia Rojas,
Jordi Puig
Url
www.cuatic.com/festivals/opelcorsacmon

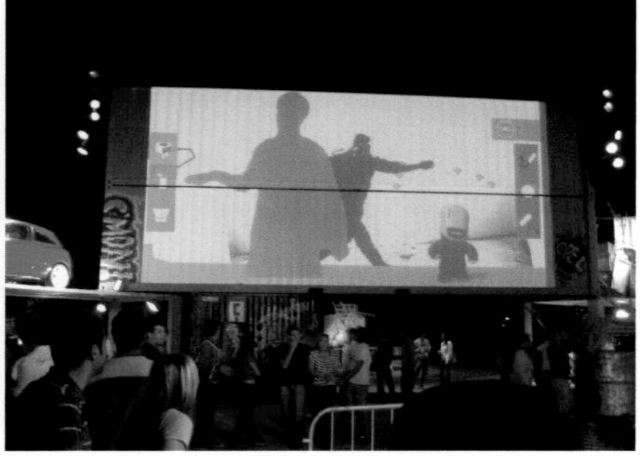

Run on Air
Air Max 360.

Duck / Washing Machine
Retailer M-Electronics added washing machines to its product line for the first time. A film loop turns each TV into a washing machine. This graphically illustrates for the consumer the new addition to the retailer's product line. "Now we have also got a washing machine".

Run on Air
Spain

National Award
Gold
Agency
Cuatic
Client
Nike
Creative Director
Natalia Rojas,
Alejandro Bica,
Jordi Puig
Art Director
Alejandro Bica
Programmer
Natalia Rojas,
Jordi Puig
Url
www.cuatic.com/festivals/runonair

Duck / Washing Machine
Switzerland

National Award
Silver
Agency
Euro RSCG Group Switzerland
Client
M-Electronics
Creative Director
Petra Bottignole
Art Director
Dominik Oberwiler
Copywriter
Cyrill Wirz
Other
Account Director:
Lukas Baumgartner

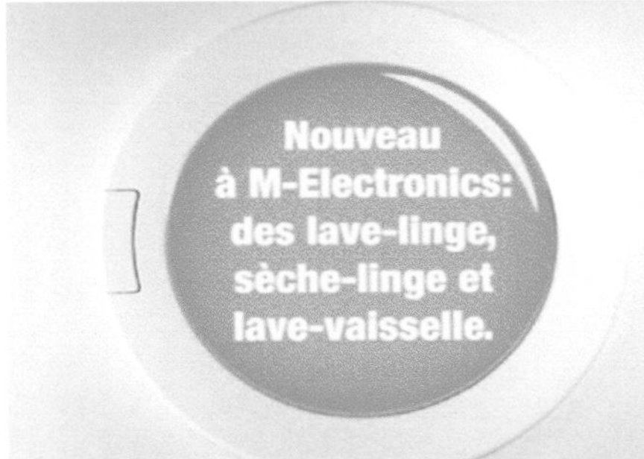

New & Mixed Media. Any Other

Austria

Poland

Czech Republic

Germany: Gold 1 Nomination

Portugal

Italy

Spain

Gold
Face2Go
(In DVD)
Germany

National Award
Shortlist
Agency
Mutabor Design GmbH Group
Client
Mutabor
Creative Director
Johannes Plass, Heinrich Paravicini
Art Director
Nils Zimmermann
Designer
Malte Schweers, Andre Kunze, Jens Meyer
Graphics
Jens Uwe Meyer, Malte Schweers, Andre Kunze
Url
www.face2go.de
Other
Frederike Putz, Strategic Planning

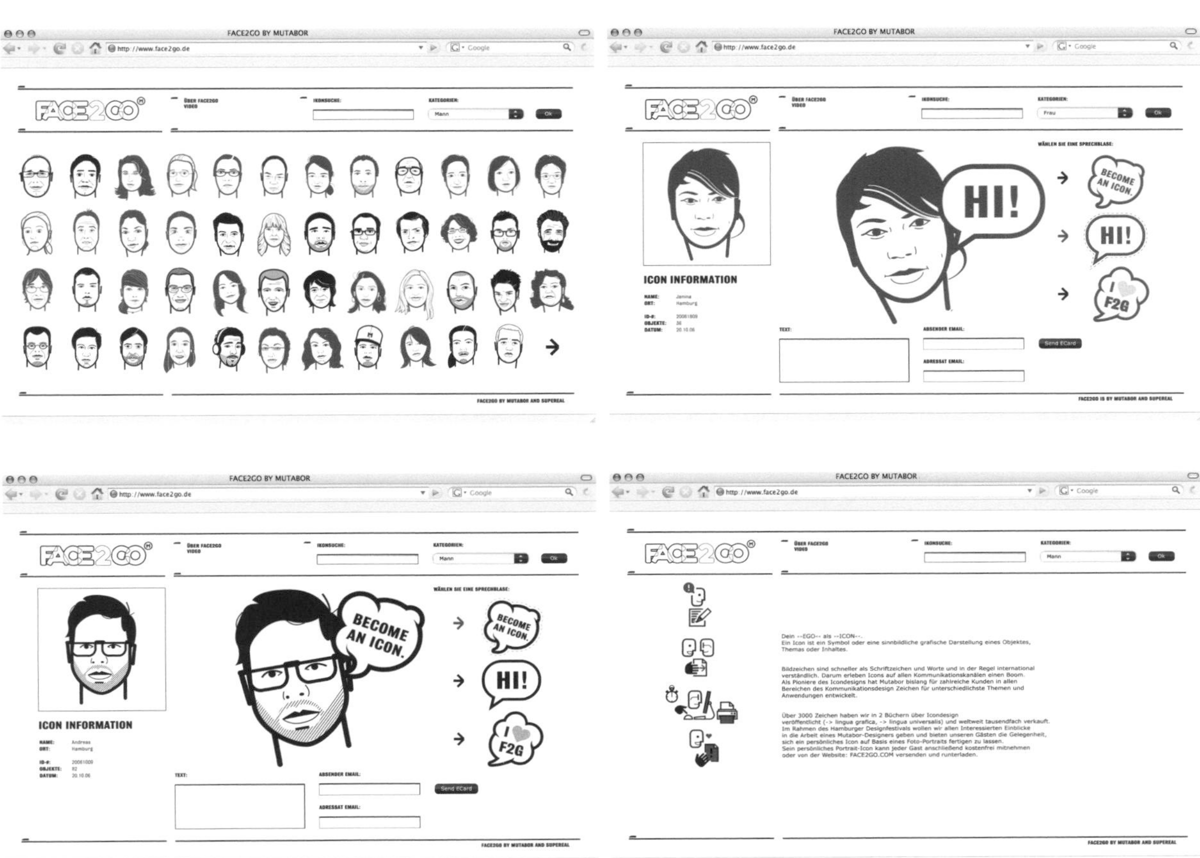
FACE2GO BY MUTABOR
http://www.face2go.de
ÜBER FACE2GO
VIDEO
IKONSUCHE:
KATEGORIEN:
ICON INFORMATION
WÄHLEN SIE EINE SPRECHBLASE:
HI!
BECOME AN ICON.
I ♥ F2G
TEXT:
ABSENDER EMAIL:
ADRESSAT EMAIL:
Send ECard
FACE2GO BY MUTABOR AND SUPEREAL
Dein --EGO-- als --ICON--.
Ein Icon ist ein Symbol oder eine sinnbildliche grafische Darstellung eines Objektes, Themas oder Inhaltes.
Bildzeichen sind schneller als Schriftzeichen und Worte und in der Regel international verständlich. Darum erleben Icons auf allen Kommunikationskanälen einen Boom. Als Pioniere des Icondesigns hat Mutabor bislang für zahlreiche Kunden in allen Bereichen des Kommunikationsdesign Zeichen für unterschiedlichste Themen und Anwendungen entwickelt.
Über 3000 Zeichen haben wir in 2 Büchern über Icondesign veröffentlicht (-> lingua grafica, -> lingua universalis) und weltweit tausendfach verkauft. Im Rahmen des Hamburger Designfestivals wollen wir allen Interessierten Einblicke in die Arbeit eines Mutabor-Designers geben und bieten unseren Gästen die Gelegenheit, sich ein persönliches Icon auf Basis eines Foto-Portraits fertigen zu lassen. Sein persönliches Portrait-Icon kann jeder Gast anschließend kostenfrei mitnehmen oder von der Website: FACE2GO.COM versenden und runterladen.

Nomination
Curtain
(In DVD)
Germany

National Award
Shortlist
Agency
Jung von Matt AG
Client
IKEA
Creative Director
Arno Lindemann, Bernhard Lukas
Art Director
Jonas Keller
Copywriter
David Leinweber
Production Company
Markenfilm GmbH
Url
www.ikea.de
Other
Graphics: Lisa Port

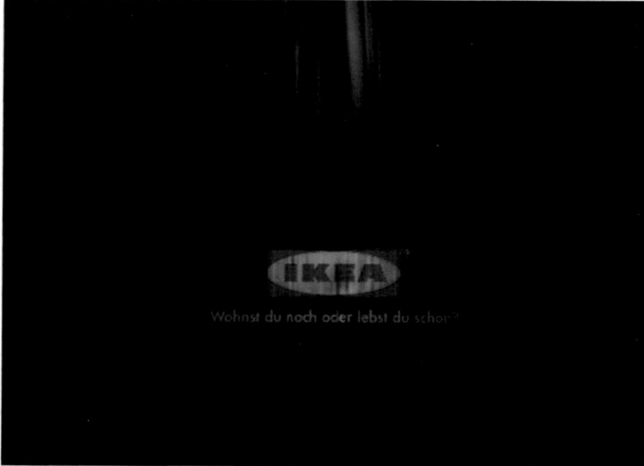

Amba Indian Goods - Guerilla Stickers
Amba. Everything from India.

Mosquitone
This year you just won't escape them.

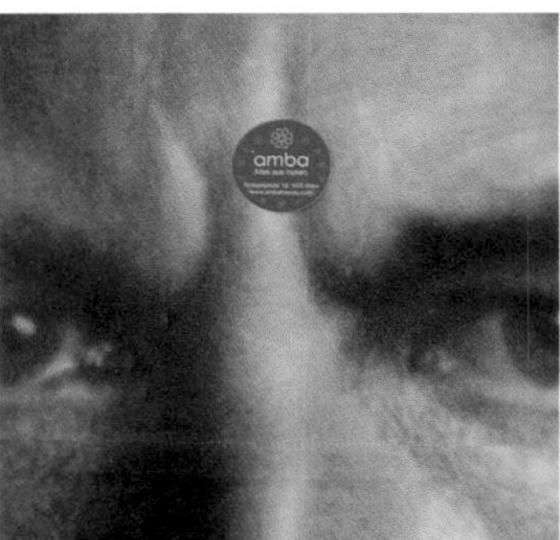

Amba Indian Goods - Guerilla Stickers
Austria

National Award
Silver
Agency
Springer & Jacoby Österreich GmbH
Client
Amba Indian Goods, Ingrid E. Jelinek
Creative Director
Paul Holcmann
Art Director
Katharina Haines
Copywriter
Jakob Würzl
Production company
Springer & Jacoby Österreich GmbH
Graphics
Katharina Haines
Other
Ralf Kober

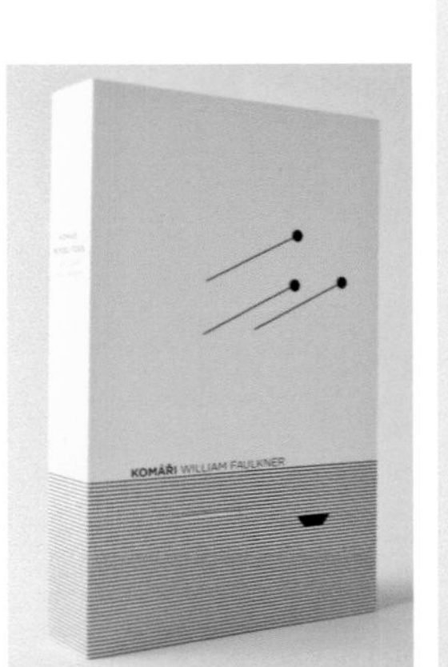

Mosquitoes
Czech Republic

National Award
Silver
Agency
WMC/Grey
Client
Novartis
Creative Director
Jan Micka
Art Director
Matej Rybak
Copywriter
Pavel Kriz
Designer
Matej Rybak
Production company
WMC/Grey
Graphics
Matej Rybak

Death Penalty
Italy

National Award
Silver
Agency
Saatchi & Saatchi
Client
Community of St. Egidio
Creative Director
Alessandro Orlandi
Art Director
Fabio Ferri
Copywriter
F. Ferri,
S. Massari,
A. Di Battista
Designer
Gianluigi Bellini
Graphics
Fabio Ferri,
Gianluigi Bellini
Programmer
Silvio Coco
Url
www.vision.saatchi-saatchi.it/work/onlineadv/penamorte/

Flags
Poland

National Award
Silver
Agency
DDB Warszawa,
Tequila Polska
Client
Kompania Piwowarska
Creative Director
Marcin Mroszczak
Art Director
Maciej Waligora,
Filip Berendt,
Robert Mendel
Copywriter
Marcin Mroszczak
Production company
Tango Productions

What
Poland

National Award
Silver
Agency
Dr. Sensitive Michal Slezkin I Slawek Wolski
Client
Interia
Creative Director
Slawek Wolski, Michal Slezkin
Art Director
Michal Slezkin
Copywriter
Slawek Wolski
Designer
Mamastudio, Marcin Rene Wawrzkiewicz
Programmer
Interia

Death Penalty
November 30, 2006: worldwide day for the petition to the UN for a moratorium on executions.

Flags
Best use of business. Tyskie Beer.

WHAT
Viral marketing for economic education.

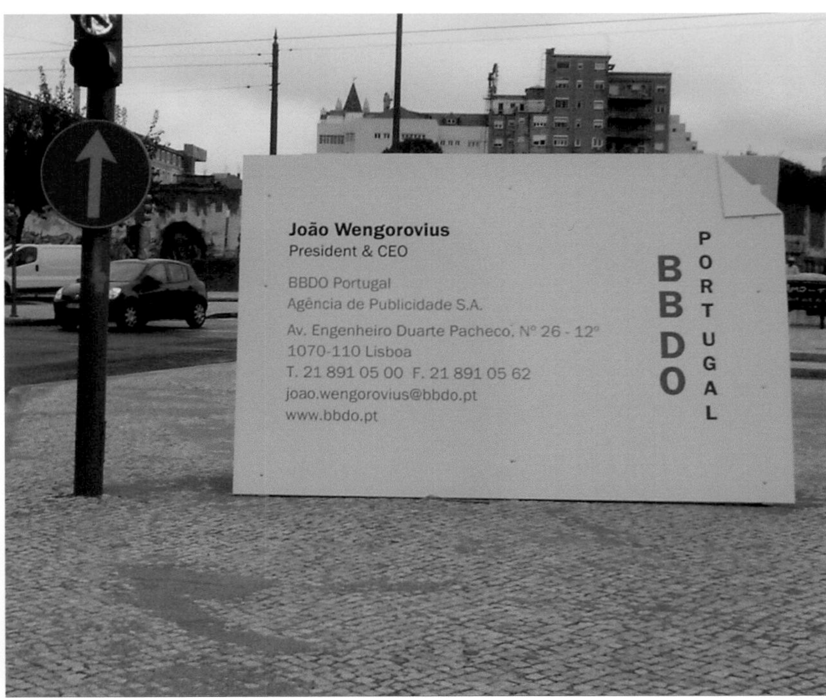

BBDO Portugal business card
Portugal

National Award
Gold
Agency
BBDO Portugal
Client
BBDO Portugal
Creative Director
Pedro Bidarra

Adivinario
Spain

National Award
Silver
Agency
Dfraile
Client
Consejería de Medio Ambiente de la Región de Murcia
Creative Director
Eduardo del Fraile
Art Director
Eduardo del Fraile
Designer
Eduardo del Fraile, Juan Jimenez, Antonio Marquez

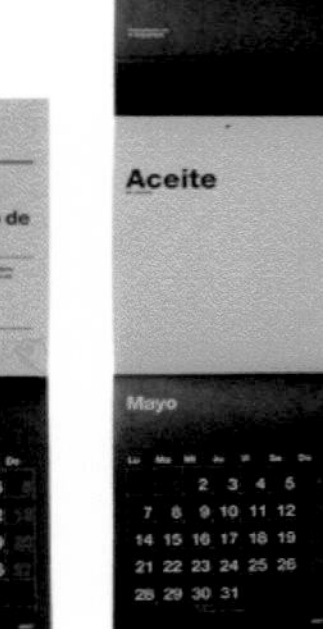

Adivinario
"Riddlar Calendar" A calendar which, month after month, suggests a riddle about an object to be recycled. The answer is described in a riddle and concludes with the impact it has on the environment when not recycled, or with the benefit that recycling brings it. It is printed using one ink and dyed paper free of chlorine or varnish, so that it is more environmentally friendly. Riddle: There are six in my family and in the parties there are dozens. We have much spark, we are very affectionate and we love people who kiss and squeeze us. The electricity that costs to make to me is three times the use of your home during a year. Answer: Tin.

Nokia Place D'Amour
Portugal

National Award
Gold
Agency
Brandia Central
Client
Nokia Portugal
Creative Director
Nelson Sinem, Elisabete Ferreira
Art Director
Sonia Gonçalves, Filipe Figueiredo
Designer
Paula Lopes
Graphics
Monica Neves
Other
Diogo Ferreira da Costa

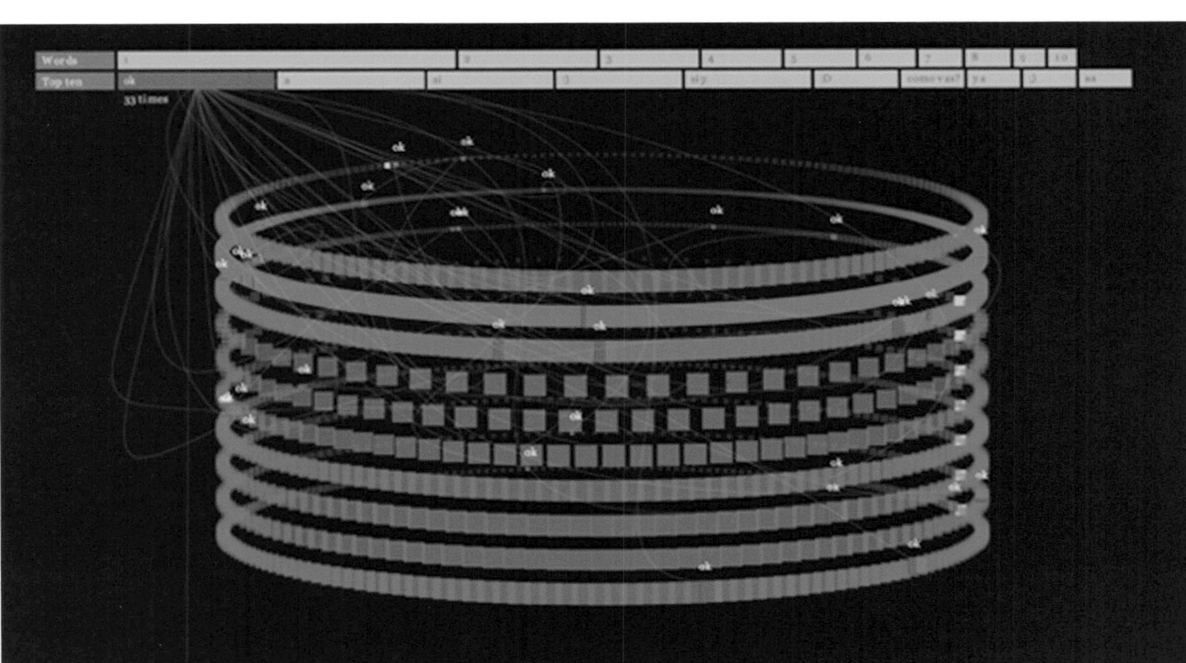

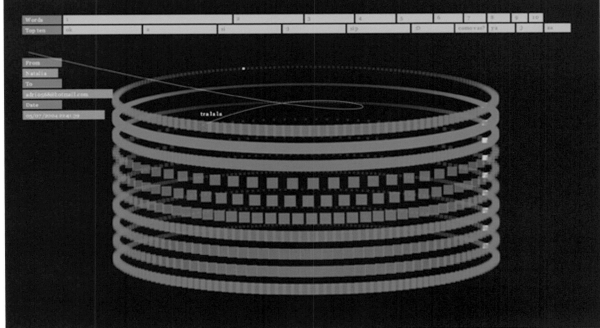

MSN history visualization v2.0
Spain

National Award
Gold
Agency
Natalia Rojas
Client
Natalia Rojas
Creative Director
Natalia Rojas
Art Director
Url
www.nataliarojas.com/p55/msn_history

Q: Who controls culture?

Q: To entertain or to educate?

Q: Can we look in another direction?

4

Design

Q: Can you define Design?

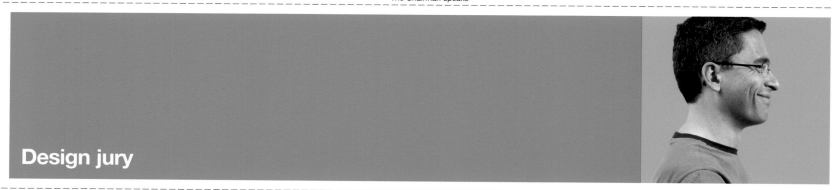

Design jury

Everybody has neighbours and they are usually quite different from us, as we are from them, unless you live in a hippie community. Different backgrounds, experiences, incomes, interests, political engagement, even different religions and we manage to live peacefully together. But how would it be, if we decided to award the block's most beautiful garden? I don't appreciate roses and dwarfs as much as bamboo and candle vases.

As Europeans, we practice 'neighbouring' on a large scale, and being together to award the best design pieces, we face the same questions brought by a diversity of criteria. With the high standards of work in competition our duty became even harder to accomplish, so we talked about it, we discussed our preferences openly, bringing up our professional values and personal considerations, changing ours or others' points of view, trying to achieve the most consensual and fair results. At the end of a long and fruitful day the best gardens were chosen. Thank you neighbours!

Mário Mandacaru
Chairman
Design Director-Brand Design
Brandia Central
Portugal

Originally from São Paulo, Brazil, in 1983 graduated in Advertising and Marketing there. In 1987 he concluded his bachelor degree with distinction in Graphic Design at the San Francisco Academy of Arts. In 1988 he moved to Lisbon and joined Massa Cinzenta as Art Director for three years. In 1991 he became Design Director at Novodesign/Brandia, and in January 2000 stepped to Maisdesign/Central de Comunicação as Associated Creative Director. At present he is one of the Creative Directors at Brandia Central and is the Vice President of the Clube de Criativos de Portugal and board member of the Art Directors Club of Europe.

Francesco Bestagno
Creative Director
Demner, Merlicek & Bergman
Austria

In 1993, he graduated under Professor Walter Luezer from the Academy of Applied Arts. He then began work at Demner, Merlicek & Bergmann as a Graphic Designer. Over his 14 years there, he has also worked as an Art Director, and since 2004 is a Creative Director.

He has received numerous honours from the world's most important award shows including Cannes, Clio, Crestas, Golden Drum, Mobius, New York Festivals, London International Advertising Awards, Creative Club Austira, Epica, Eurobest, and many more.

Roman Baigouzov
Senior Art Director
Saatchi & Saatchi
Czech Republic

He studied Graphic Design at the International Academy of Business and Banking in Togliatti, Russia. From 1998 to 1999, he was an Art Director at Ark Thompson Prague, and, from 1999-2000, was an Art Director at Ammirati Puris Lintas. He was Senior Director for McCann Erickson Prague from 2000 until 2005. Since 2005, has been the Senior Art Director for Saatchi & Saatchi, Prague.

Markko Karu
Creative Director
Velvet
Estonia

Markko Karu was born in 1974 in Tallinn and graduated from Estonian Art Academy in industrial design in 1997. From 1996 to 2002, he worked as Art Director and Creative Director at TBWA\Guvatrak, and in 2004 he went freelance; co-founding a design bureau, Velvet, where he is Creative Director. He has experience in many different design disciplines and gives lectures on design methodology in Estonian Art Academy's Open Academy. He was chosen by the British Council in 2006 as Estonian graphic designer and has won several local awards. Member of Art Director's Club Estonia and Estonian Association of Designers.

Rüdiger Goetz
Managing Creative Director
KW43 Branddesign
Germany

Rüdiger Goetz studied Communicative Design at the college of Hildesheim. After having worked as a Designer for agencies in San Francisco and Minneapolis, he joined the design agency Factor Design in Hamburg in 1992 as a Managing Partner and Managing Director Creation. In 1995 he founded the Corporate Design agency Simon & Goetz in Frankfurt as acting partner. He is holder of several international design prizes and has been teaching Corporate Design and typography for six years at the Free University of Berlin and the University of Applied Arts of Wiesbaden. In February 2005 he joined KW43, the design agency of Grey Worldwide as a Managing Director Creation.

Kristjana Sigurdardottir
Art Director
Atmo Design
Iceland

She studied graphic design at the Iceland Academy of the Arts Icelandic College of Arts and Crafts from 1993 to 1997. From 1993 to 2000, she worked at various advertising agencies in Iceland until starting her own design company, Atmo, where she is currently an Art Director and Interior Designer.

Alvin Perry
Creative Director
Fresh Design
Ireland

In 2001, Alvin established Fresh Design with partner Maria Bourke as a showcase for creative design conceived with personality and intelligence. Working on projects spanning the corporate, cultural and statutory sectors, Alvin brings an in-depth knowledge of how organisations and brands can optimise their identity and communications material through the use of insightful and informed design.

Alvin's work has received many awards and has been featured in both the national and international design press.

Michael Göttsche
Owner and Creative Director, Göttsche Agenzia di Publicità
Italy

He began his career as an Art Director at Young & Rubicam-first in Frankfurt and then in Milan. In 1972, along with E. Pirella, G. Muccini, and P. Pilla, he founded "Italia" - soon after to become Italia BBDO. Their campaigns are repaid with awards and nation-wide success. 1981 marked the birth of "Pirella Göttsche": a new, independent, and totally Italian agency. In 1985, Pirella & Göttsche joins the Lowe network bringing clients such as Volvo, British Telecom, Gatorade, Superga, and many others.
In January 2001, Michele Göttsche starts his third new agency: a creative lab and training ground for young talent.

Liene Drazniece
Art Director
"LOWE Riga"
Latvia

In the middle of the bachelor program in the Latvian Academy of Art, she was questioning herself whether she is an artist or a designer. By spending around two years of switching herself between junior designer at "Leo Burnett Riga" and young artist activities, she finally understood that working for the client is a bigger challenge for her. After three years of the experience at "McCann-Erickson Riga", she currently work for "LOWE Riga" mainly with brand identities and packaging and right now with their support she has moved to Milan to deepen her professional and practical background.

José Carlos Farias Mendes
Senior Graphic Designer
Mola Ativism
Portugal

Born in 1973 in Portugal, studied Graphic Design 7 at Ar. Co, Art Centre & Visual Communication in Lisbon. From 1996 to 1998 he worked at BBDO Portugal. He joined Novodesign in 1998, and then moved to Brandia in 2000 as a Senior Graphic Designer. He has been working at Mola Activism since 2006.

He has done work for numerous clients and during his time at Brandia he was at the core of the rebranding process of Galp Energia and the creation of the brand and graphic universe of Pluma® (gas cylinder).

He has won several national and international prizes.

Wladimir Marnich
Graphic Designer
Marnich Design
Spain

He studied at the Swinburne University, Melbourne. He moved to work for the English company for branding, FutureBrand. In 1999, he returned to Barcelona as a design director for Summa studio. In 2003, he started his own design studio: from the design of a monthly women's magazine to the creation of a corporate TV channel or a packs series for the frozen food chain- La Sirena.

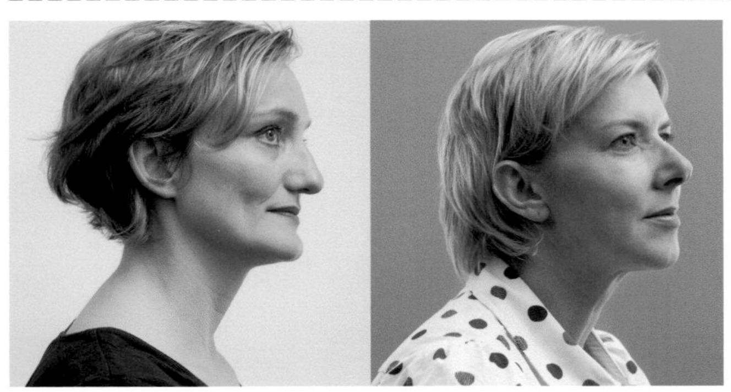

Q: No Logo, no work?

Valentina Herrmann
Art & Creative Director
Freelance
Switzerland

Harriet Devoy
Creative Director
of Graphic Design
Apple
UK

Born in 1968, Valentina Herrmann started at the Art School of Basel and Zurich and at CASH RSCG. In 1990, she moved to Milan to work at the Design Studio of Sottsass Associati. Back in Zurich, she has been working at advertising agencies Weber, Hodel, Schmid, WIRZ, Advico, Young & Rubicam and LOWE as a Freelance since January 2007.

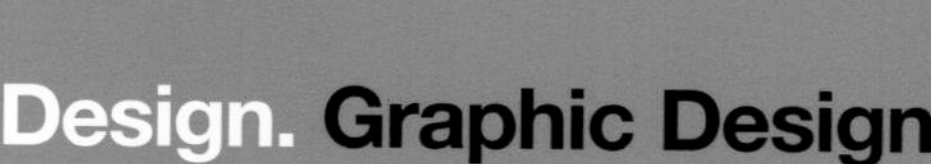

Design. Graphic Design

Austria: 2 Nominations

Estonia

Germany: Gold 2 Nominations

Iceland

Latvia

Portugal

Spain: 1 Nomination

Gold
Handmade posters
Germany

National Award
Bronze
Agency
Serviceplan
Muenchen/Hamburg
Client
Serviceplan Hamburg
Creative Director
Alexander Schill,
Axel Thomsen
Art Director
Maik Kaehler
Copywriter
Christoph Nann
Graphics
Amelie Graalfs,
Roman Becker,
Jessica Hammerich

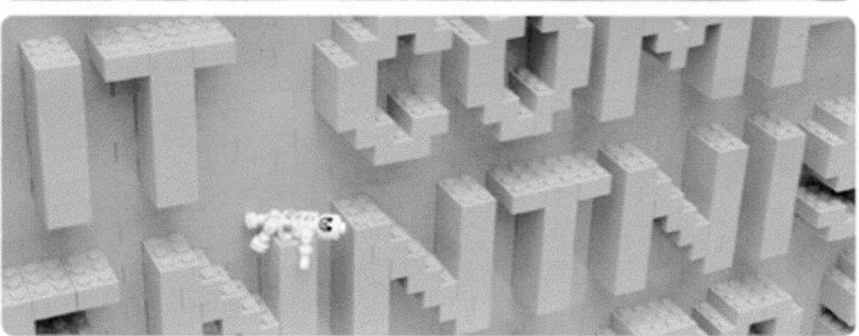

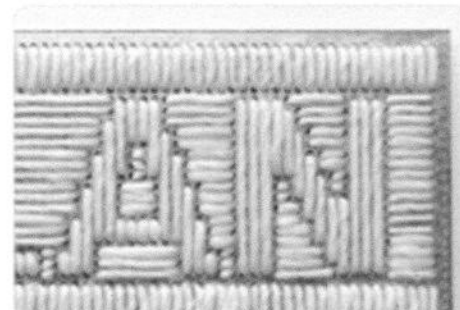

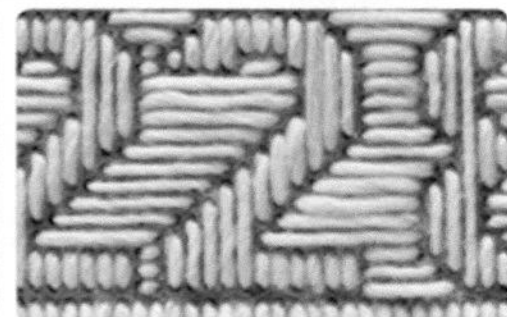

To atract graphic designers with IT skills, posters were created in design colleges. The clue: posters created with out computers. Whether build from Lego or drawing pins, sawn from wood or woven byhand, aech poster was handmade and unique.

Nomination
Modebuch Contemporary Fashion from Austria
Austria

National Award
Silver
Agency
halle34 Albert Handler / Marcus Arige OEG
Client
Unit F buero fuer mode
Creative Director
Albert Handler
Art Director
Albert Handler
Production company
Copyright
Graphics
Anouke Rehorek
Other
Ulrike Tschabitzer, Katrin Seiler

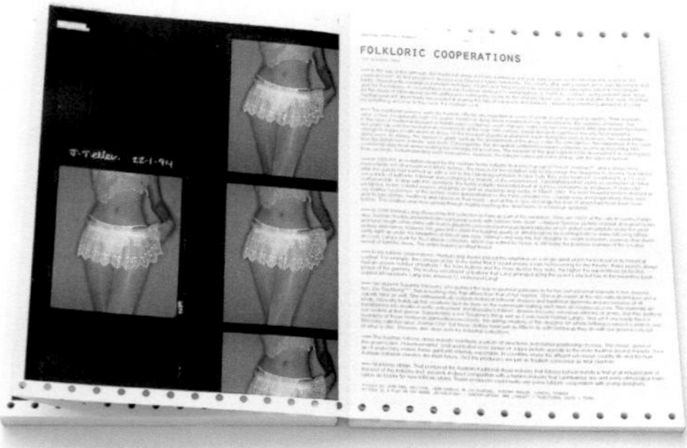

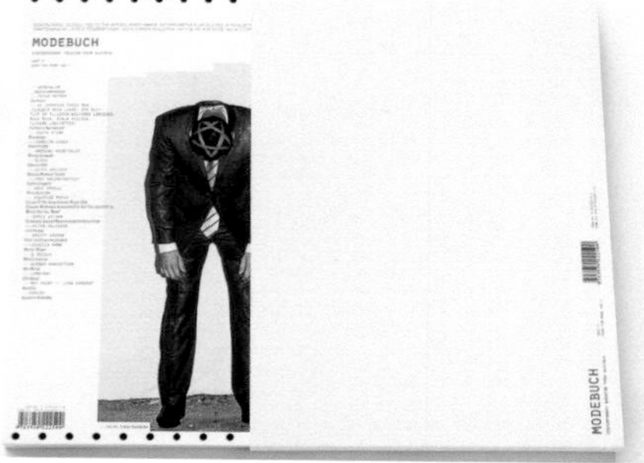

Modebuch
Contemporary
Fashion from Austria
Creative director Albert Handler and the Graphic design Agency halle34 had the target to create a German and English version which should not be designed one after another. The result is the first endless book (on 28.4 metres of endless paper).

Parabol AM #2
Parabol Art Magazine. Parabol AM is a magazine for international contemporary art. Each issue is devised by a curator. Each deviser's task is to examine a contemporary phenomenon in pictures and words on the basis of an artistic point of view.

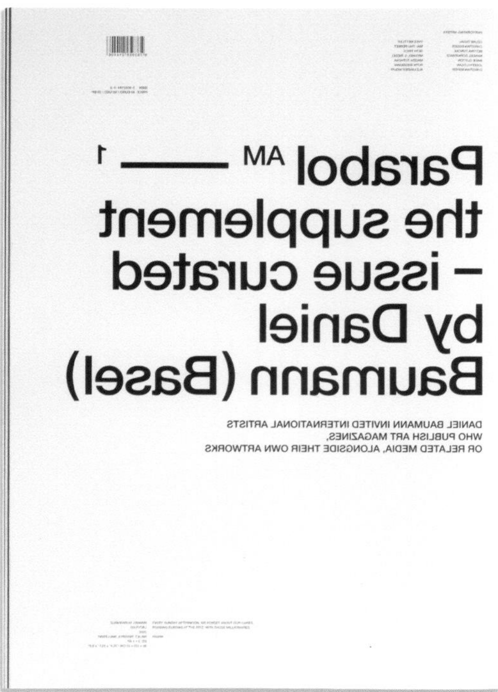

Nomination
Parabol AM #2
Austria

National Award
Silver
Agency
section.d
Client
Parabol AM
Creative Director
Chris Goennawein
Art Director
Chris Goennawein
Copywriter
Curator: Ami Barak
Graphics
Chris Goennawein

Nomination

Die kleine Schu(h)lfibel

Germany

National Award
Shortlist
Agency
Guertlerbachmann Werbung GmbH
Client
Ludwig Goertz GmbH
Creative Director
Uli Guertler
Art Director
Alexander Roetterink
Copywriter
Jens Ringena
Designer
Uli Guertler, Alexander Roetterink
Production company
Produktionsbuero Romey von Malottky GmbH
Graphics
Veronika Kieneke
Illustrator
Uli Guertler, Alexander Roetterink

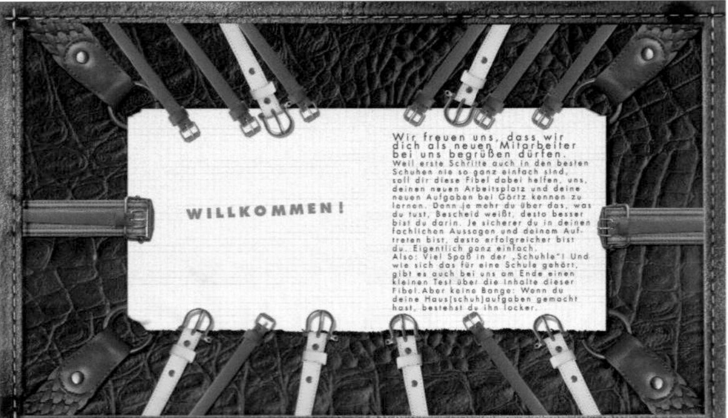

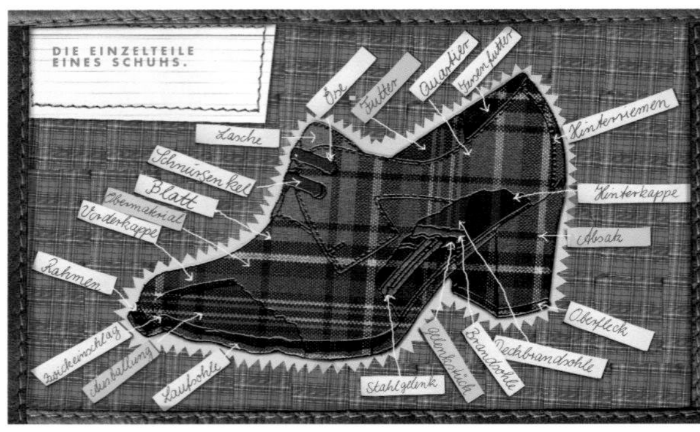

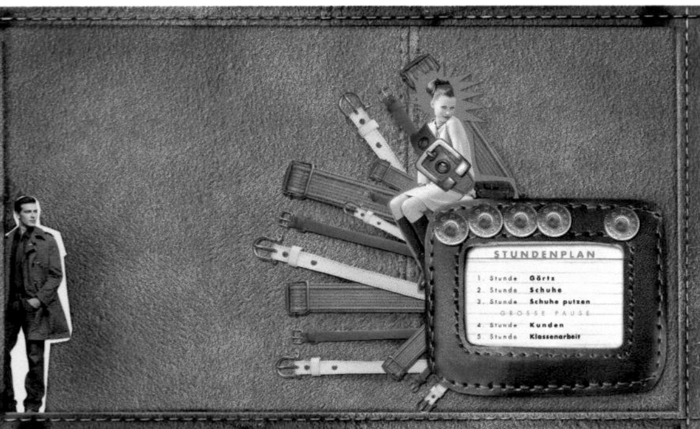

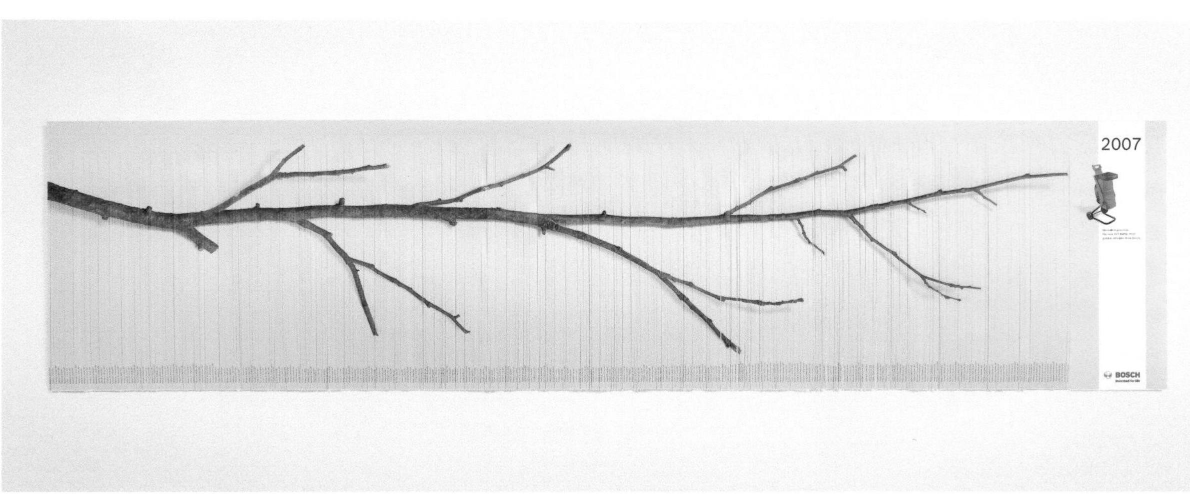

Nomination
Shredder
Germany

National Award
Silver
Agency
Jung von Matt AG
Client
Atco-Qualquast Ltd. Bosch
Lawn & Garden
Creative Director
Wolf Heumann,
Sascha Hanke,
Andreas Ottensmeier
Art Director
Olaf Scheer
Copywriter
Moritz Grub
Graphics
Kathrin Koll

Die kleine Schu(h)lfibel
It is a German word play. Schulfibel describes books that kids use in Primary School. These are learning books. Working as a shoe salesmen at Goertz 17 is an enjoyable, yet challenging job. The Book supplies new employees with the basic information for the daily work. The Book should upgrade the in-house image and encourage employees to a long-term commitment.

Shredder
"Unrivalled precision. The new AXT RAPID 2000 garden shredder from Bosch". To enable retailers and distribution partners to experience the outstanding performance of the garden shredders, recipients of the calendar were given the chance to do some shredding themselves, every day of the year. The calendar was divided into 365 thin perforated strips, and printed across all of them was a two-metre-long branch every day, the strip for that day could be torn off, shortening the branch as the year went on. The unusual dimensions (200 cm wide by 50 cm high) and the original way that people could interact with the calendar meant that it quickly became a highly desirable collector's item.

Nomination

Put Things In Order

Spain

National Award
Silver
Agency
Daniel Bembibre
Client
Daniel Bembibre
Creative Director
Daniel Bembibre
Copywriter
Daniel Bembibre
Designer
Daniel Bembibre
Production company
Salpausselän Kirjapaino
Photographer
Daniel Bembibre
Graphics
Daniel Bembibre
Other
Sponsored by UIAH and Salpausselän Kirjapaino

Put Things In Order
Visual manifesto, a self promotion one issue magazine. This is a 20 page tabloid-shaped visual manifesto. A collection of images that work independently and as a whole, in a code to be decoded by the reader. A silent way of communicating that leaves space to find your own connections within the design.

Corporate Identity Manual
Corporate Identity Manual for Baugur Group.

Art for kids
Why do we give such boring things to our clients for Christmas? Don't they deserve something better than a bottle of wine and a basket of mandarins? Why couldn't it be a valuable book? "Album For Kids", a visual conversation between twelve artists and kids is a gift from Jsc. Latvijas Gaze to its clients which is a gift to Latvian children and their parents. All the financial proceeds would be donated to children hospital reconstruction.

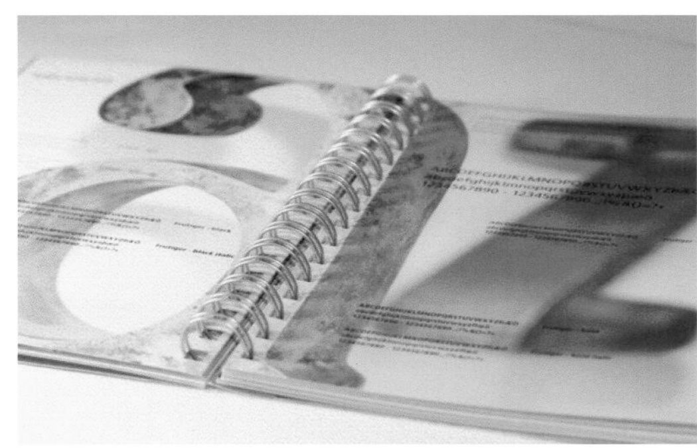

Corporate Identity Manual
Iceland

National Award
Silver
Agency
Hzeta Design
Client
Baugur Group
Art Director
Hildur H. Zoega
Designer
Hildur H. Zoega
Photographer
Hildur H. Zoega

Art for kids
Latvia

National Award
Silver
Agency
RCL Ltd. (TBWA Latvia)
Client
Jsc. Latvijas Gaze
(Latvian Gas)
Creative Director
Ivo Strante
Art Director
Mara Viska

Typofonie
Germany

National Award
Silver
Agency
Jung von Matt AG
Client
Dortmund philharmonic concert hall
Creative Director
Wolf Heumann, Sascha Hanke
Art Director
Martin Besl
Copywriter
Michael Okun, Moritz Grub
Production company
eachfilm GmbH, tisch eins, design studio

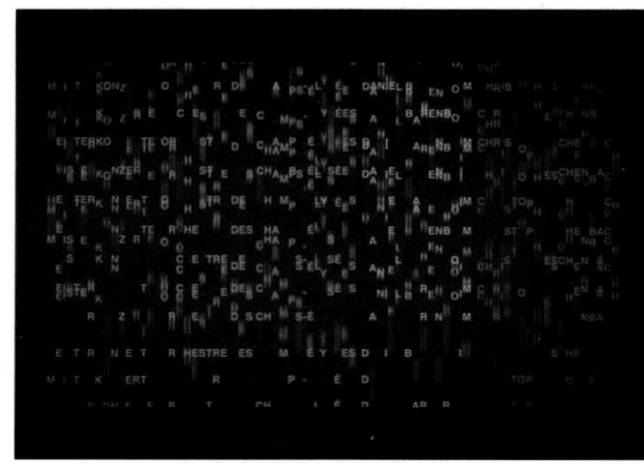

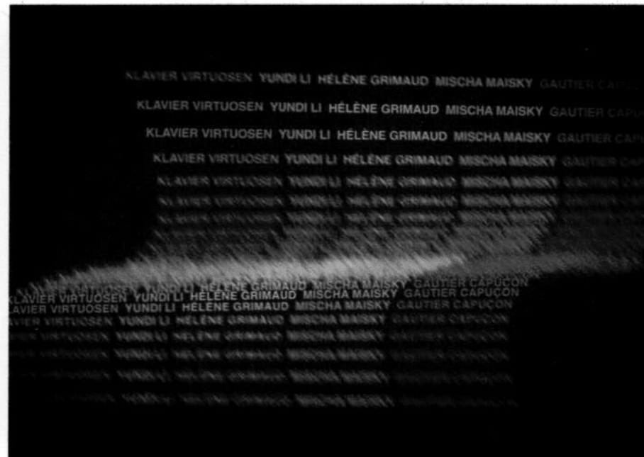

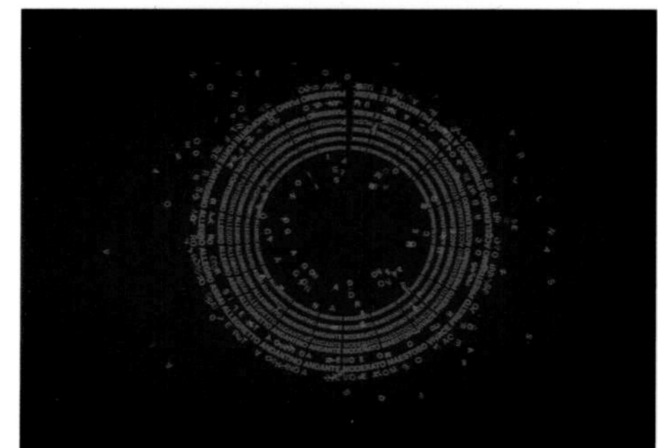

Typofonie
How do you represent music visually? By making letters move in time to a melody, we created the first-ever.

Hansabanka Open Card
Three Open paying cards for young people. Three levels: 1.level. People are young, newborn, with one eye and the whole surrounding world is like a miracle. 2.level. We grow,explore, discover. 3.level. - We become smarter. Bank helps, guides and educates.

Imagebroschüre
bauMax Imagebrochure. bauMax has been a pioneer of the do-it-yourself concept for 30 years and has effectively positioned itself as a leading brand in Central and Eastern Europe with a name recognition score of 95%. Message: "bauMax = do-it-yourself".

MSF 07
A Calendar inwhich each month is concerned with a professional skill that MSF needs to carry out its humanitarian projects.

MSF 07
Spain

National Award
Silver
Agency
Diego Feijóo
Client
Médecins Sans Frontières (MSF)
Designer
Diego Feijóo

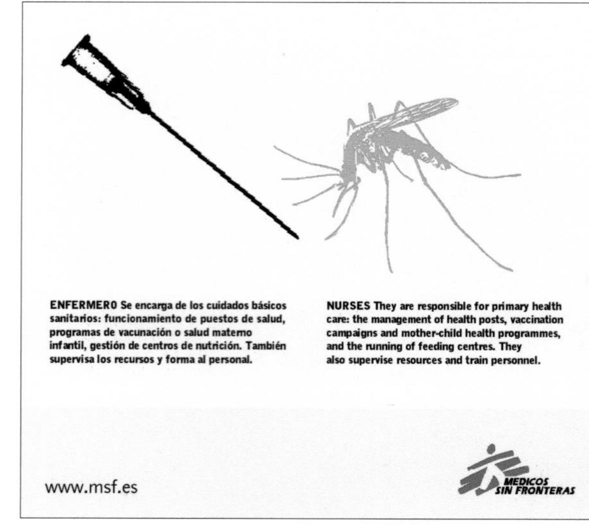

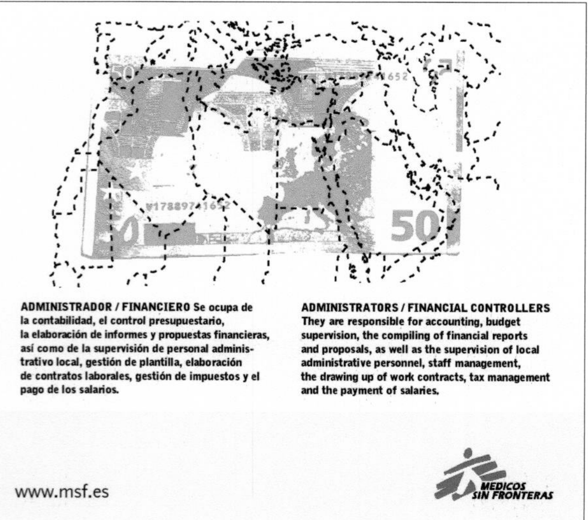

Imagebroschüre
Austria

National Award
Gold
Agency
Büro X Design GmbH
Client
bauMax AG
Creative Director
Dominik Cofalka, Andreas Miedaner
Art Director
Andreas Miedaner
Copywriter
Franziskus Kerssenbrock
Designer
Andreas Miedaner, Sascha Schaberl, Werner Singer
Production company
08/16 printproduktion
Photographer
Manfred Klimek, Klaus Vyhnalek
Graphics
Sascha Schaberl, Werner Singer, Sonja Handl,
Illustrator
Werner Singer

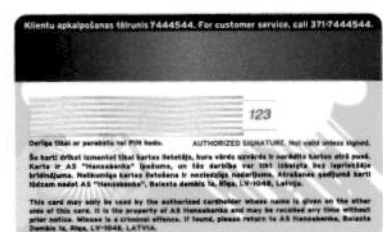

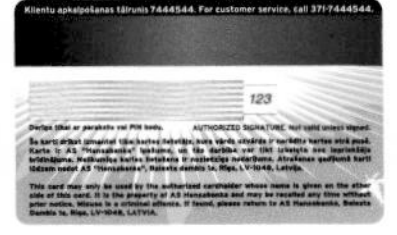

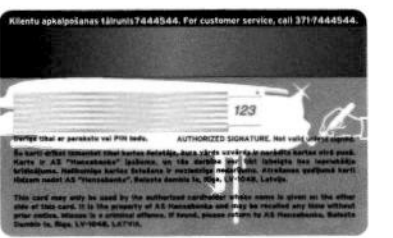

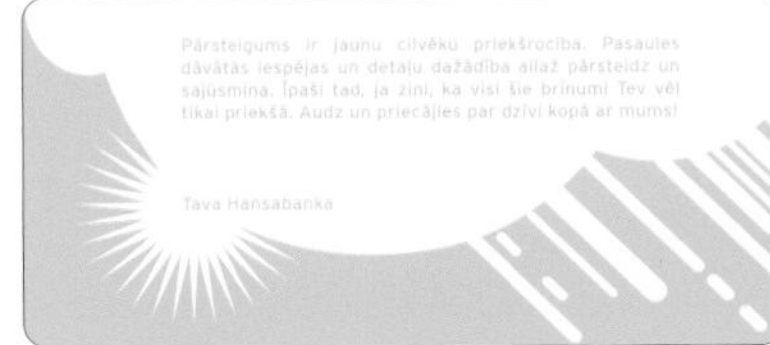

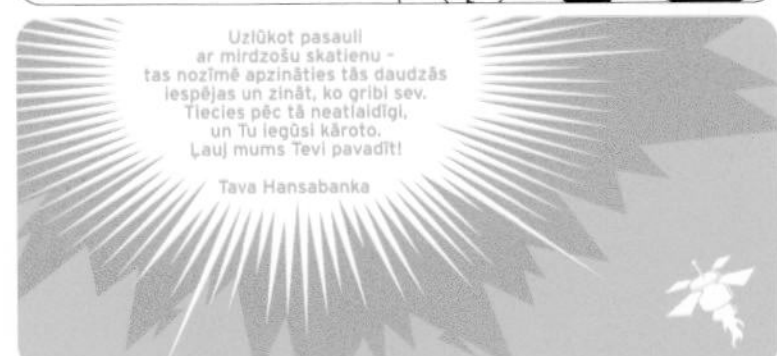

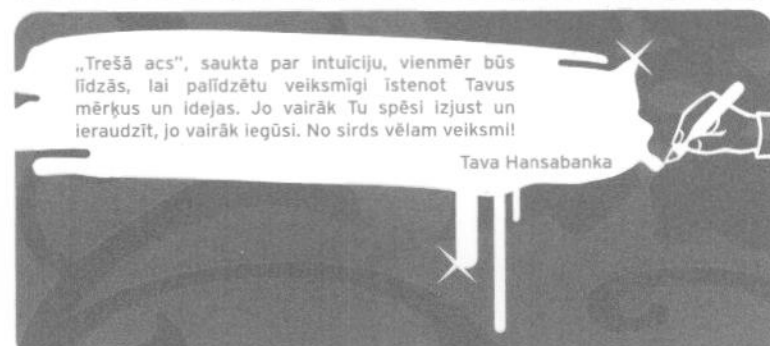

Hansabanka Open Card
Latvia

National Award
Silver
Agency
DDB Worldwide Latvia
Client
Hansabanka Jsc.
Creative Director
Kriss Salmanis
Art Director
Kriss Salmanis

Sail to the moon
Iceland

National Award
Silver
Agency
Royal
Client
Ampop
Art Director
Isak Winther and Petur Gudmundsson
Designer
Isak Winther and Petur Gudmundsson

Sail to the moon
CD cover for the band Ampop.

Breathing Prohibited
Exhibition catalogue "Breathing Prohibited" represents Evelinas Deicmanes video and photo installation where half-naked people are sitting, each in their private space, from the sundown until the moment when everything is completely dark. The catalogue's glossy surfaces causes the viewer to be reflected in the picture, so he must hide in a special black box on wheels. The goal of the catalogue was to give a sensual feeling and reflect the concept of the work.

Saeglopur
CD cover for the band Sigur Ros.

d[x]i magazine
Culture & post-design magazine, "d[x]i" is a 100% experimental platform that goes beyond the limits of editorial work, generating an independent environment of different viewpoints in contemporary culture, presented in an innovative layout. Free subscription world wide.

Breathing Prohibited
Latvia

National Award
Gold
Agency
Liene Drazniece
Client
Evelina Deicmane
Creative Director
Liene Drazniece
Art Director
Liene Drazniece

Saeglopur
Iceland

National Award
Gold
Agency
Royal
Client
Sigur Ros
Art Director
Isak Winther
Designer
Isak Winther,
Sigur Ros,
Alex Somers & Lukka
Sigurdardottir

d[x]i magazine
Spain

National Award
Gold
Agency
Equipo d[x]i
Client
d[x]i magazine
Creative Director
Alejandro Benavent
Art Director
Alejandro Benavent
Copywriter
Roger Omar
Designer
Alejandro Benavent

Calendar / Annual Report
Iceland

National Award
Gold
Agency
Tunglid
Client
Bakkavor Group
Art Director
Tomas Tomasson
Designer
Tomas Tomasson

Easily tricked
Iceland

National Award
Silver
Agency
Linda Loeskow
Client
Pineapplerecords
Art Director
Stephan Stephenssen
Designer
Linda Loeskow
Illustrator
Linda Loeskow

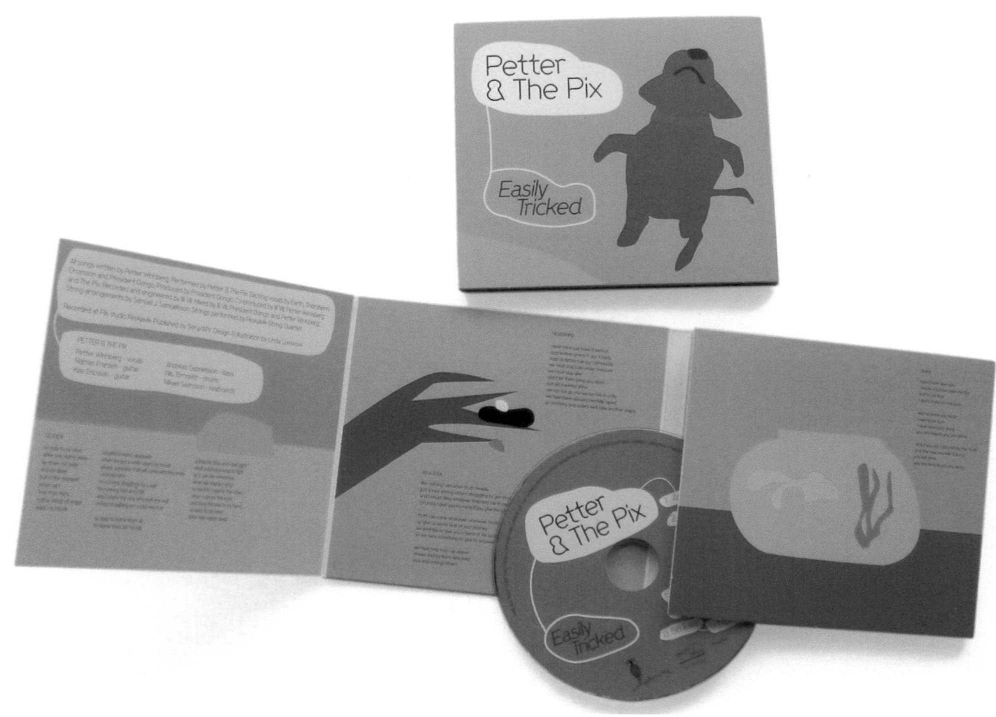

Calendar / Annual Report
Calendar and the annual report merge in one product.

Easily tricked
CD cover for the band Petter & the Pix.

Invitation "29th September"
Invitation to the centennial celebration of Siminn, the national phone company.

Adivinario
"Riddlar Calendar" A calendar which, month after month, suggests a riddle about an object to be recycled. The answer is described in a riddle and concludes with the impact it has on the environment when not recycled, or with the benefit that recycling brings it. It is printed using one ink and dyed paper free of chlorine or varnish, so that it is more environmentally friendly. Riddle: There are six in my family and in the parties there are dozens. We have much spark, we are very affectionate and we love people who kiss and squeeze us. The electricity that costs to make to me is three times the use of your home during a year. Answer: Tin.

Invitation “29th September”
Iceland

National Award
Silver
Agency
Ennemm
Client
Siminn
Art Director
Erla Gretarsdottir
Designer
Erla Gretarsdottir

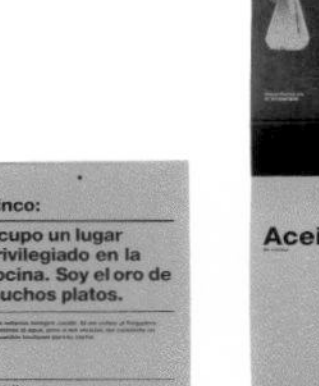

Adivinario
Spain

National Award
Silver
Agency
Dfraile
Client
Consejería de Medio Ambiente Región de Murcia
Creative Director
Eduardo del Fraile
Art Director
Eduardo del Fraile
Copywriter
Ana Leal
Designer
Eduardo del Fraile, Juan Jimenez, Antonio Marquez

Cada cosa al seu lloc
Spain

National Award
Silver
Agency
Bisgràfic
Client
Roda de Ter Town Council
Creative Director
Bisgràfic
Art Director
Bisgràfic
Copywriter
Bisgràfic
Designer
Bisgràfic
Production company
Bisgràfic
Photographer
Fotodisseny J.E
Graphics
Bisgràfic

Interferències
Spain

National Award
Silver
Agency
RUN Design
Client
Ajuntament de Terrassa (IMCET)
Creative Director
Xavier Roca Connétable
Art Director
Xavier Roca Connétable
Copywriter
Xavier Roca Connétable, Manuel Segade, Belén Simón
Designer
Xavier Roca Connétable
Graphics
Xavier Roca Connétable

Cada cosa al seu lloc
"Make no mistake: everything in its place". Roda de Ter Council's intention was to carry on encouraging the townspeople to leave their rubbish in the right kind of bin for selective collection and recycling, a system that had been started up a year before. So we cast around for an everyday image taken to absurd extremes, in order to show how easy it was to do what they were being asked to do: to put each kind of rubbish in the right place. The photo helped to achieve a sense of reality and of proximity to the people, thereby enhancing the message.

Interferències
"Interferences" Graphic campaign for a Contemporary Art festival at Terrassa (city near Barcelona). The posters show surprising minorities found in the real city statistics, ironizing of the real health of Contemporary Art in the city.Origami Visiting cards for the Take Away service.

RUN Stationery
Stationery for a Graphic Design Studio.

Origami
Stationery for a Take Away restaurant.

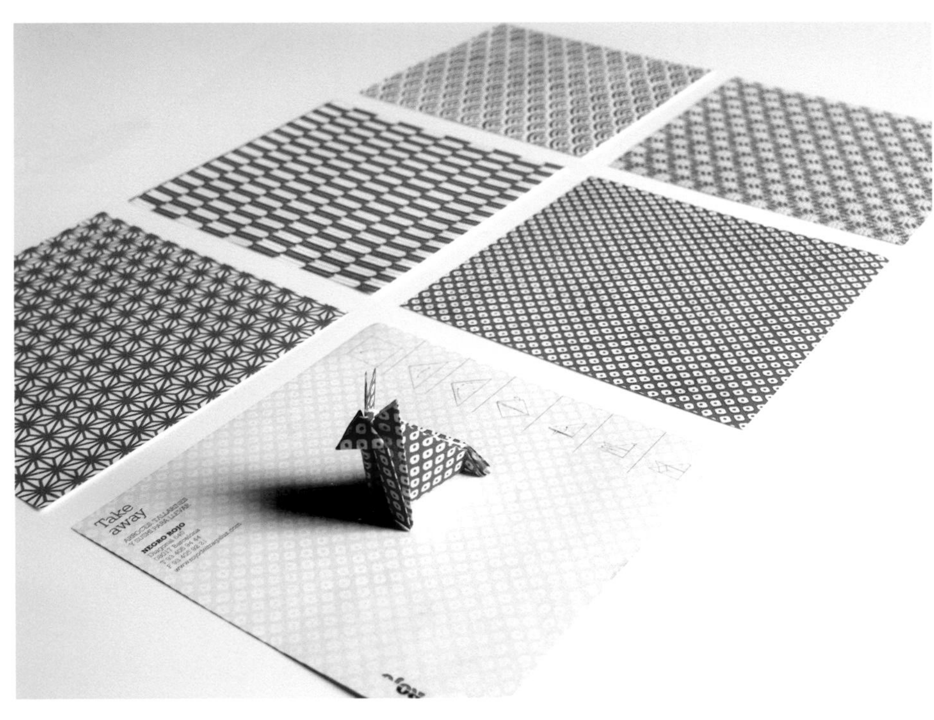

Origami
Spain

National Award
Silver
Agency
RUN Design
Client
Grupo Tragaluz, ROJO restaurant
Creative Director
Xavier Roca Connétable, Eva Balart, Sonia Estévez
Art Director
Xavier Roca Connétable, Eva Balart, Sonia Estévez
Designer
Xavier Roca Connétable, Eva Balart, Sonia Estévez
Production company
RUN Design
Graphics
Xavier Roca Connétable, Eva Balart, Sonia Estévez
Illustrator
Sonia Estévez

RUN Stationery
Spain

National Award
Silver
Agency
RUN Design
Client
RUN Design
Creative Director
Xavier Roca Connétable
Art Director
Xavier Roca Connétable
Designer
Xavier Roca Connétable, Eva Balart, Sonia Estévez
Graphics
Xavier Roca Connétable

Plat Combinat
Spain

National Award
Silver
Agency
Goroka TV
Client
Barcelona Televisió
Creative Director
Òscar López
Art Director
Santi Baró
Designer
Luz Galdeano
Production company
Goroka TV
Graphics
Aleix Abellanet
Other
Executive Producer:
Guille Cascante

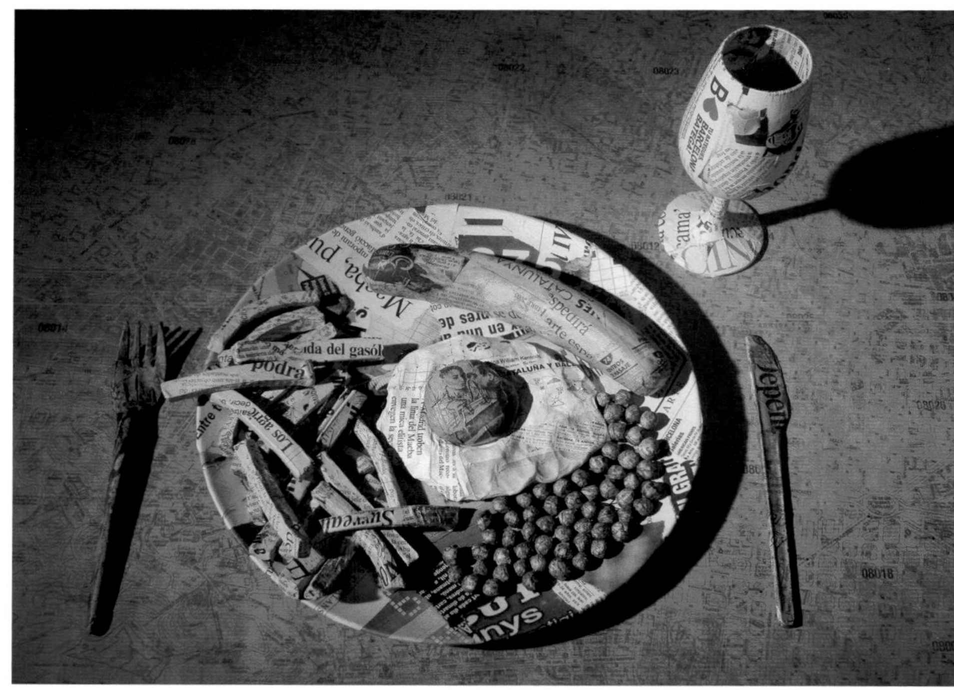

Innocent Graphics Calendar 07 Poster
Germany

National Award
Gold
Agency
Mola ativism
Client
M2
Creative Director
Rui Morais
Designer
Diogo Potes,
Pedro Carmo,
José Carlos Mendes

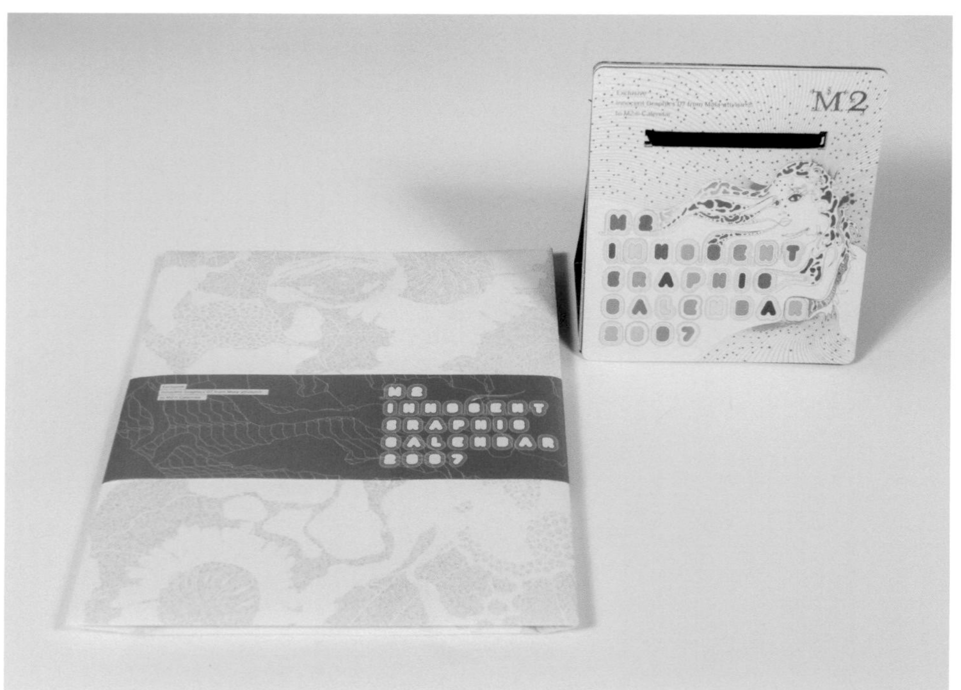

Hondas 2007 calendar/christmas card
New year's greetings and 2007 calendar. All the text is seen through perforated holes.

Innocent Graphics Calendar 07 Poster
The M2 poster is an item which incorporates and unifies all the illustrations which can be found in the Calendar. It harmoniously demonstrates how the different universes can combine and coexist.

CBasura?
"Waste?"
Promotional leaflet for demano - a firm which produces fashion accessories through recycled materials - on occasion of the Bread & Butter Barcelona fashion fair. The leaflet was a crumpled paper thrown on the floor, and it was distributed throughout the fair. This promotional element intended to promote the brand, as much as to offer an environmentally-aware point of view to the frivolous crowd which attends events of this nature.

Plat Combinat
"Combined dish". Gastronomy, culture and Barcelona are the 3 common items conducting the program. Starting out from a novel, a film or a specific disc, the audience initiates a route through the different gastronomy aspects of the city

Basura?
Spain

National Award
Gold
Agency
Mucho
Client
demano
Creative Director
Marc Català,
Pablo Juncadella
Art Director
Marc Català,
Pablo Juncadella
Designer
Marc Català
Graphics
Marc Català

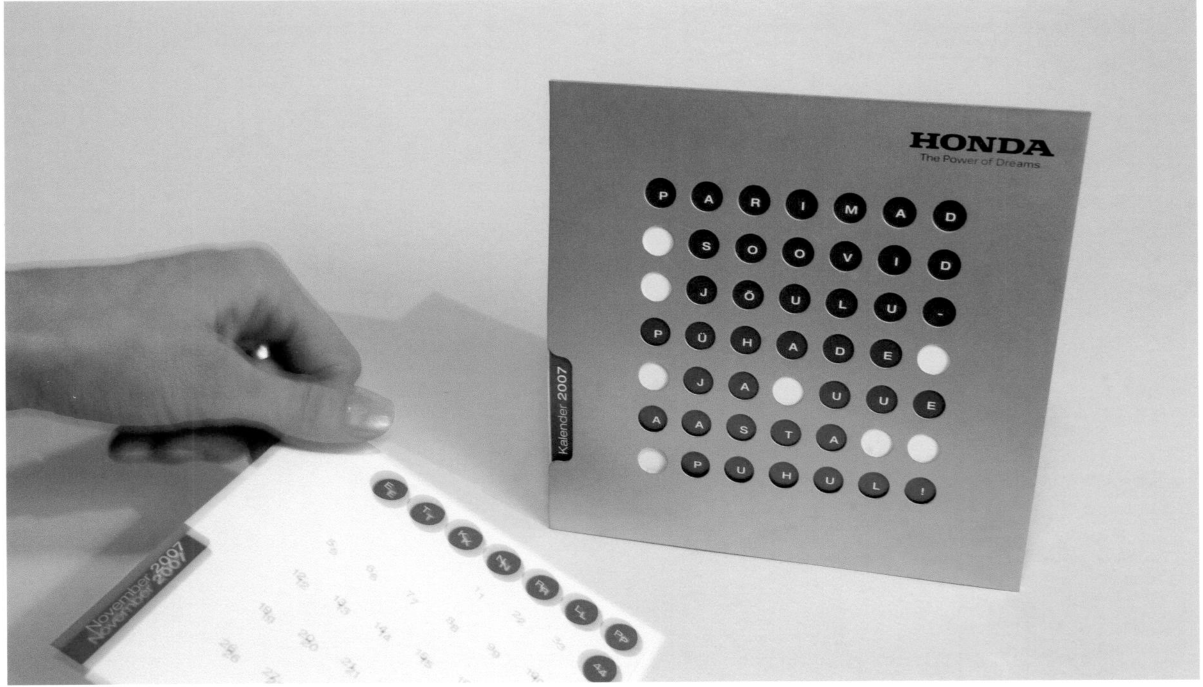

Hondas 2007 calendar/ christmas card
Estonia

National Award
Silver
Agency
Kontuur LB
Client
Honda Europe
Creative Director
Henri Jääger
Art Director
Kaia Rähn
Copywriter
Andrus Niit
Production company
Print House
Other
Project manager:
Karin Sepp

Invisible
To lean out to another world
Spain

National Award
Silver
Agency
Germinal Comunicación
Client
FEAPS. Región de Murcia
Creative Director
Jorge Martínez Pardo
Photographer
David Frutos Ruiz

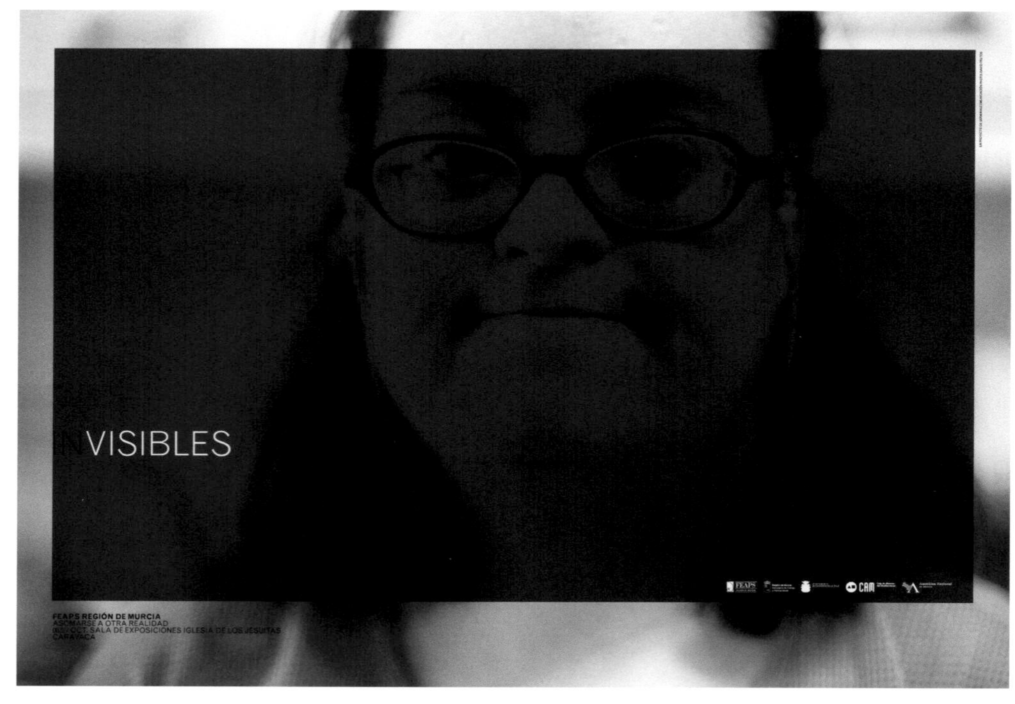

Invisible
To lean out to another world
4 billboards showing one exhibition with pictures of mentally disabled people in Murcia (Spain). To turn the invisible into visible demands an effort from the spectators. It demands a certain interest on their part and an approach to these people that don't exist for most of society. If there is no effort, there is no reading. The travelling-exhibition was held in a totally dark hall, and had to be seen with torches that were handed to the visitors at the entrance (some people complained about it and refused to enter).The best part of it was the experience shared with these families and the joy of all of the people at the event's opening. They were as happy as excited, very excited indeed- to have so many visitors coming to see them.

MSF poster
Spain

National Award
Gold
Agency
Diego Feijóo
Client
Médecins Sans Frontières (MSF)
Creative Director
Diego Feijóo
Designer
Shau Chung Shin, Diego Feijóo

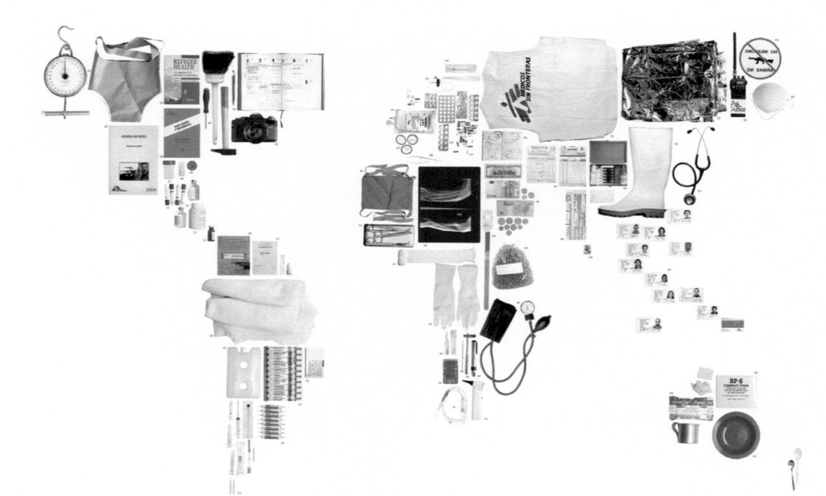

MSF poster
Equipment employed by MSF teams worldwide.

That's not entertainment
Poster of an exhibition about experimental cinema. Hollywood is ironically suggested. The design is based on the idea of type projected onto a wall. The typography is a decal which is stuck on various surfaces.

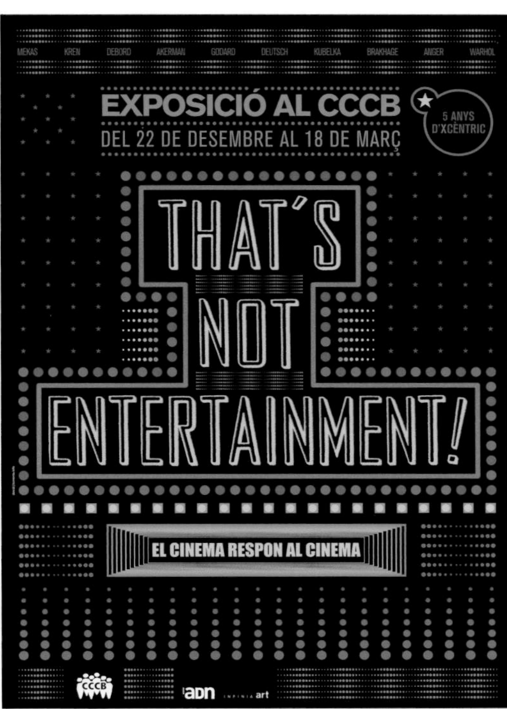

That's not entertainment! 1
Spain

National Award
Silver
Agency
David Torrents
Client
CCCB
Art Director
David Torrents
Designer
David Torrents, Anaïs Esmerado

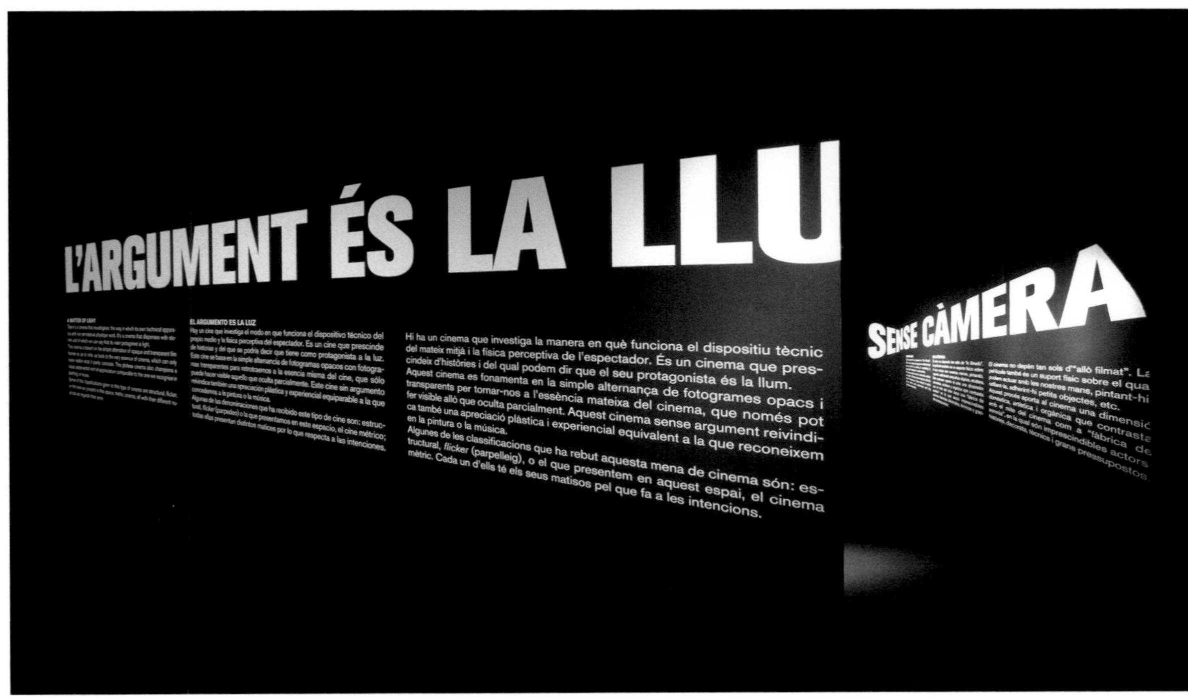

That's not entertainment! 2
Spain

National Award
Silver
Agency
David Torrents
Client
CCCB
Art Director
David Torrents
Designer
David Torrents, Anaïs Esmerado

Design. Editorial / Books / Corporate Publishing

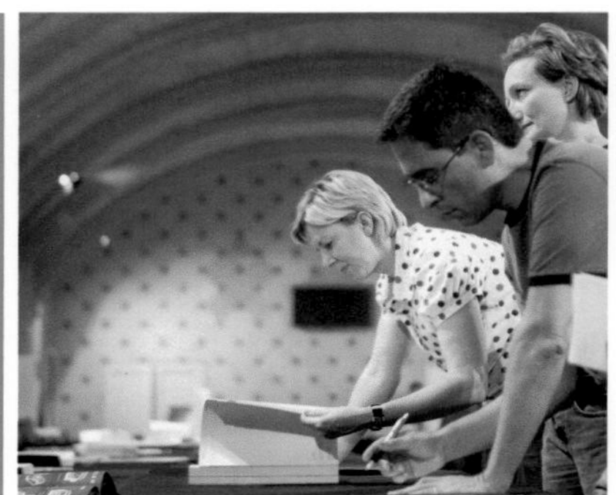

Austria: 2 Nominations

Estonia

Germany: 5 Nominations

Iceland

Italy: 1 Nomination

Latvia

Poland: 1 Nomination

Portugal

Russia

Spain: 2 Nominations

Switzerland: Gold

Gold
Fleurop Interflora Annual Report 2005
Switzerland

National Award
Silver
Agency
walker
Client
Fleurop Interflora
Creative Director
Pius Walker
Art Director
Mieke Haase
Copywriter
Rita Erb,
Sabine Manecke
Graphics
Jan-Christoph Prilop,
Oliver Griep
Illustrator
Martin Müller

the power of flowers
Geschäftsbericht 2005
Fleurop-Interflora (Schweiz)

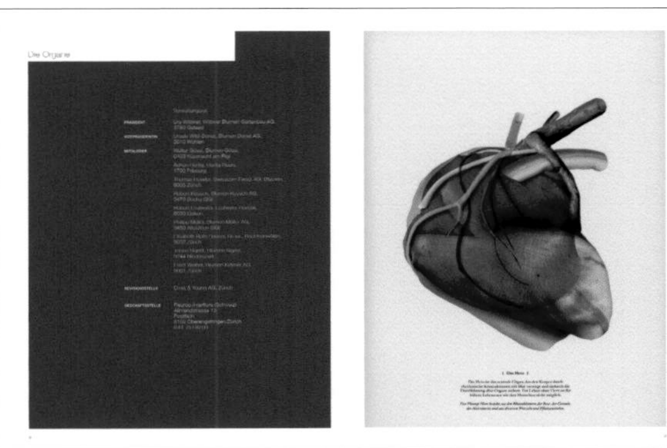

The Business report **2005** endorses the reorientation of the brand with the new corporate design and highlights the beauty and expressive power of flowers. Each graphic is illustrated exclusively with flowers.

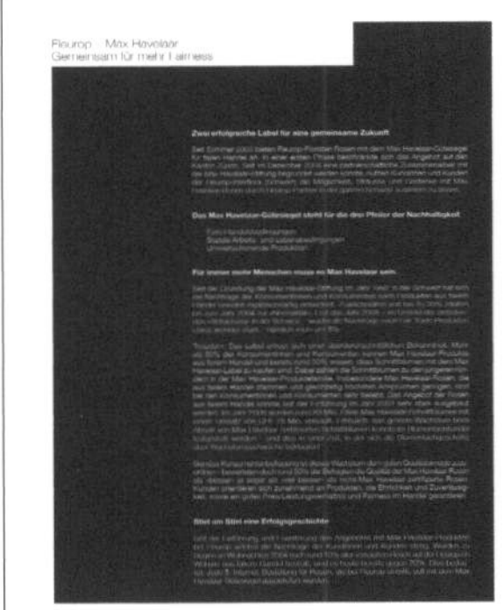

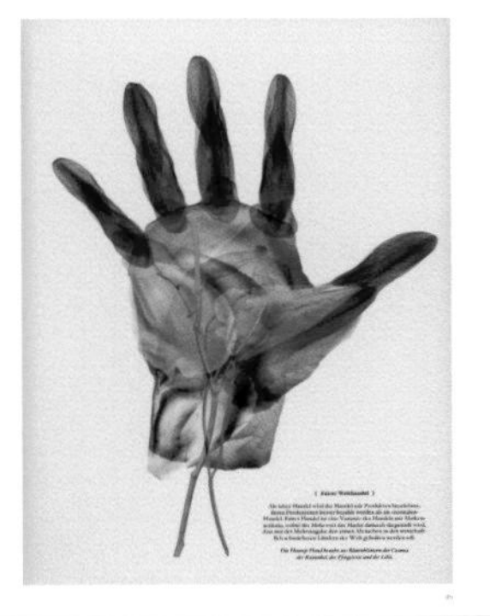

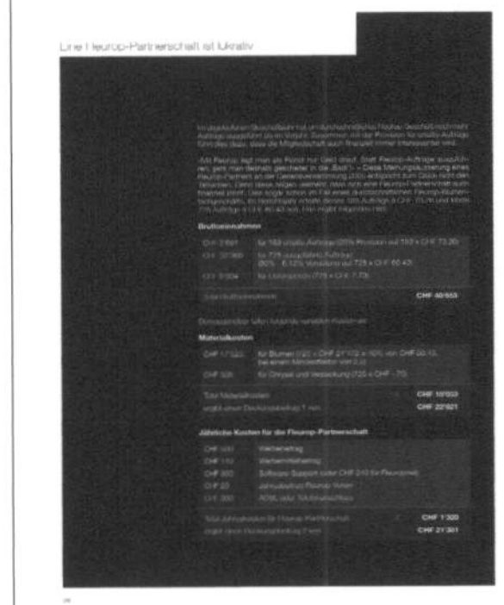

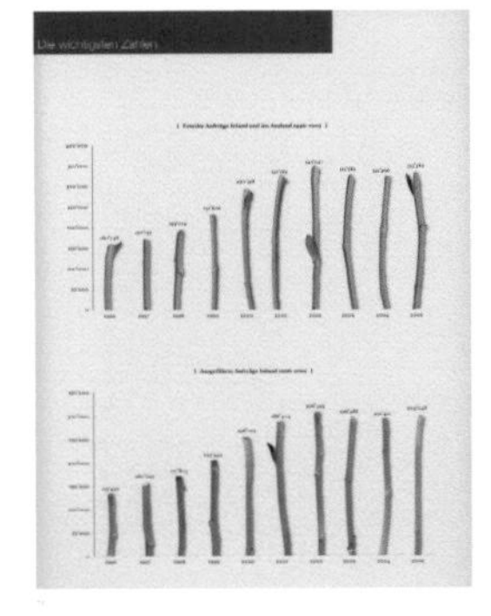

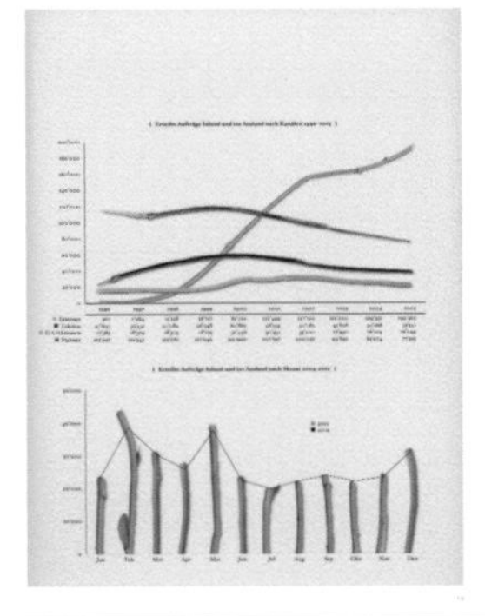

Nomination

CCA Annual 2006 - 0,36 Euro pro Idee

Austria

National Award
Silver
Agency
halle34 Albert Handler / Marcus Arige OEG
Client
Creativ Club Austria
Creative Director
Albert Handler
Art Director
Albert Handler, Emanuela Sarac
Copywriter
Christian Halmdienst
Graphics
Wolfgang Bader
Other
Ekkehard Schitter, Tibor Barci, Hans Feik

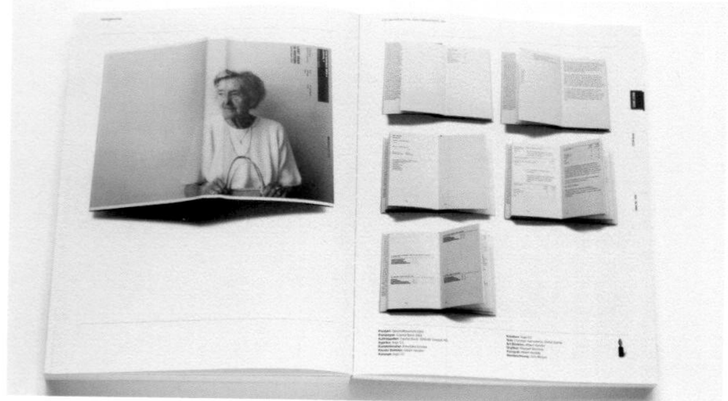

Nomination
Modebuch Contemporary Fashion from Austria
Austria

National Award
Gold
Agency
halle34 Albert Handler / Marcus Arige OEG
Client
Unit F buero fuer mode
Creative Director
Albert Handler
Art Director
Albert Handler
Production company
Copyright
Graphics
Anouke Rehorek
Other
Ulrike Tschabitzer, Katrin Seiler

CONTEMPORARY FASHION FROM AUSTRIA

—— Vienna has never been a fashion capital in the „classic" sense such as Paris, with its historical fashion roots reaching back through the centuries. And in comparison with Milan it's simply missing the economic power and industrial infrastructure.

—— Nevertheless, in the past decades Vienna has gradually managed to carve out its own place on the fashion landscape. A new generation of Austrian fashion designers is today making waves in the international trade press and conquering new terrain in the retail markets.

—— Idiosyncratic, closely tied to the artistic avant–garde, with a large dose of stock of creativity and intellectual introspection coupled with meticulous craftsmanship – these are some of the identifying features of contemporary Austrian fashion design. These properties are joined by a strong affinity for all forms of media presentation and integration into closely woven networks in the fields of fashion photography, art and music.

—— Some of today's most prominent international fashion labels of Austrian provenance are presented in the following.

---WENDY&JIM Established in 1997 by Helga Schania and Hermann Fankhauser, the Wendy&Jim label is among the „shooting stars" on the international fashion firmament. Particularly in Japan, the two former Helmut Lang students at the University of Applied Arts in Vienna have achieved something like cult status with their conceptual approach to fashion.
„We look at fashion from a very pragmatic point of view", Helga Schania and Hermann Fankhauser explain. „We try to push each garment to its limits. For example: How long can a sports jacket get before it's not a sports jacket anymore but a coat instead? It's really fun for us to deal with these kinds of questions and to make sure that journalists understand what a collection is all about. We're getting better and better at it. Our statements are becoming clearer."

—— Wendy&Jim define their brand philosophy as „a radical approach to the garment". Every piece in a collection plays a part in an overall theme. For these designers, „it's not about looking good or bad, but about following a line, a theme. We're interested in a signature style, in distinctiveness. The creative process is in the foreground. It's about being noticed. We have made ourselves visible in the international media from the very start."

—— International magazines such as i-D, Purple, Selfservice, Dazed & Confused, Flux and Surface have featured clothes designed by Wendy&Jim or interviews introducing the designer duo.

—— They display their creations not only at conventional fashion shows but also in settings verging on the art-world context, in the form of installations and performances. „We really enjoy working with people from different fields", say Schania/Fankhauser but qualify this statement by adding: „But we've realized that we run the risk of watering down our own contribution. We've now decided to work with others only on occasion – and of course to raise the standard."

—— For their 2006 summer collection, „Risk", the designers collaborated with the Viennese media artist Peter Kogler who has achieved fame with works such as his „Ameisenbilder" („Ant Prints"), shown at the documenta in Kassel. Wendy&Jim characterize this collaboration as „outstanding". „Great things came out of this: the media is still talking about it. Clothes with prints like these had never before been seen in Paris."

—— Wendy&Jim's creative network also includes photographers like Udo Titz and Michael Dürr as well as the Japanese avant-garde label Cosmic Wonder.

—— Starting with their first international appearance in 1999 at the Hyères Fashion Festival, Wendy&Jim have been presenting their collections at the prêt-à-porter shows in Paris. They have also been part of the regular fashion scene there since October 2003, as part of the „Calendrier" show selectively compiled by the Chambre Syndicale du Prêt-à-Porter des Couturiers et des Créateurs de Mode.

—— Creations by Wendy&Jim are in especially high demand on the Asian market. Today, the designers are not only represented by a press office in Paris, but also employ a press and marketing agency in Tokyo.

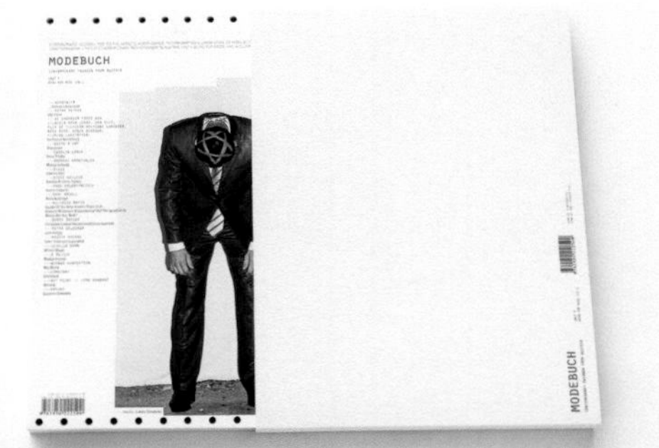

CCA Annual 2006 - 0,36 Euro pro Idee
The look and feel is as simple as it can be. The creative officers and their works are the important content of this book. If you divide the price of the book by the number of excellent ideas you get a price per idea of 0.36 euros.

Modebuch Contemporary Fashion from Austria
Creative director Albert Handler and the Graphic design Agency halle34 had the target to create a German and English version which should not be designed one after another. The result is the first endless book (on 28.4 metres of endless paper).

Nomination
Book of Independence
Germany

National Award
Bronze
Agency
Strichpunkt
Client
Papierfabrik Scheufelen GmbH & Co. KG
Creative Director
Kirsten Dietz, Jochen Raedeker
Art Director
Kirsten Dietz
Designer
Susanne Hoerner, Anika Marquardsen, Felix Widmaier
Production company
Universitaetsdruckerei Mainz
Photographer
Niels Schubert, Oliver Jung, Christian Schmidt
Illustrator
Anders Bergesen, Anika Marquardsen

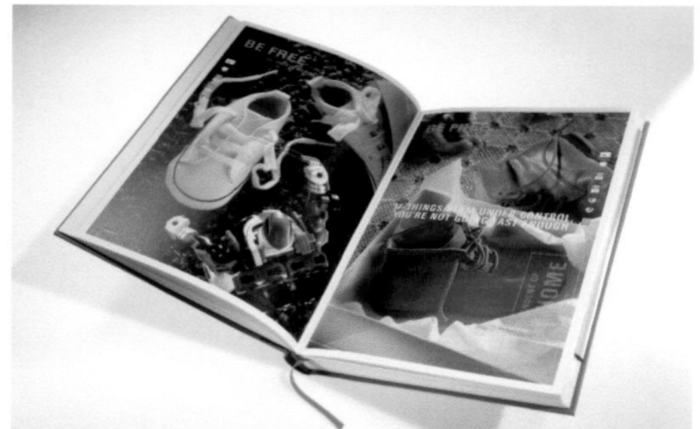

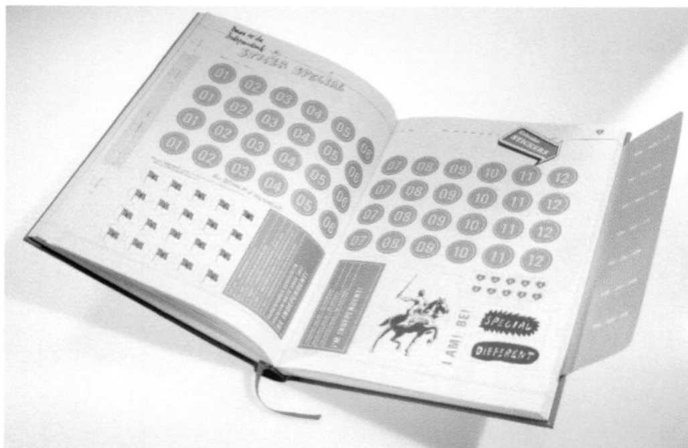

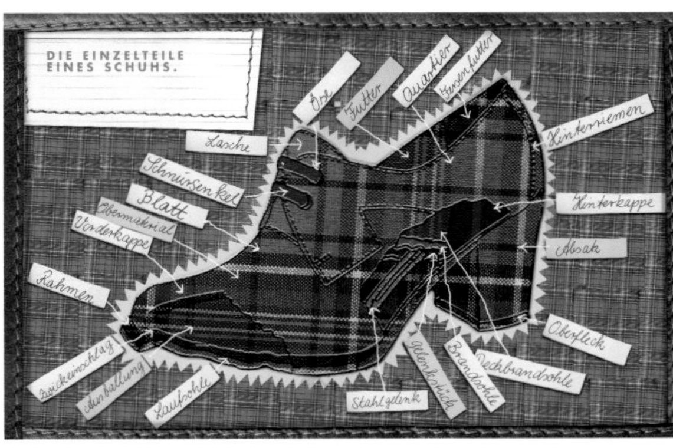

☆

Nomination
Die kleine Schu(h)lfibel
Germany

National Award
Bronze
Agency
Guertlerbachmann Werbung GmbH
Client
Ludwig Goertz GmbH
Creative Director
Uli Guertler
Art Director
Alexander Roetterink
Copywriter
Jens Ringena
Designer
Uli Guertler, Alexander Roetterink
Production company
Produktionsbuero Romey von Malottky GmbH
Graphics
Veronika Kieneke
Illustrator
Uli Guertler, Alexander Roetterink

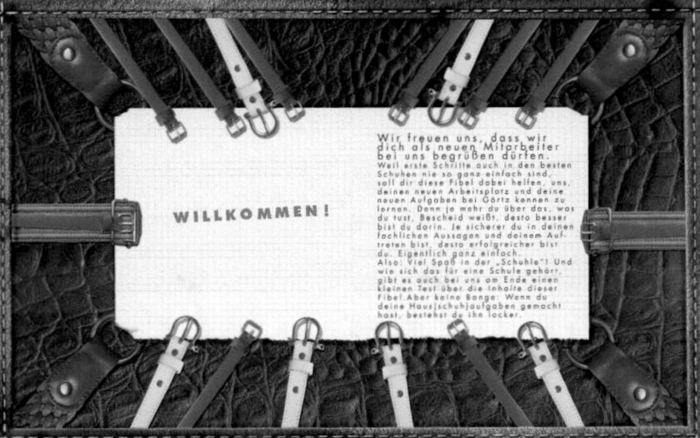

Book of Independence
Through photographs and text, the Book of Independence illustrates the various stages of life, and shows high-quality processing methods on the unique premium paper.

Die kleine Schu(h)lfibel
It is a German word play. Schulfibel describes books that kids use in Primary School. These are learning books. Working as a shoe salesmen at Goertz 17 is an enjoyable, yet challenging job. The Book supplies new employees with the basic information for the daily work. The Book should upgrade the in-house image and encourage employees to a long-term commitment.

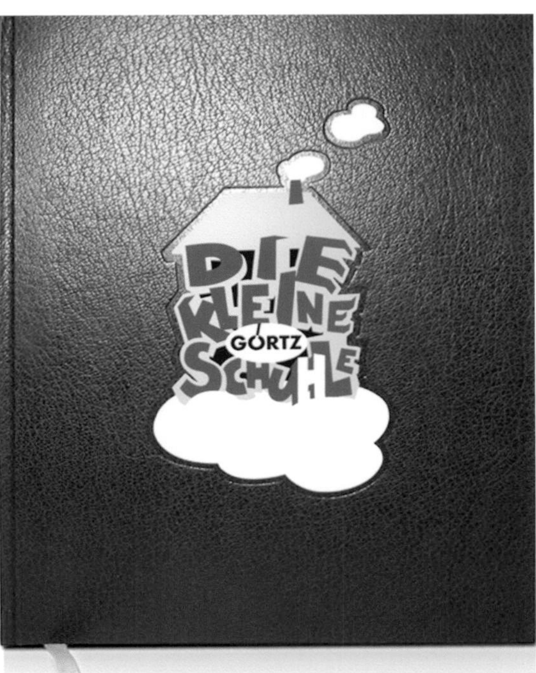

Nomination
kontaminiert
Germany

National Award
Shortlist
Agency
Alan von Luetzau
Designer
A. von Luetzau,
D. Fitzgerald,
H. Nordiek, Y. Stier

kontaminiert
"Contaminated". For the 20th commemoration of the catastrophe at Chernobyl, a book was designed including an illustrated storyline of the events that happened in Chernobyl and also a corresponding booklet of additional information and eye-witness reports.

Polyplaypylene
To mark LEGO's 50th anniversary in Germany, selected members of the press and LEGO partners were to be presented with a high-quality, unusual gift. A luxury version was to be produced for the company's 20 most important partners, and a standard version for a further 500 partners and press representatives. The Solution: Committed LEGO fan and designer Reginald Wagner used a pinhole camera to produce a book of his own personal LEGO memories, to ensure they never faded away. The book takes the form of a LEGO brick, with the luxury version featuring a cover actually made of LEGO, while the standard version is available as a paperback.

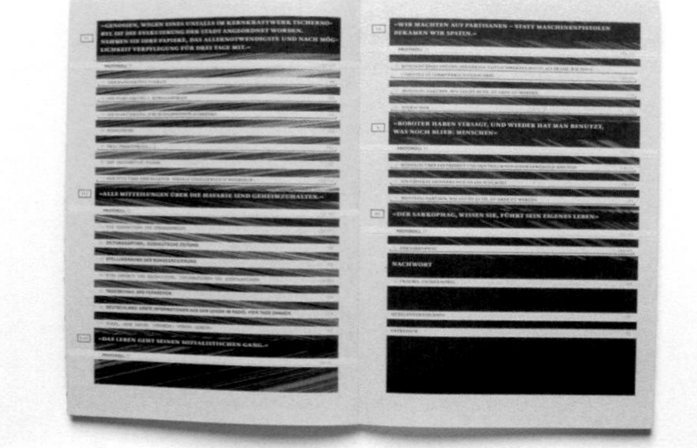

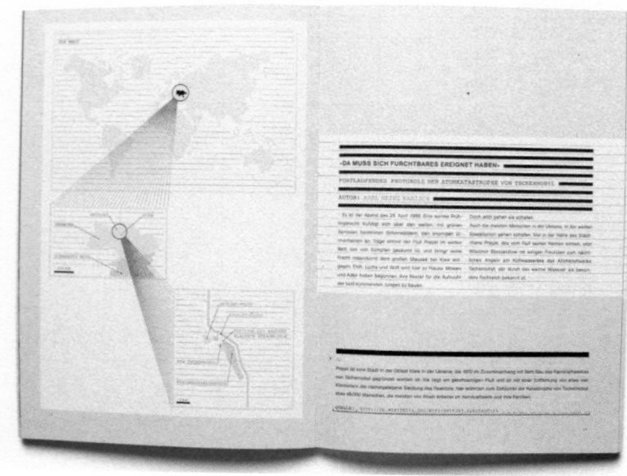

Nomination
Polyplaypylene
Germany

National Award
Bronze
Agency
Kolle Rebbe Werbeagentur GmbH/ KOREFE
Client
LEGO GmbH
Creative Director
Katrin Oeding
Art Director
Reginald Wagner
Copywriter
Alexander Baron
Designer
Reginald Wagner
Photographer
Reginald Wagner
Graphics
Reginald Wagner
Other
Account manager: Thomas Stritz, Manuela Maurer

Nomination
The Heavyweight Brochure
Germany

National Award
Bronze
Agency
BBDO Stuttgart GmbH
Client
Siegline Betzler, Personal Trainer
Creative Director
Armin Jochum, Stefan Nagel
Art Director
Stefan Nagel, Carolin Frick, Melanie Sonnenschein
Copywriter
A. Jochum, S. Dudic, A. Szymanski, J. Homoki
Production company
Cicero Werkstudio
Photographer
Niels Schubert
Illustrator
Joseph Hanopol
Other
Agency Producer:
Wolfgang Schif

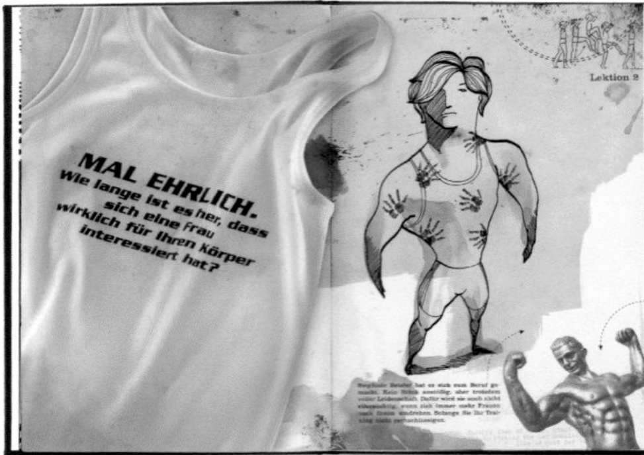

The Heavyweight Brochure
Betzler's Personal Training "The heavyweight brochure". Sieglinde Betzler will work you into a sweat right from the start. The heavyweight brochure contains solid steel plate in the binding. In order to lift it, open it and read it you have to really put in some effort: it weighs 2 kg! 200 mailings were sent out to a target audience of senior decision-makers.

Le Dictateur
Mickey Mouse in formaldheyde

A thin, linen-bound hardback brochure that holds more than it promises: it weighs an amazing 2kg!

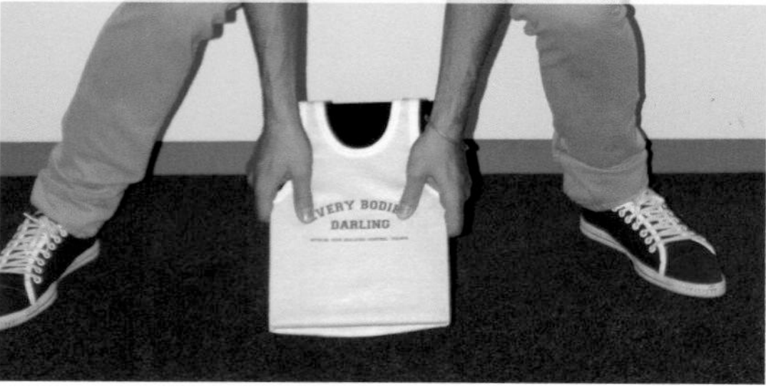

Nomination
Le Dictateur
Italy

National Award
Silver
Agency
Le Dictateur
Client
Le Dictateur
Creative Director
Federico Pepe,
Pier Paolo Ferrari

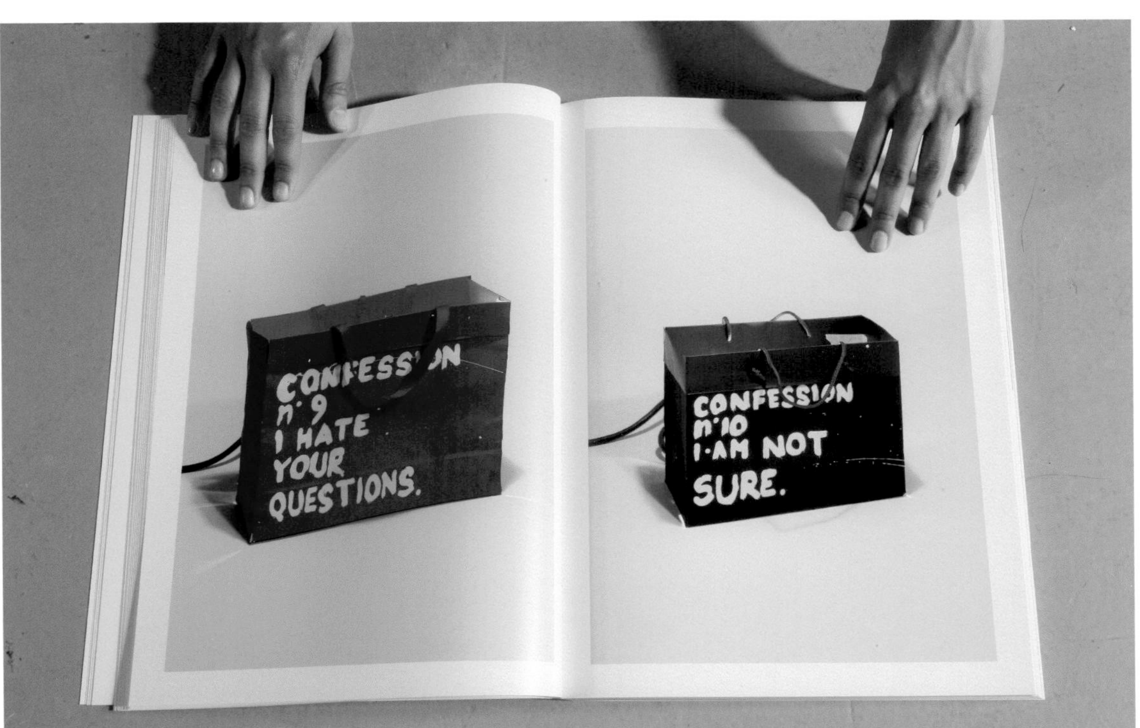

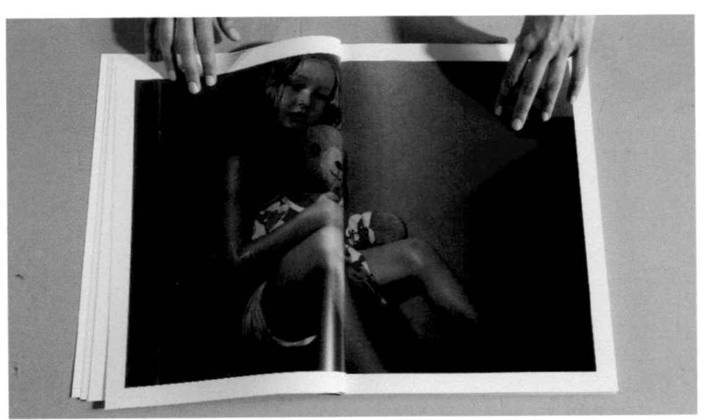

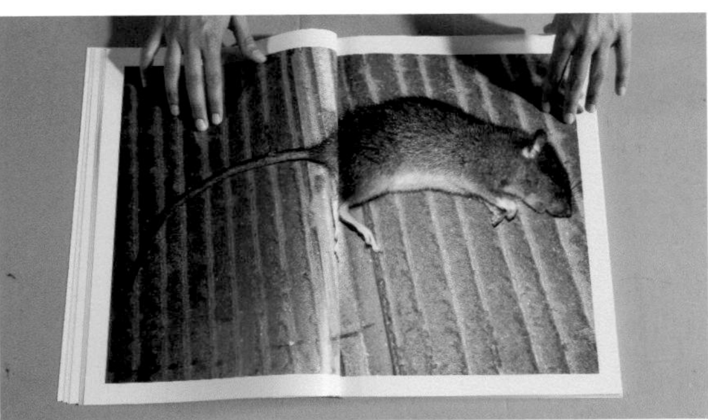

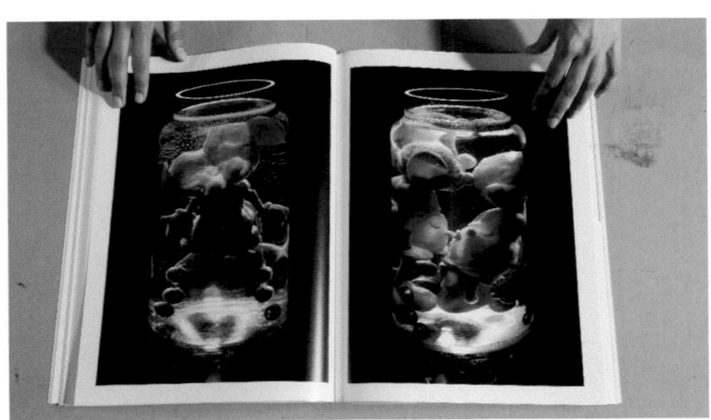

Nomination
Futu Magazine
Poland

National Award
Silver
Agency
White Cat Studio
Client
Futu Group
Creative Director
Michal Lojewski
Designer
Michal Lojewski
Production company
Futu Group:
Wojtek Ponikowski
Illustrator
Tomasz Walenta
Other
Futu Group:
Wojtek Ponikowski

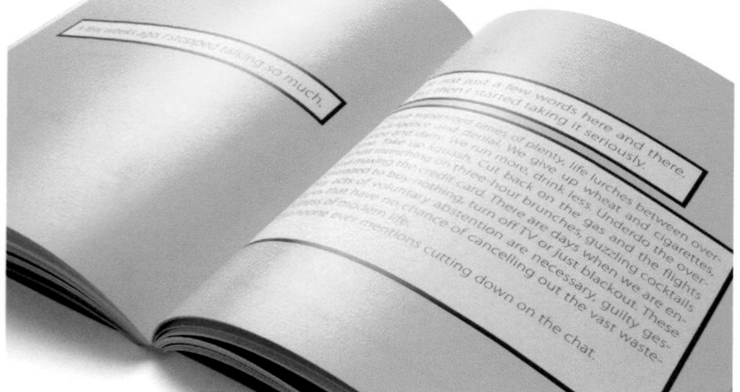

Futu Magazine
FUTU Magazine presents new forms of luxury, design and architecture. FUTU Magazine reveals the world of premium brands. FUTU Magazine is toll-free and is distributed to a select group of receivers in limited circulation. Logo, visual identity and layout design. Design of the first, second and third two-monthly issues.

El Silencio es Música
Golf, as well as a sport, can also be a nice opportunity to get closer to nature. To enjoy the landscape in all senses. Different graphic pieces were developed to communicate this concept. New corporative identity.

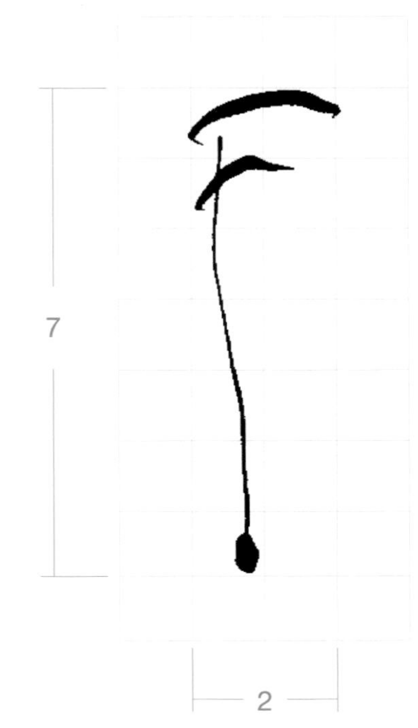

Nomination
El Silencio es Música
Spain

National Award
Bronze
Agency
ABM Serveis de Comunicació
Client
Fontanals Golf
Creative Director
Jaume Anglada
Art Director
Nuria Hugue, Nacho Tabares
Copywriter
Jaume Anglada
Photographer
Lluís Carro, Jaume Diana
Graphics
Xavi Gómez

Nomination
The Annual of Annuals
Spain

National Award
Gold
Agency
Mucho
Client
The Art Directors Club of Europe
Creative Director
Pablo Juncadella, Marc Català
Art Director
Pablo Juncadella, Marc Català
Designer
Pablo Juncadella, Carla Bahna
Photographer
Nacho Alegre
Graphics

Pablo Juncadella

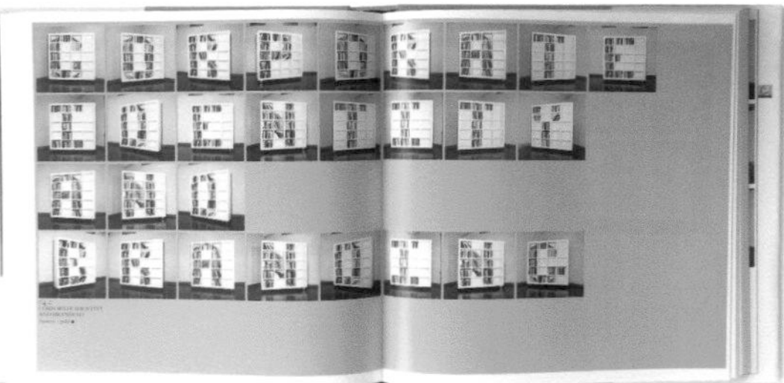

The Annual of Annuals
For "The Annual of Annuals 2007" an alphabet was designed - the Book Book - made out of books, and one single panoramic picture was produced for the cover. The Annual of Annuals is a book of books showing the best of design and advertising in Europe. The book's design is a visual solution to this definition.

Parabol AM #2
Parabol AM is a magazine for international contemporary art. Each issue is devised by a curator. Each deviser's task is to examine a contemporary phenomenon in pictures and words on the basis of artistic points of view.

Anniversary book
Anniversary book for Kalev's 200th birthday. The story of Kalev Chocolate Factory

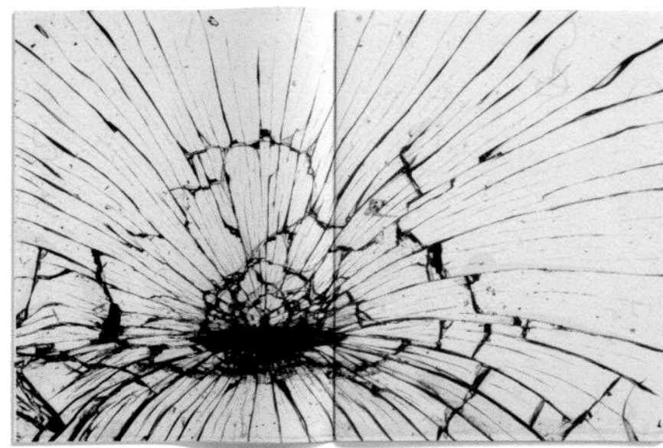

Parabol AM #2
Austria

National Award
Silver
Agency
section.d
Client
Parabol
Creative Director
Chris Goennawein
Art Director
Chris Goennawein
Copywriter
Curator: Ami Barak
Graphics
Chris Goennawein

Anniversary book
Estonia

National Award
Gold
Agency
Division
Client
Kalev Chocolate Factory
Creative Director
Dan Mikkin
Art Director
Dan Mikkin
Copywriter
Otto Kubo
Designer
Dan Mikkin
Photographer
Toomas Tikenberg
Graphics
Dan Mikkin
Illustrator
Dan Mikkin

Advertise & Sell
Germany

National Award
Gold
Agency
KNSK Werbeagentur GmbH
Client
Dummy Magazin
Creative Director
Tim Krink, Niels Holle, Christian Traut
Art Director
Oliver Fermer, Paul Snowden
Photographer
Peter Lueders

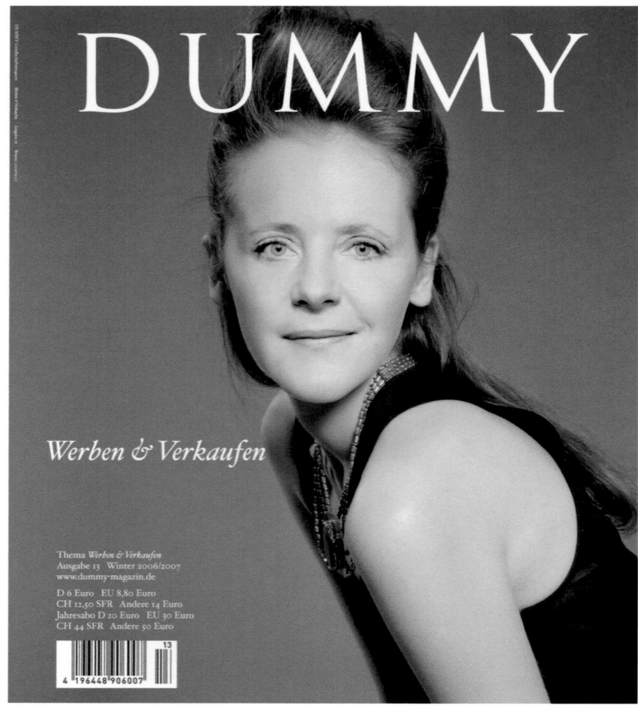

Odyssee der guten Idee
"The Odyssey of Good Ideas"
Brochure proving the client to be the most creative partner for storyboarding.

Die letzten zehn Jahre im Eiltempo - Von 1996 bis 2006 in zehn Minuten
TEMPO magazine closes the gap between the nineties and the present. A rapid look over the last ten years - From 1996 to 2006 in ten minutes. Illustrated figures show how the world has changed in the last ten years.

Danke fuer die Blumen / Danke fuer die Zeilen
"Thanks for the flowers / Thanks for the lines". Wolfgang Tillmans dared to tackle a new subject for the anniversary issue of TEMPO and we added Rainals Goetz's wishes for the coming years. Germany's most famous photo artist meets Germany's most influential writer.

Odyssee der guten Idee
Germany

National Award
Silver
Agency
Stefanscheer.com
Client
Storyboards Deutschland GmbH
Creative Director
Stefan Scheer, Gerhard Schmal
Illustrator
Elisabeth Moch

Die letzten zehn Jahre im Eiltempo

Von 1996 bis 2006 in zehn Minut en

Jetzt aber rasch! 1996 wurde TEMPO eingestellt, jetzt ist es noch einmal da. Auf den folgenden Seiten schliessen wir die Lücke zwischen damals und heute. Zuerst zeigen wir, wie sich die Welt in den vergangenen zehn Jahren verändert hat. Danach rechnen wir mit den Idolen der TEMPO-Dekade ab: Wer wurde zum Verräter, wer ist immer noch ein Held?

Die letzten zehn Jahre im Eiltempo - Von 1996 bis 2006 in zehn Minuten
Germany

National Award
Gold
Agency
Fifteen Minutes / Jahreszeitenverlag
Client
Fifteen Minutes / Jahreszeitenverlag
Creative Director
Markus Peichl
Art Director
Alexander Wiederin, Heiko Keinath
Graphics
Gaab, Gnaedinger, Hartwig, Hoff, Liebchen, Monheim, Noshe

WAHRHEIT NR. 10
Im Schönen steckt immer noch am meisten Wahrheit.
DANKE FÜR DIE BLUMEN
Vor 17 Jahren stand er plötzlich da. Mit strahlendem Lachen und einer umwerfenden Fotomappe. Wolfgang Tillmans hatte gerade sein Studium beendet. Er suchte einen Job, und wir ließen ihn Gerhard Schröder fotografieren. Es war der Beginn einer großen Künstlerkarriere: Turner-Preis, Tate-Modern-Ausstellung, legendäre Bilder von Supermodels, Partynächten, Freunden und der Concorde. Für die TEMPO-Jubiläumsausgabe wagte sich Tillmans jetzt an ein neues Sujet.

Danke fuer die Blumen / Danke fuer die Zeilen
Germany

National Award
Silver
Agency
Fifteen Minutes / Jahreszeitenverlag
Client
Fifteen Minutes / Jahreszeitenverlag
Creative Director
Markus Peichl
Art Director
Alexander Wiederin, Heiko Keinath
Photographer
Wolfgang Tillmans
Other
Text: Rainald Goetz

Generalverdacht
Germany

National Award
Gold
Agency
Sueddeutsche Zeitung Magazin
Client
Sueddeutsche Zeitung Magazin
Creative Director
Mirko Borsche
Copywriter
Sueddeutsche Zeitung Magazin
Photographer
Mirko Borsche
Graphics
A. Blaschke, M. Blomeyer, D. Bognar, O. Landgraf

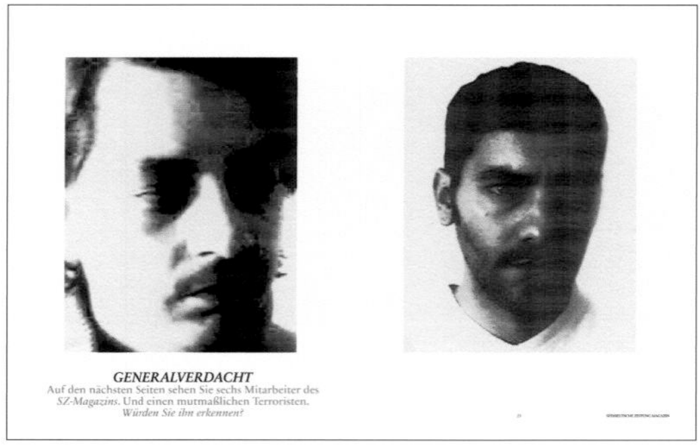

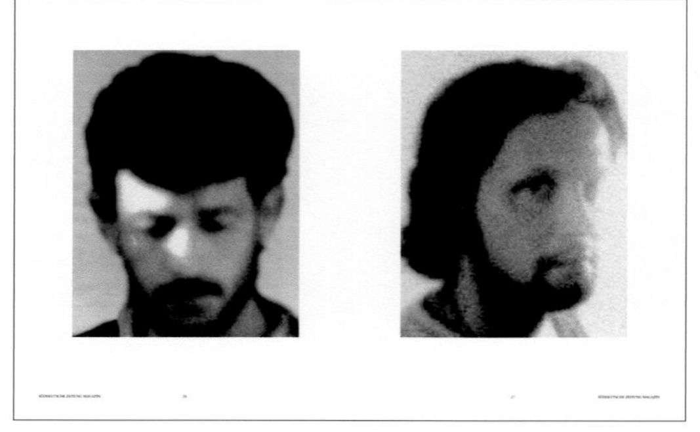

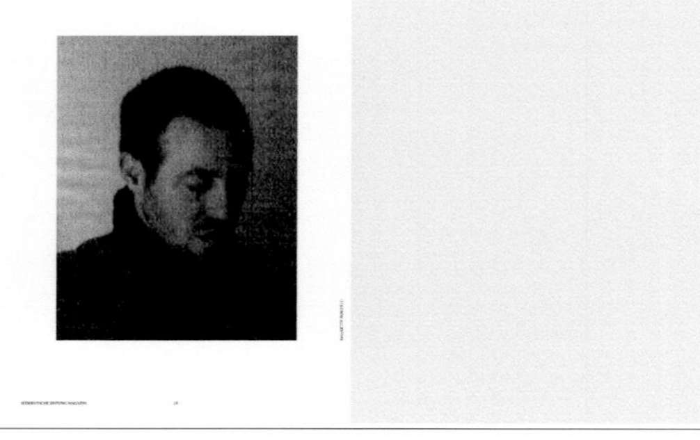

Handelsblatt 60th Anniversary Issue
Germany

National Award
Silver
Agency
KircherBurkhardt Editorial & Corporate Comm.
Client
Handelsblatt GmbH
Art Director
Brian O'Connor
Graphics
Jan Schwochow, Markus Kluger

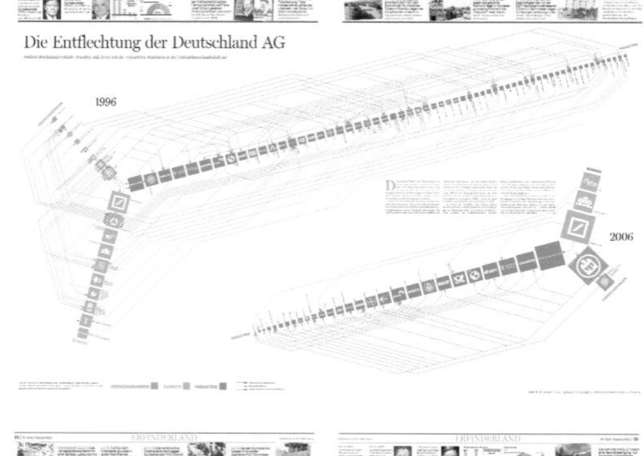

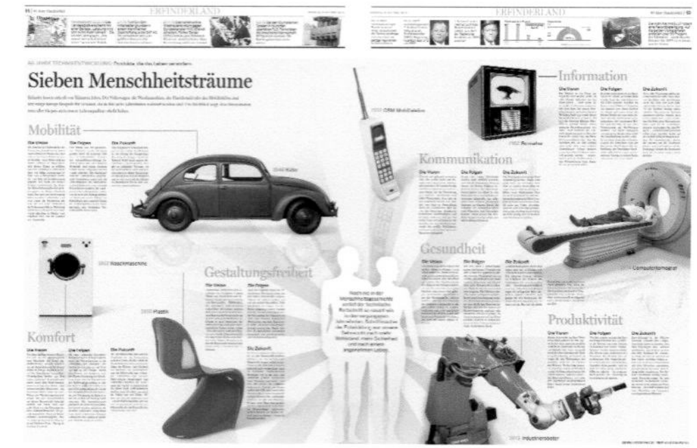

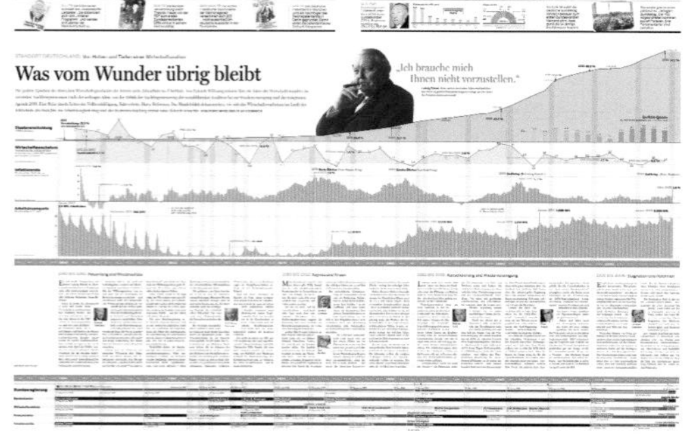

Generalverdacht
"General Suspicion"
Members of the editorial office were photographed in the fashion of Islamic terrorists to show how exchangeable the images are.

Handelsblatt 60th Anniversary Issue
Graphical rendition of four topics for Handelsblatt 60th Anniversary Issue.
1. What remains of the economic miracle
2. Bloudhounds, visionaries and hardliners
3. Seven dreams of man
4. Untangling Germany Inc.

Hier liegt ein Dorf begraben
"Here lies a village buried". Froettmanning is the location of the new Munich soccer stadium. Once it used to be a village. Traces of it can still be found.

217plus
Sal. Oppenheim is one of the leading private banks in Europe. Task was to create a premium magazine, which communicates the sophisticated self-conception of Sal. Oppenheim and the consciously lived values tradition, innovation and exclusivness. 217plus - Customer magazine of the private bank Sal. Oppenheim jr. & Cie. Issue 217plus/1 - Engagement - Issue 217plus/2 - Freedom Issue 217plus/3 - Emotion

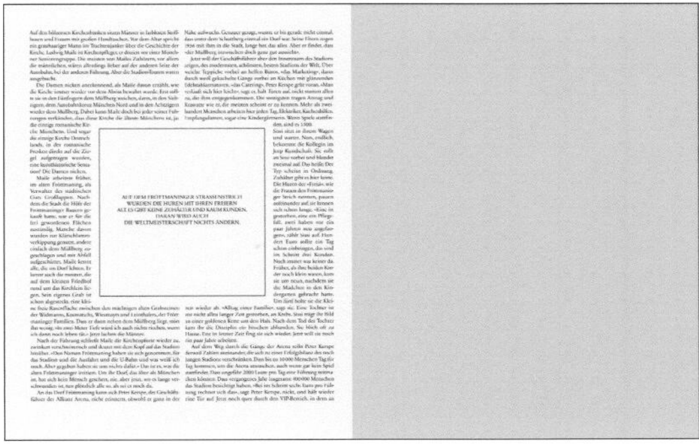

Hier liegt ein Dorf begraben
Germany

National Award
Silver
Agency
Sueddeutsche Zeitung Magazin
Client
Sueddeutsche Zeitung Magazin
Creative Director
Mirko Borsche
Copywriter
Bastian Obermayer
Photographer
Ulrike Myrzik, Manfred Jarisch
Graphics
A. Blaschke, M. Blomeyer, D. Bognar, O. Landgraf

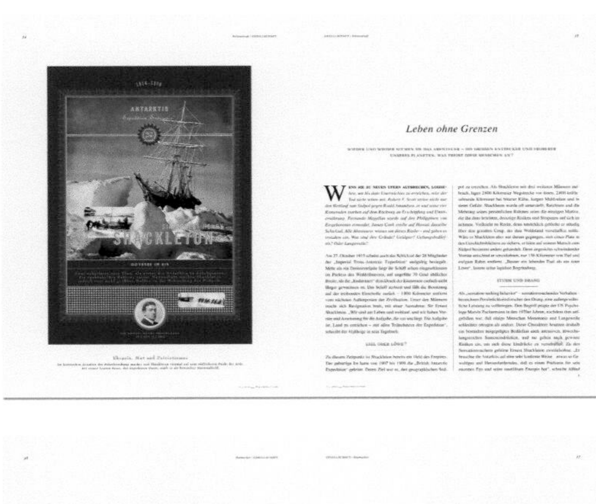

217plus
Germany

National Award
Silver
Agency
Simon & Goetz Design GmbH & Co. KG
Client
Sal. Oppenheim jr. & Cie. KGaA
Art Director
Bernd Vollmoeller
Designer
Bernd Vollmoeller

Kidswear Magazine Vol.22 Spring/Summer 2006
Germany

National Award
Silver
Agency
kid's wear Verlag
Client
kid`s wear Magazine
Art Director
Mike Meirè

Book *S,C,P,F...
Spain

National Award
Gold
Agency
*S,C,P,F...
Client
*S,C,P,F...
Project Director
Philippe Rouger
Art Director
Sandra Neumaier
Designer
Sandra Neumaier
Photographer
Jordi López
Graphics
Jordi López
Programmer
Vasava
Other
Coeditors:
Actar / *S,C,P,F

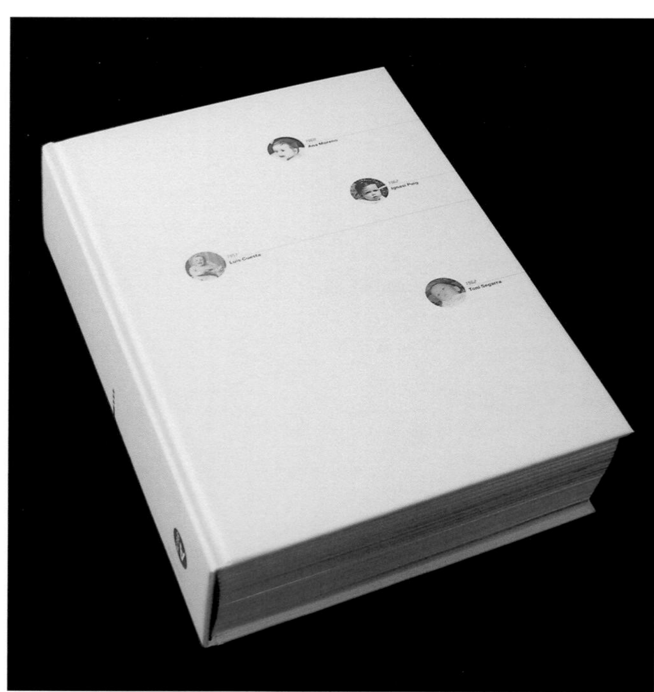

Kidswear Magazine Vol.22 Spring/Summer 2006
Kid's wear is an international style and fashion magazine for high quality kid's clothes, but it also features design, literature and art- for children and by children.

Book *S,C,P,F...
2,520 grams of advertising. The book reviews more than nine years in the life of the *S, C, P, F... advertising agency. In its 764 pages, hundreds of print campaigns and two DVDs with 356 ads produced from day to day by the agency, for brands like BMW, IKEA, Vodafone, J&B, Gallina Blanca, Toys'R'us, Evax and Damm. In addition, the book contains more than 90 recognized instances of collaboration from professionals in communication in other fields, from Spain and the rest of the world. The book comes in two versions, Spanish and English, and is distributed worldwide in selected bookshops.

Jaffa Magazine
Jaffa Magazine is an independent publicity magazine. It is more than a magazine. It is rather an art project, where design and content have something to say - purely, without any limitations, without being afraid to praise or to blame.

Rudi Carrell Interview
The entire issue is dedicated to the last interview with German showmaster Rudi Carrell.

Jaffa Magazine
Latvia

National Award
Silver
Agency
JaffaRiga Projects
Client
Jaffa Riga
Creative Director
Marija Klava
Art Director
Mareks Hofmanis

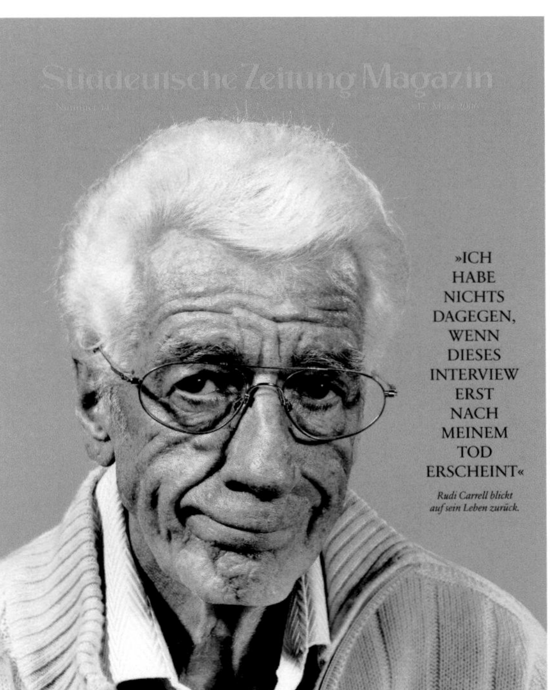

Rudi Carrell Interview
Germany

National Award
Silver
Agency
Sueddeutsche Zeitung Magazin
Client
Sueddeutsche Zeitung Magazin
Creative Director
Mirko Borsche
Copywriter
Sebastian Glubrecht, Alexandros Stefanidis
Photographer
Cover: Andreas Herzau. Private Collection Carrell
Graphics
A. Blaschke, M. Blomeyer, D. Bognar, O. Landgraf

Diary 2006
Iceland

National Award
Silver
Agency
Hzeta Design
Client
101 Hotel
Art Director
Hildur H. Zoega
Designer
Hildur H. Zoega

Menu and more
Iceland

National Award
Silver
Agency
Fiton
Client
Domo
Art Director
Oscar Bjarnason and Valgerdur Gunnarsdottir
Designer
Valgerdur Gunnarsdottir and Oscar Bjarnason

Diary 2006
The diary is illustrated by 12 artists, one for each month.

Menu and more
Cover for the menu and more.

Fraktur mon Amour
This volume brings together for the first time 300 Blackletter fonts available in digital format. 137 of them can be found on the included CD-ROM. Fraktur mon Amour is a catalogue as well as a declaration of love.

Reykjavik 871 +-2
The Settlement Exhibition Catalogue for the Reykjavik Settlement Exhibition, called Reykjavik 871 +-2.

Fraktur mon Amour
Germany

National Award
Silver
Agency
Verlag Hermann Schmidt Mainz
Client
Verlag Hermann Schmidt Mainz
Creative Director
Judith Schalansky
Designer
Judith Schalansky
Production company
Verlag Hermann Schmidt Mainz

Reykjavik 871 +-2
Iceland

National Award
Silver
Agency
Atli Hilmarsson Design Studio
Client
The Reykjavik City Museum
Creative Director
Atli Hilmarsson
Art Director
Atli Hilmarsson
Designer
Gunnar Vilhjalmsson, Daniel Claus Reuter

Protesis
Spain

National Award
Silver
Agency
Bildi Grafiks
Client
Tanit Plana,
Galeria EspaiZero1
Creative Director
Martí Ferré,
Agnès Simon
Copywriter
Tanit Plana, Bea Espejo,
Marta Gili
Designer
Martí Ferré, Agnès Simon
Production company
Galeria Espai Zero1
Photographer
Tanit Plana
Other
Print: Aubert

8º Anuário Clube Criativos Portugal
Portugal

National Award
Silver
Agency
Mola Ativism
Client
Clube de Criativos
de Portugal
Creative Director
Rui Morais
Designer
Rui Morais

Protesis
The catalogue has two parts: the exhibition (book) and the comments about Tanit Plana's work (unfolded cover). The exhibition speaks about Tanit's search of life and her grandfather's search of dead. "Today my grandmother died, she waited until my father said to her 'good morning mother' and then she died".

8º Anuário Clube Criativos Portugal
Creative Club Yearbook. The 8th yearbook of the "Clube de Criativos de Portugal" is found in a poster, which, in addition to serving as a cover, aims at forming a bridge between the graphic design realized for the festival and the yearbook itself.

DIF - Guia Cultural e Revista de Tendências Gratuito
DIF. Free Cultural Guide and Tendencies Magazine. Creating a magazine that is trendy, clean and fashionable.

Virtual Watch
"One for every moment". One is a local watch brand that asked us to develop a new way of presenting their catalogue to retailers. We've created a mailing that besides showing watches, allowed recipients to try them.

DIF -Guia Cultural e Revista de Tendências Gratuito
Portugal

National Award
Silver
Agency
Valdemar Lamego
Client
DIF magazine
Creative Director
Valdemar Lamego
Art Director
Valdemar Lamego
Designer
Valdemar Lamego
Graphics
Valdemar Lamego
Illustrator
Valdemar Lamego

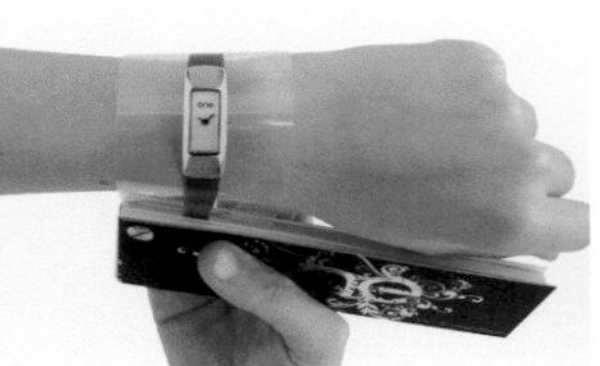

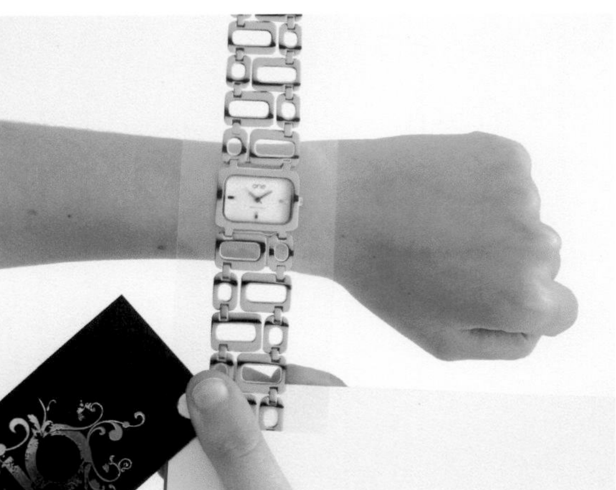

Virtual Watch
Portugal

National Award
Gold
Agency
Leo Burnett
Client
Planet One
Creative Director
Chacho Puebla,
Joâo Roque
Copywriter
Pedro Ribeiro
Designer
Pedro Roque,
Ana Ventura

Breus
Spain

National Award
Silver
Agency
Compañía
Client
CCCB
Art Director
Armando Fidalgo,
Xavier Banús
Designer
Armando Fidalgo,
Xavier Banús

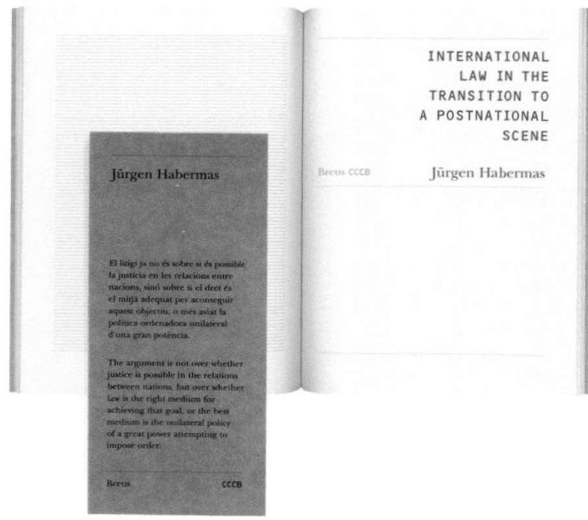

Thordis Adalsteinsdottir
Iceland

National Award
Gold
Agency
Hildigunnur & Snaefrid
Client
Reykjavik Art Museum
Creative Director
Hildigunnur & Snaefrid
Designer
Hildigunnur Gunnarsdottir,
Snaefrid Thorsteins

Breus
"Briefs". A collection of books, in a bilingual edition, that gathers lectures given at the Center for Contemporary Culture of Barcelona.

Thordis Adalsteinsdottir
"Therefore we still hear whispers" Catalogue for an exhibition of the works by the artist Thordis Adalsteinsdottir.

Lukoil Overseas Holding Annual Report
Design and layout of the annual report 2005

The Guardian
The latest pressbook for Disney-Buenavista's movie 'The Guardian'. A movie that tells the story of a very specialized group of coast-guards: people that put their lives on the line to save others under extreme conditions: storms, flooding, and so on.

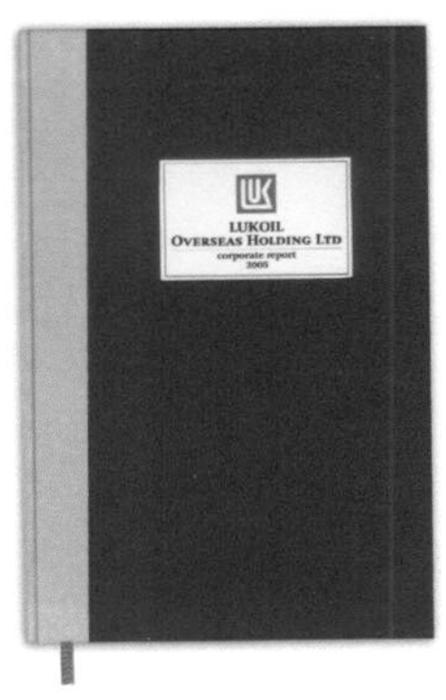

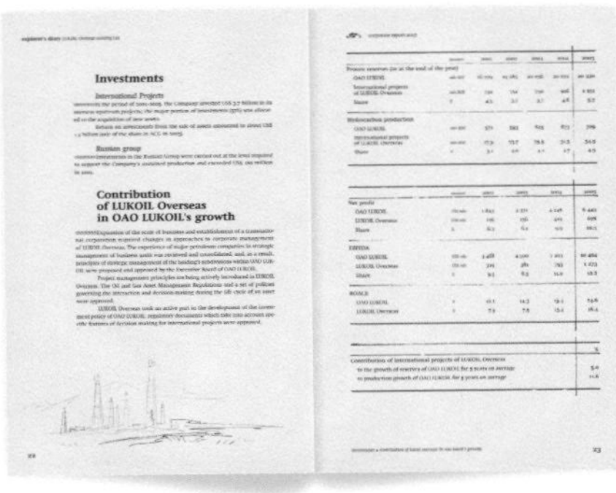

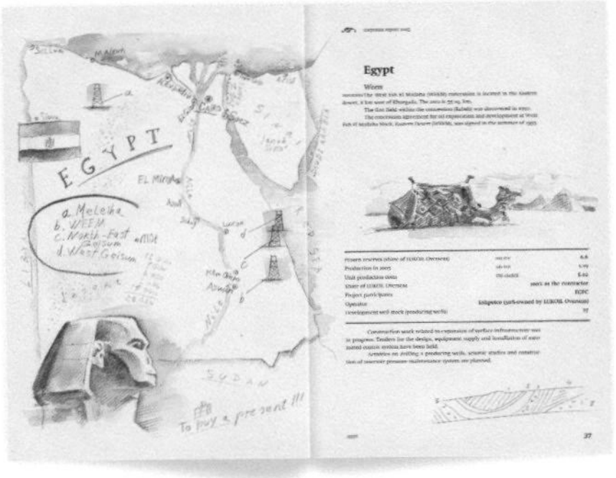

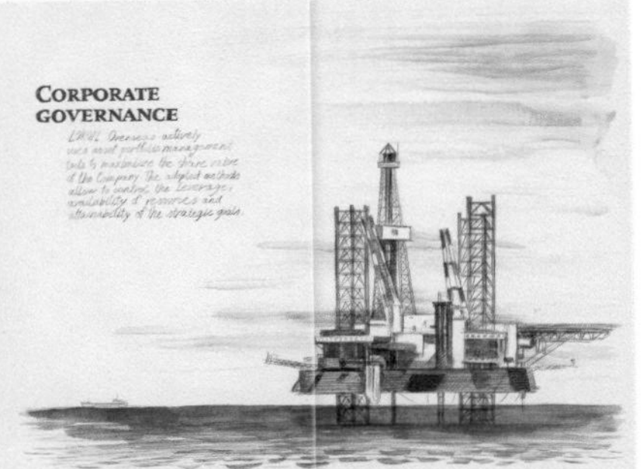

Lukoil Overseas Holding Annual Report

Russia

National Award
Silver
Agency
LLC "DesignDepot"
Client
Lukoil Overseas Holding Ltd.
Creative Director
Piter Bankov
Art Director
Eugeny Malyshev
Designer
Eugeny Malyshev
Production company
Mikhail Evstyukhin
Illustrator
Vlad Vasiliev

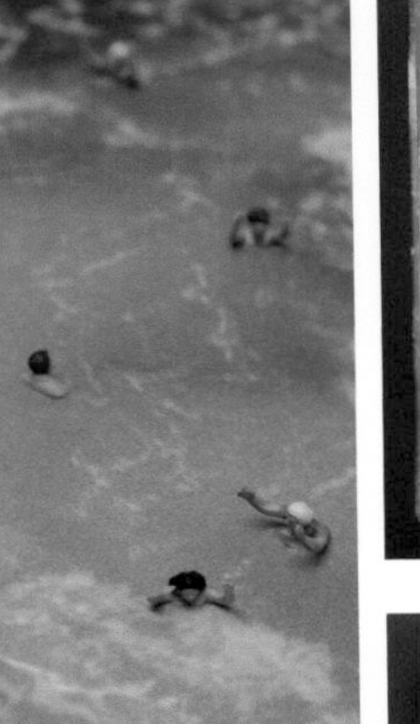

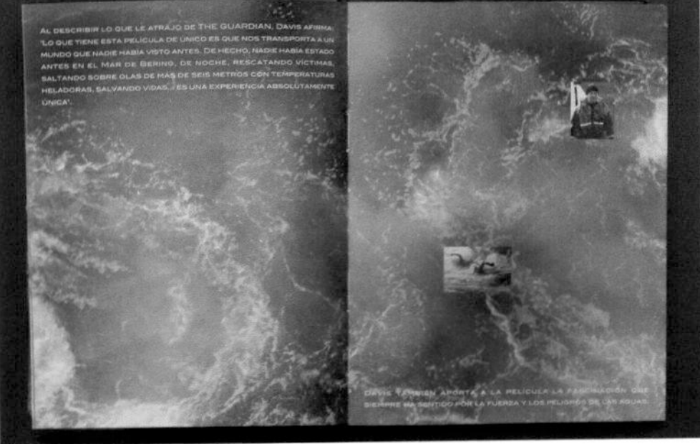

The Guardian

Spain

National Award
Gold
Agency
Zapping/M&C Saatchi
Client
Buenavista International
Creative Director
Uschi Henkes
Art Director
Uschi Henkes,
Jenny Nerman
Designer
Jenny Nerman

Guía de Iluminación 2007
Spain

National Award
Gold
Agency
Mucho
Client
Biosca & Botey
Creative Director
Marc Català, Pablo Juncadella
Art Director
Marc Català, Pablo Juncadella
Editor
Antxon Janin, Ana Varea
Designer
Marc Català, Isabel Merino
Photographer
Ferran Izquierdo, Jordi Adrià (Mocho)
Graphics
Marc Català
Other
Styling: Sonia Soms

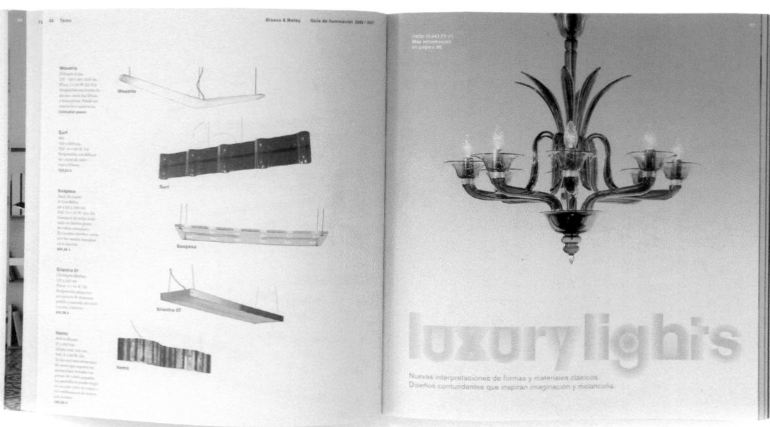

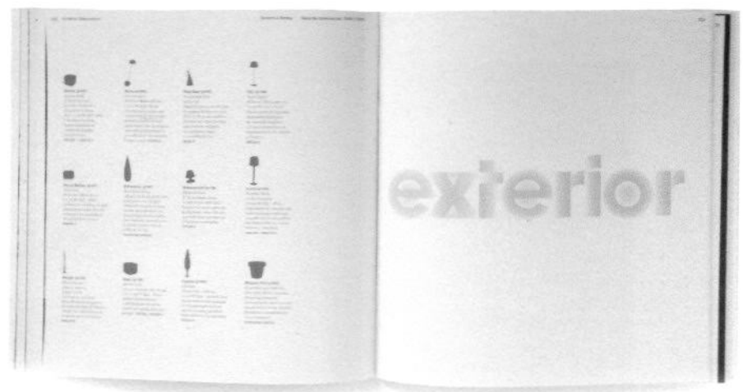

Guia de Iluminación 2007
"Lighting Guide 2007"
Lamp and lighting services catalogue, designed with the intention of producing a book with a visual interest on every page, through composition of the product, typography design and photography production.

Linóleo
Linoleum is a symphony composed of three colours, C, M and Y. A strange book illustrated by Olaf Ladousse using seals made of Linoleum.

The One Weekend Book Series
The One Weekend Book Series. Graphic Tourism Since 2003. The Collection of Volumes 1 to 5. Since 2003 Martin Lorenz travels to cities like Berlin, Milan or New York City to make 48-page books with different artists in a single weekend. In 2006 the publisher Actar asked Twopoints.Net to create a compilation of the first five books.

Quaderns Portàtils
"Portable documents"
When MACBA (Barcelona Contemporary Art Museum) thought about the need to distribute a series of interesting texts from seminars and conferences which would be hard to have printed in book format, they had the idea of creating a line of digital publications which would be accessible to anyone with a basic PC and printer. The Cosmic solution consists of designing a very simple, easy to bind format, but attractive and elegant enough for a document from a home printer to be a publication standard.

Linóleo
Spain

National Award
Silver
Agency
Olaf Ladousse
Client
Blur Ediciones
Designer
Olaf Ladousse
Production company
Blur Ediciones
Graphics
Olaf Ladousse
Illustrator
Olaf Ladousse

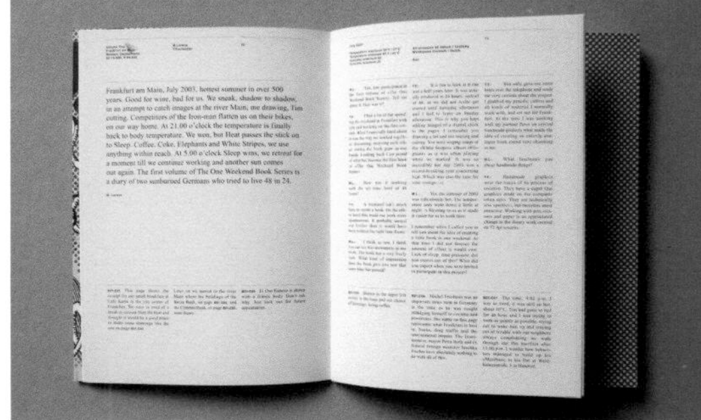

The One Weekend Book Series
Spain

National Award
Gold
Agency
Twopoints.Net
Client
Twopoints.Net / Actar
Creative Director
Martin Lorenz
Art Director
Martin Lorenz
Copywriter
Rowan J. McCuskey, Martin Lorenz
Designer
Martin Lorenz
Production company
Twopoints.Net
Photographer
Martin Lorenz
Graphics
Martin Lorenz
Illustrator
M. Lorenz, T. Faulwetter, R. McCuskey, S. Ehlers, K. Riisholt, R. Lang, E. Schulze, E. Koenig, Y. Sodeoka
Other
Project Management:
Lupi Asensio, Martin Lorenz

Quaderns Portàtils
Spain

National Award
Silver
Agency
Cosmic
Client
Museu Art Contemporani Barcelona, MACBA
Art Director
Juan Dávila
Graphics
Eduardo Manso, Joao Alves, Eugenio Borreguero
Illustrator
Joao Alves

Corporate Calendar DIRECT DESIGN Visual Branding
Russia

National Award
Silver
Agency
Direct Design
Visual Branding
Client
Direct Design
Visual Branding
Creative Director
D. Peryshkov,
L. Feygin
Art Director
D. Peryshkov,
L. Feygin

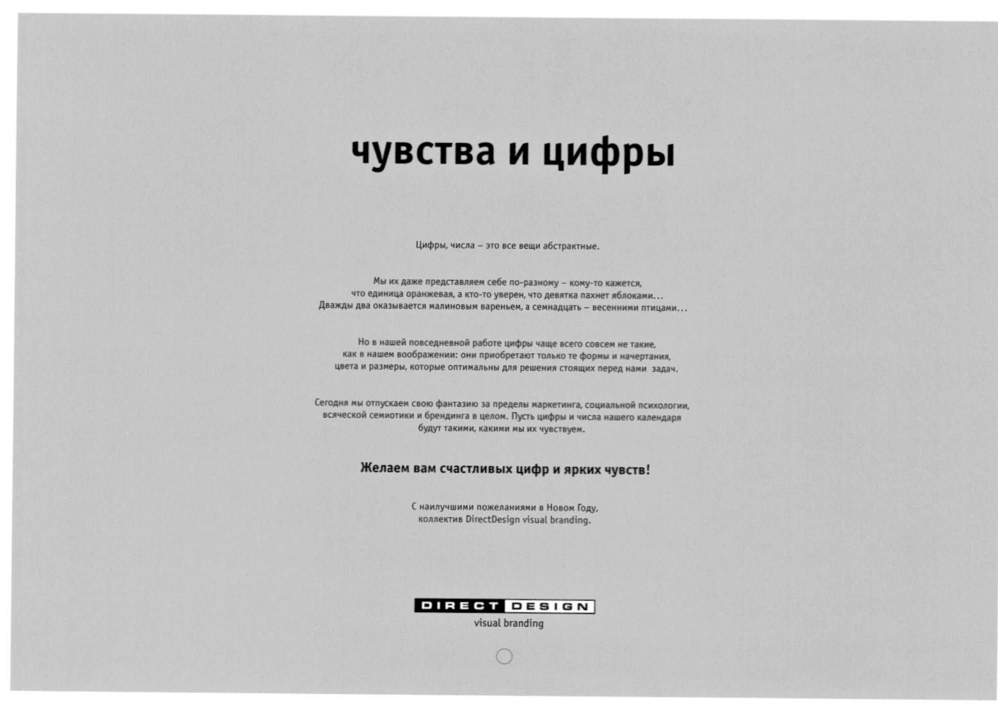

Corporate Calendar
DIRECT DESIGN
Visual Branding
Numbers and digits are abstract things. We even imagine them in different appearances. Somebody would imagine the 1 as an orange colour, another believes that 9 smells like an apple. Two times two may appear as raspberry jam, and seventeen, springbirds... But in our everyday work digits often are not like those we imagine: they acquire only that shape and stroke, colour and size that are best suited to solve our tasks. In this calendar we let our imagination run free beyond marketing, social psychology, semiotics and whole branding. Let the numbers and digits of our calendar appear as we feel them.

Suite
Free magazine about art, fashion, music, culture...

Programs
Germany

National Award
Silver
Agency
Strichpunkt
Client
Wuerttembergische
Staatstheater Schauspiel
Creative Director
Kirsten Dietz,
Jochen Raedeker
Art Director
Kirsten Dietz
Designer
Anders Bergesen,
Kirsten Dietz,
Anika Marquardsen
Illustrator
Anders Bergesen and others

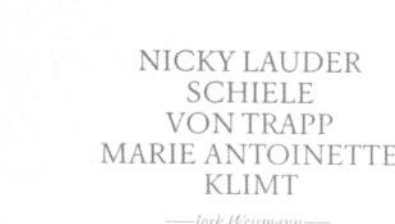

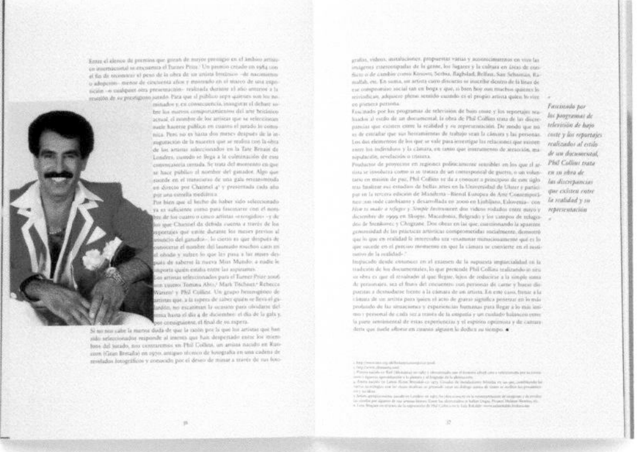

Suite
Spain

National Award
Silver
Agency
Iñigo Jerez
Client
Suite
Creative Director
Iñigo Jerez,
Marta Capdevila,
Carlos Ramírez
Art Director
Iñigo Jerez
Designer
Iñigo Jerez

Design. Corporate Identity / Branding

Austria

Estonia

Iceland

Portugal

Russia

Spain: Gold 4 Nominations

Switzerland: 1 Nomination

Gold
Limo_Kids
Spain

National Award
Silver
Agency
Emeyele
Client
Limo_Kids
Creative Director
Màrius Sala,
Laura Armet
Art Director
Màrius Sala,
Laura Armet
Copywriter
Maria Ruiz
Designer
Nika Hellström,
Laura Armet
Illustrator
Nika Hellström,
Laura Armet

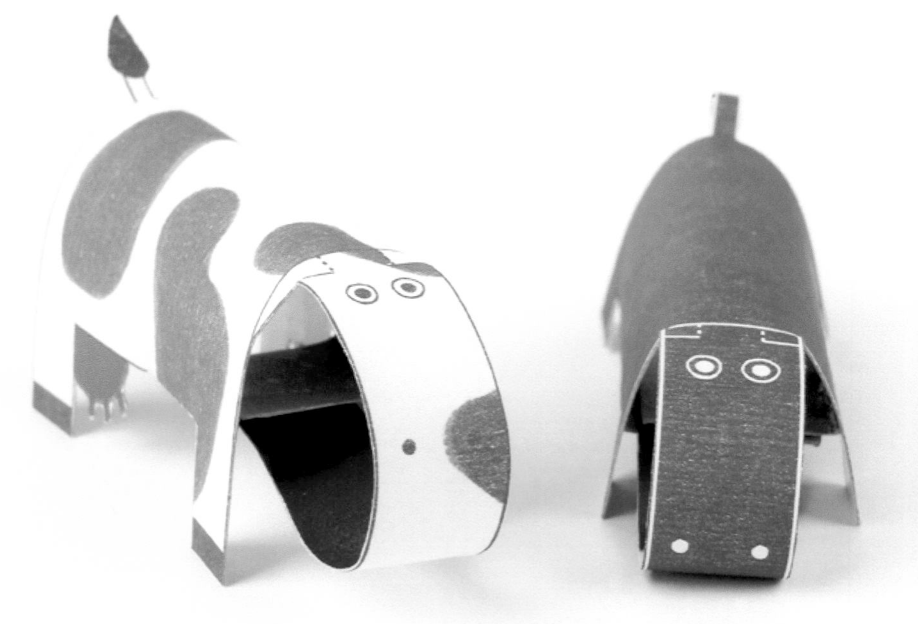

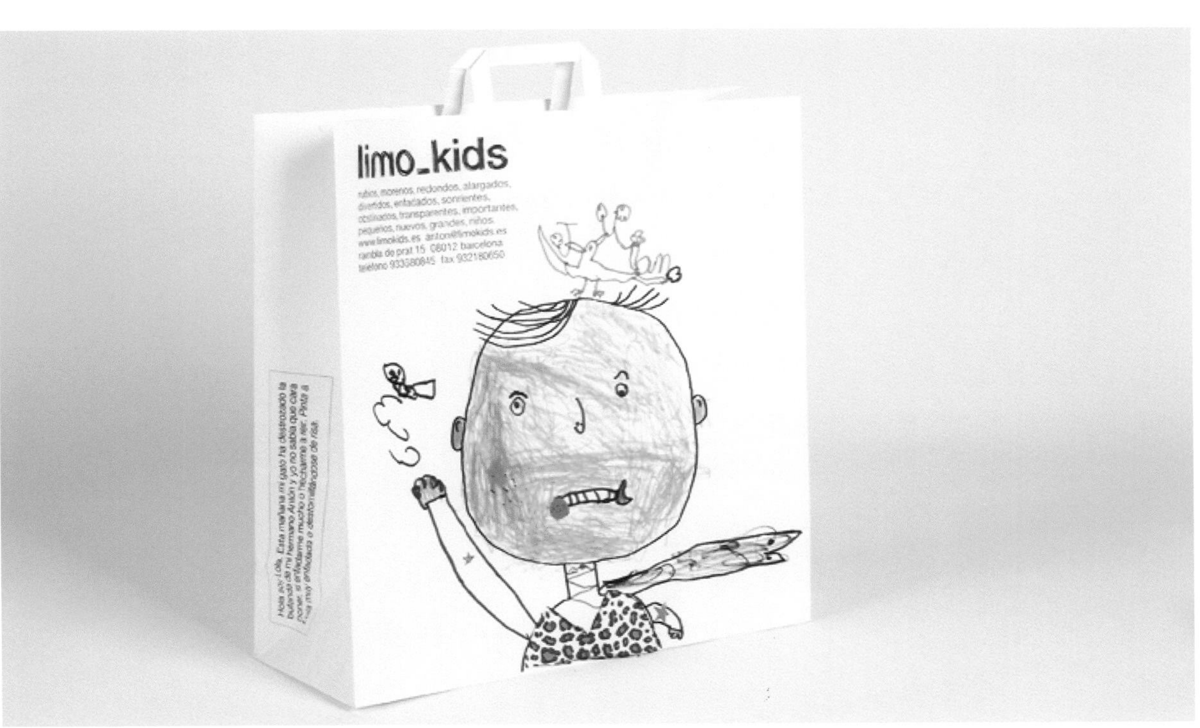

Limo_Kids is a clothing and gadget shop for children between 1 and 5 years old. A corporate identity was created using elements that kids can play with, at the same time, showing them the concept of recycling. "Limo Kids, blonds, brunettes, round, long, fun, angry, smiling, obstinate, transparent, important, little, new, big kids".

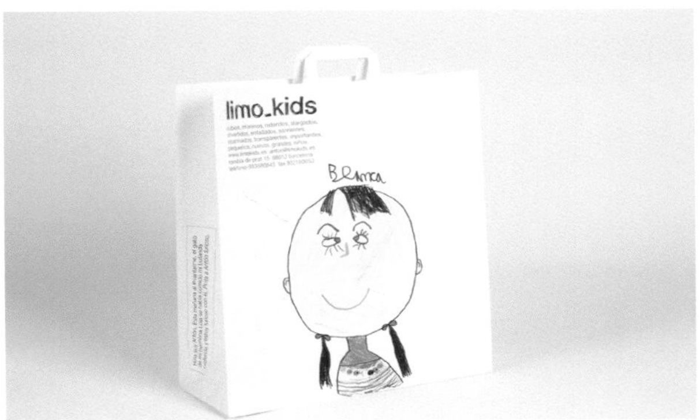

Nomination
Casa Marcelo
Spain

National Award
Silver
Agency
Cosmic
Client
Casa Marcelo
Art Director
Juan Dávila
Production company
Grafiko
Photographer
Juanjo Pascual
Graphics
Eduardo Manso,
Eider Corral

sa Marcelo
e identity for the taurant Casa rcelo (Marcelo's ace) was based on several works graffiti spread over ne of the most nous places.

masié
entity for a memade cookie nchise. The logo is e name of the and, along with a antic symbol. is form originates m the shape of a okie, and is produced as a hole ly in the shops, ile pieces of it are ed for the ckaging.

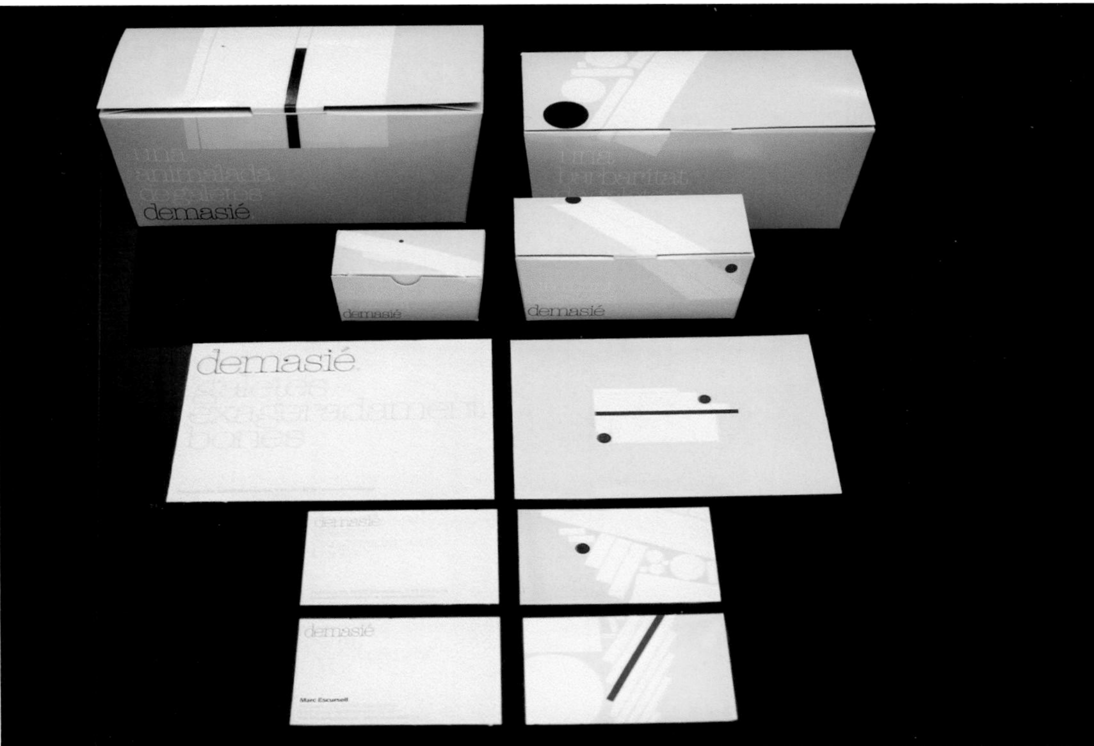

Nomination
demasié
Spain

National Award
Silver
Agency
Mucho
Client
demasié
Creative Director
Pablo Juncadella, Marc Català
Art Director
Pablo Juncadella, Marc Català
Copywriter
Marc Torrell
Designer
Pablo Juncadella
Graphics
Pablo Juncadella

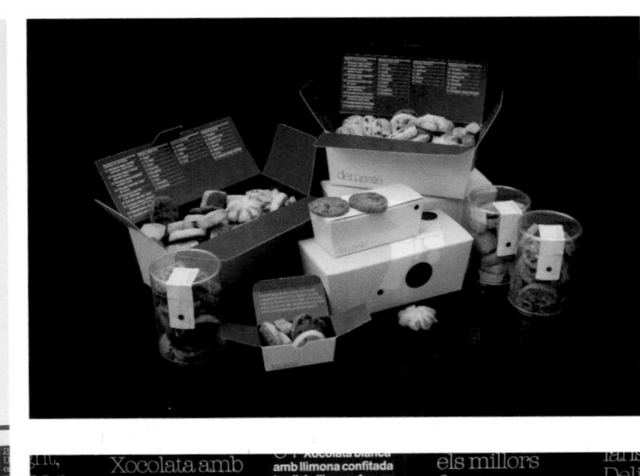

Nomination
Pedro García
Spain

National Award
Gold
Agency
Cla-se
Client
Pedro García
Creative Director
Daniel Ayuso / Cla-se
Art Director
Daniel Ayuso
Designer
Daniel Ayuso
Photographer
Daniel Riera
Graphics
Daniel Ayuso
Other
Aubergine Studio / Interior and structural design

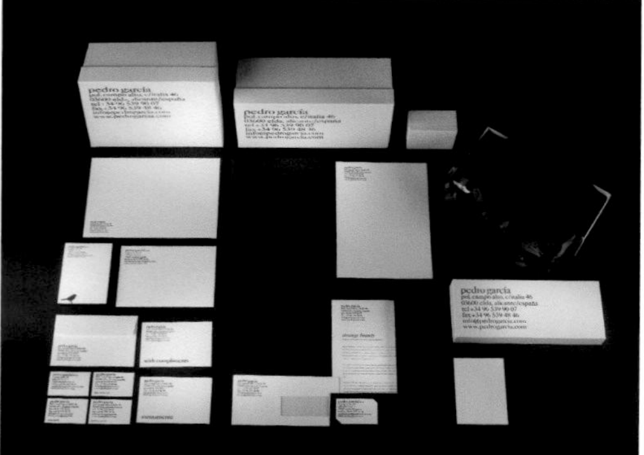

Pedro Garcia
The identity for the shoe company Pedro Garcia is a graphic system that uses only Caslon 540. All type is applied in black and white, lower case an left-aligned, with different text sizes. The printing is in termography and stamping as the shoe soles.

Terminal B
Project developed on the initiative of the FAD to conduct a census of the creative people of whatever origin (Catalonia, rest of Spain, other countries) established in Barcelona, in all areas of contemporary creation. Materialized in a web site, Terminal B is the concept under which this census has been done, with the triple aim of (1) being the showcase of the creative people who work from Barcelona and want their creativity to be seen by the rest of the world, (2) being the gateway for creative people who come to Barcelona and want to establish themselves professionally in the city and (3) bridging the gap between the worlds of creation and industry, both national and international, a meeting place between creative people and business executives

Nomination
Terminal B
Spain

National Award
Silver
Agency
*S,C,P,F...
Client
FAD
Art Director
Javi Donada
Copywriter
Angelo Palma

Nomination
Small printed Design
Switzerland

National Award
Shortlist
Agency
Ruf Lanz, Zurich
Client
Lic. iur. Ion Eglin
Creative Director
Markus Ruf, Danielle Lanz
Art Director
Lorenz Clormann
Copywriter
Ion Eglin
Other
Account Manager: Nicole Sommermeyer

Small printed Design
The lawyer Ion Eglin keeps himself very busy with the small print, for example, in contracts and law articles. This passion is already identified in his Corporate Identity.

Amonis Delicious Catering
The positioning of Wilhelm Amon Junior as the jack-of-all-trades in the catering-business, creating not only culinary delights but also arranging whole events. AMON'S delicious catering (or short ADC). Points to the creative business, as this is an important target group for AMON'S services.

Sugar Monkeys
"No brain no pain". New visual identity of an advertising agency. We take our work very seriously but we are not dead-serious about ourselves.

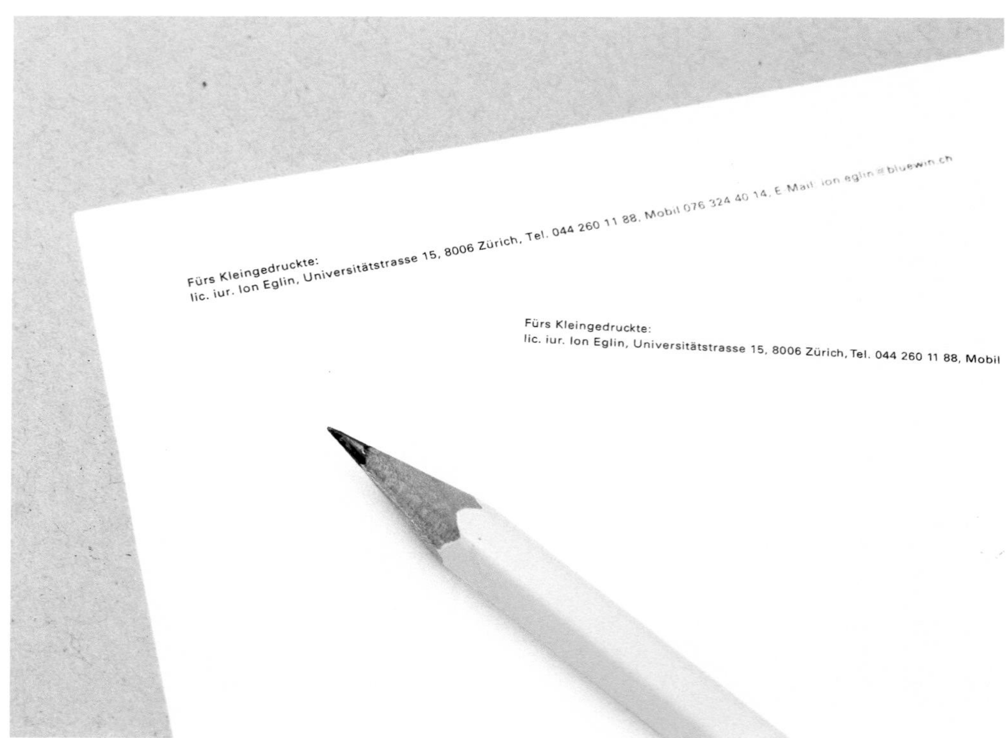

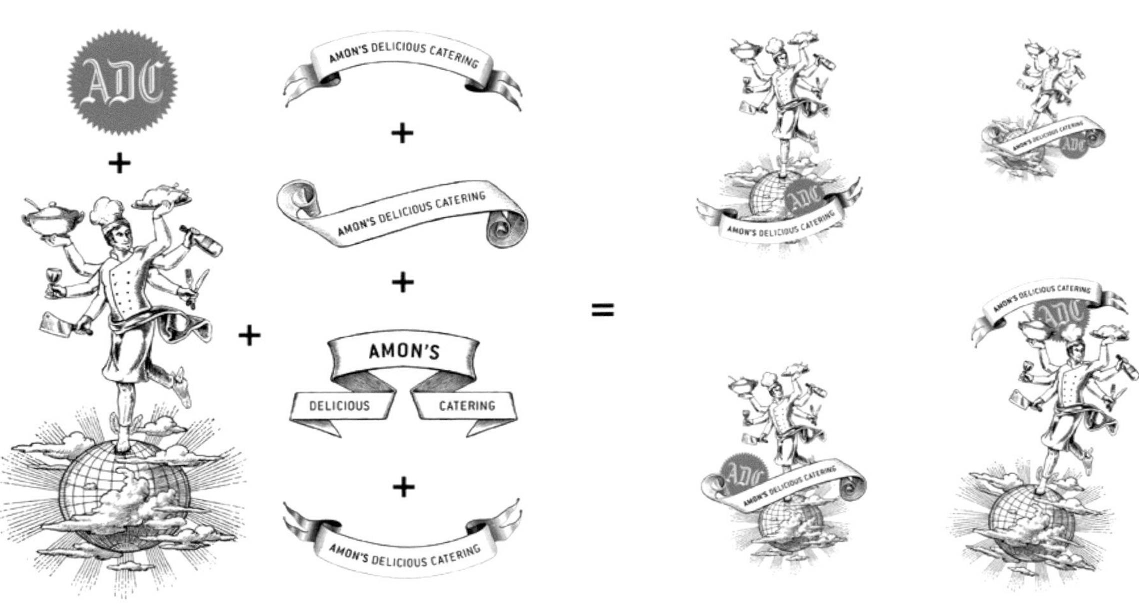

Amonís Delicious Catering

Austria

National Award
Silver
Agency
alessandridesign/Repro12
Client
Wilhelm Amon Junior
Creative Director
Cordula Alessandri
Art Director
Stephan Kirsch
Copywriter
Cosima Reif, Felix Fenz, Wolfgang Pauser, Gert Winkler
Designer
Stephan Kirsch
Production company
Repro 12
Graphics
Stephan Kirsch
Illustrator
Stephan Kirsch
Other
Concept: Cosima Reif, Felix Fenz, Wolfgang Pauser, Gert Winkler

Sugar Monkeys

Estonia

National Award
Silver
Agency
Korpus
Client
Korpus
Copywriter
Allan Hmelnitski, Hendrik Alla
Designer
Rele Liiv
Production Company
Korpus
Illustrator
Allan Hmelnitski

Di, A
Spain

National Award
Gold
Agency
Dfraile
Client
Carolina Barasoain
Copywriter
Eduardo del Fraile
Designer
Eduardo del Fraile

The Shortest route to your home
Russia

National Award
Silver
Agency
DeCafe
Client
Navigator
Creative Director
Kira Laskari
Art Director
Alexey Batalov,
Roman Klimov
Copywriter
Kira Laskari
Designer
Alexey Batalov

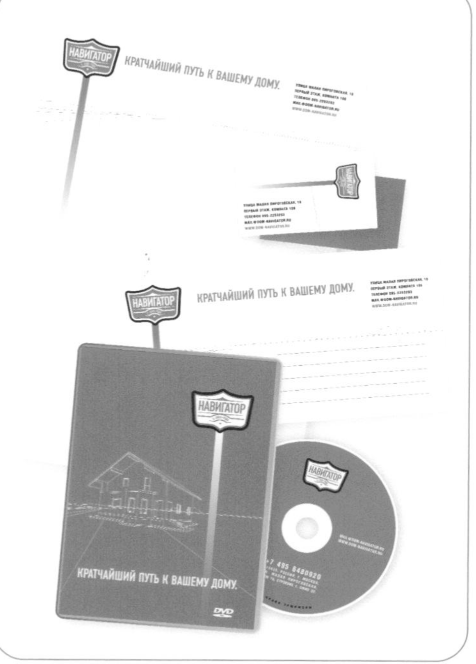

Di, A
"Say, A". Logopedics and Psychology. Letter A is the first vowel and the first letter in the alphabet. Logopedics is a discipline dealing with language disorders and providing techniques to improve one's speech. Psychology gives us guidelines to solve these behaviour problems, where the dialogue with the patient and the latter's freedom of speech is essential. Say 'A' is the beginning of a consultation appointment; the patient opens up so that the professional can help him.

"The Shortest Route to Your Home"
Logo, corporate identity, expo-materials for the cottage-building company.

Pourquoi Pas?
Why not?

Barnasalfraedistofan
Logo for the Child Psychology Clinic

Pourquoi Pas?
Iceland

National Award
Silver
Agency
Snaefrid & Hildigunnur
Client
The Ministry of Education
Creative Director
Snaefrid & Hildigunnur
Designer
Snaefrid Thorsteins & Hildigunnur Gunnarsdottir
Illustrator
Snaefrid Thorsteins & Hildigunnur Gunnarsdottir

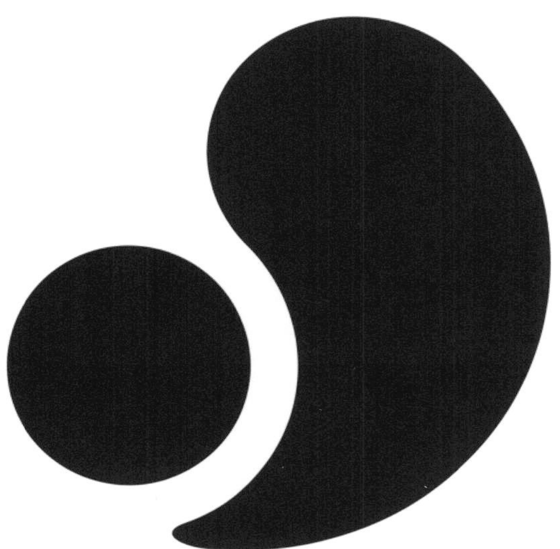

Barnasalfraedistofan
Iceland

National Award
Silver
Agency
Royal
Client
Barnasalfraedistofan
Art Director
Isak Winther, Petur Gudmundsson
Designer
Isak Winther, Petur Gudmundsson

Vegê
Portugal

National Award
Silver
Agency
Brandia Central
Client
Sovena
Creative Director
Miguel Viana
Designer
Ana Sofia Silva,
Cristina Gomes
Other
José Cerqueira

Pineapplerecords
Iceland

National Award
Silver
Agency
Linda Loeskow
Client
Pineapplerecords
Art Director
Stephan Stephenssen
Designer
Linda Loeskow
Illustrator
Linda Loeskow

Vegê
The rational and functional side of the product were the main drivers in the creation of the new brand. The new image combines the straightforwardness of the form and colours with an appealing presentation of a culinary outcome.

Pineapplerecords
Logo for Pineapplerecords

Energy of Portugal - Corporate Identity
After liberalising the energy market in Portugal, EDP realized the need to reposition the brand, steeling it in view of the challenges to come. Representing new energy with 5 dimensions, economical, convinient, closer, innovative, ecological.

DOMO
Logo for the restaurant DOMO

Energy of Portugal -Corporate Identity
Portugal

National Award
Silver
Agency
Mola Ativism
Client
EDP 5D
Creative Director
Rui Morais
Designer
José Carlos Mendes

Domo
Iceland

National Award
Gold
Agency
Fiton
Client
Kolskeggur ehf.
Art Director
Oscar Bjarnason
Designer
Oscar Bjarnason

Corporate Identity Ativism
Portugal

National Award
Silver
Agency
Mola Ativism
Client
Ativism
Creative Director
Rui Morais
Designer
José Carlos Mendes

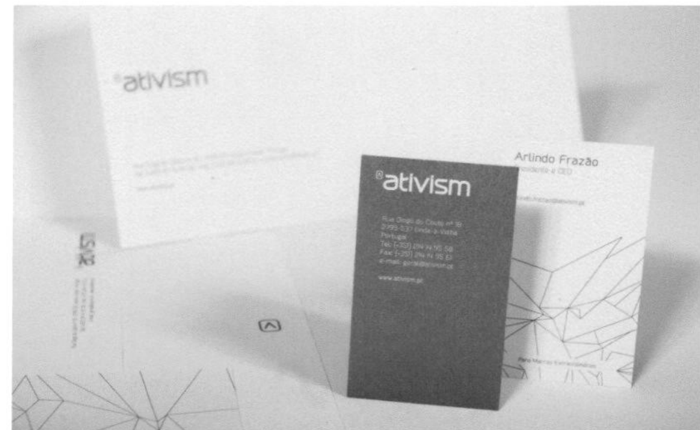

Book *S,C,P,F...
Spain

National Award
Gold
Agency
*S,C,P,F...
Client
*S,C,P,F...
Project Director
Philippe Rouger
Art Director
Sandra Neumaier
Designer
Sandra Neumaier
Photographer
Jordi López
Graphics
Jordi López
Programmer
Vasava
Other
Coeditors: Actar / *S,C,P,F

Ativism
With the formation of the Ativism group, there was a need to integrate 8 independent companies with names already known on the market into a single group.

Book *S,C,P,F...
One launch event of the book was organized in Madrid and another one in Barcelona, inaugurating a week-long exhibition in the FAD, Plaça dels Àngels. For both events an invitation was created. As for the exhibition, it consisted of 288 linear metres of canvas with the book printed at twice its actual size. In order to spread the word, we stuck posters in universities, advertising schools, restaurants and bars. The book was also the motif for the official *S,C,P,F... T-shirt for 2006. Finally, flyers and posters were distributed in the 2006 "El Sol" Festival.

Wine selection
The Eslonaut travels the world as representative for the Eselböck wine selection with the quest to find the world's finest wines. Symbolic of the Eselböck's continuous engagement regarding wines, the Eslonaut leads the observer through a fantastic world of wines.

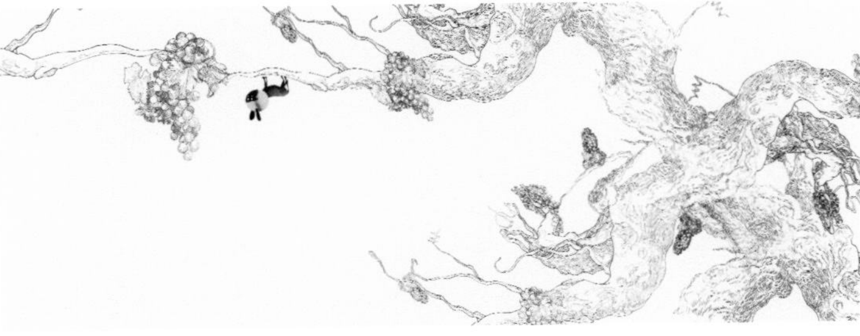

Wine selection
Austria

National Award
Gold
Agency
Jung von Matt/Donau Werbeagentur GmbH
Client
Eudard Tscheppe
Creative Director
Andreas Putz
Art Director
Wolkmar Weiss
Copywriter
Michael Haeussler, Helena Giokas, Dietmar Voll
Graphics
Dian Warsosumarto
Illustrator
Wolkmar Weiss, Dian Warsosumarto
Other
Producer:
Joerg Guenther

boba
Spain

National Award
Silver
Agency
grafica
Client
gimenez & zuazo
Creative Director
Pablo Martín
Art Director
Pablo Martín
Designer
Bárbara Castro, Ellen Diedrich
Graphics
Bárbara Castro, Ellen Diedrich

boba
Identity for a fashion brand.

Reykjavik Casting
Letterhead for the casting company Reykjavik Casting.

NY gift kit for Bartolius lawyer company
NY gift kit for Bartolius lawyer company includes wall calendar, special edition of the paper, diary, planning, pocket calendars, greeting card and packages.

Letterhead for Sagafilm
NY gift kit for Letterhead for the film company Sagafilm.

Reykjavik Casting
Iceland

National Award
Gold
Agency
O!
Client
Reykjavik Casting
Art Director
Einar Gylfason
Designer
Einar Gylfason

NY gift kit for Bartolius lawyer company
Russia

National Award
Gold
Agency
ManufaKtura Agency
Client
Lawyer company Bartolius
Creative Director
Evgeniy Charskiy
Art Director
Evgeniy Charskiy
Designer
Evgeniy Charskiy,
Konstantin Kolubin,
Ekaterina Gr

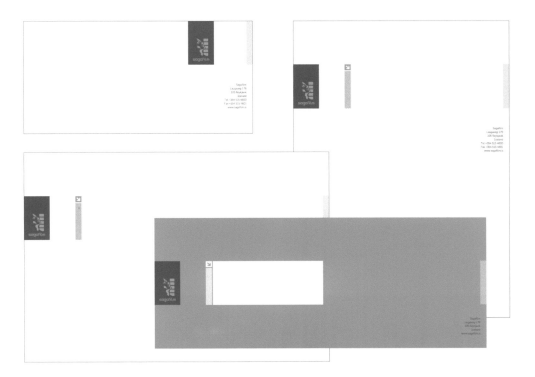

Letterhead for Sagafilm
Iceland

National Award
Silver
Agency
O!
Client
Sagafilm
Art Director
Einar Gylfason
Designer
Einar Gylfason

Olga Planas
Spain

National Award
Silver
Agency
Natalia Cuadrado
Client
Olga Planas
Designer
Natalia Cuadrado

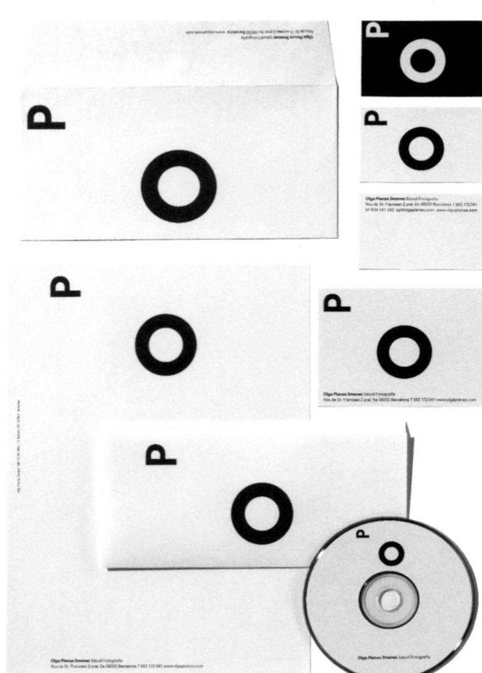

Olga Planas
The brief was to create a corporate identity for a photographer combining her initials.

Natalia Cuadrado
A corporate identity aroused by the typographic interest. The main concept was to emphasize the typographic selection converting it to an identity system.

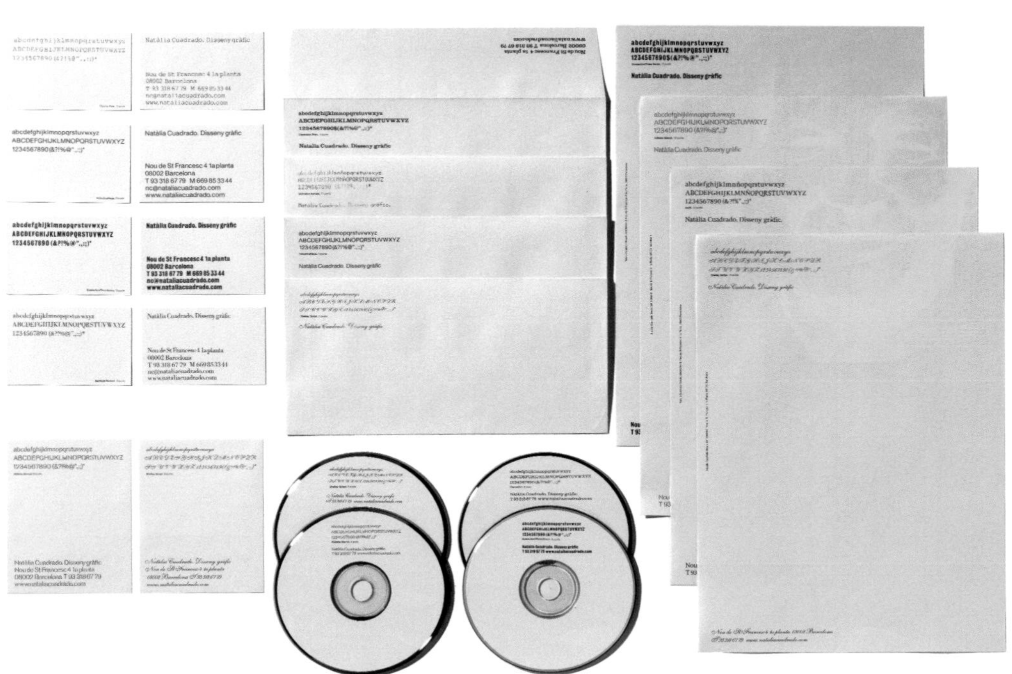

Natalia Cuadrado
Spain

National Award
Gold
Agency
Natalia Cuadrado
Client
Natalia Cuadrado
Designer
Natalia Cuadrado

Design. Illustration and Photography

Austria: 1 Nomination

Estonia

Germany: Gold 5 Nominations

Iceland

Italy: 1 Nomination

Poland: 2 Nominations

Portugal

Russia

Spain

Switzerland: Gold

Gold

War orphans

Germany

National Award
Silver
Agency
Kolle Rebbe Werbeagentur GmbH
Client
Bischoefliches Hilfswerk Misereor e.V.
Creative Director
Sven Klohk, Lorenz Ritter
Art Director
Maik Beimdiek, Jens Lausenmeyer
Copywriter
Elena Bartrina y Manns
Illustrator
Eva Salzmann
Other
Account Manager:
Jessica Gustaffson, Alex Duve

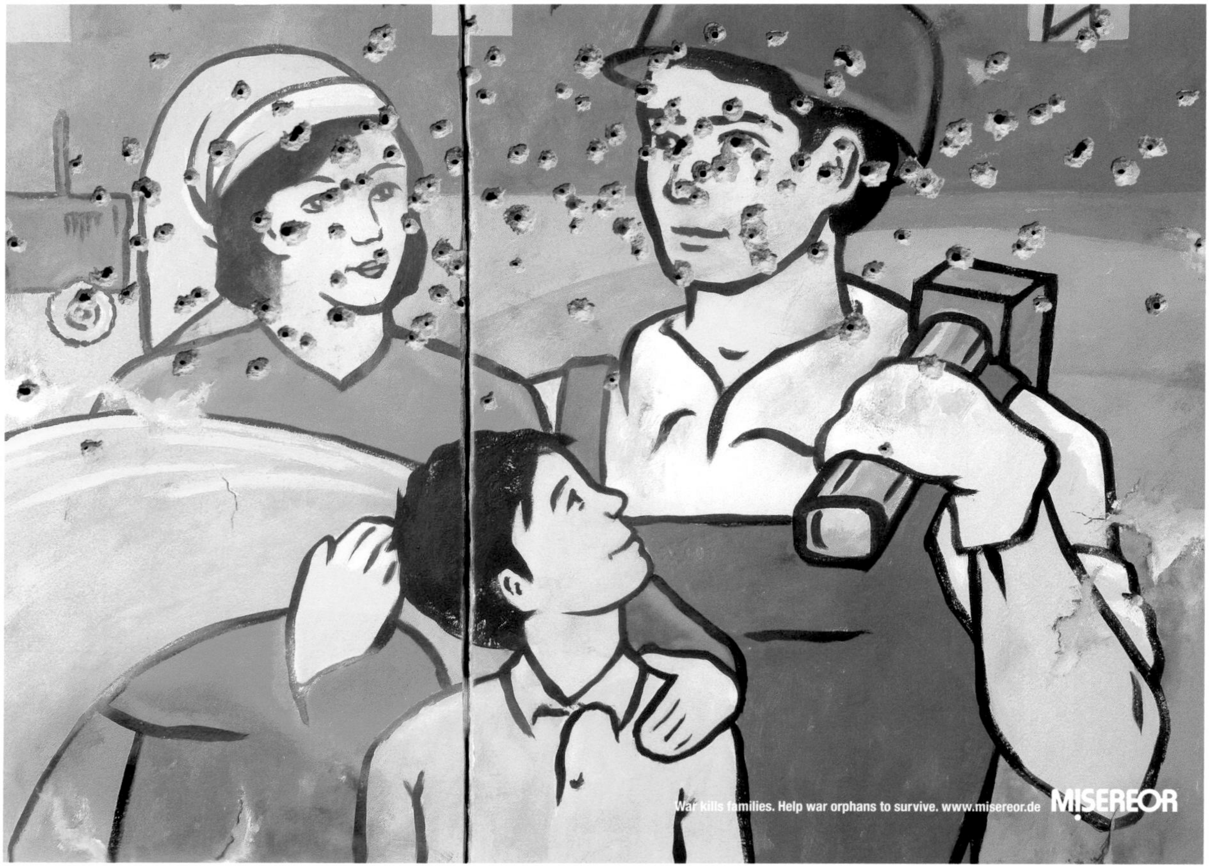

War kills families. Help war orphans to survive. www.misereor.de
MISEREOR

Misereor charity. Misereor wants to raise awareness about the topic of war orphans by means of intelligent as well as shocking treatment of the subject, in order to move viewers and encourage them to become interested in the Misereor website and maybe also to make a donation.

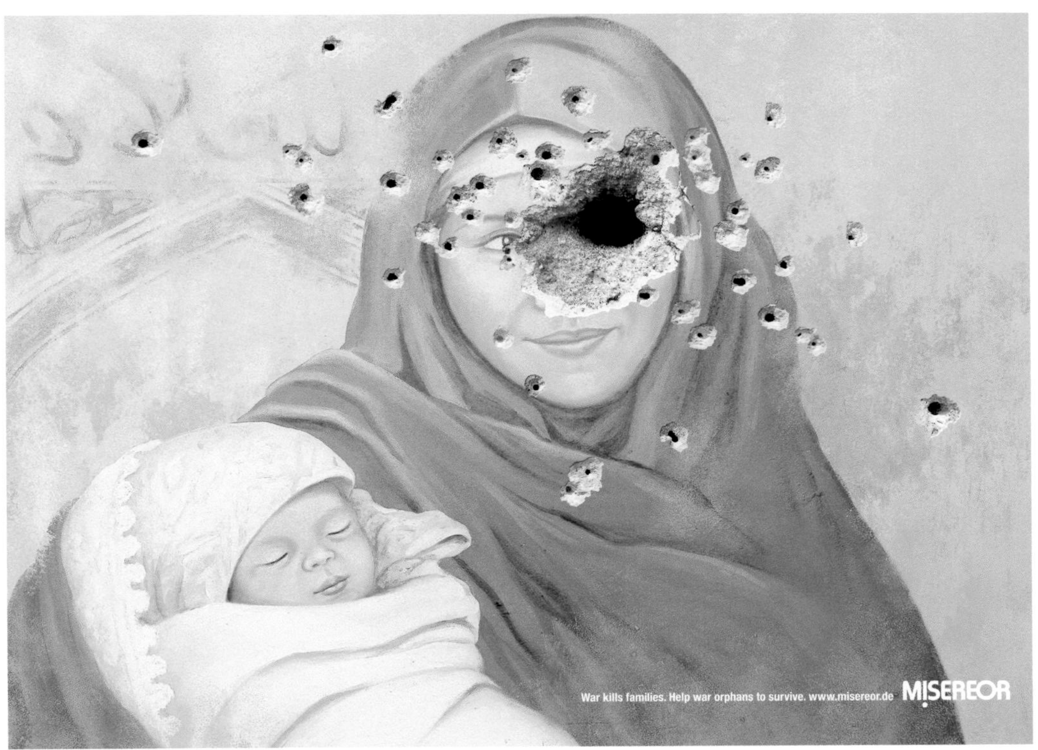

Gold
Mother's Day Campaign
Switzerland

National Award
Bronze
Agency
walker
Client
Fleurop Interflora
Creative Director
Pius Walker
Photographer
Uwe Düttmann

Fleurop-Interflora's Mother's Day Campaign for once doesn't thank mothers. It far more recalls all the little sins with which they made us suffer. The photographs imitate the target group's childhood days in the sixties and seventies.

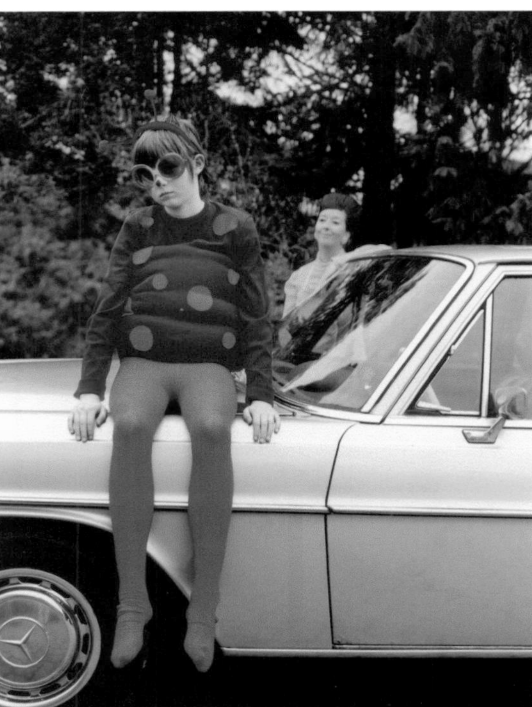

Nomination
Wine selection
Austria

National Award
Gold
Agency
Jung von Matt/Donau Werbeagentur GmbH
Client
Eudard Tscheppe
Creative Director
Andreas Putz
Art Director
Volkmar Weiss
Copywriter
Michael Haeussler, Helena Giokas, Dietmar Voll
Graphics
Dian Warsosumarto
Illustrator
Volkmar Weiss, Dian Warsosumarto

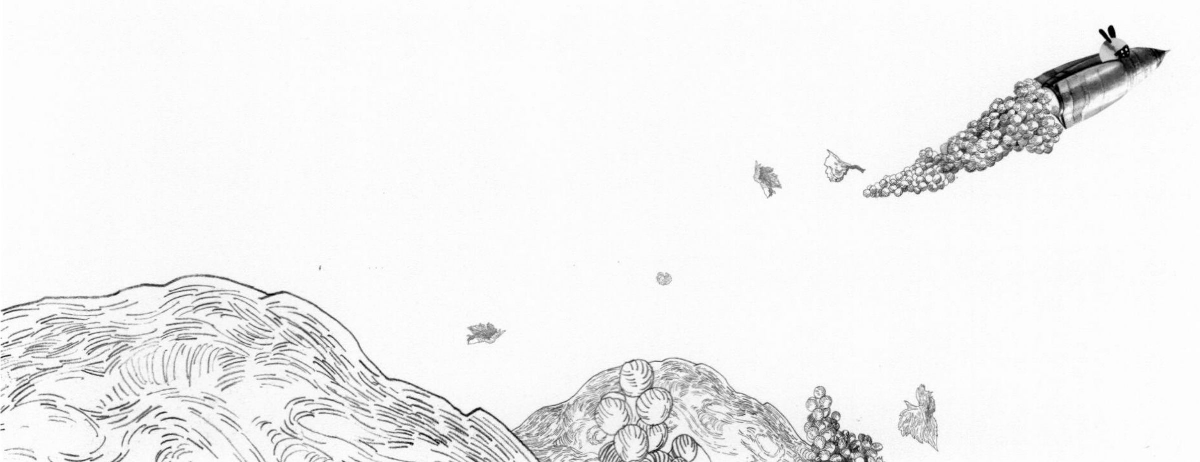

Nomination
+10 Fresco
Germany

National Award
Bronze
Agency
TBWA Germany (180/TBWA), Berlin
Client
Adidas AG
Creative Director
Kurt Georg Dieckert, Stefan Schmidt
Art Director
Boris Schwiedrzik
Copywriter
Helge Bloeck
Production company
Methodik Management & Partner
Illustrator
Felix Reidenbach
Other
Media Agency: Carat

Wine selection
The Eslonaut travels the world as representative for the Eselböck wine selection with the quest to find the world's finest wines. Symbolic of the Eselböck's continuous engagement regarding wines, the Eslonaut leads the observer through a fantastic world of wines.

+10 Fresco
Football stars like Beckham, Zidane, Raul, Messi, Kaka or Ballack are considered to be real football gods by their fans. They are simply elevated to where they belong anyway - into football heaven.. The world's largest football fresco was created in the main lobby of the Cologne central train station, which happens to be right next to the stunning Cologne Cathedral.

Nomination
ADC Junior Award: How hungry are you?
Germany

National Award
Shortlist
Agency
Ogilvy Frankfurt
Client
Art Directors Club Germany
Creative Director
Helmut Himmler, Lars Huvart
Art Director
Till Schaffarczyk
Copywriter
Ales Polcar
Illustrator
Martin Popp, Till Schaffarczyk

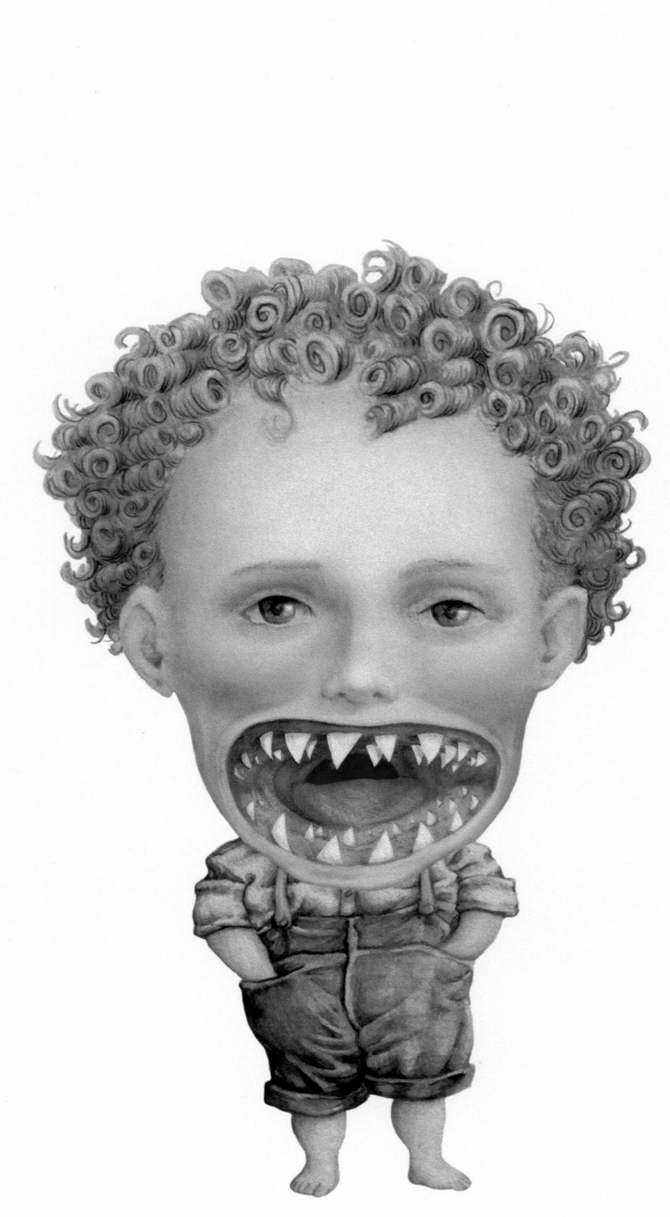

ADC Junior Award: How hungry are you?
"How hungry are you?" The posters should motivate students, graduates and junior to participate in the ADC junior award programme.

Airmail
Following a reorganisation, DHL took over the airmail service of Deutsche Post in Germany. To prevent criticism, an image campaign was launched at the point of contact: in post offices, on flyers and within the customer magazine. The campaign should involve customers emotionally by showing them that their new carrier DHL is the world's most powerful courier service. And that sending letters to every country worldwide is now as easy as throwing paper airplanes.

Nomination
Airmail
Germany

National Award
Shortlist
Agency
Jung von Matt AG
Client
DHL
Creative Director
Joachim Silber,
Paul Fleig
Art Director
Andreas Jeutter
Copywriter
Paul Fleig
Photographer
Peter Schumacher,
Thomas Baumann
Graphics
Dominic Stuebler,
Mario Loncar
Other
Joerg Macha

Nomination
UNICEF
Germany

National Award
Bronze
Agency
Serviceplan
München/Hamburg
Client
UNICEF
Art Director
Maik Kaehler
Photographer
Achim Lippoth

UNICEF
Children step out of their catastrophe: flood, earthquake, child labour, war.

When will the Middles Ages be over?
Torture of suspected terrorists in US military prisons is just one example of Western democracies' condonation of the use of torture in special cases. Reason enough for Amnesty International to launch a campaign against this medieval practice.

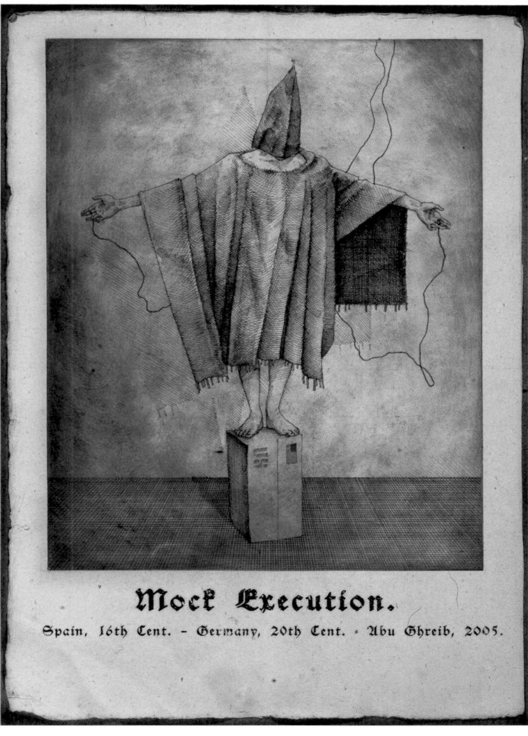

Mock Execution.
Spain, 16th Cent. - Germany, 20th Cent. - Abu Ghreib, 2005.

Torturesome Interrogation.
Also known as 'torture' or 'ordeal'. 1350-2006.

Nomination

When will the Middles Ages be over?

Germany

National Award
Bronze
Agency
Ogilvy Frankfurt
Client
Amnesty International
Creative Director
Simon Oppmann, Peter Roemmelt
Art Director
Simon Oppmann, Daniel Cojocaru
Copywriter
Peter Roemmelt, Daniel Cojocaru
Graphics
Daniel Cojocaru
Illustrator
Daniel Cojocaru

Humiliation.
Medieval method of torture, from about 1250 to 2006

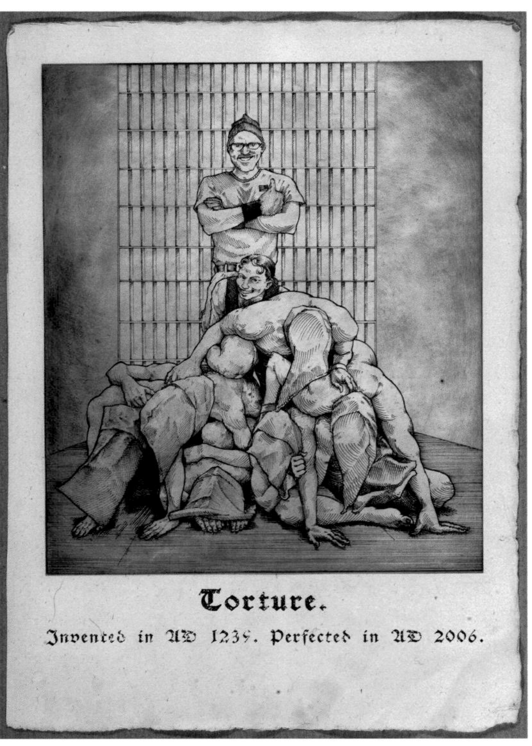

Torture.
Invented in AD 1239. Perfected in AD 2006.

Nomination
The most incredible espresso experience
Italy

National Award
Gold
Agency
Armando Testa
Client
Luigi Lavazza
Creative Director
G. Silva, E. Mendibil, H. Mendibil
Art Director
Haitz Mendibil, Andrea Lantelme
Copywriter
G. Silva, E. Mendibil, C. Nardó
Photographer
Eugenio Recuenco
Other
Post Production: Paz Otero

The most incredible espresso experience
Lavazza calendar 2007.

Nomination
Converse-couple
Poland

National Award
Silver
Agency
Photoby for JWT
Client
Converse
Creative Director
Dariusz Zatorski
Art Director
Katarzyna Macharz
Production company
Photoby
Photographer
Andzrej Dragan

Nomination
Nissan Qashqai
Poland

National Award
Gold
Agency
Photoby for TBWA/
G1 Paris
Client
Nissan
Creative Director
Chris Garbutt
Art Director
Bjoern Ruehmann,
Joakim Revemann
Copywriter
Xander Smith
Photographer
Sven Glage

Fashion Victim
Dresses by the Austrian designer Linda Zlok are look so great that women would die for them.

Innocent Graphics Calendar 07
Total freedom to create. M2's objective was to come up with an item using free and creative illustrations in order to illustrate the best possible way to use print techniques to distinguish an item.

Fashion Victim
Austria

National Award
Silver
Agency
Friendly Fire
Client
Linda Zlok
Creative Director
Norbert Horvath, Thomas Schmid
Art Director
Norbert Horvath
Copywriter
Thomas Schmid
Photographer
Klemens Horvath
Graphics
Hannes Kosina, Manuel Godetz
Illustrator
Norbert Horvath

Innocent Graphics Calendar 07
Portugal

National Award
Gold
Agency
Mola Ativism
Client
M2
Creative Director
Rui Morais
Designer
Diogo Potes, Pedro Carmo, José Carlos Mendes

Lukoil Overseas Holding Annual Report
Russia

National Award
Silver
Agency
LLC "DesignDepot"
Client
Lukoil Overseas Holding Ltd.
Creative Director
Piter Bankov
Art Director
Eugeny Malyshev
Designer
Eugeny Malyshev
Illustrator
Vlad Vasiliev

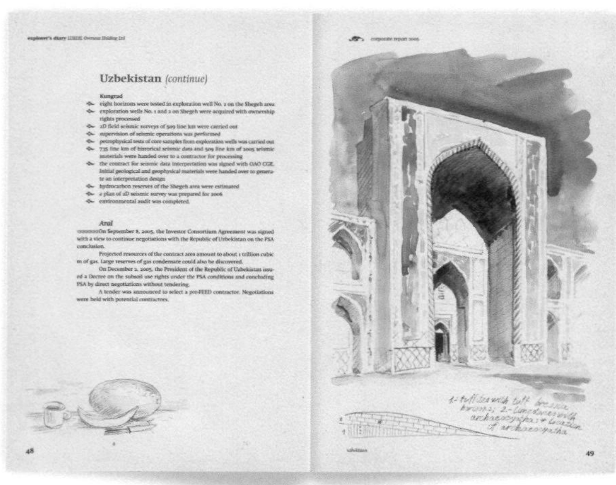

National holidays
Iceland

National Award
Gold
Agency
Gott folk McCann
Client
Landsbanki Islands
Creative Director
Jon Arnason,
Gary Wake
Art Director
Amundi Sigurdsson
Illustrator
Amundi Sigurdsson

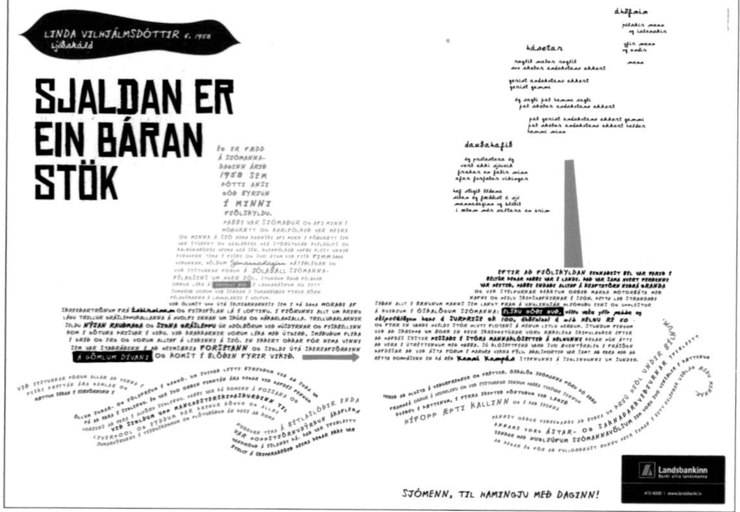

Lukoil Overseas Holding Annual Report
Design and layout of the annual report 2005

National holidays
Illustrations for different national holidays.

Pourquoi Pas?
"Why not?" Illustrations for a French cultural event program, called Pourquoi Pas? - a French spring in Iceland.

The Classics of Opera - 400 years
"Collectable book and CD for periodical newspapers". Both cover and book illustrations are centred on key-moments of the libretti. The main concept is the dramatic and passionate nature of the intrigue, reflecting the expressions and emotions of the characters.

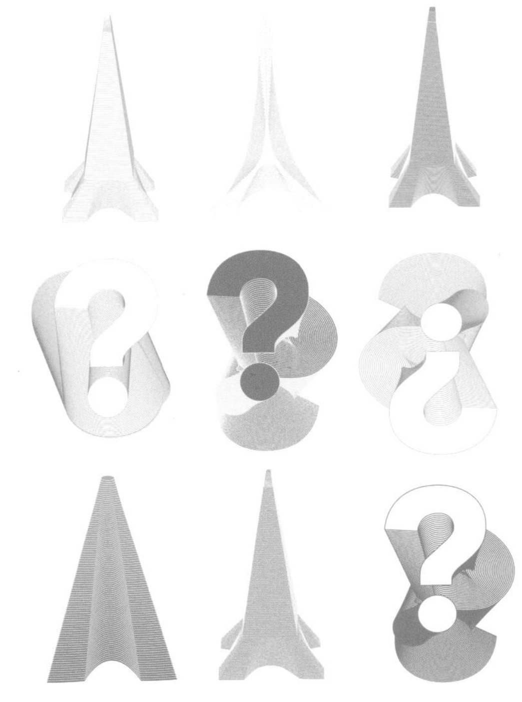

Pourquoi Pas?
Iceland

National Award
Silver
Agency
Snaefrid & Hildigunnur
Client
The Ministry of Education
Creative Director
Snaefrid & Hildigunnur
Illustrator
Snaefrid Thorsteins & Hildigunnur Gunnarsdottir

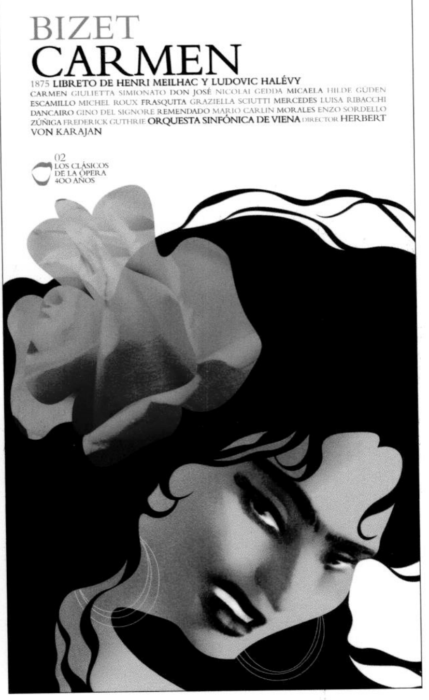

BIZET
CARMEN
1875 LIBRETO DE HENRI MEILHAC Y LUDOVIC HALÉVY
CARMEN GIULIETTA SIMIONATO DON JOSÉ NICOLAI GEDDA MICAELA HILDE GÜDEN ESCAMILLO MICHEL ROUX FRASQUITA GRAZIELLA SCIUTTI MERCEDES LUISA RIBACCHI DANCAIRO GINO DEL SIGNORE REMENDADO MARIO CARLIN MORALES ENZO SORDELLO ZÚÑIGA FREDERICK GUTHRIE ORQUESTA SINFÓNICA DE VIENA DIRECTOR HERBERT VON KARAJAN
02
LOS CLÁSICOS DE LA ÓPERA 400 AÑOS

The Classics of Opera - 400 years
Portugal

National Award
Silver
Agency
Silva! Designers
Client
Prisa Innova
Creative Director
Jorge Silva
Art Director
Jorge Silva
Designer
Silvia Pacheco
Illustrator
Ana Juan, Alain Corbel, André Carrilho, Miguel Rocha

AUDI
Poland

National Award
Silver
Agency
Photoby for FCB
Wilkens Hamburg
Client
Audi
Creative Director
Alexander Gutt
Art Director
Alexander Gutt
Photographer
Anatol Kotte

Cinema Book
Spain

National Award
Silver
Agency
DFraile
Client
Consejería de Medio
Ambiente Región de Murcia
Creative Director
Eduardo del Fraile
Art Director
Eduardo del Fraile
Designer
Eduardo del Fraile,
Juan Jimenez
Photographer
Javier Urosas,
Eduardo del Fraile

Fight sleep
Italy

National Award
Silver
Agency
Giovanni Settesoldi-
Luissandro Del Gobbo
Client
Sasch - SHS
Creative Director
Giovanni Settesoldi,
Luissandro Del Gobbo
Art Director
Giovanni Settesoldi
Copywriter
Luissandro Del Gobbo
Photographer
Riccardo Bagnoli
Illustrator
Claudio Luparelli
Other
Post Production:
Claudio Luparelli

Cinema Book
With a photographic sequence, this shows a metaphor of distributing culture, and thus we capture the attention of the general public to participate in an humanitarian project which consists of donating used books to Spanish-Speaking countries.

Fight sleep
Fight sleep man - Fight sleep woman

Birthday calendar
Synterra
"SYNTERRA Birthday calendar"
This illustrated calendar was created by Design Bureau Volga Volga for Syntrerra, Group of Russian national telecommunications companies. "Friendly connection" – the company slogan – became the creative framework for the product which is called "Name Day Calendar". The idea was to remind people of their friend's name days according to the Russian Orthodox Church calendar. There are 360 illustrated characters with different names in the calendar. They represent a typical occupation for every season and also a social connection between people.

Birthday calendar Synterra
Russia

National Award
Silver
Agency
Design Bureau
Volga Volga
Client
Synterra
Art Director
Sivohin Pavel
Copywriter
Koltyga Philip
Designer
Sivohin Pavel
Illustrator
Pivko Natalia

Kunsthalle Wien/More than you can bear
Austria

National Award
Gold
Agency
Jung von Matt/Donau Werbeagentur GmbH
Client
Kunsthalle Wien
Creative Director
Andreas Putz
Art Director
Volkmar Weiss
Copywriter
Christoph Gaunersdorfer
Photographer
Martin Klimas/Bransch
Graphics
Eva Jordan
Other
Art Work:
Albert Winkler/Vienna Paint

Kunsthalle Wien/More than you can bear
An image campaign for the Kunsthalle Wien, THE place in Vienna for contemporary and modern art.

Ultra Wallpapers
"Ultra prepaid phonecard". Wallpapers at Ultra web site for different users of Ultra phonecard with different tastes.

I'm not an artist
"Poster campaign" First element of the new design school communication campaign that questions the perception of the designer as an artist, re-qualifying him as a professional, from whom qualified training and hard work should be demanded. All by means of an ironically "artistic" illustration.

Guia de Iluminación 2007
"Lighting Guide 2007" How to create four different photographic edits for four lighting themes, each including many different lamps? This is the aim of this series of pictures. The themes: Modern Classics, Luxury Lights, Scandinavian Design, Outdoor decorative.

Ultra Wallpapers
Estonia

National Award
Gold
Agency
Age McCann
Client
Tele 2
Creative Director
Kaarel Grepp
Art Director
R. Martinson,
V. Loginov, M. Loginov
Designer
R. Martinson, V. Loginov,
M. Loginov
Production company
Age McCann

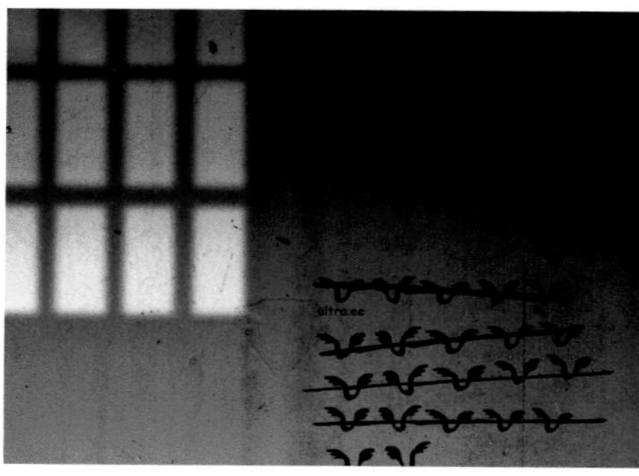

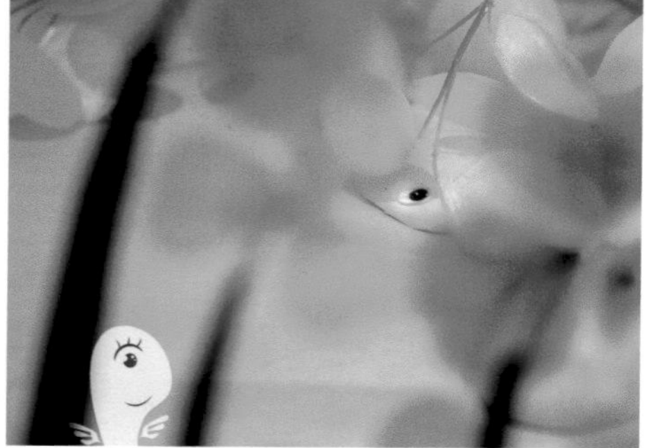

I'm not an artist
Spain

National Award
Silver
Agency
*S,C,P,F...
Client
Elisava
Art Director
Javi Donada
Copywriter
Angelo Palma
Illustrator
Cristóbal Vera

Guía de Iluminación 2007
Spain

National Award
Gold
Agency
Mucho
Client
Biosca & Botey
Creative Director
Marc Català,
Pablo Juncadella
Art Director
Marc Català,
Pablo Juncadella
Editor
Antxon Janin,
Ana Varea
Designer
Marc Català,
Isabel Merino
Photographer
Ferran Izquierdo,
Jordi Adrià (Mocho)
Graphics
Marc Català
Other
Styling: Sonia Soms

Cinema Curtain
Austria

National Award
Gold
Agency
TBWA Wien
Client
Beiersdorf GmbH
Creative Director
Elli Hummer,
Robert Wohlgemuth,
Gerd Turetschek
Art Director
Sabina Karasegh
Copywriter
Tanja Trombitas
Production company
Film Factory
Photographer
Renée Del Missier
Other
Concept: Niki Link,
Maik Wollrab

Cinema Curtain
Smooth Skin in an instant.

Fleurop Interflora Annual Report 2005
The Business report 2005 endorses reorientation of the brand with the new corporate design and highlights the beauty and expressive power of flowers. Each graphic is illustrated exclusively with flowers.

Fleurop Interflora Annual Report 2005
Switzerland

National Award
Gold
Agency
walker
Client
Fleurop Interflora
Creative Director
Pius Walker
Designer
Mieke Haase
Illustrator
Martin Müller

Design. Packaging

Austria: 2 Nominations

Estonia

Iceland: 1 Nomination

Slovenia

Germany: 1 Nomination

Portugal

Spain: 1 Nomination

Nomination
Bottling date / calendar sheet
Austria

National Award
Silver
Agency
Max Jurasch
Client
Weingut M. Machalek
Creative Director
Max Jurasch
Art Director
Max Jurasch
Designer
Max Jurasch
Production company
Rotfilter
Graphics
Max Jurasch

Bottling date / calendar sheet
The label on the bottle is a calendar sheet, the date on the sheet is the one when the bottle was filled with wine.

Niepoort Comic Edition
Gestolen Fiets (NL) = Stolen Bicycle, Sarvet (FL) = Horn. Visual concept for different countries: famous cartoonists tell a country-specific story in 12 images with a fatal end.

Nomination
Niepoort Comic Edition
Austria

National Award
Shortlist
Agency
alessandridesign
Client
Dirk van der Niepoort
Creative Director
Gert Winkler
Art Director
Cordula Alessandri
Designer
Stephan Kirsch
Illustrator
(NL) Willem Holtrop, (FL) Juba Tuomola

Nomination
delishop
Spain

National Award
Silver
Agency
Enric Aguilera Asociados
Client
delishop
Creative Director
Enric Aguilera
Art Director
Enric Aguilera
Designer
Jordi Carles,
Mercè Fernández
Graphics
Jordi Carles,
Mercè Fernández

delishop
Global project of packaging design for alimentary products, selected by delishop. The objective of this project was very simple, to make labels for all packaging products with a minimum cost. As a solution we proposed to convert the barcode into the graphic system.

Super
For the spirits range of ANTHONY'S GARAGE WINERY we developed a campaign to persuade Munich's number one address for delicacy foods, Dallmayer, to order the liqueurs. Solution: We designed and realised ANTHONY'S SUPER range. In keeping with their origin from the GARAGE, they are filled into handy schnapps canisters. The packaging concept for distribution to Dallmayer included finding a name and designing ANTHONY'S SUPER Z (plum liqueur), SUPER K (cherry schnapps), SUPER W (Williams Christ peach liqueur). Result:The new ANTHONY'S SUPER range was highly convincing. The three fruit liqueurs were taken into the Dallmayer range.

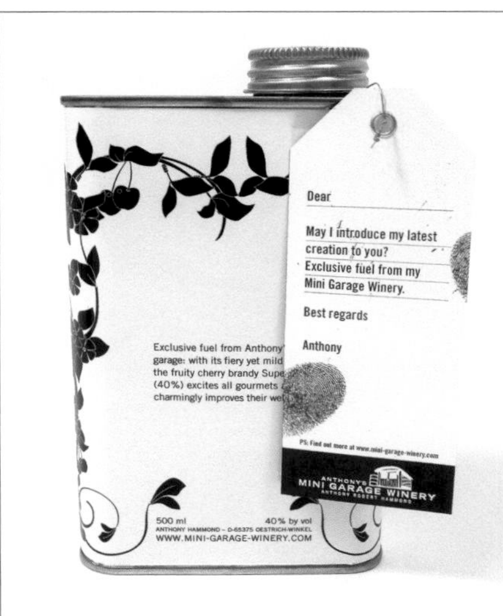

Nomination
Super
Germany

National Award
Silver
Agency
Kolle Rebbe Werbeagentur GmbH
Client
Anthony Robert Hammond
Creative Director
Katrin Oeding
Art Director
Reginald Wagner, Benjamin Pabst
Copywriter
Sabine Manecke
Graphics
Sonja Kliem

Nomination
Woollen Sock
Iceland

National Award
Gold
Agency
Fiton
Client
Olgerdin Egill Skallagrimsson
Creative Director
Halla Helgadottir
Art Director
Halla Helgadottir
Designer
Arnar Geir Omarsson

Woolken Socks
Brennivin is a traditional Icelandic schnaps. So, what better packaging than a traditional Icelandic woollen sock!

Gold Andres Sarda
"Packaging for limited edition bathing suit". The suit is decorated with Swarovsky glasses. The pack imitates the effect these provide to the content by incorporating them to the graphic code.

Prodiet
Prodiet diet food helps us to have and keep a slim and healthy body-line. This product is available as 5 different meals / flavours.

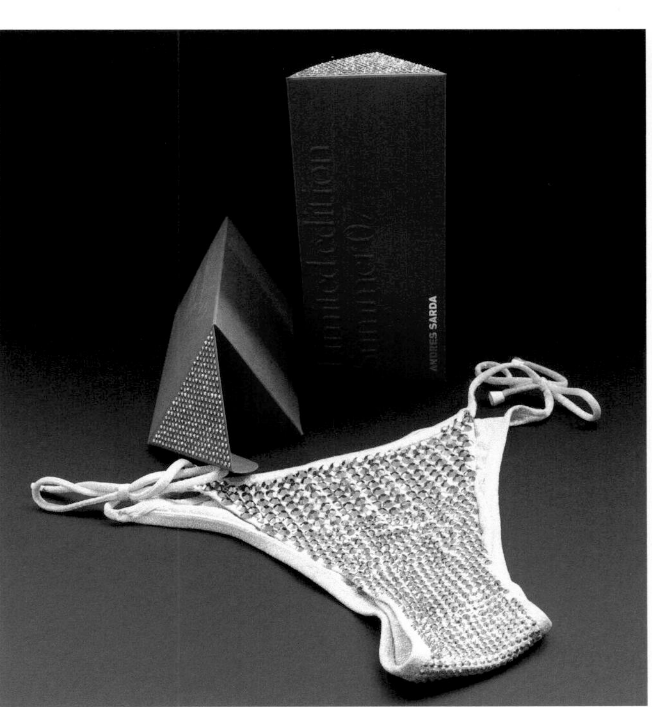

Gold Andres Sarda
Spain

National Award
Gold
Agency
Mucho
Client
Andres Sarda
Creative Director
Pablo Juncadella,
Marc Català
Art Director
Pablo Juncadella,
Marc Català
Graphics
Pablo Juncadella

Prodiet
Slovenia

National Award
Gold
Agency
Studio 360 d.o.o.
Client
Difar d.o.o.
Creative Director
Vladan Srdic
Art Director
Vladan Srdic
Designer
Vladan Srdic
Production company
Eping d.o.o.
Photographer
Luka Kase
Graphics
Vladan Srdic
Illustrator
Vladan Srdic

Atugusto
Spain

National Award
Gold
Agency
Marnich Design
Client
La Sirena
Creative Director
Wladimir Marnich
Designer
Griselda Martí
Illustrator
Bo Lundberg

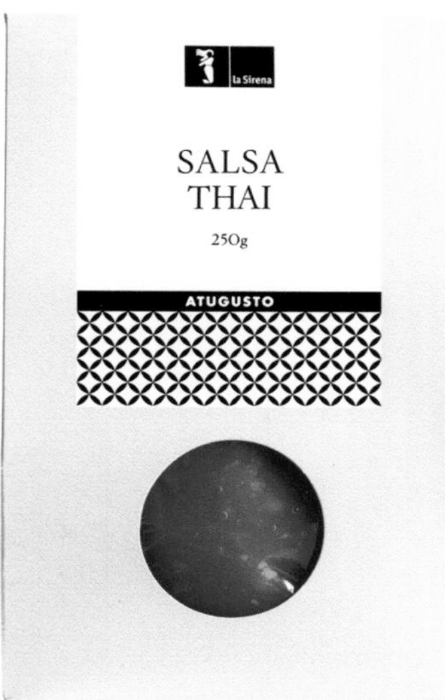

Ensaimades Ca'n Paco
Spain

National Award
Silver
Agency
Damià Rotger Miró
Client
Panaderia Ca'n Paco
Creative Director
Damià Rotger Miró
Art Director
Damià Rotger Miró
Designer
Damià Rotger Miró
Production company
Editorial Rotger
Graphics
Damià Rotger Miró

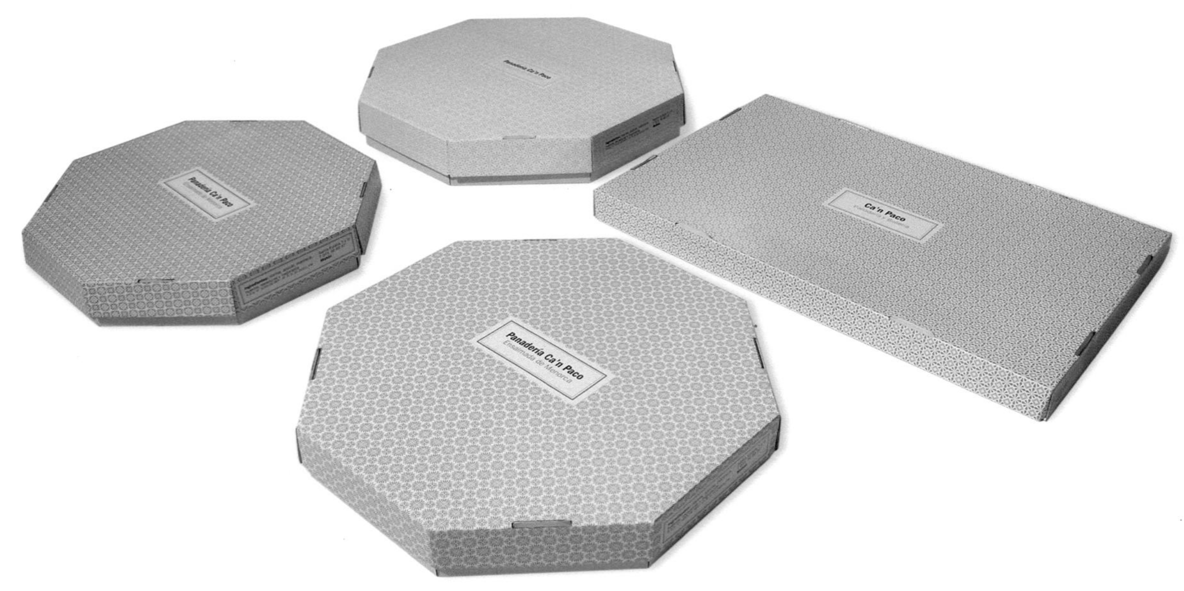

Atugusto
La Sirena stores are a frozen food specialists in Spain. The company requested a family brand design for a new range of non-frozen products to make their regular products look tastier.

Ensaimades Ca'n Paco
The proposal consists of a corporative graphic system to lend own identity to a typical gastronomic series-collection product of the Balearic Islands that are handmade : ensaimadas, coca, carquinyols, tortells, pastisssets, etc. The series-collection began with boxes for ensaimada and coca. Each box consists of two auto set individual pieces. The material that was chosen is micro ecological cardboard for food, authourised by the country's authorities. With this set of packs we tried to provide the product with a unique graphic identity that concurs with sensitivity of the craftsmen who produce the delicate pastry. Through a chromatic system and varied textures the elegance of the folk can be represented, the exquisiteness of the handmade and revaluation of anthropological confectionery.

Estonian Air cognac
A special cognac for Estonian Air that is only sold on board its airplanes.

1944
Line of packaging for ready-meals.

Estonian Air cognac
Estonia

National Award
Gold
Agency
Division
Client
Estonian Air
Creative Director
Kristian Kirsfeldt
Art Director
Kristian Kirsfeldt
Designer
Kristian Kirsfeldt
Graphics
Kristian Kirsfeldt
Illustrator
Kristian Kirsfeldt

1944
Iceland

National Award
Silver
Agency
Gott folk McCann
Client
Slaturfelag Sudurlands
Art Director
Amundi Sigurdsson
Designer
Asgerdur Karlsdottir
Photographer
Addi

Oliveira da Serra Packs
Portugal

National Award
Silver
Agency
Brandia Central
Client
Sovena
Creative Director
Miguel Viana
Art Director
Cristina Gomes
Designer
Rui Sampaio de Faria

Oliveira da Serra Labels
Portugal

National Award
Silver
Agency
Brandia Central
Client
Sovena
Creative Director
Miguel Viana
Art Director
Cristina Gomes
Illustrator
Rodrigo Filipe

Oliveira da Serra Packs
The bottles kept the square base, and present a formal coherence with all the products with an exclusive design. The personalisation factor was also considered, through the placement of leaves (brand element) with huge emphasis.

Oliveira da Serra Labels
The repackaging of the labels was created in a way that transmitted a more contemporary, organic and innovative image. The labels now contain information regarding the usage of each kind of olive oil, with distinctive, trendy and urban graphics.

12"
A series of sleeves for 12".

O de Oliva
Organic Extra Virgin Olive Oil. Objective: Aimed at the European market and looking for a consumer concerned with the manufacturing process and quality of oil. This oil will be included in the range of products bearing an environmental certificate. It will accurately reflect how beneficial it is for our health. Solution: By choosing a pack from the pharmaceutical market, it is implied that the product is beneficial for our health. In an opaque coloured bottle in order to preserve the quality of the oil. To place the bottle as a point of reference in the environmentally friendly market, going for a minimalist design that shows its purity of content.

12"
Iceland

National Award
Silver
Agency
Linda Loeskow
Client
Pineapplerecords
Art Director
Stephan Stephenssen
Designer
Linda Loeskow
Illustrator
Linda Loeskow

O de Oliva
Spain

National Award
Silver
Agency
Dfraile
Client
Export Olive Oil
Creative Director
Eduardo del Fraile
Art Director
Eduardo del Fraile
Designer
Eduardo del Fraile

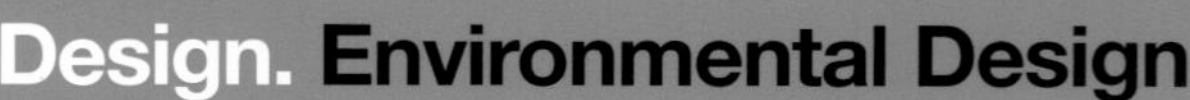

Design. Environmental Design

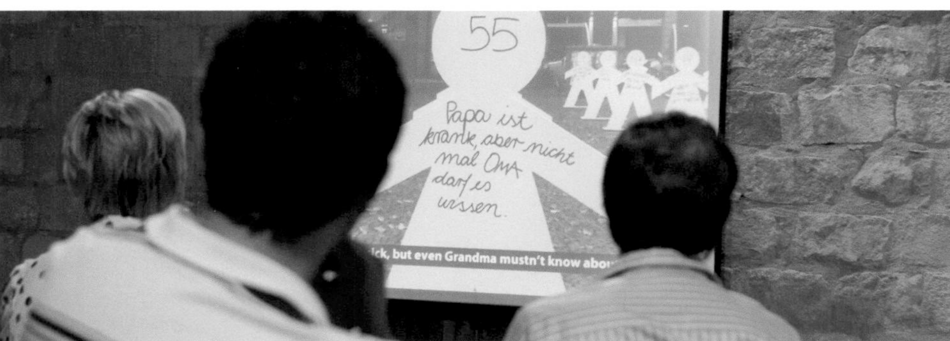

Germany: Gold 4 Nominations

Iceland

Gold
kids and aids installation
(In DVD)
Germany

National Award
Shortlist
Agency
Jung von Matt AG/
Miami Ad School Europe
Client
AJS - kids and aids
Creative Director
Oliver Voss,
Goetz Ulmer
Art Director
Tugba Kantarcioglu,
Marta Nin Llansen,
Jennifer Chen,
Lisa Port
Copywriter
Philipp Barth,
Daniel Pieracci
Designer
Lisa Port
Graphics
Lisa Port

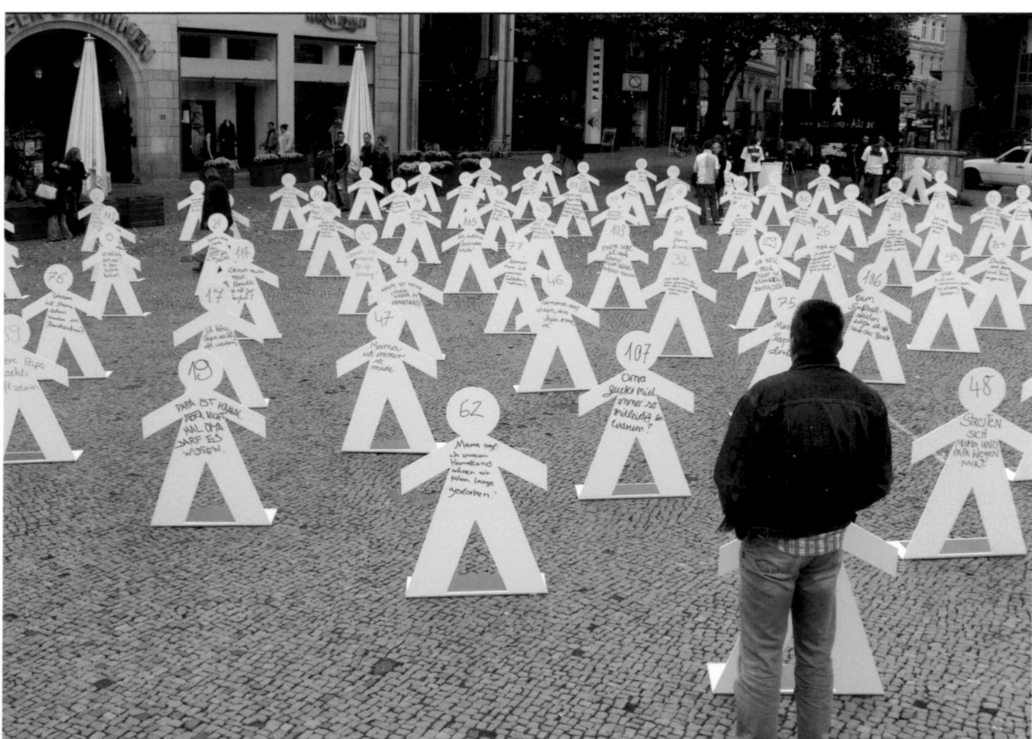

114 Ikonen auf dem Hamburger Gänsemarkt.

HAMBURG

114 Mahnmale für Kin

Weiße Männchen auf dem Gänsemarkt

"Challenge: The non-profit organization "AJS" supports kids in Hamburg, whose families are affected by HIV. "ASJ"'s finances were cut. They needed donations.

Solution: An installation of 114 statues was placed in Hamburg's main square. Each one symbolizes a child. A personal statement from a kid is written on every statue. For example: "Mum has to go to the hospital. Do I have to live with strangers again?". For 114 euro, each statue can be adopted symbolically.

Result: The people of Hamburg were deeply moved. Following coverage from local newspapers, over 25.000 euro was donated, enough to finance another year."

Nomination
+10 Fresco
Germany

National Award
Bronze
Agency
TBWA Germany (180/TBWA), Berlin
Client
Adidas AG
Creative Director
Kurt Georg Dieckert, Stefan Schmidt
Art Director
Boris Schwiedrzik
Copywriter
Helge Bloeck
Production company
Methodik Management & Partner
Illustrator
Felix Reidenbach
Other
Media Agency: Carat

Adidas mi Innovation Center (MIC)
MIC is a multi sensory digital installation inside the Adidas flagship stores. Its purpose is to communicate and strengthen the high-tech and innovation power of the Adidas brand by using all possible digital media.

Nomination
Adidas mi Innovation Center (MIC)
(In DVD)
Germany

National Award
Bronze
Agency
Mutabor Design GmbH
Client
Adidas AG
Creative Director
Heinrich Paravicini
Art Director
Axel Domke
Designer
Thomas Huth
Production company
Fraunhofer HHI Institute, Berlin
Other
Media Planning:
NIYU, Berlin

Nomination

SkyArena Frankfurt - Overture to the FIFA World Cup 2006 in Germany

(In DVD)
Germany

National Award
Silver
Agency
Atelier Markgraph
Client
Tourismus+Congress GmbH Frankfurt am Main
Creative Director
Roland Lambrette, Stefan Weil
Art Director
Alexander Hanowski

SkyArena Frankfurt - Overture to the FIFA World Cup 2006 in Germany
Whitsun 2006: Frankfurt opens the FIFA World Cup one week early. A 45-minute light and media show transforms the city skyline into a huge stage for soccer images that travel the world. An 11-stage journey through soccer's great emotions.

Walk of Ideas
The Federal President Koehler set the task: "Germany should be the Land of Ideas". So, in 2006 during the World Cup 6 gigantic sculptures built a unique outdoor exhibition in the centre of Berlin and represent ideas "Made in Germany".

Nomination
Walk of Ideas

(In DVD)
Germany

National Award
Shortlist

Agency
Scholz & Friends

Client
FC Deutschland GmbH

Creative Director
Wolf Schneider, Tobias Wolff, Sebastian Turner

Art Director
Juergen Krugsperger, Danielle Sellin, Alf Speidel

Copywriter
Mirko Derpmann

Designer
Claus Potthoff (Audi AG)/ Stephan Dietrich (adidas)

Production company
BASF Coatings AG/ EDAG Engineering/ Design AG

Graphics
Andreas Bergmann, Ralph Bremenkamp

Other
Nicolaus v. Hantelmann, Christian Ruehe

Pineapplerecords
Iceland

National Award
Silver
Agency
Linda Loeskow
Client
Pineapplerecords
Art Director
Stephan Stephenssen
Designer
Linda Loeskow
Illustrator
Linda Loeskow

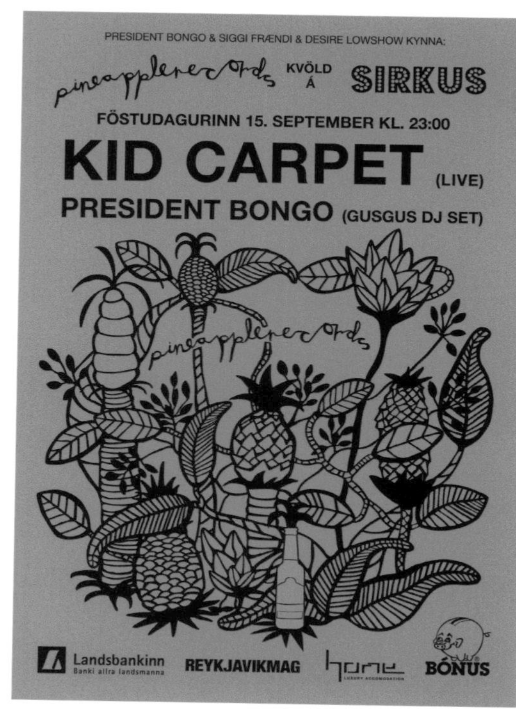

Sofakynslodin
Iceland

National Award
Silver
Agency
Ragnar Freyr (FRONT)
Client
Young Activists
Art Director
Ragnar Freyr Palsson
Designer
Ragnar Freyr Palsson,
Helgi Laxdal

Pineapplerecords
Poster for a musical event.

Sofakynslodin
The sofa generation

Table of Free Voices
On September 9, 2006, 112 individuals came together in central Berlin to tackles 100 questions. Each person was recorded simultaneously. The 700 hours of footage can now be viewed and discussed on the dropping knowledge website.

Holidays
"Posters to mark holidays". Each poster marks a different holiday.

Table of Free Voices
Germany

National Award
Silver
Agency
dropping knowledge e.V.
Client
dropping knowledge e.V.
Creative Director
Ralf Schmerberg, Andreas Laeufer
Art Director
Johannes Koblenz
Designer
dropping knowledge creative think tank
Production company
dropping knowledge e.V.
Photographer
S. Roth, Justine, D. Wenders, R. Pfisterer
Graphics
dropping knowledge creative think tank

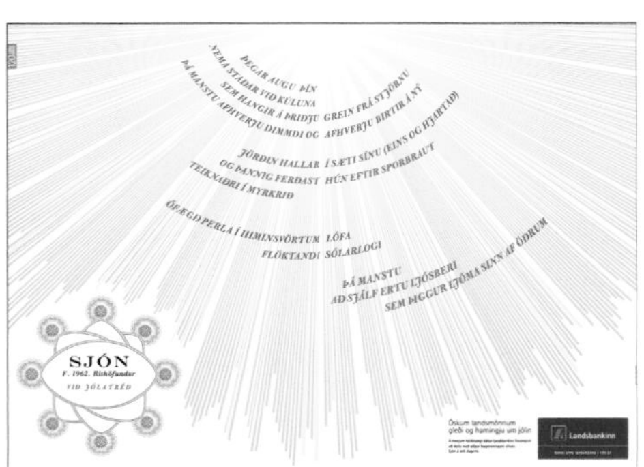

Holidays
Iceland

National Award
Silver
Agency
Gott folk McCann
Client
Landsbanki Islands
Creative Director
Jon Arnason, Gary Wake
Art Director
Amundi Sigurdsson
Illustrator
Amundi Sigurdsson

Nordic Music Days
Iceland

National Award
Gold
Agency
Hordur, Siggi & Sol
Client
Nordic Music Days
Art Director
Hordur Larusson, Siggi Orri & Sol Hrafnsdottir
Designer
Hordur Larusson, Siggi Orri & Sol Hrafnsdottir

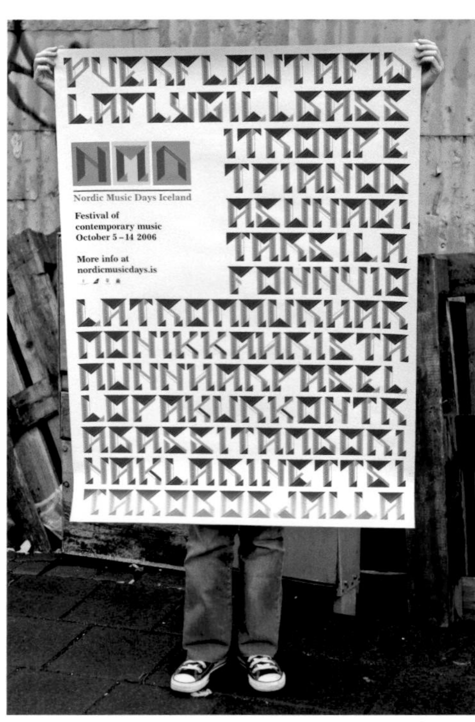

Nordic Music Days
Very old Icelandic font, mainly used for wood carving, is used as a design element.

Museum X
Mix of 3D billboard, urban revitalization project and art sculpture. Transformation of the former central theatre into an illusionary museum at the central city plaza. Placeholder for the real museum whilst under 14 month reconstruction. Catalyst for political debate on urban development.

Museum X
Germany

National Award
Silver
Agency
realities: united
Client
Museum Abteiberg Moenchengladbach / M:AI Museum für Architektur und Ingenieurkunst NRW
Creative Director
Jan Edler, Tim Edler
Designer
Christoph Wagner, Tim Edler, Milena Monssen
Production company
realities:united
Illustrator
Malte Niedringhaus

Design. Any Other

Germany: Gold 4 Nominations

Estonia

Iceland

Latvia

Portugal

Russia

Spain: 2 Nominations

Gold
365 on Death Row
Germany

National Award
Bronze
Agency
Serviceplan
Muenchen/Hamburg
Client
Alive e.V. gegen Todesstrafe
Creative Director
Christoph Everke
Art Director
Veronika Broich
Copywriter
Helmut Huber
Production company
Pinsker Druck und Medien
Graphics
Anja Krumrein,
Ivo Hlavac,
Massimo Petrolli
Other
Account Executive:
Carla Nothhelfer

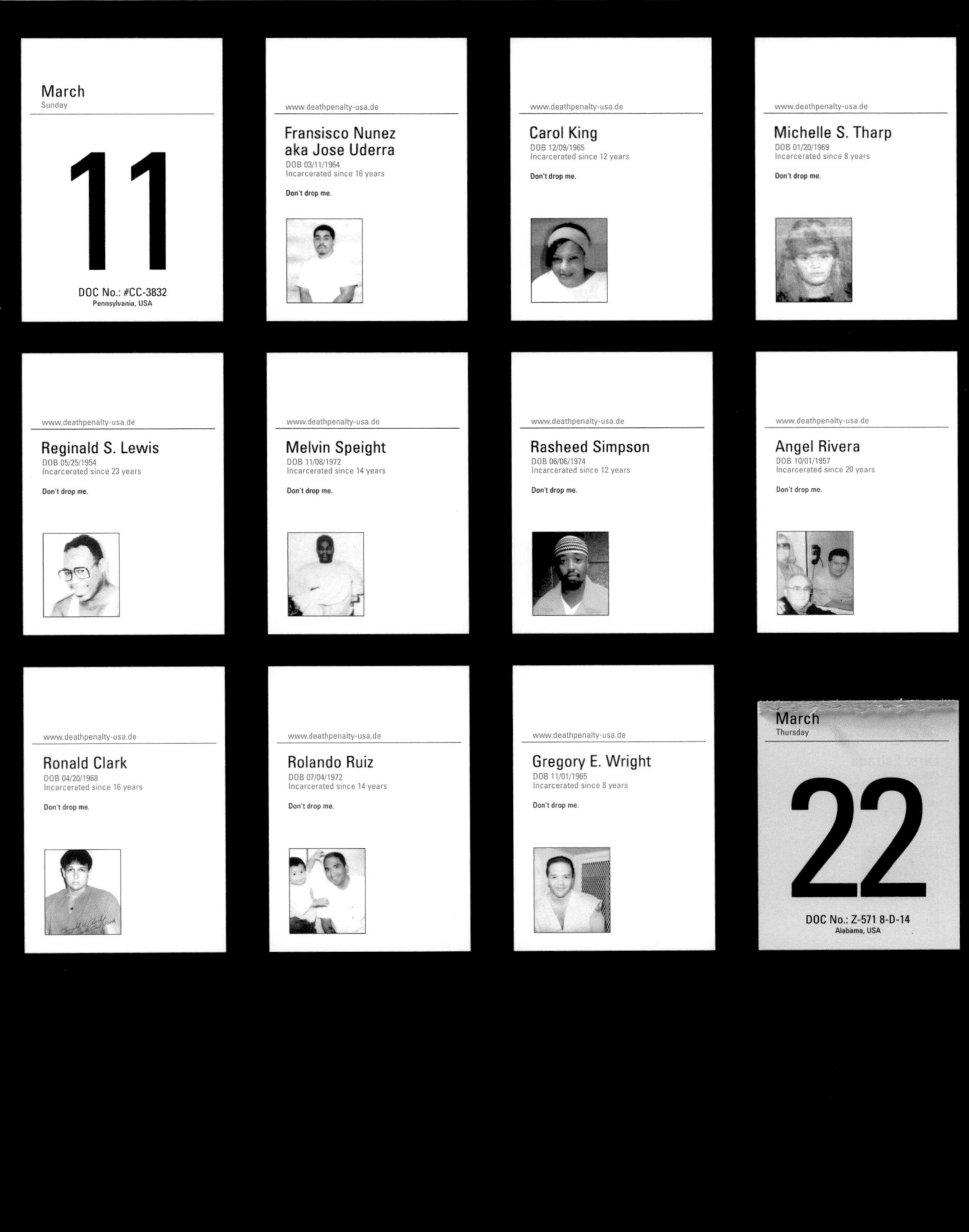

March
Sunday
11
DOC No.: #CC-3832
Pennsylvania, USA
www.deathpenalty-usa.de
Fransisco Nunez
aka Jose Uderra
DOB 03/11/1964
Incarcerated since 16 years
Don't drop me.
www.deathpenalty-usa.de
Carol King
DOB 12/09/1965
Incarcerated since 12 years
Don't drop me.
www.deathpenalty-usa.de
Michelle S. Tharp
DOB 01/20/1969
Incarcerated since 8 years
Don't drop me.
www.deathpenalty-usa.de
Reginald S. Lewis
DOB 05/25/1954
Incarcerated since 23 years
Don't drop me.
www.deathpenalty-usa.de
Melvin Speight
DOB 11/08/1972
Incarcerated since 14 years
Don't drop me.
www.deathpenalty-usa.de
Rasheed Simpson
DOB 06/06/1974
Incarcerated since 12 years
Don't drop me.
www.deathpenalty-usa.de
Angel Rivera
DOB 10/01/1957
Incarcerated since 20 years
Don't drop me.
www.deathpenalty-usa.de
Ronald Clark
DOB 04/20/1968
Incarcerated since 16 years
Don't drop me.
www.deathpenalty-usa.de
Rolando Ruiz
DOB 07/04/1972
Incarcerated since 14 years
Don't drop me.
www.deathpenalty-usa.de
Gregory E. Wright
DOB 11/01/1965
Incarcerated since 8 years
Don't drop me.
March
Thursday
22
DOC No.: Z-571 8-D-14
Alabama, USA

Brief: In 2005 at least 2,148 people worldwide were executed. The aim is to show that the death penalty is nothing abstract –people are dying every day.

Idea: A tear-off calendar was created for ALIVE e.V. to demonstrate this fact. On the back of each page there is a picture of a condemned person as that day's representative victim. The tearing off a sheet every day communicates that peoples' lives are literally being torn apart and thrown away.

Implementation and result: One thousand calendars were printed. 200 calendars were sent to the press, politicians, especially to Governors of States where executions occurred in 2006. Another 700 were sent to the condemned, their families and lawyers.

The response exceeded expectations. To give an example, the following e-mail was received from one of the condemned: "The calendar – it's tough but that's how it is. I know that my life lies in the hands of others and they will decide when it will be over".

Nomination
Light Regular
Spain

National Award
Silver
Agency
Mucho
Client
Biosca & Botey
Creative Director
Marc Català,
Pablo Juncadella
Art Director
Marc Català,
Pablo Juncadella
Graphics
Marc Català

abcdefg
hijklmn
opqrstuv
wxyz

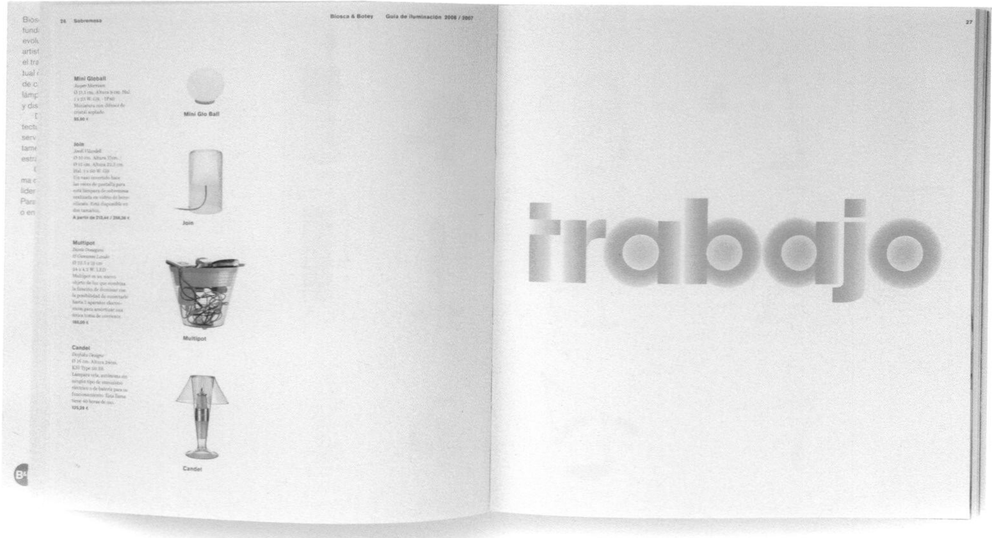

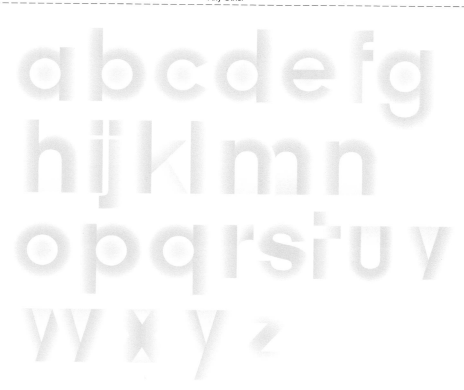

Light Regular
Typography for the lamp retailers catalogue. Light Regular has been specifically created to set the headlines for the "Guía de Iluminación 2007", published by Biosca & Botey, a firm dedicated to selling lamps. Light Regular is an attempt to design type with light, using light beams as a reference.

The Annual of Annuals
Font designed to type set "The Annual of Annuals". The concept of the book is based on the construction of a photographic alphabet formed by books, being the annual an awarded selection of what the annuals of the member countries publish.

Nomination
The Annual of Annuals
Spain

National Award
Silver
Agency
Mucho
Client
Art Directors Club of Europe
Creative Director
Pablo Juncadella, Marc Català
Art Director
Pablo Juncadella, Marc Català
Designer
Pablo Juncadella, Carla Bahna
Photographer
Nacho Alegre
Graphics
Pablo Juncadella, Carla Bahna
Other
Furniture:
Gloria de Pallejà

Crack it!
Estonia

National Award
Gold
Agency
Leo Express
Client
Elion Ettevõtted
Creative Director
Anti Naulainen
Art Director
Aive Blond
Copywriter
Anti Naulainen
Other
Rivo Räim

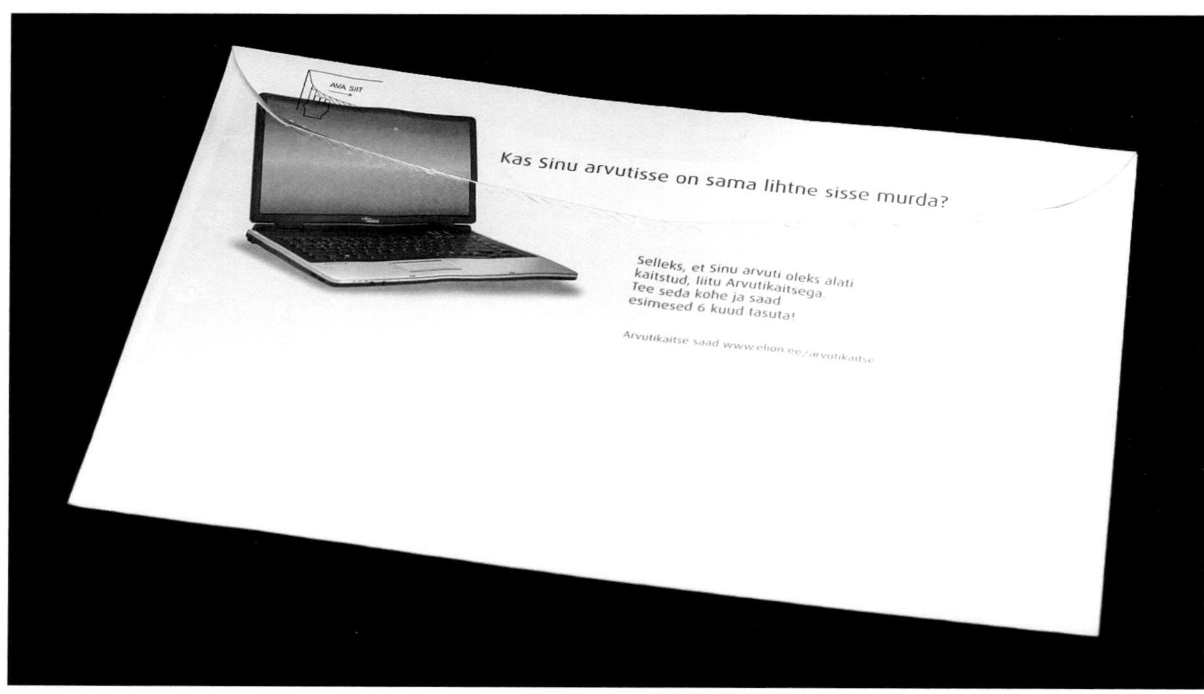

Opened letter
Estonia

National Award
Gold
Agency
Leo Express
Client
Elion Ettevõtted
Creative Director
Anti Naulainen
Art Director
Aive Blond
Copywriter
Anti Naulainen
Other
Rivo Räim

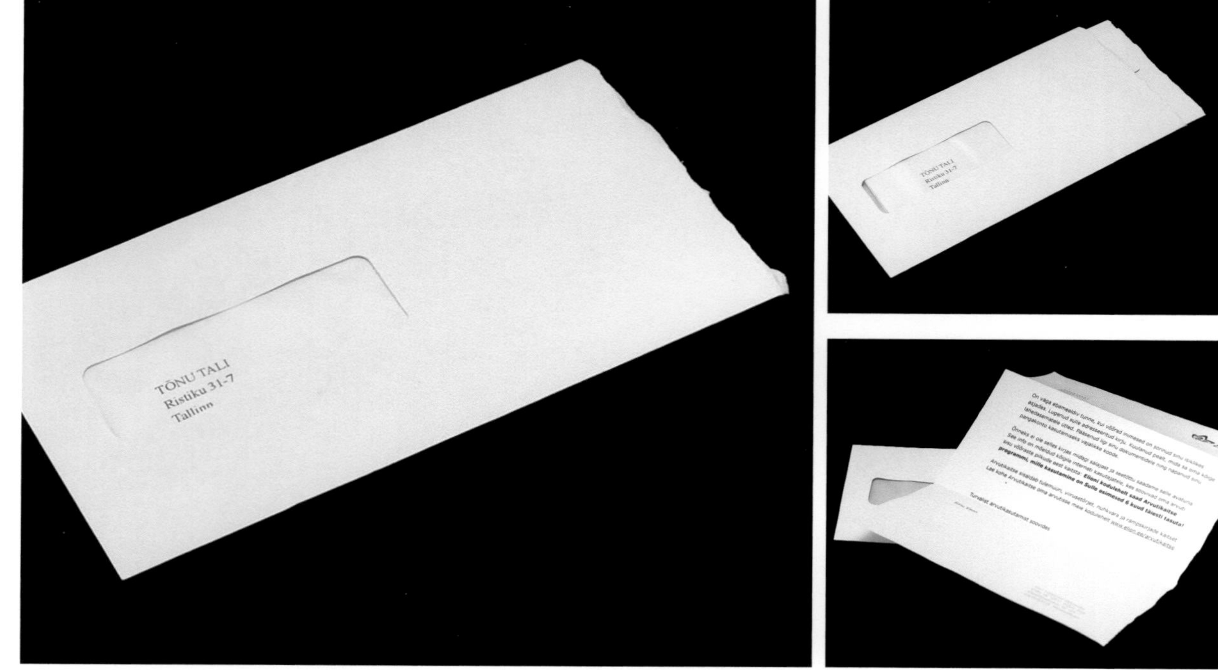

Crack it!
This highlights the idea that breaking into a computer without a firewall is as easy as opening an envelope. Protect your computer, take computer protection.

Opened letter
Customers of Elion found a letter addressed to them in their mailbox. The letter was already opened and contained an offer: "if you don't want anyone to read your letters take computer protection".

Bus route
Proposal for a new bus route map.

Coffee Menu
Coffee menu at a coffee house.

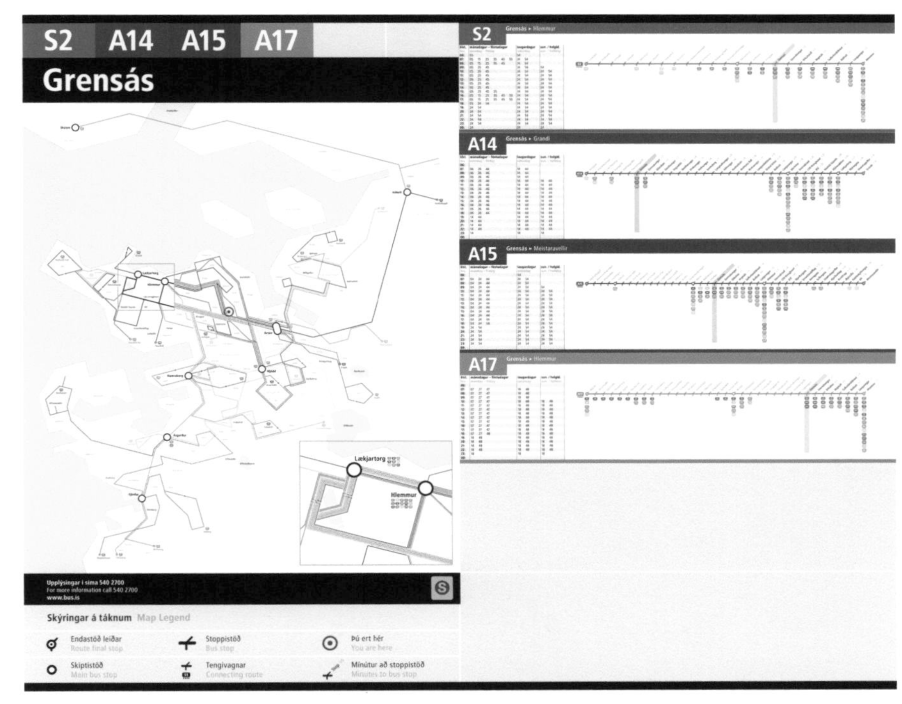

Bus route
Iceland

National Award
Silver
Agency
Hordur Larusson
Client
LHI
Art Director
Hordur Larusson
Designer
Hordur Larusson

Coffee menu
Iceland

National Award
Silver
Agency
Royal
Client
Kaffiheimur
Art Director
Isak Winther,
Petur Gudmundsson
Designer
Isak Winther,
Petur Gudmundsson

Invitation
Iceland

National Award
Gold
Agency
Hzeta Design
Client
Baugur Group
Art Director
Hildur H. Zoega
Designer
Hildur H. Zoega

Once I had it good
Iceland

National Award
Gold
Agency
Hunang
Client
Smekkleysa
Art Director
Sigrun Sigvaldadottir
Designer
Sigrun Sigvaldadottir
Illustrator
Halldor Baldursson

Invitation
Invitation to a fishing trip.

Once I had it good
Book cover.

The Ambassador
Book cover.

Staklis table set collection
Staklis stool/table is influenced by the Latvian ethnography that offers to create different shapes of surfaces - triangles, stars, etc. Staklis table is ideal for the rest area. It is easily mountable and dismountable, consisting of 3 similar surface details and legs. Very comfortable when dismounted. A 1 euro coin should be used as a turnscrew.

The Ambassador
Iceland

National Award
Silver
Agency
Hvita Husid
Client
Edda publishing
Art Director
Bjarney Hinriksdottir
Designer
Bjarney Hinriksdottir, Sigrun Palsdottir
Illustrator
Bjarney Hinriksdottir

Staklis table set collection
Latvia

National Award
Silver
Agency
Elina Busmane
Client
Elina Busmane
Designer
Elina Busmane

Type Ativism
Portugal

National Award
Gold
Agency
Mola Ativism
Client
Ativism
Creative Director
Rui Morais
Designer
José Carlos Mendes

type//////////
ativism//////

type ativism-light
ABCDEFGHIJKLMNOPQRSTUVWXYZ
abcdefghijklmnopqrstuvwxyz
0123456789

type ativism-Normal
ABCDEFGHIJKLMNOPQRSTUVWXYZ
abcdefghijklmnopqrstuvwxyz
0123456789

type ativism-Medium
ABCDEFGHIJKLMNOPQRSTUVWXYZ
abcdefghijklmnopqrstuvwxyz
0123456789

type ativism

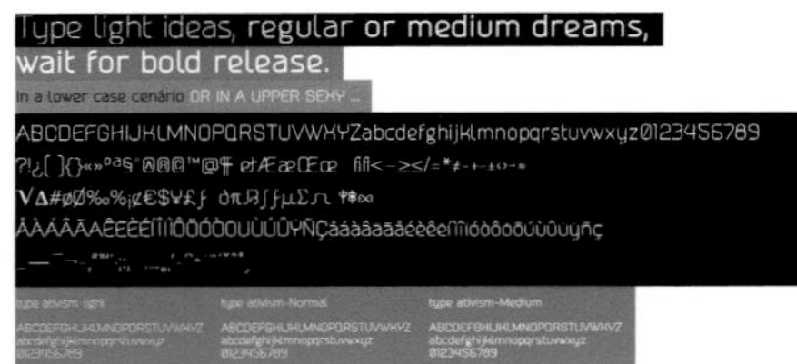

Innocent Graphics Calendar 07
Portugal

National Award
Silver
Agency
Mola Ativism
Client
M2
Art Director
Rui Morais
Designer
Diogo Potes, Pedro Carmo,
José Carlos Mendes

Type Ativism
The ativism typeface was designed for the ativism network of agencies. This is revealed in the strength of the diagonal lines, in the design of the letters and in the name.

Innocent Graphics Calendar 07
Total freedom to create. M2's objective was to come up with an item using free and creative illustrations in order to illustrate the best possible way to use print techniques to distinguish an item.

Anduaga
The project Anduaga is the revival of a digital format of 18th century Spanish handwriting. The typographical project includes the edition of a published book for the prestigious publishing company Campgrafic, which features an article by the expert Albert Corbeto about the origins and history of the calligraphy.

What's Next?
We live in a world in which various trends and languages exist and almost anything is allowed: pasting, superimposing, mixing.

Anduaga
Spain

National Award
Gold
Agency
Can Antaviana
Client
Campgrafic Editors
Creative Director
Josep Patau Bellart
Designer
Josep Patau Bellart

Ciclostatil
Master de tipografía litográfica
la Nueva Escritura
Tractorada
l'Aplec del Cargol
les aparences són precisament, això
Mr. Gromenauer

What's Next?
Portugal

National Award
Silver
Agency
Mola Ativism
Client
Creative Club of Portugal
Creative Director
Rui Morais
Designer
Rui Morais

gatcpac
Spain

National Award
Silver
Agency
grafica
Client
Museu d'Història de la Ciutat/Col.legi d'Arquitectes de Catalunya
Creative Director
Pablo Martin
Art Director
Pablo Martin
Designer
Meri Iannuzzi
Graphics
Meri Iannuzzi

Table-board
Latvia

National Award
Silver
Agency
Baiba Lindane
Client
Ugis Gailis
Designer
Baiba Lindane

Gatcpac
Graphic design for the GATCPAC exhibition (Museu d'Història de la Ciutat/Col.legi d'Arquitectes de Catalunya exhibition).

Table-board
The folding table has two functions: it's a table but you can move it so that it doesn't take up space - that's how the second function comes up - by hanging the surface on a wall you get a note board. The multi-function folding table is unique, it is as interesting as it is comfortable and easy to use.

Metalarte
Graphic design of the Metalarte Stand at the Frankfurt Fair.

Cinema Book
Objective: Capture the attention of the general public to participate in a humanitarian project. Look for a format illustrating the delivery of books to Spanish-speaking countries. Solution: With a photographic sequence, it shows a metaphor of distributing culture, this way aiming at a greater level of public awareness-raising. A cinema book format has been chosen in order to represent the object to be delivered in a more expressive way.

metalarte
Spain

National Award
Silver
Agency
grafica
Client
metalarte
Creative Director
Pablo Martin
Art Director
Pablo Martin
Designer
Meri Iannuzzi
Graphics
Meri Iannuzzi

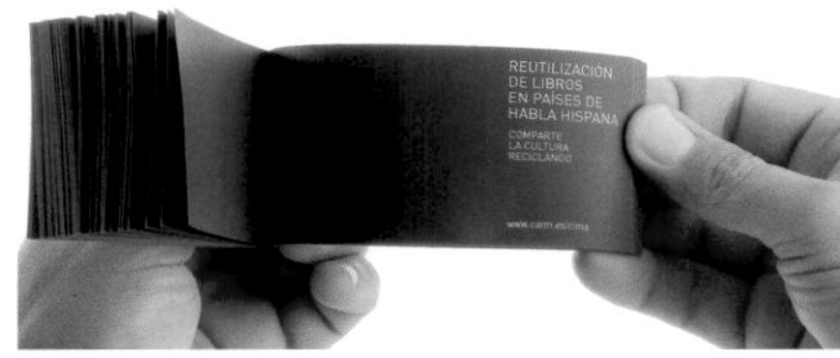

Cinema Book
Spain

National Award
Silver
Agency
Dfraile
Client
Consejería de Medio
Ambiente Región de Murcia
Creative Director
Eduardo del Fraile
Art Director
Eduardo del Fraile
Designer
Eduardo del Fraile,
Juan Jimenez
Photographer
Javier Urosas,
Eduardo del Fraile

Covers for book series "History for young"
Russia

National Award
Silver
Agency
Ribakov Andrei
Client
B.S.G.-press
Creative Director
Ribakov Andrei
Art Director
Ribakov Andrei
Copywriter
Ribakov Andrei
Illustrator
Ribakov Andrei

Covers for book series "History for young"
Book covers for book series.

Put Things In Order
A visual manifesto, a self promotion one issue magazine. This is a 20 page tabloid-shaped visual manifesto. A collection of images that works independently and as a whole, in a code to be decoded by the reader. A silent way of communicating that leaves space to find your own connections within the design.

The Settlement Exhibition - Shop
Iceland

National Award
Gold
Client
The Settlement Exhibition
Creative Director
Snaefrid & Hildigunnur
Designer
Snaefrid Thorsteins & Hildigunnur Gunnarsdottir
Photographer
Gudmundur Ingolfsson and Vigfus Birgisson

Put Things In Order
Spain

National Award
Silver
Agency
Daniel Bembibre
Client
Daniel Bembibre
Creative Director
Daniel Bembibre
Copywriter
Daniel Bembibre
Designer
Daniel Bembibre
Production company
Salpausselän Kirjapaino
Photographer
Daniel Bembibre
Graphics
Daniel Bembibre
Other
Sponsored by UIAH and Salpausselän Kirjapaino

Q: What is more realistic, a High or a Low Res Image?

Q: Must every experience have the right to an audience?

Q: Is the third screen too small for big ideas?

5

Epilogue

Q: What will remain?

Young Creative of the Year

Austria

Germany

Latvia

Poland: Gold

Portugal

Gold
No administrator
(In DVD)
Poland

National Award
Gold
Creative
Rafal Gorski,
Adam Smerecynski,
Konrad Grzegorzewicz
Copywriter
Rafal Gorski,
Adam Smerecynski,
Konrad Grzegorzewicz
Category
New and Mixed Media - Online Advertising
Company
Arc Warsaw,
Leo Burnett Group

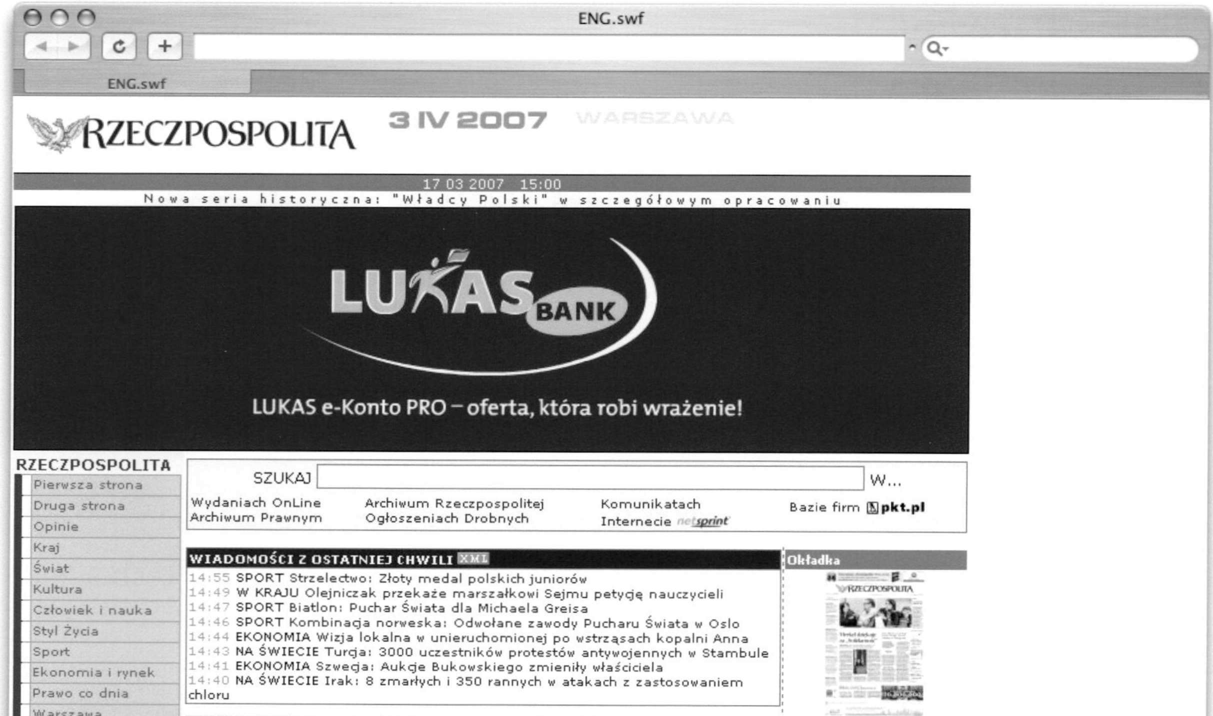

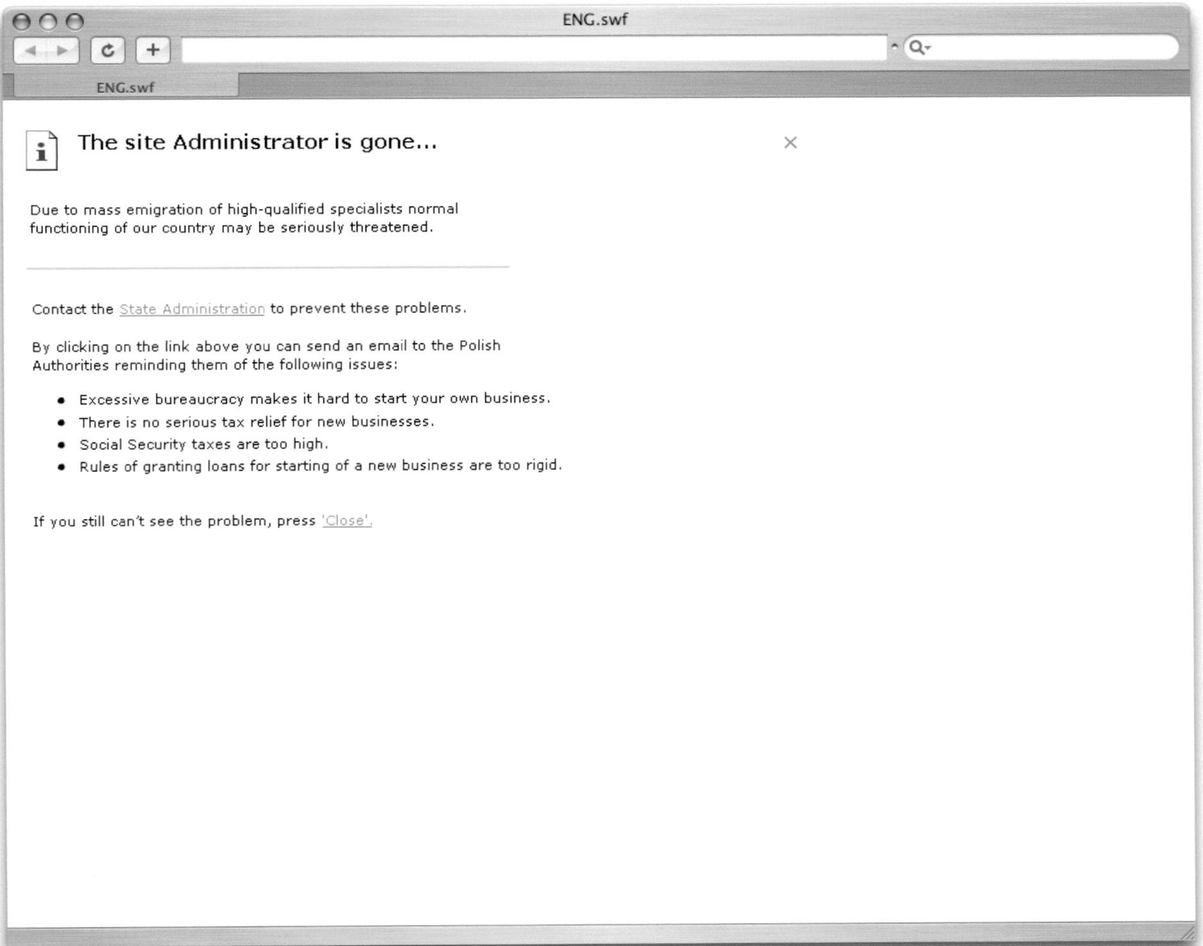

ENG.swf
ENG.swf
The site Administrator is gone...
Due to mass emigration of high-qualified specialists normal functioning of our country may be seriously threatened.
Contact the State Administration to prevent these problems.
By clicking on the link above you can send an email to the Polish Authorities reminding them of the following issues:
Excessive bureaucracy makes it hard to start your own business.
There is no serious tax relief for new businesses.
Social Security taxes are too high.
Rules of granting loans for starting of a new business are too rigid.
If you still can't see the problem, press 'Close'.

No administrator
After joining The European Union many young, educated people left Poland to find a job in Western Europe, a fact that gave rise to a shortage of specialists in the Polish market. The aim of the campaign was to draw the attention of the Polish authorities to the problem of the "brain drain" in Poland. To encourage the government to take action to reduce the emigration of highly qualified workers.

Calling without thinking
Germany

Creative Director
Tanja Schulze
Category
Film
Company
BBDO Berlin GmbH
Creative team
Andreas Manthey,
Ines Bärwald,
Benjamin Schwarz

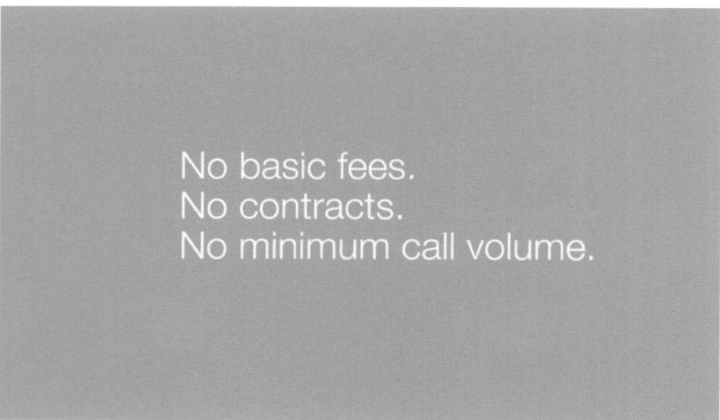

Baptismo
Portugal

Art Director
Victor Sousa
Copywriter
Miguel Durao
Category
Print
Company
BBDO Portugal /
McCann Erickson Portugal

Baptismo
Launch of the new Prize water bottle in the market. Work: The idea in this piece is based up in the habit of inaugurate something like a ship or a boat by breaking a bottle against this new arrived thing. In this case is the bottle that is new and the boat that breaks against it.

Adwards
This mixed media campaign was for this year's Latvian Advertising Festival ADWARDS. The three symbols of th festival -eye, ear and mouth- represented the three main elements of communication all absolutely indispensable in advertising.

Adwards
Latvia

Creative
Peteris Lidaka
Category
Mixed Media Campaigns
Company
Zoom!

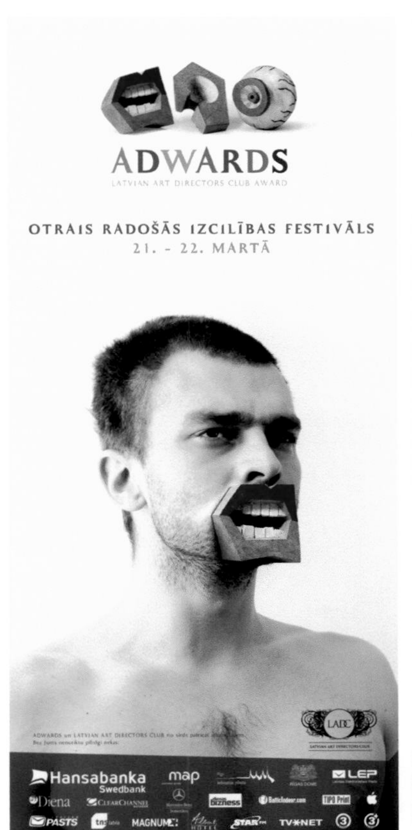

One loves Music
Austria

Agency
Jung von Matt/Donau
Creative Director
Christian Begusch,
Andreas Putz,
Christoph Gaunersdorfer
Category
Mixed Media Campaigns

Pol-end
After joining The European Union many young, educated people left Poland to find a job in Western Europe, a fact that gave rise to a shortage of specialists in the Polish market. The aim of the campaign was to draw the attention of the Polish authorities to the problem of the "brain drain" in Poland. To encourage the government to take action to reduce the emigration of highly qualified workers.

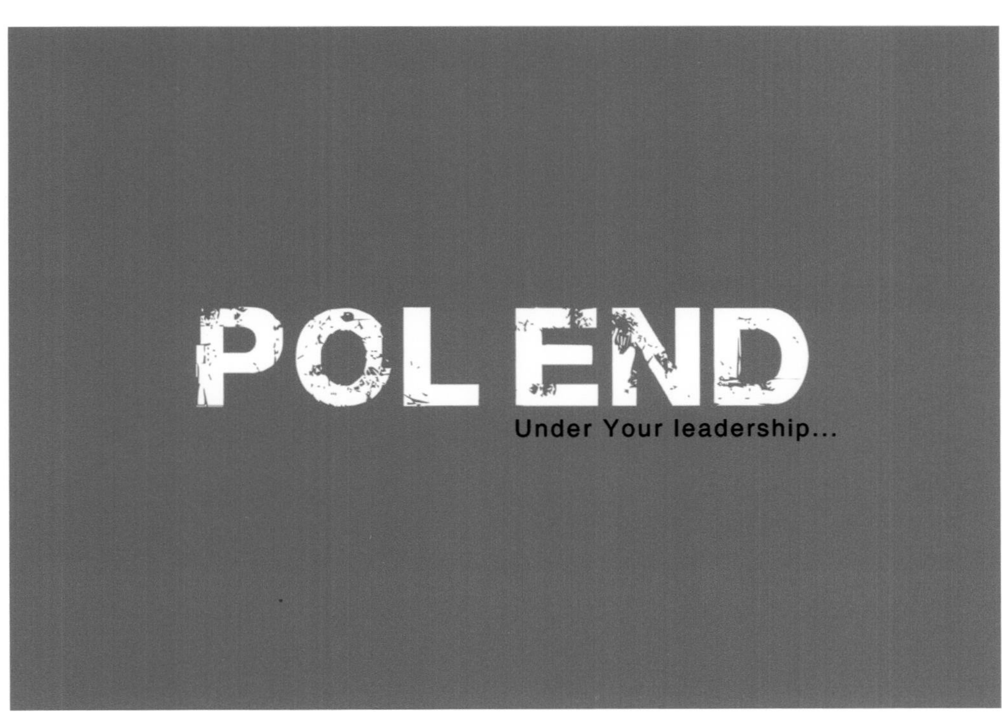

Pol-end
Poland

National Award
Gold
Creative
Ewa Trzewikowska, Sabrina Samulska
Category
Print - Public Service and Charity
Company
Tequila/Poland
Url
www.ktr.org.pl

European Student of the Year

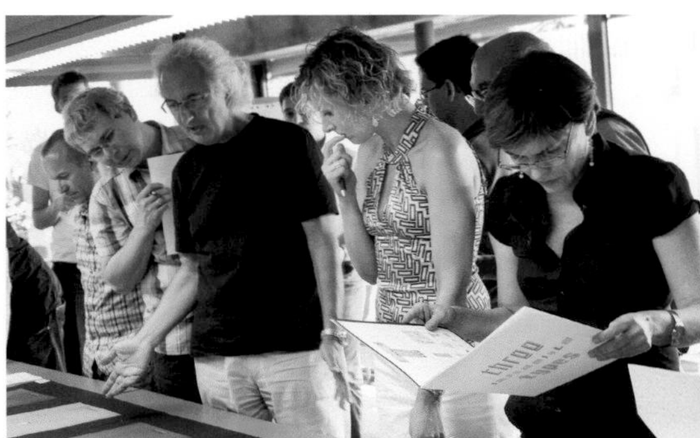

Austria

Germany: Gold

Portugal

Spain

Russia

Gold

Clusters-tracking everyday life

Germany

National Award
Talent des Jahres
Student
Eva Klose
Category
Print
School
University of Applied Sciences Mainz

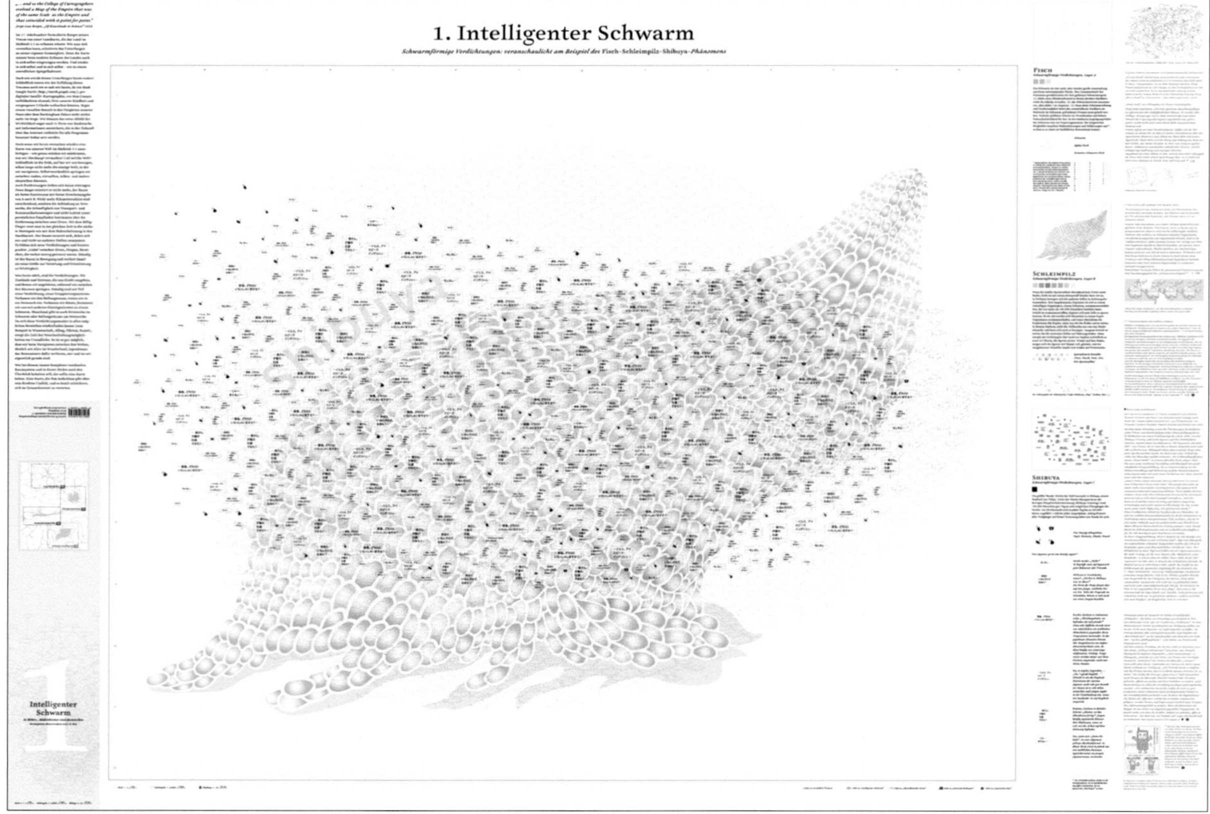

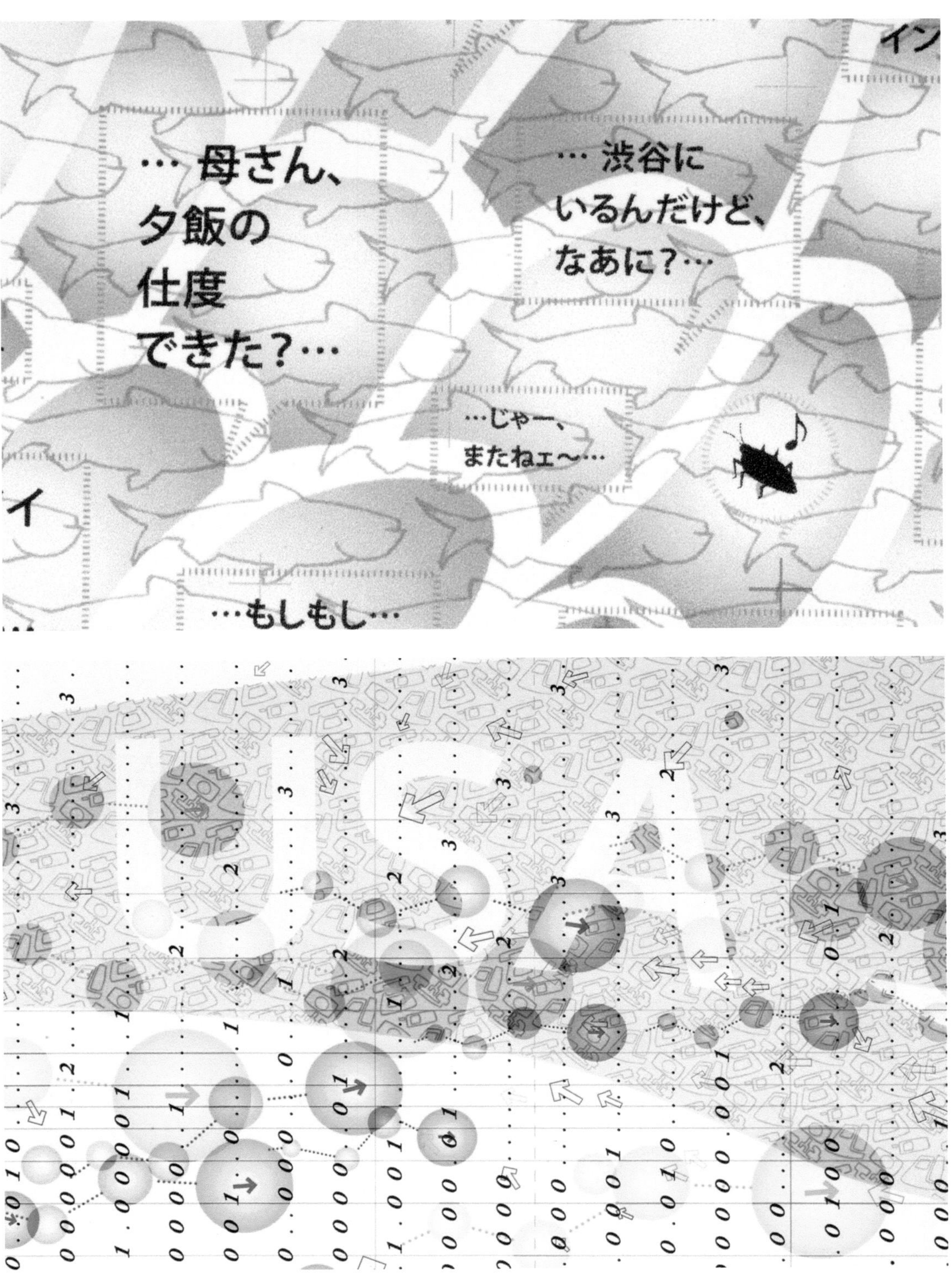

In four maps, she has measured the everyday life and discovered the following types of clusters: swarms, networks, currents and concentrations. Each map condenses three visually similar phenomena through an overlay into a basic form. Extracted from independent data, the cards show unexpected similarities and connections between contents and events, that were thought to have nothing in common. The developed typology serves the viewer, on one hand, as starting point to continue the given observations in his own everyday life. On the other hand it serves him as a register, where he can fit his own situation and experiences in order to more easily locate himself in the total context of realisty an provide a beter overiew of the world.

"Magic Box - Caixa Mágica"

Portugal

Student
Ana Carina Martins
Ricardo, Andreia Brizio
Duarte Castelo de Campos
Category
New Media
School
Lisbon Ad School

Try Before You Order Online

Austria

National Award
Gold (CCA- Rookie of the Year)
Student
Julia Newmann
Category
Print
School
Miami Ad School

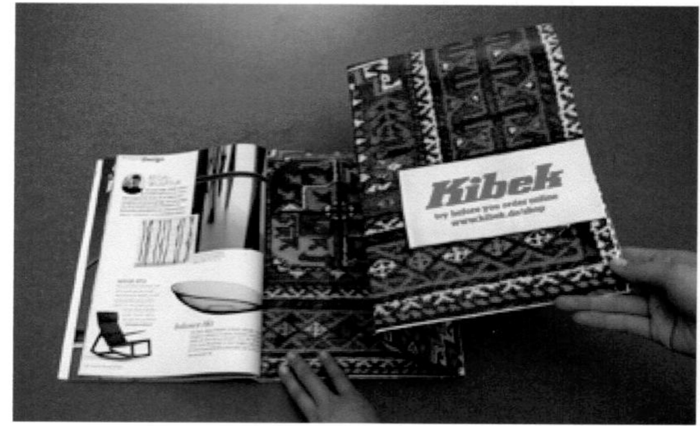

"Norbert"
Germany

Student
Anne Julia Nowitzki
Category
Film - Animation/flash
School
HFG Offenbach

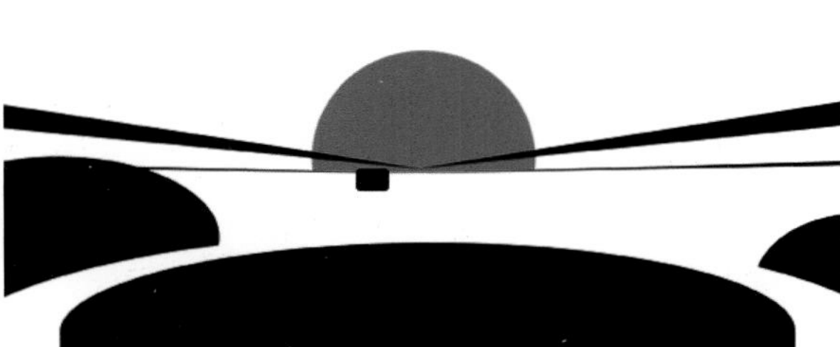

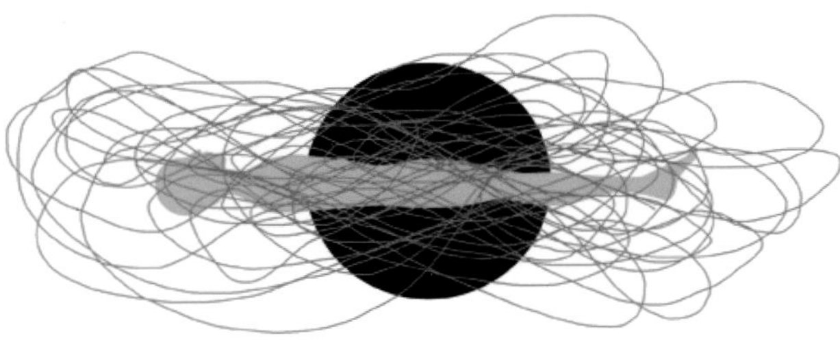

Magic Box - Caixa Mágica
The first time you open the box, you can see Frizes' new bottle. Then you close the box. The next time you open it, it's just an empty drawer. This process shows what will happen when the new Frize will be on sale.

Norbert
Animated short story, based on a summary of the booh sex II (author: Sibylle Berg)

"Try for free" Wempe
Austria

National Award
Gold (CCA-Rookie of the Year)
Student
Julia Newmann
Category
Print
School
Miami Ad School

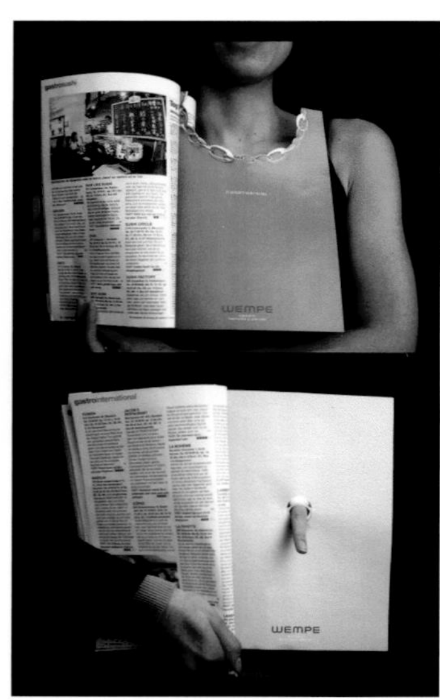

Three impossible types
Spain

National Award
Laus Estudiants 07
Student
Héctor Olivares
Category
Graphic Design - Typography
School
Eina, Design & Art School

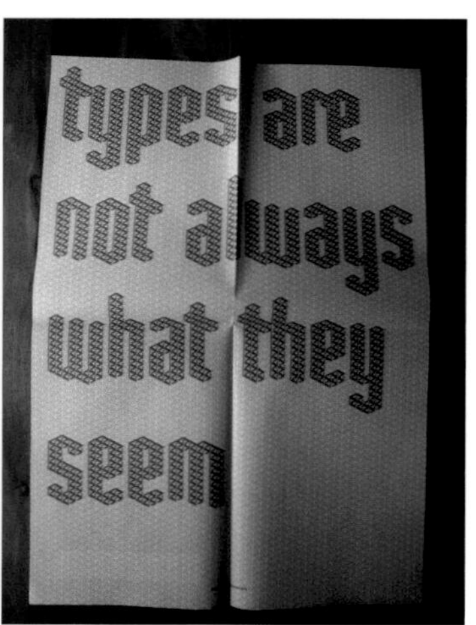

Three impossible types An approach and analysis of the world of impossible figures, visual tricks and M.C. Escher's work. Let us build a system of modules, the root of each one of the three alphabets.

Apple, think different
Spain

National Award
Laus Estudiants 07
Creative
Cristian Jiménez, Arnau Aloy
Category
New and Mixed Media
School
Escola BAU

TO BUY SOMETHING JUST
~~TAKE YOUR MONEY FROM THE CASH MASHINE AND~~
GO TO THE PAY DESK
MasterCard

Mastercard
Russia

Creative
Anton Kazakov, Galina Luppo, Maria Hisamova, Andrey Levin
Category
Print
School
Russian State Social University (Galina, Maria), Moscow State Universtity (Andrey).

Index

Agencies

Agency Producers

Art Directors

Clients

Copywriters

Creative Directors

Designers

Film Directors

Graphics

Illustrators

Photographers

Production Companies

Schools

Students

Various

Young Creatives

Sponsors

IMPORTED
BOMBAY
SAPPHIRE
Distilled
LONDON
DRY GIN
Distilled from 100%
Grain Neutral Spirit
from a 1761 recipe
THE BOMBAY SPIRITS COMPANY,
London W1B 5HH
PRODUCT OF ENGLAND
IMPORTED
"SAFE KEEPING" credenza design by JUN AOKI
UNA COMBINACIÓN DE 10 ELEMENTOS BOTÁNICOS Y UN PROCESO ÚNICO
DE ELABORACIÓN MEDIANTE "INFUSIÓN DE VAPOR" CONSIGUEN DAR A
BOMBAY SAPPHIRE SU CARACTERÍSTICO SABOR: SUAVE Y EQUILIBRADO.
BOMBAY SAPPHIRE
INSPIRED
Bebe con moderación. Es tu responsabilidad. 47º
Bombay Sapphire es marca registrada.

Genius
Loci
The first
serious
meeting
of three
continents'
advertising
THE
CUP
INTERCONTINENTAL
ADVERTISING
CUP
ADC*E
goldendrum
ADFEST
FIAP
DEDICATED TO 'GENIUS LOCI'
Valencia
November
22–24
2007
www.thecupawards.com

Sponsors & Supporters

ADC*E collaborating
Associations & Companies

ADC*E Collaborating Schools

MIAMI AD SCHOOL EUROPE

ADC*E Collaborating Media

CONTROL